D0867732

A HISTORY
of
THE CURE OF SOULS

HARPER'S MINISTERS PAPERBACK LIBRARY

A HISTORY
of
THE CURE OF SOULS

———••———

JOHN T. McNEILL

HARPER & ROW, PUBLISHERS
New York, Hagerstown, San Francisco, London

A HISTORY OF THE CURE OF SOULS

Copyright, 1951, by Harper & Row, Publishers, Inc.

Printed in the United States of America

All rights in this book are reserved.
No part of the book may be reproduced in any manner whatsoever without written permission except in the case of brief quotations embodied in critical articles
and reviews. For information address Harper & Row, Publishers, Inc., 10 East
53rd Street, New York, N.Y. 10022. Published simultaneously in Canada by
Fitzhenry & Whiteside, Toronto.

First Harper & Row paperback edition published in 1977.

ISBN: 0-06-065540-2

Library of Congress Catalog Card Number: 76-62926

77 78 79 80 81 10 9 8 7 6 5 4 3 2 1

CONTENTS

PREFACE

IN THE phrase "cure of souls" the word "cure" has something like the range of meaning of the Latin *cura* from which it comes. The primary sense of *cura* is "care," and it is readily applied either to the tasks involved in the care of a person or thing, or to the mental experience of carefulness or solicitude concerning its object. Occasionally the former direction of meaning is further specialized to signify "healing," or the means by which healing is effected. It was natural that the Latin Church should employ the expression *cura animarum* in such a way as to comprehend these variations of the meaning of *cura*, and it is in this comprehensive sense that the term "cure of souls" has come into common use in English.

We have no need in this connection to undertake an examination of the various philosophical conceptions of the soul. In the sources employed in this volume the word is ordinarily used in a way that is sufficiently clear to every reader. The soul is the essence of human personality. It is related to the body, but it is not a mere expression or function of the bodily life. It is capable of vast ranges of experience and susceptible of disorder and anguish; but it is indestructible and endowed with possibilities of blessedness within and beyond the order of time. The cure of souls is, then, the sustaining and curative treatment of persons in those matters that reach beyond the requirements of the animal life.

Man is a seeker after health, but not health of the body alone. Health of body may be contributory to, but it does not guarantee, health of personality. It may be possessed by a man who suffers painful disorders of mind and spirit. On the other hand, it may be destroyed by mental or emotional disease. The health that is ultimately sought is not something to be secured by material means alone; it is the well-being of the soul. In our day the science that heals the body has advanced far beyond that which aims to restore the soul. Yet the function of the healer of the soul is not less ancient than that of the physician of the body. In primitive societies both functions are commonly assumed by the same person. The *shaman* of American Indian or primitive Siberian tribes is at once healer, sorcerer, priest and teacher. The African medicine man is consulted alike by the sufferer from insupportable anxieties and the victim of gastric pains, and has his weird recipes for both. In higher cultures some connection of bodily healing with the therapy of mind and soul is still often assumed, but in practice there has been greater specialization. Distinctive qualifications of training and wisdom have been required of those who would undertake the guidance of souls. In ancient times the advance of medicine did not keep pace with the progress of philosophy and religion, and the healer of souls who emerges in the advancing culture is not typically a member of the medical guild. In Greece he belongs instead to the fraternity of philosophers; in Israel he is the "wise man" who rests his instruction upon religion and is a near relation of the prophet.

Socrates was, and wished to be, *iatros tēs psuchēs*, a healer of the soul. These Greek syllables have been recast to form the word "psychiatrist." But Socrates would hardly recognize the medical psychiatrist as a member of his fraternity. A scientific psychiatry indifferent to religion and philosophy is a new and strange phenomenon. Whatever may be the future importance of this new science, it is abundantly evident that the role of the religious physician of souls is not played out. In the stresses of the present century, his function seems, indeed, to be expanding. He stands in a long and honorable tradition, although, through the neglect of historians, the record of it has been largely concealed from him. The danger of obsession with the contemporary besets him. It is my hope that this book will enable him to see his own difficult task in something like its true historical perspective, and to gain an invigorating awareness of his membership in a unique and sacred profession that spans the centuries. This book is designed, too, to introduce to a wider class of readers a province of history of which there exists no other general treatment.

Both aims and methods in the cure of souls have varied with the flow of history. They have reflected the changing philosophies of the relation of the individual to the group (or church). Where high interpretations of group authority prevail, the individual who breaks the pattern is subjected to an authoritative corrective discipline. The object sought is the subjection of the individual, and concern for the group interest rather than the interior recovery of the personality becomes the determining factor. Close attention is paid to specific acts, and there is a corresponding neglect of the more fundamental concept of personal character as a whole, of which acts are but symptoms and indices. "Sins" become more important than "sin," legal restraint than inner motivation.

In Christianity, I believe, this trend has never been completely dominant, but it was strongly marked in the medieval system and has appeared in varying degrees within Protestant communions. New Testament Christianity, despite its intense group loyalty, unfailingly, sought the spiritual vitality of the individual and achieved a wholesome co-ordination of individual and group interests. Luther's guidance of souls marks a restoration of this balance, and, relatively to the preceding era, an invigoration of personality. Much as he stressed the devastation wrought by sin, he was not minutely anxious about separate sinful acts. He had in view the integral liberation, health and enrichment of souls.

The Reformation, in its Lutheran, Reformed and Anglican branches, adopted this new orientation, and substituted for obligatory and exhaustive confession a voluntary confiding of sins and "griefs" to a minister or other suitable adviser, for relief and counsel. The favorite Reformation doctrine of the priesthood of all Christians encouraged mutual or group procedures in guidance. These have not always been given recognizable organized form, but the principle has found notable expression in Pietism, Methodism and Quakerism, and in the Reformed, Presbyterian and Baptist churches. Even in their stern and often unwholesomely authoritarian discipline, the Calvinist communions sought to embody the principle of the mutual cure of souls. Not without some loss and danger, but on the whole with great advantage, the Protestant churches have largely abandoned the legalism that has at times attended their methods, and are free to advance along new lines with the aid of modern scientific knowledge.

The chapter headings will suggest the range and proportion of the book, but a brief notice of the chief matters treated may be useful here. While Christianity is the main field of investigation, Jewish and classical-pagan guidance are briefly examined. Both had much influence upon Christian developments, and both are independently important. The inclusion of data from the Asiatic religious cultures is justified, I believe, as opening a window on a wide realm of phenomena comparable with those of the Christian cure of souls, and affording perspective for the evaluation of aspects of the latter. The New Testament phase is described with reference to the Gospels and passages from the Epistles, and with stress on the elements of inner renewal and mutual spiritual help. The writings of the Church Fathers and early monastics yield evidence of the Christianizing of some pagan methods, of increased attention to the duties of pastors, and of a drift toward externalization and emphasis upon sins in detail. The completion of the latter tendency appears in medieval penance as revealed in the Penitential Books and in the later authorized practice of the confessional. Amid the deterioration that accompanied this development we find some arresting new elements, such as formal instruction in the virtues and the interest in "the art of dying well."

Chapters VIII to XII treat the cure of souls in the Reformation churches and later Protestantism. The reader will observe here a wide variety of types of method and a good deal of experimentation in which notable persons participate, but also a certain family resemblance arising from a common debt to the Reformation founders. The resemblance extends to early Anglicanism; but in the last century that communion has shown a marked trend toward the revival of medieval practices. Features of the chapter on modern Roman Catholicism are the attention given to the provisions of the Council of Trent and illustration of the work of the great seventeenth century spiritual directors. A survey of the cure of souls in Eastern Orthodoxy and in the Armenian Church forms the last historical chapter of the book. The most distinctive elements here are found in the functions of the Russian "elder" (*starets*), a unique type of spiritual guide. In the Conclusion an attempt is made to establish contact between the historic religious guidance of souls and the pastoral counseling of today with its use of scientific methods.

The available materials for such a book as this are almost limitless, and I have striven to exclude all that seemed unimportant. I have also endeavored to treat proportionately the various historical phases of the subject, and to reach a fair judgment of the persons and methods considered. I can only ask indulgence for the omission of many matters that on a larger plan might legitimately have been included. Numerous Protestant and Eastern Christian denominations and sects, the modern offshoots of Roman Catholicism in Europe, and the whole series of new churches that have grown out of modern foreign missions, receive no consideration. The history of physical healing by exorcism and prayer is merely touched upon: the ministry to the sick is rather incidentally treated, and the ministry to prisoners comes to notice at a few points only. I abandoned a design to include a critical review of the history of casuistry—a topic that tends to expand unmanageably when one tries to grasp it—and have contented myself with references to its more prominent aspects. The need of casuistry in the cure of souls, and the peril of its abuse, are at least suggested in what is said about it in connection with Stoicism, Judaism, Roman Catholicism and Puritanism. The formal seventeenth century Lutheran casuistry, which is represented by a fairly large, if now forgotten literature, is not considered, since it can hardly be regarded as typical of the Lutheran spirit. My judgment of what might be omitted or lightly stressed in the development of the theme of the book may differ from that of the critical reader. But in order to complete the work within a volume of moderate size, some such economy as I have practiced was requisite.

It was incumbent upon me throughout to present the essential data, and I have been more concerned to set down the facts than to induce the reader to interpret them by my own standards. But the element of evaluation is never wholly absent, and not only in the Conclusion of the book but also in the closing section of each chapter generalizations and comparisons appear. A selected list is appended of the more useful books and articles consulted.

The volume has been half a lifetime in preparation, but it is only about twelve years since I resolved to complete it in the form of a general history. A doctoral thesis, *The Celtic Penitentials*[1] constituted my first essay in the field. A second stage was reached with the book *Medieval Handbooks of Penance*[2] in which Dr. Helena M. Gamer cooperated. Since that volume appeared, labor on the present one has occupied an ever-increasing proportion of my time.

I have been generously permitted by the publishers of the second of these volumes to make a number of quotations from it in Chapters V and VI. The editors of *Church History* have permitted a similar use in Chapter VI of an article, "Medicine for Sin as Prescribed in the Penitentials," which appeared in that journal (Volume I, 1932); and this privilege has been extended by the editor of *Christendom*, for my study, "Personal Counselling in Early Protestantism" (Volume VI, 1941), some paragraphs of which appear in Chapter IX, and by the editor of *Religion in Life* for "Casuistry in the Puritan Age" (Volume XII, 1943), which was drawn upon in a part of Chapter XI.

In lecture courses and seminars in the Divinity School of the University of Chicago and in Union Theological Seminary, I have profited by

[1] Chicago, 1920, published in Paris, 1923.
[2] Columbia University "Records of Civilization" series, edited by Austin P. Evans, Vol. XXIX, New York. 1938.

the stimulating response of competent students. My colleagues in Union Seminary, Professors James Muilenburg, Frederick Clifton Grant, August Karl Reischauer and John Knox have placed me greatly in their debt by reading and commenting on the drafts on Chapters I, II, III, and IV, respectively, while Professor Arthur Jeffery has given invaluable criticism of the section on Islam in Chapter III. Professor Seward Hiltner, who read the manuscript for Harper & Brothers, not only called my attention to several minor defects but also very helpfully raised some points of general interpretation. Numerous faults were eliminated as a result of this generous and expert help; the defects that remain are, of course, chargeable to me alone. Father George Florovsky of St. Vladimir's Orthodox Theological Seminary and Professor Matthew Spinka of Hartford Seminary have also given indispensable aid in suggesting literature and points of emphasis for Chapter XIV. My wife has read the entire manuscript and made many valuable suggestions. I wish to express my sincere gratitude to all those named, and to others who in chance conversations have stimulated my thought on aspects of the study. I have exploited the exemplary patience of many busy librarians. The text employed in New Testament quotations is that of the Revised Standard Version, published by Thomas Nelson and Sons; copyright, 1946, by the International Council of Religious Education, and reprinted by permission. The labor of the writing has been relieved by the joy of learning: may the reader share this delight.

J. T. M.

Chapter I

THE GUIDES OF ISRAEL:
WISE MEN, SCRIBES AND RABBIS

I

The conscience of a man is the lamp of the Lord, searching the innermost chambers of the being." This couplet in Proverbs (20:27) vividly expresses a cardinal principle of developed Judaism, the moral responsibility of the individual. Each man had to do with Yahwe, his maker and judge, the sovereign Lord of his conduct. In late pre-Christian Judaism the growing stress upon the sacredness of the Torah, as the utterance of Yahwe and the guide to action, may have reduced to some extent the sense of this relationship. Yet the Jew continued to feel that his God was the guide of his soul. It was to Yahwe that he said: "Thou shalt guide me with thy counsel" (Psalm 73:24). And one of the Wisdom writers affirms that God is "the guide even of wisdom and the director of the wise" (Wisdom 7:15). God was available to the devout, and His authoritative Word was an unfailing light. It is for this reason that the spiritual and moral counselor, even in the period of his highest authority, appears rarely to have acquired the peculiar intimacy with and control over his disciple that was characteristic of the direction of souls in Hinduism and in the Christian confessional. His exhortations were addressed to groups, and while he sought obedience from individuals, this obedience was rather to his reasoned teachings and interpretations of the Law than to himself as bearing divine authority. Evidence of this attitude is to be recognized in the fact that in the Midrash the judgments of one rabbi are habitually balanced against those of another.

Obedience to the divine Lord was the great task of life. The need for counsel arose from the fact that the task was beset with difficulties and complexities. It involved not only a battle against natural perversity but

1

also the observance of manifold rules of ritual and social behavior. "The imagination of man's heart is evil from his youth" (Genesis 8:21). The dutiful Jew often felt the need of direction and correction. Those whose consciences were dull could hardly escape rebuke. There was no lack in Hebrew society of specialists qualified to guide candidates for a righteous life, and to admonish the ungodly.

From early times there had existed in Judaism three distinct classes of experts in religion: the Priests, a hereditary class whose work and teaching were connected with public worship and ceremonies; the Prophets, who gave utterance in the name of the Lord on religious and moral issues and sometimes rebuked and directed prominent individuals; and the Wise Men (*hakhamim*) who counseled their fellows of all ranks and callings on the principles of the good life and details of personal conduct. Some prophets, such as Amos and Ezekiel, appear at times to have performed the functions of the sages, but in general their roles were distinct. These three well-established vocations are expressly mentioned together in one passage—that in which Jeremiah's enemies assure one another that when his message is repudiated "the law shall not perish from the priest, nor counsel from the wise, nor the word from the prophet" (Jeremiah 18:18). When in later times prophecy declined and the priesthood became impaired by political pressure, the scribes and rabbis maintained, with variations, the functions of the wise men of earlier days, and became the dominant force in Jewish religion. It should also be remembered that at all periods parents were expected to impart religious training to their children. In Deuteronomy (6:6-7; cf. 11:19) we read: "And these words, which I command thee this day, shall be in thine heart: And thou shalt teach them diligently unto thy children, and shalt talk of them when thou sittest in thine house . . ." Such passages reveal an important aspect of Judaism.

II

Since the wise men chiefly gave guidance to individuals, we are especially concerned with them. Modern historians recognize in the wise man of Israel a common phenomenon of ancient Semitic cultures. Egypt and Babylon had a similar class of dispensers of guidance. Some of these are known by name, and have left collections of their teachings that are remarkably similar to the Wisdom books of the Bible and Apocrypha. Egyptian books of this class are, in fact, among the earliest extant writings of mankind. *The Teaching of Kagemma*, possibly the earliest of these, survives only in a fragment of five paragraphs enjoining humility and condemning arrogance. *The Wisdom of Ptah-hotep* is preserved in a papyrus written nearly two thousand years before Christ and claims to have been composed eight hundred years earlier. It consists of a series of moral maxims set in a reported discourse before the king of Egypt. The author is represented as a very aged official of Memphis who is about to hand on his office to his son. Having feelingly discussed the distresses of old age—in a passage comparable to Ecclesiastes 12:1-8, though lacking the rich imagery—he begs the king's permission to speak counsel to his son and successor. Ptah-hotep's commendable purpose is "that sin may be banished among persons of understanding." Because he addresses to his son precepts for successful living, he has been called "a primaeval Chesterfield." His views suggest comparison with those of Benjamin Franklin, and appear to resemble those typical of men of the Enlightenment in Western Europe. He speaks of "the God" as approving the good actions recommended. Thus his morality has the sanction of religion; but he shows little interest in religion for its own sake. Good behavior has its reward in the present life. The prudential morality of Ptah-hotep amounts to this: avoid arrogance, conceit, ill-temper, covetousness and entanglements with women; then do as you please, and don't overwork. Although Ptah-hotep lived nearly five thousand years ago, he was far from thinking of himself as an innovator. He modestly desires to hand on "the weighty sayings of the ancestors and of those who have obeyed the gods." He is not the originator but the continuator of a tradition, the beginnings of which are lost in the deeps of prehistory. The fact that many of his precepts seem applicable to people of relatively humble rank strengthens the impression that the author has drawn upon traditional materials of popular teaching.

The most intrinsically important of Egyptian books of guidance is *The Teaching of Amen-em-apt* (or Amen-em-ope) who calls himself "Scribe of the Grain," or superintendent of agriculture. About 1000 B.C. he compiled his thirty chapters of precepts. The manual was designed for the moral training of government officials like himself and, in the words of Sir E. A. Wallis Budge, "to teach a man how to live to God and to love his neighbor." It proved attractive to Jews, and, probably before the Exile, was translated into Hebrew. The Book of Proverbs (especially 22:17 to 24:22) and the Wisdom of Solomon show numerous striking parallels to it. These may be borrowings by the Jewish writers; but some scholars think that a body of floating Wisdom material was

drawn upon by both Egyptian and Hebrew compilers, or that Amen-
em-apt, who leans strongly to monotheism, felt the influence of Hebrew
religion. Like the Hebrew Wisdom classics, this is a book of penetrating insight into men's motives, and of fear of the judgments of a God
who rewards justice and beneficence. The author seeks to teach a man
how he may "steer his course away from evil" and win the applause
of the wise. The reader is counseled to avoid an arrogant and angry
bully. On the other hand, he is to set the discouraged sinner on his feet,
giving him generous help, and then committing him to "the hands of
God," who may have in store for him "a new occasion of beneficence."
Strict honesty in weights and measures and in boundaries, consideration
for widows, debtors, the poor and the handicapped, truthfulness of
speech, are among the principles enjoined; while cheating, bribery, anger,
slothfulness, indulgence in meat and protracted sessions in beer parlors
are emphatically condemned. Amen-em-apt insistently deprecates all
harsh treatment of the weak and unfortunate, which he calls "being
valorous against the man of broken arm." The afflicted are spoken of
as "in the hand of God," which apparently means under divine discipline for their sins (the suggestion that it is a kindly way of saying
"mentally deficient" seems misleading). They are not to be incon-
siderately treated: "Laugh not at a blind man, nor tease a dwarf. . . .
Tease not a man who is in the hand of God, nor be fierce of countenance
against him when he has transgressed." As in Christian social idealism
the poor are in a sense "God's poor," and wealth without love is vanity.
"Better is a beggar who is in the hand of God, than the rich who are
safely housed in a comfortable dwelling. Better are bread-cakes of flour
and water with a loving heart than rich meats that carry with them
bickering and quarreling." When Amen-em-apt observes that "the
heart of a man is the nose of God" he seems to affirm the divine
authority of conscience: in Proverbs conscience is "the lamp of the
Lord."

That schools of wise men flourished in Edom, southeast of the Dead
Sea, is evident from Jeremiah's reference (49:7). The wise man had
his place also among the Babylonian and other peoples of the Euphrates
region. Here the tradition in its later stage is well represented by the
Maxims of Ahikar, a work of about 500 B.C., which appeared in Aramaic,
Syriac, Armenian and Arabic versions and is reflected in Proverbs and
other Hebrew Wisdom books. Ahikar reaches a peak of ethical counsel
in such precepts as: "My son, if thine enemy meet thee with evil, meet

thou him with good"; but much of his advice is on a purely utilitarian plane. In the Arabic version especially, we find emphasis laid upon a subdued voice and manner: "O my son, bind thy head . . . and soften thy voice and be courteous . . . and raise not thy voice when thou laughest, for if it were by a loud voice that a house was built the ass would build many houses every day" (cf. Proverbs 24:3). Ahikar is represented as a sage who is secretary to Sennacherib, king of Assyria, and his discourses are set in a fascinating Oriental tale.

The common features of this didactic literature have been summarized by Paul Humbert. He notes that they tend to take the form of

the warnings of a father to his son or of a king to his heir, later of a teacher to his pupil. From the fatherly or scholastic type of this instruction are to be explained its traditional, authoritative, apodictical character, its strict stylistic unity, the repeated warnings to the hearer, the emphasis laid on reward and success, the practical tone of the teaching, the importance of the instruction motif.

He observes that as the genre developed, there came a change of literary form from distich to strophe and from artless utterance to composed collections of sayings.

III

Elements of such instruction break into Old Testament narrative and prophecy at an early time. An example is seen in the conversation between David and Saul, in I Samuel 24. When David remarks: "As saith a proverb of the ancients, wickedness proceedeth from the wicked," and when Saul, touched by his rival's magnanimity, replies, "thou hast rewarded me good, whereas I have rewarded thee evil," we detect the very word and spirit of the wise man. The psalmists made use of the typical expressions and ideas of the sages. Some of their verses, like the Wisdom books, exhibit striking parallels to non-Jewish materials. Thus the comparison of the righteous man to a flourishing tree in Psalm 1 (cf. Jeremiah 17:5-8); the words in praise of the righteous poor in Psalm 5:16 and the warning: "If riches increase, set not your heart upon them" in Psalm 62:10, are related to passages in Amen-em-apt, who wrote centuries earlier. The great prophets reflect the Wisdom lore, and may have taken differing attitudes to wise men among their contemporaries. Thus Amos, whose vehement sermons enforce the ethical gospel of Wisdom, condemns the people for despising them. "They hate him that rebuketh in the gate, and abhor him that speaketh uprightly" (Amos 5:10). On the other hand, we may perhaps discern in Isaiah 29:13-14 the impatience of the inspired prophet over the traditional, stale and undisturbing counsel of the wise men who made no claim to be directly prompted by Yahwe. The people "taught by the precepts of men" have come to honor the Lord with their lips only; their punishment—"a marvelous work"—is to be that "the wisdom of their wise men shall perish, and the understanding of their prudent men shall be hid." And it is the enemies of Jeremiah, who say that "counsel shall not perish from the wise."

The wise men of Israel, unlike the prophets, did not challenge their contemporaries on public issues, and few of them came to such prominence as to obtain lasting fame. The names of four early Israelitish wise men are preserved to us in I Kings 4:31 and I Chronicles 2:6. In the former of these passages we are told that "Solomon was wiser than all men; than Ethan the Ezrahite, and Heman and Chalcol and Darda, the sons of Mahol." In the other passage the same names appear as four of the five sons of Zerah, a son of Judah and Tamar: this would make them great-grandsons of the patriarch, Jacob. It is probable that "Zerah" is to be identified with "Ezrah" in "Ezrahite." To Heman "the Ezrahite" is attributed Psalm 88, and to Ethan Psalm 89. The former of these Psalms so parallels the thought of Job that its writer has been credited with that book. The word "maschil" used in the descriptive headings of these (and eleven other) Psalms apparently meant a set of verses for use in instruction; but the word may have lost its exact meaning in these cases. In I Chronicles 15:17, 19 Heman and Ethan are mentioned as singers in charge of the brass instruments. Otherwise we can only conjecture why these men became celebrated for wisdom. If their wisdom had been thought of as musical skill only, they would hardly have been classified with Solomon. If they were "singers" they may have been composers of psalms embodying the teaching of the wise. We may reasonably take the mention of their names with that of the paragon of wise men as evidence of the recognized status of their guild in Israelitish life of the period.

While the prophets worked upon men's emotions to arouse repentance and a transformation of life at its deeper levels, the moralists of the Wisdom books, like their non-Jewish forerunners, relied upon argument and reasoned admonition. They despaired of, or despised, the "prating fool," and the arrogant scorner of their message. Yet they were in no respect esoteric or aristocratic. In her house of seven pillars Wisdom prepares a feast for all comers: "She crieth upon the highest places of the city, whoso is simple, let him turn in hither" (Proverbs 9:1-4). Ben Sirach has her say: "Come unto me, all ye that be desirous of me, and fill yourselves with my fruits" (Ecclesiasticus 24:20), and in the Wisdom of Solomon "she goeth about seeking such as are worthy of her" (6:15).

IV

The writer of I Kings 4:30, "the wisdom of Solomon surpassed the wisdom of the eastern Arabs," evidently had some awareness of the wider range of the Wisdom literature. His comparison is a patriotic boast, but would be justified if Solomon were the author of the books credited to him. Solomon's reputation for wisdom is to be understood in the light of the custom of ascribing moral precepts to kings and great administrators. These eminent personages may have had even less to do with books that bear their names than had James I with the "King James Version." The Book of Proverbs, though ascribed to Solomon and transmitting much early lore, is in its extant form a postexilic compilation. It contains sections of quite separate origin bearing their own titles: "The words of the Wise" (22:17); "The words of Agur" (30:1); "The words of Lemuel" (31:1). Lemuel is called "king of Massa" and Agur is of the same tribe—progeny of the seventh of the twelve sons of Ishmael (Genesis 25:14). Thus these portions are admitted to be non-Hebrew in origin.

The Jewish Wisdom writers felt also the influence of the sages of Greece, and the Book of Ecclesiastes (ca. 200 B.C.) not only shows a strain of Epicureanism but, as Harry Ranston points out, has numerous apparent borrowings from the moralizing poet Theognis of Megara who lived in the sixth century B.C. Jesus Ben Sirach, who wrote the Book of Ecclesiasticus about 180 B.C., while censuring Solomon's lasciviousness holds his wisdom in respect (Ecclesiasticus 47:13-20). His grandson and namesake, who wrote the prologue to the book and may have inserted some matter of his own (ca. 132-116 B.C.), states that he went to Egypt where he found, and profited from, "a book [literally, "a copy"] of no small learning." From certain parallels Dr. Oesterley has suggested that this may possibly have been the treatise of Amen-em-apt. The text is uncertain, but a resemblance is at least discoverable. In Ecclesiasticus the typical elements of Jewish family discipline are asserted, and expressed with an unusual severity (30:1-13):

> He that loveth his son causeth him often to feel the rod . . .
> Give him no liberty in his youth,
> And wink not at his follies. . . .

Another aspect of parental responsibility is revealed in a striking passage (42:9-14) which begins:

> The father waketh for the daughter, when no man knoweth;
> And the care of her taketh away sleep.

A somewhat contradictory discourse on servants authorizes severe measures in dealing with the lazy and disobedient, but ends on a note of kindness (33:24-28):

> If thou have a servant, entreat him as a brother:
> For thou hast need of him, as of thine own soul.

There is a remarkable passage (38:1-15) in praise of devout physicians, in which the sick man is urged, after prayer, repentance and offerings, to:

Give place to the physician, for the Lord hath created him.
Let him not go from thee, for thou hast need of him . . .
For they shall also pray unto the Lord
That He would also prosper that which they give for ease and remedy to
    prolong life.

Ben Sirach has weighty advice on the type of counselor to be consulted, and on those who are disqualified from giving guidance by self-interest or prejudice (37:7-15):

> Hearken not unto these in any matter of counsel.
> But be continually with a godly man
> Whom thou knowest to keep the commandments of the Lord,
> Whose mind is according to thy mind,
> And will sorrow with thee, if thou shalt miscarry.

It is characteristic of pre-Christian Judaism that self-direction is here reserved against the counselor's authority:

And let the counsel of thine own heart stand:
For there is no man more faithful unto thee than it.
For a man's mind is sometime wont to tell him more than seven watchmen
That sit above in an high tower.
And above all this pray to the Most High
That He will direct thy way in truth.

Thus the traditional way of life is commended to Jews confronting a pagan world. Herford regards Ecclesiasticus as superior to Proverbs "in the quality of its ethical teaching."

The Wisdom of Solomon was composed in Alexandria, at a date not agreed upon by scholars between 50 B.C. and A.D. 50, and written in cultivated Greek. It may have been intended as a corrective of the un-Jewish pessimism of Ecclesiastes; one of its points of emphasis is stated in the words: "In the world to come the righteous shall enjoy eternal felicity in the presence of God" (3:8). It is in the main an affirmation of Hebrew religion, in opposition to idolatry, for the benefit of people exposed to paganism. It contains extended references to Israel's bondage in and escape from Egypt; the crossing of the Red Sea calls forth a remarkable passage on pagan fear and the conscience made cowardly by sin. But it has also marked traces of classical influence. Thus the four cardinal virtues are extolled (8:7), and God is called "the first author of beauty" (13:3). St. Paul was evidently a careful reader of this book, as numerous passages in his epistles, especially in Romans, attest.

V

All these books present an accumulation of the sayings of wise men who were practical counselors of souls, proclaiming reverence for God and justice to men, and making plain the path of right conduct. This material has the marks of moral maturity and combines broad human interests with concern for traditional values. It represents the experience of graybeards seeking to mold the lives of the young and the morally immature. It tends to present a cautious and stereotyped morality as pleasing to God and advantageous for life. The sayings of the wise men are often impressive, but rarely profound.

Regarding the past with reverence and themselves as the faithful transmitters of it, they encouraged parental authority, and urged the obligation to follow the instruction of father and mother. "How beautiful it is," says Ptah-hotep, "when a son receives what his father says." In the same spirit a much later wise man enjoins: "My son, hear the instruction of thy father, and forsake not the law of thy mother" (Proverbs 1:8). The counselor may represent himself as reiterating the precepts of his own father (as in Proverbs 4:1-4) or he may assume the role of a father and address his hearer as "my son." The framework of the family relationship creates an impression of personal intimacy and warm concern:

> My son, if thine heart be wise, my heart shall rejoice, even mine. . . .
> The father of the righteous shall greatly rejoice. . . .

Thy father and thy mother shall be glad. . . .
My son, give me thine heart, and let thine eyes observe my ways.
(Proverbs 23:15, 24-26)

The "me" in the last sentence here may be the teacher himself; or it may refer to Wisdom whose spokesman he is. In Proverbs, Ecclesiasticus and the Wisdom of Solomon, Wisdom becomes a kind of subordinate female deity, while set against her is Folly, the "instruction of fools" (Proverbs 16:22). Folly is also personified as the insolently seductive Strange Woman. Like Wisdom she invites the passerby to her house, but "her guests are in the depths of hell" (Proverbs 9:18).

The wise man was the counselor of the young, but it would be erroneous to suppose that he confined his exhortations to them. He gave much attention to the duties of parents, and of persons in positions of responsibility. The pursuit of wisdom is to be maintained throughout life:

> My son, gather instruction from thy youth up;
> So shalt thou find wisdom till thine old age.
> Come unto her as one that ploweth and soweth,
> And wait for her good fruits.
> (Ecclesiasticus 6:18-19)

The wise man was convinced that his message was in accord with divine wisdom, and, without claiming the charisma of inspired utterance, he demanded attention, assent and imitation of his own example. "I give you good doctrine," says the speaker in Proverbs 4:2; "Forsake ye not my law." The eloquent passage in the Wisdom of Solomon (chapters 6 to 8) which begins "Wisdom is glorious and never fadeth away" well illustrates the appeal for imitation and discipleship:

As for Wisdom, what she is, and how she came up, I will tell you. . . .
Receive therefore my instruction through my words, and it shall do you
    good . . .
I loved her, and sought her out from my youth . . .
Knowing that she would be a counsellor of good things,
And a comfort in cares and grief.
(Wisdom 6:22, 25; 8:2, 9)

Although the Wisdom teaching is prevailingly addressed to the individual, it is apparent that the wise men were public teachers, holding forth to knots of listeners "in the chief place of concourse, in the openings of the gates" (Proverbs 1:21), or wherever people congregated.

They also received inquirers in their houses and taught in the houses of others. Ben Sirach advises the seeker of wisdom to make the most of the various opportunities to gain it:

Stand in the multitude of the elders,
And cleave to him that is wise.
Be willing to hear every godly discourse . . .
And if thou seest a man of understanding, get thee betimes to him,
And let thy foot wear the steps of his door.
(Ecclesiasticus 6:34-36)

In public and in private, the wise men of Israel stressed godliness not less than moral rectitude. "They never dreamed," says Dr. Oesterley, "of such a thing as ethics without religion." Evidently they earnestly inculcated faith in God, and gave lessons in prayer. We have notable examples of their prayers in Ecclesiasticus 23 and in Wisdom 15. They were deeply conscious of the righteousness of God. Yet they could not compete with the prophets in vigor and impressiveness. The prophets were the crisis theologians of their era: the wise men were the educators of conscience. They supplied the daily bread of instruction in reverent attitudes and moral habits, and gave stability to the character of their people.

VI

While teachings of the wise men were being recorded in the Wisdom books, there arose a new leadership in the *Sopherim* or Scribes. The wise men had always exalted the Law, and the scribes were its interpreters. We read of scribes as early as the time of David (2 Samuel 8:17). In II Samuel and in I and II Kings certain scribes are named with priests and other officials. They may have functioned mainly as secretaries: there is no suggestion that they were teachers. Scribes are not mentioned in the passage in II Chronicles 17:8-9 where Jehoshaphat (king of Judah about 940 B.C.) sends Levites and priests through the cities of Judah to teach the people from the book of the Law. Ezra is regarded as the principal founder of the order of scribes, who were not only "bookmen" or writers, but experts in the Law, and its revered interpreters. Ezra is called both a priest and "a scribe of the words of the commandments of the Lord"; in the letter of Artaxerxes to him he is designated "a scribe of the law of the God of heaven" (Ezra 7:11, 12; cf. Nehemiah 8:1).

Thus the scribes may have arisen from the priest class, without connection with the wise men. Whatever their original relation to the priests, they soon became a separate guild of scholars. The groups that gathered to hear their interpretations of the Law were molded into the earliest synagogues, and in these the scribes were the most important members. They were, indeed, sometimes called by the old name "wise men" (*hakhamim*) for their skill in the Torah. By the first century of our era they were addressed by the honorific title of Rabbi (my master) and were held in great esteem. Their decisions were taken as law, and sometimes, as S. Zeitlin remarks, "even favored above the Torah."

The scribes were the authors of the voluminous materials of the Midrash, which comprises the Haggadah (narration) consisting of direct expositions of the text, and the Halakha (tradition; derived from a verb which means "to walk"), or commentary on the Oral Law. The latter was the originally unwritten but authoritative scribal amplification of the written Torah. It was alleged to have been secretly imparted to Moses on Sinai and was esteemed no less authoritative than the scripture itself. In the critical years of Judaism during the second century A.D. the scribes recorded the accumulated traditions and the Oral Law was reduced to writing. It is sometimes held to comprise the entire rabbinical literature; but it is especially represented by the Mishnah (authoritative though nonscriptural instruction), the received text of which was shaped about A.D. 190 by Rabbi Jehudah "the Prince" (d. 220). The numerous tracts of the Mishnah contain the collected *halakhoth*, or scholastic and casuistical definitions of scribes, chiefly of the period A.D. 70-170. The Mishnah is combined in the Talmud with the (later) Gemara (conclusion), which is a commentary on the Mishnah and thus one stage farther removed from the scripture itself. These materials appear in their most expanded form in the Babylonian Talmud which represents the labor of rabbis of the fifth and sixth centuries.

VII

The Jewish scribes of the first century A.D. were somewhat clearly divided into lenient and rigorous schools. These were respectively represented by Hillel and Shammai, two eminent teachers of the period of Herod the Great. Their opposed opinions are frequently cited in the Mishnah. Often Hillel permits what Shammai forbids, though on some special points these roles are reversed. Dr. Louis Finkelstein has shown that Hillel represented the townsfolk, Shammai the rural and provincial elements in Palestine. Well known is Hillel's way of easing the problems of a commercial age and giving stability to credit. To accomplish this, he had to circumvent the requirement in Deuteronomy 15 for the release of debtors in the seventh year. His invention of a *prosbol*, or form of declaration, in which the lender stated in advance that he would be free to demand payment when he chose, made legal collection in a sabbatical year. Many such ingenious evasions were employed, often with advantage to social life, sometimes merely in relaxation of a hard demand of the Law.

The presupposition that life is to be regulated by an unalterable law inevitably leads in time to interpretations designed to make the law more comfortable in altered social conditions. Changing conditions also require the application of the law to countless situations not contemplated in its original provisions. These elements can be observed in Rabbinical Judaism, where a major intellectual effort was devoted to the interpretation of the Torah. Much of this effort seems to us misdirected, but it was unavoidable on the assumption of the unalterability of the Law. Many scholars have exhibited examples of the minutiae to which the rabbis descended. Many pages of their judgments in the Babylonian Talmud show only refinements of casuistry with a sprinkling of mildly humorous anecdotes but scarcely a gleam of any profound wisdom or lofty piety. Thus they discussed the duration of twilight, the order in which to pour hot and cold water for the bath, the wearing of hairnets by women while bathing, fowl and cheese on the same table, the amount of the thirty-nine labors forbidden on the Sabbath. It was an offense to weave three threads or to sew two stitches, and salt might not be mixed with water in such density as to float an egg. If a cask of oil bursts open, an amount sufficient for three meals may be saved. A sheaf of grain may not be moved but a spoon may; if a spoon is inserted into the sheaf, harvesting may proceed. Some rabbis devised ways of extending the limits of the Sabbath day's journey of two thousand cubits: one might set his starting point at a distance from his position.

In various tracts of the Talmud; the conduct of mourners and their comforters is ordered in detail, on wise principles no doubt, but with excessive formality. As in Job 2:13, one may not speak to a mourner until he has spoken. For thirty days he is to receive words of consolation but not to be questioned concerning his peace; after that he is to be so questioned, but not to be tendered words of consolation (*Mo'ed Katan*).

VIII

The small change of casuistry ought not, however, to distract attention from the higher principles that are here to be discovered. Many of these are treasured up in the *Pirke Aboth*, or Sayings of the Fathers, an anthology of about four centuries (200 B.C. to A.D. 200). In this famous tract we find the Wisdom strain combined with that of the scribes. It also bears evidence of the functions of the rabbis. The Torah is represented as handed down from Moses through Joshua, the elders (Joshua 24:31), the prophets, and the men of the "Great Synagogue," a college of scribes supposedly founded by Ezra. Three special instructions were said to have been transmitted to the scribes and accepted by them:

> Be deliberate in judgments;
> Raise up many disciples;
> Make a fence about the Torah.

The function of the rabbis as guides of conscience is well expressed in the problem of tithes by a saying of Rabbi Gamaliel, a grandson of Hillel and the tutor of St. Paul: "Provide thyself with a teacher (*rab*), be quit of doubt, and accustom not thyself to give tithes by a conjectural estimate" (*Pirke Aboth* i, 16). Thus the interpreter of the Law relieved the doubtful conscience of the taxpayer by estimating his payment. We have secularized in modern life what for the Jew remained within the sphere of religion. Ben Sirach advised: "Let thy foot wear the steps of [the wise man's] door." It was also commendable to have the experts come freely to one's house and hold discourse there. "Let thy house be a meeting-place for the wise," said Rabbi Jose, "cover thyself with dust at their feet, and drink in their words with thirst" (i, 4). The first century Jewish scholar, Philo of Alexandria, in a book on the Sabbath, reports his observation of a typical scene of scribal instruction: "The listeners sit in perfect stillness eagerly drinking in most excellent doctrines."

The rabbis made it a point of conscience to be available at all times for consultation, and to answer inquirers patiently. The story is told of Hillel that on a Friday, when he was preparing for the Sabbath, he was thrice approached by a man who had wagered that he could make the holy man angry. Each time the visitor asked a foolish question, but Hillel answered with unfailing kindness, good humor, and humility. An incident of the time of Trajan illustrates the readiness of the rabbis to be interviewed even at inconvenient times. When Rabbi Ishmael and Rabbi Simeon were about to be executed, the former asked the latter whether any woman or man who had sought his advice while he was sleeping or eating had been kept waiting. Simeon replied that his servant had orders not to prevent anyone from reaching him even when he was asleep or at a meal.

The higher element in the rabbinical teaching may be suggested by brief quotation from the *Pirke Aboth*. To avoid sin, said Rabbi Jehudah "the Prince" (the chief editor of the Mishnah), "remember that there is above thee an all-seeing eye, an all-hearing ear, and a record of all thy actions" (ii, 1). "Be a disciple of Aaron," said Hillel; "love peace and pursue peace; love all men too, and bring them nigh unto the Law. . . . Pass not judgment upon thy neighbor until thou hast put thyself in his place. . . . Where a man is needed, endeavor that thou be the man" (i, 12; ii, 5, 6). "Let thy friend's honor be as dear to thee as thine own," said Rabbi Eliezer (ii, 15), and Rabbi Jose has the same advice about a friend's property (ii, 16). "This world," said Rabbi Jacob, "is like a vestibule before the world to come. Prepare thyself in the vestibule, that thou mayest enter into the hall" (ii, 21). Humility and charity, and indifference to riches and worldly honor, are frequently praised. It appears that the guides of Israel did not wholly neglect "the weightier matters of the Law."

In their teaching on confession and repentance the rabbis also expressed a truly religious spirit. The day of Atonement was preceded by nine days of penitential preparation. But in addition to public repentance the rabbis stressed individual and inward penitence. The words of Numbers 5:6, 7 were interpreted as requiring oral confession, along with restitution to the injured. The injunction, "Repent one day before thy death," uttered by Rabbi Eliezer and others, was a demand for daily repentance, since the day of death is not known. The dying were expected to make a special act of confession and repentance. The rabbinical authority, S. Schechter, and the Jesuit scholar, J. Bonsirven, have called attention to the practice of confession of personal sins in late pre-Christian Judaism. Societies were formed whose members were pledged to a weekly confession.

Palestinian piety was fed by the Wisdom books. It brought forth the Psalms of Solomon, written during the woes of Pompey's conquest of Jerusalem, from which calamity lessons of humility and repentance are drawn; relief is found in the hope of a Messiah King: "He shall bless the people of the Lord with wisdom and gladness . . . for God shall cause him to be mighty through the Holy Spirit, and wise through counsel and understanding." A century later, stress was laid by Philo, in his essay *On Penitence*, upon conversion and amendment of life. The lessons of the Psalms and the prophets were not forgotten: God was represented as always willing to pardon repentant sinners.

IX

"Wisdom is justified of her children," said Jesus, when he was accused of being a friend of sinners. Yet he vigorously denounced the scribes of his time. He called them "blind guides," and charged them, along with the Pharisees, to whose party most of them were attached, with self-glorification, pretense, and oppressive legalism. If his words are correctly reported in Matthew 23, he delivered judgments upon them as caustic as any utterance of the eighth or seventh century prophets upon the ungodly of their times. To St. Paul also, a former student of one of the most honored of the rabbis, their system was "a yoke of bondage." They burdened men's consciences with innumerable requirements. With endless refinements of casuistry, they obscured the moral vigor of the Law to which they affirmed their devotion. It is remarkable that men of their intellectual gifts often employed them in trivial and peripheral matters, and that they nevertheless retained for centuries their sway over a well-schooled people. Yet the preservation of Judaism was in the main their achievement. If judged alone by their minute and scrupulous legalism, they were indeed blind guides. By their own testimony, true religion moves in another sphere. Even their casuistry had, however, the valid objective of bringing the common life of men under the control of religious principles. "Let all thy deeds," said Rabbi Jose, "be done in the name of God" (*Pirke Aboth* ii, 17). As we look back upon their work, it is not their casuistical determinations but their higher spiritual wisdom that deserves lasting admiration and marks them as the heirs of the wise men of former days.

Chapter II

PHILOSOPHERS AS PHYSICIANS OF THE SOUL

I

RELIGION in ancient Greece lacked the support, and the restraint, of dogma. Belief was fluid, and philosophical thought was able to assert its independence of religious presuppositions. The Greeks were not strangers to theological ideas: they may be said to have invented the concepts of Christian theology. But their theological ideas did not coalesce into a theology; they fell within the framework of free philosophical inquiry. Religion remained naïve while philosophy reached maturity. "The poetic conceptions of early religion," says Edward Caird, "could not stand for a moment the shock of criticism . . . Socrates was the only martyr of philosophy in the ancient world."

The philosophers, too, were to take over from religion the moral direction of daily life. It is true that in the early period, to the end of the sixth century B.C., the Delphic oracle of Apollo exercised a remarkable moralizing influence. The Pythia, speaking for the god, demanded exacting purificatory rites for homicide, which in Homer was a relatively casual matter. The guilty man before his purification "was debarred," says M. P. Nilsson, "from all association with gods and men." This excommunication, and the severity of the rites of atonement, gave a new seriousness to the pollution of blood-guilt in the consciousness of the Greeks. The Apollo cult also induced the states to act in prevention of private revenge, and to bring manslayers to a court trial. The fact that in the Apollo cult no merely formal penance but inward and sincere repentance was required, is illustrated by Dr. Nilsson from Herodotus' story of Glaucos who was rebuked and condemned by the oracle because, while willing to seek pardon, he wished to escape by perjury the repayment of misappropriated money. The oracle of Apollo had also much

17

to do with the development of justice and sanctioned many legal reforms. In its stress upon such mottoes as "Know thyself" and "Nothing too much" which were inscribed on the temple at Delphi, the Apollo cult schooled its adherents in humility before the gods and rebuked that arrogant aggressiveness (*hubris*) that would bring the divine vengeance (*nemesis*) upon men.

In the Platonic dialogue *Protagoras,* Socrates refers to the above-mentioned inscriptions as having been dedicated by the Seven Sages "as the first fruits of their wisdom." His list of the Seven Sages differs from others, but all include Thales, who flourished about 600 B.C. and was a contemporary of the prophet Jeremiah. According to Socrates, as here reported, the Sages were followers of the primitive philosophers of Sparta and Crete, who met their pupils in closed sessions and pretended to foreigners that they were ignorant. The Sages spoke in "short memorable sentences." The discussion between Socrates and Protagoras the Sophist turns on the meaning of one such sentence propounded by the sage Pittacus, "Hard it is to be good." There is no reason to doubt that a band of early teachers of the Greeks imparted to their people a body of homely maxims of this sort. Nearly related to these were the sententious moralizing poets of the two centuries and a half (*ca.* 750-500) from Hesiod to Theognis and Simonides, whose extant compositions present many utterances of practical wisdom coupled with reverence for the gods. The ease of the road to wickedness and the labor of the steep ascent to virtue, the need of dependence upon the gods, the inevitability of justice though it be delayed, and the melancholy darkness that surrounds death, are themes presented by these singing sages as they sought to find a way of life. There are close parallels between some utterances of the sages and gnomic poets of early Greece and of the wise men and psalmists of Israel. But we must not infer from each resemblance that there has been borrowing. One major difference lies in the fact that the God of Israel was clearly understood as one, holy, and righteous, while the loftiest ideas of deity among the Greeks were vague, or complicated by polytheism.

In the same dialogue Protagoras presents what Werner Jaeger calls a "sociological" argument for the thesis that virtue can be taught. (This topic had been made familiar by Theognis and other philosopher poets.) Protagoras recites a detailed description of the teaching of virtue as it is practiced among the Greeks. The process of instruction lasts from early childhood to old age. Mother, nurse, father and tutor vie with one another in seeking the child's improvement. They continually set forth to him "that this is just and that is unjust; this is honorable, that is dishonorable; this is holy, that is unholy; do this and abstain from that." They punish his disobedience, to straighten him as they would a warped piece of wood. He is sent to teachers who are enjoined to give attention to his morals. He is given moral tales to memorize. Later the youth obtains moral lessons and training for citizenship from the study of the laws. Though there are bad sons of good fathers, the worst of civilized men are superior to savages. All men are in some degree teachers of virtue. The criticism by Socrates of the main contention that virtue can be imparted by teaching does not call in question the Sophist's description of the efforts to teach it, or remove the impression that strong educational forces were actively directed to the building of character.

The ascetic followers of Pythagoras (d. *ca.* 500 B.C.) were vegetarians not, as a satirist charged, because they were too poor to buy meat, but because they believed in man's brotherhood with all animals and in the reincarnation of souls. They taught the necessity of purification, and projected the purgatorial process into future existences. There is some resemblance here to Hinduism, but their ethics did not partake of the quietism of the latter. They gave expression to maxims of practical morality such as are contained in the late Pythagorean poem known as "The Golden Verses." It contains a section entitled *Katharsis* (purification), in which loyalty to family and friends, mastery of the passions, self-reverence, reflection before action, sincerity and moderation are enjoined. As a religious fraternity, the Pythagoreans laid emphasis also on a dutiful attitude to the gods and the ceremonies of worship.

II

With Socrates (469-399 B.C.) we reach a new beginning both in philosophy and in the guidance of souls. Our knowledge of his life, aims and teaching comes largely from Plato's *Dialogues*, especially the *Phaedo* and the *Apology*, and from Xenophon's *Memorabilia* and *Defense of Socrates*. Xenophon's interpretation differs considerably from Plato's. It has usually been regarded as less authoritative, and sometimes as almost valueless, but it has had its defenders. The difference may be due not to intentional misrepresentation but to the special interests and limitations of the writers. Xenophon makes Socrates a useful citizen and a saintly man, while Plato makes him the propounder of philosophical principles that coincide with Plato's own. Both, however, show us with fair clearness his labors as a physician of souls, and both lead us to believe that he felt this to be his divinely appointed calling. "It is primarily," says James Adam, "as the ἰατρὸς τῆς ψυχῆς—the physician or healer of the soul—that he regards himself."

In the *Phaedo*, a dialogue on immortality, a long passage of an auto-biographical nature is attributed to Socrates (who has already been condemned by his judges). In youth he had been captivated by philosophers who engaged in the investigation of nature and in the study of the mind, but had found these studies unprofitable since they failed to show him what he himself was, or the nature of the good. "I thought," he states, "that I ought to be careful that I did not lose the eye of my soul. I was afraid that my soul might be blinded." The argument for immortality that follows relies on the doctrine of ideas, and Socrates exclaims: "But then, O my friends, if the soul is immortal what care should be taken of her." She will take with her the fruits of her nurture in this life; thus the cultivation of the soul is the first concern.

In the *Apology*, Socrates testifies that, having survived the dangers of war in his youth, he was set apart by God to the life of philosophy. "Men of Athens, . . . I must obey God rather than you." He will not cease while he has breath to follow wisdom, and to warn every man who cares for money and fame while caring not at all for truth and the welfare of his soul.

> This will I do for old and young—for every man I meet, foreigner and citizen. . . . It is God's bidding; you must understand that. . . . I have gone about doing one thing and one only,—exhorting all of you, young and old, not to care for your bodies or for money above and beyond your souls and their welfare.

They will do harm to themselves, not to him, by putting him to death—one "who, at God's command, clings to the city as a gadfly clings to a horse." God has given him to the Athenians, to urge and prick each one, and never cease. He has never required payment from his listeners (he had described a Sophist as "one who deals wholesale and retail in the food of the soul"); he is ready for questions from rich and poor, and to question them in turn. "An unexamined life is not worthy of a man."

Dr. Jaeger regards the *Apology* as a composition of Plato made under the shock of the "colossal wrong" of his master's death, but as, nevertheless, a true representation of Socrates' character. He holds that Socrates' summons to men to care for their souls "turned the mind of

Greece toward a new way of life," and he attributes the emergence of the idea of the care of the soul in Christianity to the influence of Socrates as Plato interprets him. Socrates was like many a Christian in that, having keenly felt his own soul endangered, he spent his life admonishing others to attend to the welfare of theirs. In the *Protagoras* young Hippocrates knocks at his door very early in the morning, excitedly reporting the arrival of Protagoras the Sophist whose (fee-paying) pupil he proposes to become. "Young man, what are you doing?" asks Socrates; "are you aware of the danger to which you are about to expose your soul?" You would not take such risks with your body, he argues, but you hastily endanger your soul "on which all depends."

The soul, for Socrates and Plato, was the divine element in man, and was immortal. It was properly lord (*kuria*, "mistress") over the body. Socrates gave to the word *psyche* those "moral and religious overtones" (Jaeger) that "soul" has for Christian minds. It subsists upon instruction, and the instruction that is hawked about by merchants may be quite unwholesome. Such men may not know what is good or bad for the soul, and their customers, too, may be ignorant, unless one of them happens to be himself a physician of the soul. As a qualified physician, Socrates goes with the youth to test the skill of Protagoras, whom they find walking to and fro and discoursing to a group of listeners. The whole dialogue is a battle for the soul of young Hippocrates.

The *Dialogues* show us many scenes in which the sage is casually drawn into the conferences in which he took delight. The opening paragraph of the *Lysis* is an example:

> I was walking straight across the Academy to the Lyceum, by the outside road close under the wall, when, on reaching the little gate by the fountain of Panops, I met Hippothales . . . and Ctesippus . . . and several other youths gathered together in a group. As he saw me approaching Hippothales called out, "Ho, Socrates . . ."

But in other instances, Socrates took the initiative, and in either case, he assumed leadership of the discussion. Xenophon stresses his habit of going to the market place when it was thronged, seeking to be where people congregated, that he might inquire of them and discuss with them what they thought.

He appears as a relentless examiner of men's states of mind, a surgeon who probes before he heals. Often he seems primarily concerned to disturb and confuse those who rely on ill-considered opinions, forcing them into untenable positions and convicting them of self-contradiction.

True to his principle of examining himself as well as others, he often admits that he is as ignorant and mistaken as his pupils. He is much in the habit of saying "we," or "you and I," as he nimbly leads the course of argument. This, however, in no sense lessens the frustration of the victim. By the masterly swordplay of his dialectic he reduces his interviewer to a state of complete perplexity (*aporia*) and self-distrust. It is the intellectual counterpart of "conviction of sin" in Christian evangelism. In the *Theaetetus* he admits that he has a reputation for this habit of bringing men "to their wits' end." This dialogue is very revealing with regard to his method of soul guidance. Having quickly, on the question of the nature of knowledge, forced young Theaetetus to admit his complete discomfiture, he proceeds, with a paternal tenderness, to prompt him to think his way out: "If God be favorable, and you show a manful spirit, you will be able." In this connection he speaks of his art as that of a midwife who brings to birth the thoughts of men. In the end some progress is made by the youth under this treatment and, recovering from his mental paralysis, he says to Socrates in grateful surprise: "By Zeus, through your help, I have said more than there was in me."

Perhaps none of his interlocutors received a more grueling cross-examination than Euthydemus, who fancied himself highly talented for government. Midway in the inquisition Socrates enforces the lesson of the temple inscription, "Know thyself." The victim finally exclaims, "I seem to know absolutely nothing." He became a devoted pupil: but Xenophon notes: "Of those who were thus treated by Socrates, many came to him no more." (*Memorabilia* IV, ii.) Probably some "went away very sorrowful." In a celebrated passage of the *Symposium* Alcibiades (whose later life was made a reproach to his teacher) declares how Socrates amazed and possessed the souls of his listeners, and how his own heart leaped and his tears flowed under the master's instruction until he could hardly endure the life he was leading, neglecting the wants of his soul. He tears himself away, and many a time has wished that Socrates were dead; yet he knows that would be greater sorrow. So he concludes, "I am at my wits' end." In the case of Alcibiades this experience of *aporia* did not lead on to virtue, as doubtless Socrates hoped. No method of guiding turbulent youth can be guaranteed never to fail. But there is an abiding truth in the view that inordinate self-esteem stands in the way of true self-fulfillment and must be overcome at the cost of pain. Epictetus realized the purpose of Socrates when he wrote: "Arrogance is removed by confutation, and Socrates was the first who practiced this." (*Discourses* III, xiv.) He felt it important to strip men of their armor of self-confidence and compel them to abandon all security in "the unexamined life."

Xenophon labors to show that Socrates not only pointed the way to virtue but actually induced his disciples to follow it. He reports a conversation with Aristodemus, who has become religiously an unbeliever and ceased to attend worship. Socrates leads him to admit that the adaptation of the structure of the human body to its functions, the instinct of motherhood, the soul's direction of the body, and man's powers of understanding can be taken as evidence for the concern of the gods for mankind. Aristodemus is urged to offer them worship and to discover for himself that the divinity is present everywhere and has a care for all things.

By delivering such sentiments, Socrates seems to me [says Xenophon] to have led his associates to refrain from what was impious or unjust or dishonorable, not merely when they were seen by men, but when they were in solitude, since they would conceive that nothing which they did would escape the knowledge of the gods. (*Memorabilia* I, iv)

That Socrates suited his medicine of the soul to the needs of the individual is everywhere apparent. Xenophon may have wished to illustrate this by placing in immediate context the conversations with Glaucon and with Charmides (*Memorabilia* III, vi, vii). The former seeks political responsibility without preparation for it. He is stopped on the street and put through a humiliating interrogatory, in which he shows a complete ignorance of what every citizen ought to know, and is then roundly lectured on the necessity of such knowledge on the part of one who desires public office. Charmides, on the other hand, is capable of civic service but shrinks from speaking in public. He is chided for his timidity and urged both to examine himself and to improve the affairs of the state. Xenophon also reports a dialogue in which Socrates seeks to persuade his own son to revere his mother (Xantippe) who, the youth complains, "says such things as no one would endure" (*Memorabilia* II, ii); and another in which he strives to reconcile two brothers by prompting the younger to approach the elder in brotherly affection and so challenge him to a contest in kindness (II, iii).

Socrates spoke of the *daimon* or supernatural inward monitor that often restrained him from wrong courses and held him to his vocation.

That it did not warn him to desist from teaching and take flight when he was being brought to his death he took as proof of divine approval of his resolution; and Xenophon makes him say that when he began to prepare a studied defense, "the *daimon* testified disapprobation." Xenophon represents the *daimon* as prompting his exhortations to his companions to do certain things and leave others undone. The *daimon* was distinct from conscience, which for Socrates was linked with reason. In Xenophon's report of his defense, it is called "the voice of God." It represented a direct breaking in from a supernatural realm, and was wholly personal to himself. He does not seem to have expected a corresponding manifestation in his disciples.

Socrates keenly resented the charge that his teaching had corrupted the youth of Athens. He disclaimed the name of "teacher" partly because other teachers seemed to him mercenary, and partly because he felt himself a fellow searcher with those who engaged in discussions with him. He claimed that many citizens and aliens who made virtue their pursuit took delight in his talk, and challenged his accusers to show that anyone had been led by him to drunkenness, idleness or vice. Yet his method must have been disturbing to society. It set men on a new quest for salvation by education, and encouraged a questioning habit of mind which tended to bring all existing order to the bar of reason. His assumption that virtue necessarily flows from knowledge has been criticized from Aristotle down. Socrates did not reckon sufficiently with the strength of man's passions, or realize the force of the moral impulses that spring up in the emotional realm. On the other hand, the knowledge he sought was not a set of factual data but a reverent grasp of life and of one's true place in it. Thus his position has a certain affinity to that of those Christian reformers who asserted the priority of faith to works. However we may estimate his philosophical position, we must regard him as the most eminent and original of those men of ancient Greece who devoted themselves to the guidance of souls.

III

The lasting impression made by Socrates is attested by countless references of later philosophers, especially of the Academicians and the Stoics, and of such eclectic geniuses as Cicero and Plutarch. The idea of the philosopher's function as physician of souls, of which he had been the most original exponent, was given fresh expression by many writers. It was probably the Academician Crantor (d. 268 B.C.), who supplied the earliest example of a new literary *genre*, the consolatory essay.

The modern studies by Carl Buresch, C. Martha, Charles Favez, Sister Mary Evaristus [Moran] and Sister Mary Edmund Fern have shed much light upon the ancient literature of consolation. In its fullest extent it includes many passages in poets and philosophers before and after Crantor's time. The writers of consolation treatises strew their pages with quotations from Homer, the tragic poets, and the Dialogues of Plato. Certain of the Dialogues—the *Phaedo* and the *Apology*—in which Socrates consoles the friends whom he must leave, and the *Menexenus* which contains a funeral oration, approach closely to the Consolation type. The latter, however, has for its essential purpose the lifting of the weight of sorrow from a bereaved or stricken friend.

Crantor, a native of Soli in Cilicia, became a teacher in the Athenian Academy. His *Peri Penthous* (On Grief), although Cicero says, "We have all read it," is extant only in quoted fragments. Cicero used it in his book *On Consolation*, but of this also only fragments remain. Its contents can best be understood from references and quotations in Cicero and Plutarch. Crantor's consolation was written to comfort a father on the deaths of his children. But it evidently went beyond this to discuss a wider range of life's sorrows and disappointments. He opposes the Stoic demand for *apatheia*, the rejection of emotion. The affections are grounded in human nature and are of use to man for virtue. Without fear there would be no foresight, without suffering no kindness, without anger no valor. Moderation in, rather than annihilation of, grief is held desirable. "I am by no means in agreement," he says, according to Cicero, "with those who highly praise a sort of painless state that cannot and ought not to exist. . . . If I should be ill, let me have the feeling I had before, whether something is to be cut away or extracted from my body. For this rejection of feeling comes only at the great cost of barbarity of soul and insensibility of body." In a work attributed to Plutarch he is quoted as agreeing with "all the old philosophers" that human life is full of woe, fortune is inconstant and, indeed, the bitter potion of our misfortunes was mingled for us as soon as we were born. From the defects of our mortal nature our judgment is depraved and disease and care afflict mankind. But comfort comes not only through acquiescence in the common lot of mortals: "To be innocent is the greatest comfort in affliction." Crantor evidently held a belief in an immortal life in which the good are rewarded.

IV

The versatile Marcus Tullius Cicero (d. 43 B.C.) was much concerned with the task of consolation. He is remarkable for having written a consolation for his own sorrows. In February, 45 B.C. his beloved daughter Tullia died. She was only thirty-two, but had suffered much unhappiness and had very recently been divorced by her third husband. Her father had hoped to have her companionship in his old age. His friends now sent letters of consolation, and he recalled much that he had read on bereavement. "Nothing has been written for the lessening of grief that I have not read at your house" (he confided to his friend Atticus); "but my sorrow breaks through it all." He has taken up his pen to write a "consolation" for himself and is laboring at it daily all day long. In this way Cicero compiled his now lost treatise *On Consolation*. Some sentences of this book are quoted by the author in his *Tusculan Disputations*, written late in the same year at his villa beside the then thriving city of Tusculum. Evidently he argued in it for the immateriality, divine origin and immortality of the human soul (*T.D.* I, xxvii). He wrote so impressively that the book caused one reader to wish to depart from this sorrowful world (I, xxxi). He refers to examples of the constancy of eminent men in bereavement (III, xxviii). In the *Consolation*, he undoubtedly drew suggestions from Crantor, and favored his admission of moderate grief as against Stoic apathy.

The *Tusculan Disputations* as a whole is nearly related to the Consolation literature, since it deals with death and pain as problems of the individual, and discusses methods of healing afflicted souls. It presents in five leisurely dialogues, the substance of which is delivered by a character who is obviously Cicero himself, critical analyses of the opinions of Greek philosophers, and makes fruitful use of both Greek and Roman poetry. Thus the work provides a feast of ideas rather than a closely woven argument. Cicero stresses the view that the soul is imperishable and that death for the good man is release into a better life. God forbids our willful departure from life, but where, as in the cases of Socrates and Cato, God gives a sound reason for dying, the wise man will go forth gladly "from this darkness to that light." For philosophers, as Socrates said (in *Phaedo*) "the whole of life is a consideration of death" (I, xxx).

But supposing for the sake of argument that there is no afterlife, should we shrink from death as an evil? Death takes us from the ills of life in a moment of time. Pompey would have been happier if he had died earlier. If there is no consciousness after death, there is no consciousness of deprivation. Nature has granted us the loan of life; we have no cause of complaint if she calls it back when she will. The virtuous live on in fame and glory, and in the esteem of good men. Thus whether death brings a change of our situation or a perpetual sleep, it is not to be thought of as evil, but as good. Let us at God's bidding go gladly and thankfully, as those loosed from chains (xxiv-xlix).

The second disputation treats of the endurance of pain, along with the hardships of toil, military exposure and athletic training. Cicero here so far favors the Stoics as to say that disgrace is an evil worse than pain. He extols the four cardinal virtues, prudence, temperance, fortitude and justice, and shows that they imply the soul's conquest of pain. It is in the third disputation that he is most directly a physician of souls. The art of healing the body has, he believes, advanced beyond that of healing the soul. The soul that is sick cannot rightly prescribe for itself, except by following the instruction of wise men. The evil we drink in with the milk of our nurse, and the later corruptions that assail us from our environment, bring on disorders that need treatment no less than bodily ills. The diseases of the soul are more pernicious and more numerous than those of the body. With the poet Ennius, Cicero observes that the sick soul is wandering and frustrated, and dogged by ceaseless desire (III, i-iii).

The discussion here becomes too detailed for us to follow as it turns upon the use of terms such as "affliction" (*aegritudo*), "terror," "lust," "wrath," "unsoundness of mind" (*insania*), "fury." "We are not born from rock" and although the wise man will not yield to the despondency of affliction, he may suffer many disorders and perturbations by which his soul is shaken as by a tempest. While Crantor's recognition of this fact, against the Stoics, is accepted, Cicero would have us not merely acquiesce in it. He is courageous enough to demand that we uproot these evils from our souls. Unless the soul is healed, and without philosophy it cannot be, there will be no end of miseries. Cicero examines the Stoic theories in which the wise man is free from pity and envy, and turns to the Peripatetic doctrine of the mean. He has criticisms of both. He rejects the views of the Epicureans, who would merely redirect the sufferer's attention from troublous thoughts to pleasing ones; and he agrees with Carneades against the Cyrenaics and the Stoic Chrysippus, that affliction is not relieved by contemplation of the sorrows of others.

Cicero notes that the position here opposed was supported by a quotation from a (lost) play of Euripides. "To me it seems quite otherwise," says Cicero, finding for another reason a healing value in the common sorrow; "for the necessity of bearing the human condition forbids me to contend, as it were, against God, and warns me that I am a man; and this thought greatly relieves sorrow." Cicero does not voice the thought which Tennyson expresses in the words:

> That loss is common would not make
> My own less bitter, rather more.

But he does indicate that instead of taking a crude satisfaction in seeing others suffer, we should be encouraged to bear the burdens we see them quietly bear. We must support those who are staggering under the weight of affliction. Perhaps there is some smugness in his remark, that a career spent honorably and with distinction itself brings such "consolation" as to ward off affliction or make slight the wounds of the soul (III, vi-xxv). Cicero condemns as detestable the barbarous rites of mourning that are performed from a sense of duty, and the likewise dutiful but artificial gloom of formal days of mourning in which children are whipped for any outbreak of merriment. Men have ceased to mourn when startled by fear; shall reason then have no power to resist affliction?

In the concluding sections (xxxi-xxxiv) of Book III, Cicero seeks to summarize the duties of comforters in the light of philosophy. What Aeschylus in *Prometheus* called "healing words" (*iatroi logoi*) should be spoken at the proper season. The comforter should (1) show the slightness of the evil suffered; (2) discuss the common state of human life, and the individual's own special sorrow; (3) show the folly of yielding to grief when it obviously profits nothing. Merely to say, "This [sorrow] is not peculiar to you," is not sufficient: one must adapt the treatment to the individual case, as lawyers do in dealing with the persons in court. The states of poverty, obscurity, exile, the "death" of one's country, slavery, weakness, blindness, and all the ills the flesh is heir to, severally require their own special consolations.

In the fourth book Cicero moves on to discuss the uses of philosophy for the "perturbations" that assail the soul. On the basis of Stoic writers an elaborate catalogue of these is set forth which will remind the Christian reader of Gregory the Great's tabulation of the Deadly Sins and their attendant vices. Yet the psychopathic states referred to are not thought of as sins in the Hebrew and Christian sense. The soul, which Cicero always regarded as in some sense divine, is offending against itself, not against God. Excessive joy, and lust, as derived from anticipations of what is good, are set over against fear and that desperation in affliction called *aegritudo,* which arise from considerations of evil. Compassion (*misericordia*) is among the perturbations to be cast out, no less than the malice that rejoices in another's woe. Cicero, here confessedly reciting Stoic teachings, regards compassion as affliction caused by the undeserved misery of another: nobody, he supposes, has compassion for a parricide or a traitor. Men have as individuals a "proclivity" to special faults, just as they are each subject to attacks of different bodily diseases. But there are robust and gifted souls who repel distempers as Corinthian bronze resists rust, and, if affected, are cured more readily than the dull and sluggish (IV, i-xiv).

When the soul's irrational agitations tend to mount and to burst all restraint, their cure lies in virtue alone, virtue being always associated with reason. At this point he uses the term "frugality" as expressing what is characteristic of the virtuous and well-ordered soul. It is, we may say, the quality of a man whose moral economy is sound and free from excesses. The man who possesses it measures human affairs by his awareness of eternity, and of the vastness of the universe. Watchful amid life's vicissitudes, he is unperturbed when ill-fortune comes, and knows the fullest happiness. The Peripatetics are wrong in trying to confine the soul's disorders within permitted limits: as well permit some measure of injustice or vice—a course which leads down the slippery slope to moral ruin. The argument that the passions are useful for virtue, e.g., anger for courage, is rejected. Cicero is not sure that he has ever acted courageously; but if he has he is sure that it has not been from anger—though he has not thought it unbecoming to simulate anger as a pleader in court.

Some of Cicero's letters, and of his treatises, are replete with materials that might be studied with profit for his method as a philosophic guide. The *De Officiis (On Duties),* for example, offers much casuistical direction of conscience. But we must make room for other eminent guides of souls. The *Tusculan Disputations* sets forth very well the approach to distressed souls made by a moderate, unoriginal and eclectic philosopher. Cicero is sensitive and considerate. He is firm but never harsh. The trouble within us must be wholly uprooted and cast out; but, hardly less than medieval guides, he recognizes that each person and each disorder must be treated in a special way. He makes discriminating use of earlier writers, leaning now to the Stoics and now to the Academicians, showing respect for the Aristotelians, but sternly opposing the easy prescriptions of the Epicureans. Where there exists that grave condition which he calls *aegritudo*, he urges that it be directly combatted with arguments of reason. He appears to think that a reasoned exposition of the unworthiness of yielding to this experience is sufficient to eradicate it. This view accords with the conception of Socrates that virtue depends upon thinking. Cicero, indeed, cites an incident in which Socrates agreed with a critic that he was disposed to certain vices, but claimed that he had cast them out by reason (IV, xvii-xxx). The soul, he repeats, comes from God, and is like God himself; if not blinded by error, it would become absolute reason (V, xiii). Whereas the Aristotelians had given something of an ethical function to the emotions, Cicero gives them only that tolerance demanded by the principle of humanity, and follows Socrates in linking virtue, the life of moral wholeness, with right thinking and true knowledge.

V

Before turning to the Stoics we note two consolatory writings found in a later eclectic philosopher. Plutarch (A.D. 46-120) was a native of Chaeronea in Boeotia, and wrote most of his works there in his later years. His authorship of the *Consolation to Apollonius* is only a probability, but there is no question of the genuineness of his *Consolation to His Wife*. The former is the ampler essay. We have already noted the evidence it provides concerning Crantor's *On Grief*. It repeats, too, some of the favorite ideas of Cicero set forth above. It is addressed to a father who has been bereaved of a son, a model youth. At a seasonable time the author brings "healing words" (Aeschylus: see above p. 28) to lessen the grief of his friend. With the aid of passages from philosophers and poets, and biographical references, he presents the topics suitable for consideration in such a case. Sorrow must have some expression, but is not to be nursed and clung to. In our insecurity and mortality, reason is its sovereign remedy. The calamities of others should be considered, not in order to find satisfaction in their miseries, but to remove the feeling of peculiar affliction. Death, as a remedy for life's ills, or as a far journey of the soul, ought not to be deplored. The measure of our life is not its length but its quality. Remembrance of the worthy life of the departed calls for gladness rather than mourning. The old piety of

Greece, that excludes complaint of what the gods decree and dreads the nemesis entailed by pride, finds fresh expression in this product of late Hellenism.

"To be obstinate in our grief is the resolution of madness." It is deplorable that men charge the gods with cruelty and prompt themselves to mourning; they even treasure the last words of the departed as fuel to rekindle their sorrow. Who knows but that God has taken some away in fatherly tenderness, protecting them from the world's evils? We soon follow those we mourn for, and should avoid the company of those who "flatter our tears." Numerous anecdotes are recited to show how heroically the loss of sons and daughters has been borne by men of exemplary character. An eloquent panegyric is pronounced upon the young man, who is now numbered among the blessed dead, the darling of the gods, and will not be pleased to see his father and mother grieve for him.

Plutarch's relatively short letter to his wife, Timoxena, contains many of the arguments of the epistolary essay just examined. The occasion was the death of a two-year-old daughter bearing her mother's name. The father has learned of this bereavement during a protracted absence from his home. In this letter the evidence of a remarkably Christian-like relationship of husband and wife is more striking than the terms of the advice. We are again, he says, as we were before she was born, save that we now number her two years of happy life among our blessings. He is sure that his wife will resist foolish people who visit her only to revive her grief. The child, knowing nothing of the experiences she is deprived of, has felt no loss. He reminds his wife of what together they had been assured of in the Eleusinian mysteries—that the soul is deathless. It is set free by death as a bird from a cage.

VI

A number of Stoic philosophers before Seneca contributed to the literature of consolation; notably Cleanthes (d. 252 B.C.), Chrysippus (d. 206 B.C.) and Panaetius (d. 108 B.C.). The works of all these are, like those of Crantor, preserved mainly in the fragmentary quotations and casual comments of later writers. Chrysippus was, perhaps, most directly concerned with the cure of souls. Émile Bréhier compares him with Socrates in the fact that he "undertook a mission to individuals and became a director of souls," and adds that he sought an intimate transformation of the soul which assures to it not only wisdom but happiness.

Cleanthes and Chrysippus held that the true sage has perfect happiness, and that the state of happiness is consummated in a union with the will of Him who guides the universe. Their perfectionist views accorded with a stern note in the treatment of grief: it has no place in the mind of the true philosopher. Cicero owed much to Panaetius and his Roman pupils, and represents him as under the influence of Crantor and as the author of a letter *On Bearing Sorrow*.

Lucius Annaeus Seneca (d. A.D. 65), most famous of the Stoics, holds a place of distinction as a guide of souls. A considerable number of his voluminous writings fall within that branch of philosophy which he called the "department of precepts." This comprises such matters as advice, dissuasion, admonition, exhortation, consolation, praise, reproof. Seneca, while requiring the subordination of precepts to basic principles (chief of which is "life according to nature"), insists, against Aristo, that they are not superfluous but necessary. He defends, too, the office of the "monitor," or counselor, who lays down precepts for inquirers; even if he points only to the obvious he may do a valuable service. Good precepts benefit us as do good examples. The weak need someone to go before them and say: "This you shall avoid, this you shall do." "One must be directed even while he is beginning to be capable of self-direction." Each of us needs a guardian (*custos*) to tweak his ear when he is careless. With success and admiration, vices grow rank. Amid the noise of city life we need a monitor to contradict the assumptions of worldlings (Letter xciv).

Seneca lived in affluence unbecoming to a Stoic, but met with misfortunes and in the end committed suicide at Nero's command. Different judgments have been made on his character. He is the earliest of a great trio of Stoic directors of souls. He was probably less uncompromising than his younger contemporary, Musonius Rufus (d. A.D. 100) and the latter's eminent disciple Epictetus (d. A.D. 120). His writings mark a new reforming emphasis in Stoicism and he has been called by Samuel Dill "the apostle of a moral revival." The earnest moralism of Seneca was manifestly rooted in religious belief. "Truly no man is good without God," he once wrote. . . . "It is He who gives noble and upright counsel" (Letter xli). It is not surprising that there was invented a friendly correspondence between him and St. Paul, and that many later Christians felt toward him much as Zwingli did when he called Seneca "*vir sanctissimus.*" There is, however, a baffling vagueness about his use of the term "God." His theology lacks a Redeemer, and trust in God as an ever present help in trouble is scarcely discoverable in his ministry of guidance.

Many of Seneca's moral essays are expanded letters addressed to persons well known to him and offering advice of a personal kind. *To Marcia on Consolation* is such a treatise. This prominent Roman lady had been bereaved in turn of a noble father, whose death was self-inflicted in defiance of a tyrant, and of four sons. The death of the last of these sons cast her into such a settled state of despondency that Seneca felt impelled to proffer his advice. He uses at the outset two contrary examples of bereaved mothers, that of Octavia who sorrowed until death for her son and was morose toward her other children, and that of Livia who after a season of mourning cast off her sorrow, and lived cheerfully, cherishing her son's memory and speaking frequently of his good life. To follow the first example is disastrous; to follow the second is worthy of the dead and helpful to the living. Another bereaved lady is also cited who consulted the philosopher Areus and obtained relief through his guidance. Some paragraphs are devoted to the (conjectured) advice of Areus in this instance: the material is commonplace, but not the adroitness with which Seneca breaks through Marcia's resolute gloom. At the end he calls in her departed father to speak to her from his heavenly home where, with the young man now so unwisely lamented, he enjoys the unalloyed bliss and limitless knowledge of the immortals. Seneca plies Marcia with persuasions against nursing her grief longer, and urges the common argument of the fickleness of fortune and the prevailing misery of life. We must accept the insecurity of our blessings: our stage is set with properties loaned and returnable. The injunction, "Know thyself," calls attention to man's mortality. What is man? A frail, anxious, mortal creature—though he makes a great uproar, reflects upon things eternal, and plans for his great-grandchildren!

Seneca examines what he supposes to be in Marcia's mind as she defends the sanctum of her sorrow. Is she lamenting the loss of the pleasure her son has given her, and unthankful that she once enjoyed it? A chain of examples follows, of those who assuaged their afflictions by bearing them calmly. These are of men only: does she then reply: "You forget that it is a woman whom you are comforting?" He accordingly presents numerous cases of the heroic bearing of Roman women in bereavement. The mother of the Gracchi, having seen her two sons murdered, said to those who would have commiserated with her: "Never shall I, who bore the Gracchi, call myself unblest."

The children of her son should remind Marcia of him and not of her sorrow. While our loved ones are alive we do not weep at their absence. We should think of the dead as only absent; we have sent them on before, whither we shall soon follow. The popular beliefs concerning a future world of terror are idle fancies of the poets. Death is release from pain, a bound that our ills cannot pass, an entrance to everlasting peace. It frees the slave, lifts the captive's chains, and brings men back to the equal state they were born in. Pompey, Cicero and Cato would have been happier if they had died earlier. Had the young man lived to ripe years he might have been corrupted from his modest purity. There is no need to visit the tomb where his bones lie: he himself has departed, pausing near the earth for a season of purification, then to be borne up to highest heaven and welcomed by a holy company of such as Scipio and Cato.

Another of Seneca's consolations was written to comfort his mother Helvia over his exile in Corsica (A.D. 41-48). It is a poignant essay, since the comforter's own affliction is the cause of the recipient's grief. Seneca rarely exhibits the orthodox Stoic apathy, least of all here. He feelingly recalls family sorrows: his own son had died in Helvia's arms. This catalogue of bereavements is a part of his healing method: "I resolved," he says, "to conquer, not to minimize your woe." He is happy amid conditions that usually make men miserable. He has been taught by wiser men never to trust fortune, and has habitually kept outward goods separated from his inner self. He has lost his wealth but true wealth is of the mind and of virtue, which the exiled take with them. His environment is forbidding, but he can behold the stars, whose motion suggests that God delights in movement. Innumerable people by compulsion or desire have changed their place of abode. By numerous examples he encourages her to give herself to the study of philosophy, sovereign remedy for sadness. Nevertheless he lays emphasis upon the support she will find by welcoming the kindness of her other sons, of her brilliant little grandson, Marcus, and of her women relatives. The highest praise is bestowed upon the fine womanly qualities and lifelong devotion to duty of Helvia herself. She must think of him as cheerful in his exile and really in the best of circumstances, since he is engaged in an uninterrupted, eager search of truth.

Seneca wrote about the same time a consolation to Polybius, a highly responsible official, who was mourning for a brother. Here Seneca uses such arguments as we have noticed above, and in addition advises the

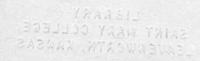

concealment of grief if it cannot be quite overcome, for the sake of example to the many who constantly observe the conduct of so great a man as Polybius, and for his master the emperor's sake. The departed brother has only gone before us into a realm of joy and light. True pleasures are those enjoyed in retrospect; the remembrance is more than the present experience. The words with which this piece closes have reference to the author's situation: while not despairful they are far from being so brave as those with which he comforted his mother. Had he practiced toward her that dutiful dissimulation which he suggests to Polybius?

Seneca's letters contain a vast amount of material that would merit examination did space permit. Many were written in his later years to Lucilius, the procurator of Sicily. Although valuable for Seneca's ripe observations, these letters interest us especially for the moral advice and direction they contain. "It will be my glory," he says, "if I can draw you out of the depths in which you flounder without hope of escape." Philosophy teaches deeds, not words: one must live according to his own principles, and deeds must agree with words. Let Lucilius get rid of the ostentation of a great household, so that no one will pay him lying compliments. The soul softened by ease and dreading hardships must be aroused out of sleep (*Epistulae*, xx). We do not need to pray with hands raised toward heaven: "God is at your side, with you, within you." There dwells within us a holy spirit (*sacer spiritus*). No one is good, no one rises above his fortune, without God's help. A spirit is sent down to illumine us, as sunbeams from the sun. When we witness human character at its highest, we know that it is supported by the divine (xii).

The shortness of life and the preciousness of every hour, are themes of frequent emphasis in Seneca as in many of his predecessors. Life is all too brief, they said, for the attainment of virtue: let us then be up and doing. Men forget, and Seneca reminds them, that by nature they die daily and have already partially died. An idle, aimless life of eighty years is far less desirable than a short and serviceable one (Letter i). In his essay *On Anger* and elsewhere he recommends a thorough self-examination at the end of every day. This was not new; it was the method of Pythagoras—and it appears in the *Analects* of Confucius. Benjamin Constant Martha, in his *Études morales* has an interesting chapter on the history of this practice in antiquity; he notes its revival by the Theophilanthropists of the French Revolution. We shall see it frequently illustrated in Christian piety.

In his treatises on consolation Seneca repeatedly denies what earlier Stoics had affirmed, that the wise man never feels grief. Rather, like Crantor and Cicero, he permits it to be entertained for a limited time. *"Fluant lacrimae, sed eaedem et desinant"*—let the tears flow, but let them also cease! Yet on the whole his prescriptions partake of the Stoic heroism. He does not try to heal wounds too lightly. All elements of the grief felt are searched and considered. Man's life is full of woe, and we must gain strength to bear it. We may not seek relief in frivolities, or in anything external. We ought, indeed, to accept the ministries of friends and relatives, but we must vigorously take ourselves in hand and live undisturbed by the flux of circumstance. In his essay *On Tranquillity*, he is responding to the confession of a young military officer who in his manner of life has fulfilled the whole law of the Stoic sages, yet finds himself inwardly unstable. Seneca urges him to withdraw his mind from all outward affairs, yielding up if need be the plans he has cherished, and to retire into himself in order to find, or recover, tranquillity. This is not by intention an unsocial repudiation of the common life, but (along with diversions necessary to our well-being) a means of recruiting the resources of personality required to face our duties. Yet the common tasks of life are hardly thought of as an opportunity for helpful service to mankind. They are significant in the education of the soul chiefly as a part of the inevitable, to which our attitude should always be acceptance.

VII

Musonius Rufus (whose surviving utterances have been edited and translated by Cora Lutz) approached closely to the teachings of the New Testament, especially on forbearance and forgiveness. He, too, was a Stoic counselor of souls. The fact that Musonius had suffered exile and imprisonment for his ideals qualified him as an adviser. He sought to persuade one under sentence of exile that exile itself is not an evil. The whole world is our fatherland, and not even at home do we enjoy it all or share all possible good companionship. It is only the evil in us that makes exile an evil. When we see men endanger themselves for gain (e.g., acrobats turning somersaults over upturned swords), should we not be willing to endure hardship for the sake of happiness? To live well we should regard each day as our last. He is blessed who dies not late but well. Musonius challenges one depressed by his own defects:

"What are you waiting for? . . . Until God in person shall come to you?
. . . Cut off the dead part of your soul and you will recognize the presence
of God."

Epictetus, a liberated slave, sickly and lame, having been expelled
from Rome by Domitian (A.D. 90), taught for an unknown period at
Nicopolis in Epirus (now Palaeoprevesa, Albania). His *Discourses* were
preserved in the careful notes of a learned disciple. They are informal
homilies on the conduct of life. There is extant also a short *Manual* in
which his teaching is presented in condensed form. Whereas Seneca, like
Fénelon and William Law, was a director to men and women of the
higher social class, Epictetus addressed unclassified groups of hearers. His
practical ethics rests on a religious foundation, and his sense of the
presence of God as maker, father and judge is strong and constant. If
we could feel the truth that we are children of God we should be proud
and happy. Failing this, we develop our lower natures and become
beasts (*Discourses* I, iii). It is not enough to be familiar with the
treatises of Chrysippus: one must get rid of mourning and sighing over
his misfortunes, and be able to say with Socrates, "If it please the gods,
so be it" (I, iv). God knows all things and knows us altogether. "Never
say that you are alone: you are not alone, God is within." Let us swear
allegiance to him as soldiers to Caesar, and swear to find no fault with
his gifts (I, xiv). We ought to praise him continually. "What else can a
lame old man as I am do but chant the praise of God? . . . This is my
task" (I, xvi). When you stand before a man of worldly power, remember that it is God and not he whom you should seek to please (I, xx).
To cast out our passions and vices we must look to God alone and obey
Him. We must have the courage to pray: "Do with me as Thou wilt,"
whether this means retirement or office, poverty or riches. Epictetus
repeatedly urges the appropriateness of praise to God; but leaves little
room for prayer. Stoic prayer is essentially a summoning of the soul to
acquiescence in God's will. The God addressed is the God within, or
the God discoverable in nature's law (II, xvi). Yet, more than his
predecessors, Epictetus recognized the need of divine guidance. Casti-
gating unqualified lecturers he remarks that the teaching function "demands mature years, a certain way of life, and the guidance of God"
(III, 21).

The Stoic tradition comes out in Epictetus' insistence that conditions
that lie beyond reach of our will are to be dismissed from our concern.

Such matters are *adiaphora*, things indifferent. At times, however, he stresses the importance of a right judgment of things indifferent. The Stoic note appears, too, in his severity toward offenders. When a scholar who had become an adulterer came to his lecture, Epictetus excoriated him as an unsocial monster, likening him to a wasp, a wolf and an ape (II, iv). This stern view of sex offenses is connected with the doctrine of the fatherhood of God, which is the bond of society. Why, he asks elsewhere, are you not aware of your divine origin? Will you not remember this in eating, and in your relations with women? You would shrink from doing what you do if an image of God were present: but God who sees all, is within you (II, viii). In another case he dwells upon the unmanly loss of self-respect that go with acts of profligacy, and urges the offender to return to the disciplined life (IV, x).

The instances just given suggest a characteristic of the *Discourses*; they were free and easy discussions of a theme, in which opportunity was taken to deal with individuals. He interrupts a lecture to tell a Roman visitor how ignorant he is of God and man; here he likens the function of the philosopher-guide to that of a mirror reflecting an ugly face, or of a physician diagnosing a serious illness (II, xiv). Sometimes, too, Epictetus in his lectures reports his private conversations with those whom he has counseled. He recounts how he urged a man who had "decided" to starve himself, to re-examine his decision rather than to feel himself bound by it (II, xv). Sometimes the lecture resolves itself into a dialogue with an opponent. In a very frank discussion with a Roman city magistrate, an Epicurean, he asks: "Can you imagine a city of Epicureans?" (III, vii). In other cases the thought is developed by objection and reply in the manner of a dialogue. The topic of freedom is treated in the form of an argument with a hypothetical senator who looks upon freedom and slavery as external things (IV, i). A highly satirical discourse in the same style disposes of the aspirants to philosophy who ostentatiously come to lectures unwashed (IV, xi). Epictetus was a celibate and in a good sense an ascetic; he practiced and preached a rigid discipline of the body, but not its degradation. And he warned against boasting of physical self-restraint or austerity. If you are a water drinker, he is reported to have said, do not proclaim it. Train yourself by taking cold water when very thirsty, casting it forth again—and saying nothing about it. The whole of life is for him a training of the soul under the eye of God, to make it pure and steadfast and quite indifferent to good or evil fortune.

VIII

That the Stoic directors offered valuable help to many of their sorrowing, perplexed and misguided contemporaries, cannot be gainsaid. They furnished many suggestions, too, to the Christian Fathers. The later Stoics, including Marcus Aurelius, who is rather an inspiring writer than a practicing guide of souls, show a departure from the harsher early positions, and share the prevailing eclecticism. The Stoics are very fond of citing the example of Socrates: Epictetus sometimes makes use of his great example almost as a Christian preacher would use the example of Christ. Seneca shows a thoughtful searching of the human heart, and accords a restricted place to natural feeling. But too much remains of the negative temper of early Stoicism, and of Cynicism with which it was closely linked. (Zeno, the founder of the Stoics, had been a pupil of the Cynic, Crates.) Socrates failed to reckon with the emotions; the Stoic counselors either repudiated them or restricted them very narrowly. Salvation, the making whole of the personality, was in the Academy a matter of the intellect, in the Stoa a matter of the will, which becomes a stern policeman of the emotions. Men are exhorted to beware of forming attachments which may be suddenly broken, to refrain from hearty laughter, to avoid scenes of excitement. Amid the challenges to a heroic self-control are suggestions of an ethic of escape. "You can be invincible," says Epictetus (*Manual* 19), "if you never enter a contest where victory is not in your power." If you make jokes you may forfeit the respect of others (33). Such advice seems hardly consistent with the oft-emphasized Stoic indifference to reputation. Epictetus at times lays himself open to the charge of assuming a moral pose. When you see a man in grief for a dead or absent child, he says, you may sympathize with him in words and groans; "but take heed that you do not groan in your inner being" (*Manual* 17). Probably the philosopher would explain this too brief statement so as to escape the charge of downright hypocrisy. In the context he reminds us of the Stoic view that the distress lies not in the event but in the man's judgment of the event. But there remains a certain unreality and insufficiency in this approach to the sorrows of our fellow men. The modern therapist would try to combine objectivity with a real personal interest.

The Stoic acceptance of everything that happens as a determination of nature or as a judgment of God may mean acquiescence in avoidable evils. The sages partially realized this, but did little to correct it. They

aimed to reform the inner life; they held a vision of a brotherly humanity or "City of the Universe" in which each would fulfill his duty; but
they failed to show how this could be realized. Epictetus grows eloquent
on this theme (e.g., *Discourses* III, xxii), but he often points to the
widespread failure of Stoics to live by their own precepts, or to carry
their principles into political and social action (IV, iv). In such passages
there is a note of defeat. In their world of moral confusion the Stoic
minority bore a wholesome witness to the values of tranquillity and restraint. But, seeking to suppress the emotions, they failed to arouse men
to those great loyalties which are needed both to resolve the anxieties of
the individual and to transform the spirit of a society that burdens him
with anxiety.

In all this philosophical direction of souls there lurks a recognition of
the fact of sin which rarely comes to clear expression and hardly at all
to poignant realization. When Seneca in his work *On Clemency* (I, 6)
says, *"Peccavimus omnes"* (we have all sinned), the statement is merely
the prelude to a reminder that we are too prone to censure others. The
concept of sin, so prominent in Judaism, like the concept of God, here
remains vague. The prevailing notion of what is wrong with the soul
is based on the analogy of bodily disease. It is rather in the cults that
entered the West from Egypt and Asia Minor that the notion of sin
begins to approach that of the Hebrew-Christian tradition.

Raffaele Pettazzoni finds evidence of the confession of sins with penitential prayers and satisfactions in classical writers, particularly in Ovid
(d. A.D. 17). Ovid's references are largely to the religion of Isis as
practiced in Rome, but are by no means confined to this. The instances
of King Midas in the *Metamorphoses* xi, and Claudia Quinta in the
Fasti iv, are connected with practices long prevailing in Anatolia in the
worship of the Great Mother. Plutarch in his essay *On Superstition* (vii)
tells of penitents who might be seen sitting in sackcloth or in filthy rags,
or rolling naked in the mud, reciting their misdeeds—or at the very least
fumigating themselves within doors. Their sins were of the nature of
violations of tabu, such as eating or drinking what was forbidden, or
walking on a forbidden road. Devotees of the Dea Syria practiced self-
mutilation and engaged in orgiastic dances in which under great excitement they loudly accused themselves of sins. In Samothrace certain
priests performed rites which appear to stem from the pre-Greek in-
habitants of the island, for the purification of homicides. Confession of
sins, according to Pettazzoni, where it appears in the Greco-Roman

world, arises from non-Greek and non-Indo-European influences. That Western men of the classical age adopted it, however, may be inferred from Pettazzoni's own reference to the first of Ovid's *Pontic Letters* (versified epistles from his place of exile in Pontus) in which the aged poet expresses a bitter and profound contrition for his misdeeds. One passage may be translated:

> Oh, I repent . . . I repent, and I am tortured by my deed.
> Though exile is sorrow, guilt is to me a greater sorrow . . .
> Death will end my exile, but will not make me not to have sinned.

The occasion of Ovid's deep sense of guilt is a puzzle to his editors. His apparent contrition may be genuine, even though it was affirmed in the hope of a relaxation of sentence. Exile was for him a kind of excommunication.

In Greek and Roman society philosophy and piety could not in the cure of souls draw upon such a body of fixed belief as Judaism and Christianity possessed. Yet in this realm the debt of later ages to the philosophers is immeasurable. Socrates was a great forerunner of the many who have searched out and sifted the thoughts of men for the healing and well-being of their souls. Later philosophers established a tradition, particularly in the realm of "consolation," which the Christian Fathers could not ignore. The cults that flourished during the first age of the Church accustomed men's minds to ideas and practices in matters of penance and purification that in some respects anticipated those which were to become characteristic of Christianity. Yet the human soul craved more, and required more, than these could supply.

Chapter III

SPIRITUAL DIRECTION IN HINDUISM, BUDDHISM, CONFUCIANISM, AND ISLAM

I

AMONG ancient civilizations, that of India seems to have given the greatest prominence to the spiritual director. In the sacred books of Hinduism this functionary is the *guru*, a term still in use with similar meaning among many Hindu sects. While *guru* is the common name for the authoritative and revered moral and religious counselor and guide, numerous distinct classes of *gurus* are referred to in the Vedic literature. Seven of these are specified by Professor S. V. Venkateswara. Among them are the *āchārya* and the *kulaguru* who were preceptors of numerous pupils in one school. Other types of *guru* were ascetics and mystics of various sorts. In early times the *āchārya* (or *ākārya*) presided over the elaborate three-day initiation rites of the young Brahman, whispered in his ear a secret formula (*mantra*) and invested him with the triple cord which was the badge of his membership among the "twice-born." In the age of the writing of the *Sūtras*, the last half-millennium before the Christian era, the *āchārya* is the superior teacher, the *guru* more especially the moral instructor and personal director. I am informed that this corresponds in a general way to modern usage. But in Edgar Thurston's monumental *Castes and Tribes of Southern India*, there appear some quotations from nineteenth century rituals in which the two words are certainly used interchangeably.

Initiation in the eighth or ninth year of boyhood was regarded as normal, but it might be postponed even to the age of twenty-two. In the ensuing stage of studentship the youth lived with his *guru* under instruction and in respectful obedience. This relationship ordinarily lasted for twelve or more years, and in many cases was broken only by death.

Numerous early and later texts represent the *guru* as a man of exalted virtues and superior attainments. In the *Vedanta Sara* there occurs an extended description of "the true guru" of the medieval Siva sect. He is "a man who habitually practices all the virtues, who with the sword of reason has lopped off the branches and torn out the roots of sin . . . who behaves with dignity and independence; who has the feelings of a father for all his disciples." He treats his friends and enemies alike; he strives to enlighten the ignorant, and he rejects even in thought every sinful action. A faithful worshiper of Siva, he has visited all the sacred places and bathed in the sacred streams. He is perfectly acquainted with the *Vedas* and with many other sacred books. The Abbé Dubois, who quotes this passage, adds out of his own close personal observation of early nineteenth century Hinduism: "This is what *gurus* ought to be, but are not," and he proceeds to depict their corrupt, tyrannical and mercenary habits of which he has been a witness. That the ideal was not forgotten, however, is attested by his later quotation from a current "Hindu catechism" which consists of a set of stanzas in Sanskrit. One of these is rendered:

Pride and arrogance suit no one; constancy, humanity, sweetness, compassion, truth, love for one's neighbor, conjugal fidelity, goodness, amiability, cleanliness, are all qualities that distinguish really virtuous people. He who possesses all these ten qualities is a true *guru*.

One could easily compile from the early writings a similar character sketch of the *guru* as he ought to be. Dr. Venkateswara has in fact done something of this sort. It is altogether likely that, like other clergy, those of Hinduism often failed to reach, or even approach, the standards set for them. The very authority of the *guru* was his temptation. I shall illustrate this by reference to works of the *Sūtra* period. Over his young disciple he exercised a mastery so absolute that it may often have been oppressive. Living with his preceptor, the pupil was also his servant, performing household tasks and supplying his needs by systematic begging. In this quite respectable employment he was expected to avoid the homes of his own and his *guru's* relations. Toward his master he was required to pay unfailing ceremonial deference in speech, gesture and posture. According to the *Institutes of Vishnu* he may eat, when the *guru* permits, some of the food he has obtained by begging; he must rise before him and go to bed after him; on meeting him he must "embrace his feet with crossed hands," and (perhaps an equally exacting requirement for a boy) he must always avoid mimicking the good man's gait and speech. He must also prostrate himself before the *guru's* wife. Similar statements are found in the *Laws of Manu* and in the *Aphorisms of Apastamba*. Apastamba, however, rejects the last mentioned provision, and in other respects shows some inclination to protect the pupil. According to the *Laws of Manu* the pupil who censures his teacher, though justly, will be reborn an ass, while one who falsely defames his teacher will become a dog. Penance must be done by the pupil if the sun rises or sets while he sleeps.

The framers of the *Sūtras* were *āchāryas* whose functions were those of professors in the schools of Hindu learning; they were the scholastics and canon lawyers of ancient Hinduism. We may suppose that their students frequently became what we may call the local priests and pastors and the *gurus* or preceptors of young pupils. In their instruction the *gurus* would be largely guided by the *Sūtra* materials imparted in the schools. Both Manu and Apastamba indicate that the pupil is bound to revere, equally with his teacher, the teachers of his teacher. The firmness of the tradition is seen in such regulations, as also in those which attach and restrict the system to the three "castes of the first-born," Brahmans, Kshatriyas and Vayshas. The order of *gurus* was in fact almost exclusively Brahman.

In Gautama's *Institutes of the Sacred Law* the author refers to another venerable *ākārya* with too much respect even to name him. In numerous documents the *guru*, his wife, and his children are protected by heavy penalties imposed for crimes and torts committed against them. The *guru* was also held to possess extraordinary powers as an agent of salvation. He is often compared to his advantage with the pupil's parents. One of the more modest of these comparisons may be quoted from the *Institutes of Vishnu* (there is an earlier formulation of the statement in the *Laws of Manu*):

A man has three *atigurus* [or specially venerable superiors] his father, his mother, and his spiritual teacher. By honoring his mother he gains the present world; by honoring his father, the world of the gods; by honoring his spiritual teacher, the world of the Brahmans [i.e., exemption from rebirth, the highest attainment].

In the celebrated poem, probably of the second century B.C., the Bhagavadgita, Arjuna at the beginning hesitates to fight in battle where his "two honored *gurus*" are with the enemy. One of these has been his instructor in military science; the other, a more typical *guru*, a moral teacher of boys. The Lord Krishna is himself addressed as "revered, most venerable *guru,*" or, in the paraphrase by Sir Edwin Arnold, "*Guru of gurus.*" Among the virtues enjoined by Krishna in this poem is devotion to one's teacher (here *āchārya*). In a note on a passage of the Bhagavadgita the French editors, A. Auvard and M. Schultz, describe the *guru* as "spiritual master, director of conscience, instructor, to whom . . . the disciple owes service, obedience, respect, devotion and veneration."

II

The austere and meticulous rectitude of behavior proper to the sincere *guru* or *āchārya* was to be imparted to the pupil by example and precept. The teaching was based on explicit concepts of virtues and sins, which were regarded, e.g., in the *Laws of Manu,* as divinely given. These laws according to tradition were recited by the sage Bhrigu at the command of the divine Manu. In this code we find the "ten-fold law" which all the twice-born, in all four orders or stages of life (students, householders, hermits and ascetics), must obey. This is an impressive list of virtues: contentment, forgiveness, self-control, abstention from theft, purification, coercion of the ten bodily organs (five of sense and five of action), wisdom, knowledge, truthfulness, abstention from anger. These laws, and numerous other codes, such as the *Vāsishtha Dharmasāstra,* are replete with insistent demands upon the twice-born to be faithful in life and study, sometimes on penalty of loss of caste. The *Aphorisms of Apastamba* presents a list of fourteen "sins which destroy creatures," and a corresponding list of their opposite good qualities which are to be acquired by the practice of *yoga.* The vices include exultation, grumbling, covetousness, injuriousness, hypocrisy, lying, gluttony, lust, secret hatred, neglect to control the senses, and to concentrate the mind. The virtues are liberality, uprightness, affability, peace with created beings.

Avoidance of sin is a constant emphasis, but the conception of sin is affected by primitive notions of ceremonial uncleanness. In the *Vedas,* according to A. B. Keith, sin is thought of as something that sticks to a man from without, and Raffaele Pettazzoni calls it "a kind of fluid that invests the person of the sinner from without and has to be eliminated by material means such as water and fire." More ethical conceptions of sin are often in evidence, however, and these enter the language of the cults. In the *Institutes of Vishnu* "carnal desire, wrath and greed" are "the three most dangerous enemies" of man. In the worship of Varuna we see a well developed belief in a deity who is all-seeing, all-judging, and merciful to the praying sinner. Keith finds, too, in this ancient cult, a sense of "a universal moral law," which excludes gross vices.

In connection with ritual sacrifices, confession and penance in many forms come to assume high importance as means of delivering the sinner from his predicament. In one Vedic ritual, the *Satapatha Brāhmana*, the wife of the sacrificer is required by the officiating priest to declare what lovers she has had, "lest she should sacrifice with a pang in her mind." She is obliged to name her paramours, or at least to hold up as many stalks of grass as their number. The explanation here is that "where confessed, sin is diminished since it becomes truth." The adulteress becomes pure when she abandons the falsity of concealment, and then only may the sacrifice be conducted on behalf of the family without impairment of its purificatory effect. Should she fail to confess truthfully, her children would suffer grave spiritual penalties from the destructive wind-deities that in this instance are being propitiated.

Participation in the religious rites often involves correction of sin by penances and deprivations, and the declaration of future punishment. As in the medieval Christian penitential manuals, special penances are assigned for special offenses. The codification of penances is widely illustrated in the codes of Manu and Apastamba and in Gautama's *Dharmasāstra*. Gautama lays down the rule that "a secret penance must be performed by him whose sin is not publicly known," and prescribes such penances for various faults and crimes. Offenses for which confession and penance have not been performed doom the sinner to one of the "hells" to be endured before his next human reincarnation. In the *Institutes of Vishnu* one who has stolen meat is appropriately reborn a vulture; one who has stolen perfume becomes a muskrat. The Western reader is sometimes surprised by the implied estimate of the relative gravity of sins; for example, to smell spirituous liquor is an offense as heavily penalized as homosexuality. Despite such peculiarities, the sins identified are in most cases actions or attitudes universally condemned. The principle of composition, or payment to the injured by the offender, as in early medieval Western codes, is employed with regard to the distinction of rank. Thus the composition for a kshatriya's life is set by Apastamba as one thousand cows, for a Vaysha's one hundred, for a Sudra's only ten. A passage from the *Institutes* of Gautama illustrates how moral values emerge against a background of required rites. The learned Brahman is instructed in the "forty sacraments" which include sacrifices to gods, *manes*, men and goblins and to the new moon. However, the "eight excellent qualities" of the soul have more weight of merit. These eight virtues are: compassion; forbearance; freedom from anger; purity; quietism or avoiding painful activity; auspiciousness, or doing what is praised by good men; freedom from avarice; freedom from covetousness. He who possesses these, though he is satisfied with only a few of the sacraments, "will be united with Brahman and will dwell in his heaven."

It is apparent that the ancient Hindu guide of souls had a vocabulary of the moral life comparable to that of the West, and that attempts were made by his authorities to give to morality the sanctions of religion and of tradition. The system extended only to the privileged castes, but the principles enjoined are often stated in universal terms. They are also prevailingly negative, designed to subdue natural impulses and desires rather than to encourage active goodness. Thus, in the stage of studentship the *Laws of Manu* declare:

Let him not, even though in pain, (speak words) cutting (others) to the quick; let him not injure others in thought or deed; let him not utter speeches which make (others) afraid of him, since that will prevent him from gaining heaven.

And again, of the ascetic:

Let him not desire to die, let him not desire to live; but let him wait for (his appointed) time, as a servant (waits) for the payment of his wages. . . . Against an angry man let him not in return show anger, let him bless when he is cursed, and let him not utter speech devoid of truth. . . . The only friend who follows men even after death is justice. . . . Justice must not be violated lest justice destroy us.

With such precepts, souls were guided and molded by the Hindu *gurus*.

Reverence for the *guru* has remained, at least until very recently, a constituent element in Hindu social life. The obedience accorded by his disciples sometimes finds expression in acts of unreserved self-abnegation and in ascriptions of authority so extravagant as to amount to deification. Dayānanda, the founder of the Arya Samāj, when already more than thirty-five years of age, was so submissive to his blind Brahman *guru* that he submitted to severe beatings by him and thereafter remained for three years (1860-63) under his instruction. The Chaitanyas, founded at the beginning of the sixteenth century, sometimes entrust all their possessions to the *guru* and look upon him as a deity more to be revered than the Lord Krishna himself. The founder of the Brāhma Samāj (1866), Keshab Chandra Sen, felt the influence of this sect, and, although he resisted (according to J. N. Farquhar) "the extreme dangers of guruism" in his own movement, he had moments of self-appreciation in which he likened himself to Christ. In some modern sects the devotee performs a solemn act of lifelong dedication to his *guru*. The *guru's* voice "is declared to be the voice of God," says G. A. Grierson, "and the fullest devotion . . . must be rendered to him." H. H. Wilson notes that of all obligations recognized by religious Hindus "the *guru padasraya*, or servile veneration for the spiritual teacher, is the most important and compulsory." R. L. Hume remarks that the excessive regard for the *guru*, while springing from a commendable motive, is nevertheless "a fatal defect" rather than an excellence in Hindu life.

The word *guru* assumes a large significance through its application to the founders and leaders of reforming sects. The Sikhs were long ruled by a succession of chief *gurus*. In the year 1690 the tenth of these, Gobind Singh, militarized the sect in resistance to the Moguls and declared that the *Granth Sahib*, the holy book of the Sikhs, should henceforth be their *guru*, or spiritual guide. In time the book itself became an object of worship, and the ten *gurus* of the earlier period came to be thought of, against the founder's teaching, as incarnations of deity. The Rādhā Soāmi sect takes its name from the title adopted by its first *guru*, a former banker, who died in 1868. It teaches that the founder was the Supreme Being in human form; he had referred to himself as *Sant Satguru*, perfect saint and preceptor, and as the manifestation of the impersonal Supreme Being. Shrines of the sect are called "the *guru's* chamber," and photographs of the *gurus* (and of the wife of the founder) are used in meditation.

Christians have naturally appropriated the idea of *guru* reverence and related it to Christian doctrine. I have seen an anonymous and undated Christian tract for Hindu readers which presents Christ as the true *guru* who alone can satisfy the universal need for direction of the soul and is supremely to be obeyed. The saintly Christian Sadhu Sundar Singh had the habit of "discoursing in the informal, somewhat rambling style of the Indian *guru*"; in order to avoid *guru*-worship he declined to be addressed as "*Swami*," lord.

III

The sixth century B.C. gave rise to the two historic movements, Jainism and Buddhism. Both of these repudiated the authority of the

Vedas and the religious domination of the Brahman caste and, discarding Sanskrit, utilized the current speech. They drew their recruits largely from the Kshatriya or military caste, yet they are far from being militaristic religions. As in the relation of Western monasticism to feudalism, these movements stood in contrast to the class from which they obtained their following, and offered an escape from its secular violence. The close resemblance of Jain and Buddhist teachings has often been observed, and is explained on the ground of their common inheritance from Hinduism; but the differences are also striking. Mahāvīra, the founder of the Jains, began his work a few years earlier than Gautama Buddha. The discipline he employed was rigorous, and included the practice of nudity which has been retained by the "sky-clad" branch of the sect. Gautama, on the other hand, sharply revolted from intense bodily austerities and abandoned these to adopt a "middle path," or moderate discipline. Both, however, earnestly sought inward escape from the dominion of sin, and from the consequent reincarnation which was regarded as its penalty. And both provided for the guidance of the seeker, and for exercises of repentance and penance.

The *Uttarādhyayana Sūtra* of the Jains, which has been translated from Prākrit by H. Jacobi, requires that "obedience, praise, devotion and respect" be paid to the *guru*, and that confession of sins be made before him. By this confession the soul "gets rid of the thorns of deceit, misapplied austerities and wrong belief," which would obstruct the way to final liberation. As in Hinduism, escape from the necessity of rebirth is the end devoutly sought in the struggle: "He who does not comprehend and renounce the causes of sin . . . is born again and again." Confession is to be followed by repentance, first in private, and then before the *guru*, and by the practice of penance. This includes fasting, mendicancy, exposure to weather, and other austerities. The young Jain monk must engage earnestly in study under his preceptor. The pedagogic method employs five exercises: saying the lesson; questioning the teacher, repetition of the lesson; pondering over it, and "religious discourse." In Jainism there appears a notable effort to establish the best natural relations between teacher and taught. "Politeness" on the part of the pupil includes not only ceremonial behavior but also "loving the *guru*"—this despite the fact that love is generally, like hatred, regarded as injurious. Ill-behaved pupils exasperate even a gentle teacher, while polite pupils win a hot-tempered one. These humane ideas were, however, accompanied by regulations of discipline severe to an extreme degree, and especially minute on actions that involve the taking of life in its lower forms. According to Albert Schweitzer, it is in Jainism that *ahimsa*, the avoidance of injury or death to all living things, "first becomes a great commandment." For this reason members of the sect avoid occupations such as agriculture that make impossible its fulfillment. The motive is not compassion but purification. The intensity of the discipline of Jainism is seen in the word *tapo* used for asceticism in its sacred books, a word which means "consuming heat," and suggests that the bodily impulses must be burned away.

IV

The Buddhist doctrinal system rests upon basic principles, derived from the suffering in the universe and called the Four Noble Truths: the universality of suffering; its origin; its cessation; and the way of escape from it. The Eightfold Path by which the soul attains "Arahatship" of the state of Nibbana (Nirvana) consists of: right belief, right aspiration, right speech, right conduct, right employment, right effort, right remembrance, and right concentration.

Buddhism is a religion not of gods but of morality and discipline, based upon these conceptions of the world and of life. At the core of the moral system are the Five Precepts which (in accord with Hindu teaching) forbid killing, stealing, adultery, lying and the drinking of intoxicants. These simple principles are refined upon and applied to innumerable details of conduct. The Ten Good Actions add to the above five abstinences the condemnation of slander, abusive language, foolish talk, covetousness, malice and ignorance. S. Tachibana, in *The Ethics of Buddhism*, stresses particularly the Buddhist revulsion to lying and covetousness. The latter is for Buddhists "the evil of evils"; his list of near-synonyms for covetousness in Buddhist literature occupies two pages. Lying too is condemned, and truthfulness enjoined. Dr. Tachibana warns us against concluding from the negative form of the rules of conduct that the system was purely negative. The virtues opposed to the faults condemned were expressly or by implication approved and embraced. The Buddha himself was revered and celebrated for great virtues such as truthfulness, tolerance, benevolence and justice, and was declared to have sent forth his missionaries "for the benefit and welfare of the multitude, and out of compassion for the world." Nevertheless, Schweitzer seems to be justified in his insistence that Buddhism rests upon a "negation of the world and of life," despite its tendencies to a positive morality.

While the Brahman ordinarily spent a period as a "householder," the Buddhist devotee was vowed from boyhood to perpetual celibacy. Around the group of ascetics there was a wider circle of lay adherents who were subjected, like the Franciscan Tertiaries, to rules of discipline suited to their status, and were guided by ascetics in their personal lives. The Buddha himself frequently exhorted laymen. On fast days the *upāsaka* or Buddhist layman observed certain abstinences. At other times he was obligated by the Five Precepts only. He was instructed in social duties, particularly those of family life. Buddhist lay morality is regarded by Professor L. de la Vallée Poussin as more positive than that of the monks. Novices, or candidates for monkhood, were required to observe the Ten Precepts. The *bhikkhu*, or mendicant ascetic, the Buddhist monk, was under the much more elaborate system of the *Pāti-mokkha*, with its 227 rules. It is doubtful whether the layman was encouraged to hope for Arahatship by any endeavors in this life, but the degree of his purification was at least significant for his status in his next rebirth. Professor A. K. Reischauer's treatment of the Buddhist sects of Japan indicates their variety and suggests the peril of generalization on this point. The thirteenth century Shin sect broke from the conception of merit and affirmed salvation by faith alone, good works being regarded as fruits of faith.

The Buddha himself was the teacher and guide of a band of disciples, and may be regarded as the greatest of Indian teachers. Early narratives state that the young Gautama in his search for truth placed himself in turn under the guidance of two houseless or hermit *gurus*, Alāra Kālāma and Uddaka, but dissented from them, and after his illumination proposed to convert them, only to hear that they had died. It would appear that converts were won to Buddhism by private instruction or exhortation. In an early story of the institution by Gautama of the Sangha, or community of *bhikkhus*, we are told of the conversion of Yasa, a noble youth who, in distress at the emptiness of an indulgent life, has come for counsel to the Buddha. The Blessed One talks to him of the merits of almsgiving, the moral duties, heaven, the sinfulness of desires and the blessings of the abandonment of desire. After further instruction and the fuller enlightenment of Yasa, the Buddha ordains the convert with the words, regularly used in similar instances: "Come O *bhikkhu*, well taught is the doctrine; lead a holy life for the complete extinction of suffering." Yasa's father is induced to consent; his mother and his former wife receive instruction and become the first female members of the order (*bhikkhunîs*).

Another tale illustrates how Gautama was believed to have dealt with the problem of bereavement. He was visited by a mother who in a distraction of grief begged for medicine for her dead child. He required her to bring to him some mustard seed from any house she could find where no one had died. Finding this impossible, she entered on the Path as a disciple, and soon attained Arahatship. This is Buddhist consolation: the universality of suffering and the necessity of denying the ego that demands exemption from it.

Buddha's disciples by devout study and discipline followed the Eight-fold Path. They adopted the practice of holding semimonthly gatherings for mutual confession and undertaking of penance. At these meetings there was read a long list of offenses to be confessed if committed by a brother or sister. The list is called the *Pātimokkha*, a Pali word of uncertain origin; the interpretation "disburdening" has been disputed. The document has been called by J. F. Dickson, editor of the Pali text, "the Buddhist office of the confession of priests," and by the editors of the translation, T. W. Rhys-Davids and Hermann Oldenberg, a "liturgy of confession." Sukumar Dutt, however, in his critical study *Early Buddhist Monachism*, holds that it was originally a code and not a liturgy. Mr. Dickson was admitted to a recitation of the *Pātimokkha*, January 2, 1874, in the Brazen Palace of Anurādhapura (Ceylon), in a room that he calls "the oldest chapter-house in the world."

This impressive liturgy opens with a solemn warning against lying to conceal offenses:

> Therefore a fault, if there be one, should be declared by that bhikkhu who remembers it and desires to be cleansed therefrom. For a fault when declared shall be light to him.

The question is then put three times to the assembled fraternity: "Are you pure in this matter?" Thus a real "disburdenment," on the part of any distressed in conscience by lapses from the rule, is insistently sought.

The faults of the brethren are classified under eight heads arranged in descending order of their gravity. Carnality, theft, homicide and false claims of knowledge are "defeats" for which the offender is expelled from communion. Dickson calls them "the four deadly sins." The section of ninety-two offenses requiring repentance has special interest for the student of confession of sins, and has been featured by Pettazzoni in his extended history of that subject. Dickson noted that during the night the brethren kneeling in pairs whispered mutual confessions. Like Western monastic rules and penitential books, these regulations indicate a well-ordered fraternal asceticism, carefully guarded at vulnerable points. Sample occasions of penitence are these: deliberate lying; abusive language; slander of a fellow *bhikkhu*; driving out another in anger; exhorting one of the sisters after sunset; eating delicacies when in health; watching a military display; journeying to the next village with robbers, or with a woman. In many related documents the authority of the *Pātimokkha* is upheld. We read a condemnation of the lax habit of reading it in abridged form: this is permitted only in imminent peril of attack by savage people. Nor is the *Pātimokkha* to be recited before laymen.

In the ordination rites alleged to have been received from the Buddha we obtain information on the pupil-instructor relationship. By way of correction of undisciplined and rowdy conduct, directions are given for the choice of two sorts of personal instructors, the *upagghāya* and the *ākariya*. In other documents these Pali words are translated respectively "preceptor" and "teacher." *Ākariya* is of course the Sanskrit *āchārya* of Hinduism; in Buddhism he appears to be inferior to the *upagghāya*. The acts and words in which the disciple chooses, and offers himself to, a master are here the same for both types of spiritual guide. He is to adjust his robe, salute the director's feet, then squatting down raise his joined hands and say thrice: "Venerable sir, be my *upagghāya* (or *ākariya*)." Another Pali text, the *Kullavagga*, gives ample and complicated regulations for probation and penance in the order of *bhikkhus*. In certain circumstances a period of probation in which privileges were withdrawn preceded the assigned period of penance. Either probation or penance itself might be interrupted on request of the subject. In case of a fresh offense during either, the offender was set back to the beginning of his term of discipline. If the fault has been concealed for a time, this time is added to the ordinary time of probation.

When contention has arisen between two parties of *bhikkhus*, confession of the offense must be made before all by a discreet representative of each side, to the end that the faults of both parties "may be covered over as with grass." Some disputed cases were to be referred to a commission or jury composed of experts in the *Pātimokkha* and in legal matters. The evolution of rules for the confession of the women of the order can be seen in the *Kullavagga*. Their confession to a *bhikkhu* in their own residences, and even out of doors, proving occasions of scandal, selected *bhikkhunîs* were instructed by qualified *bhikkhus* in the art of hearing confessions, and thereafter acted as confessors for their sisters.

The difficulty of maintaining this rigorous system of confession is indicated by the fact that in the reforming council of Pātaliputra, by which King Asoka instituted the reform of Buddhism (*ca.* 245 B.C.), a vast number of *bhikkhus* who had habitually neglected it were expelled.

The attempt to secure the best relations between the guide and the guided is apparent. In the ordination rites the master is to consider the disciple as a son and the disciple to regard the master as a father. "Thus these two, united by mutual reverence, confidence and communion of life, will progress, advance, and reach a high stage in this doctrine and discipline." Exacting and detailed rules are given for the disciple's personal service to his master. Yet he may have recourse to the *Sangha* (community of ascetics) for the discipline of his superior if the latter is guilty of a grave offense. The *upagghāya*, on the other hand, was enjoined to dismiss a pupil for any lack of affection, reverence or devotion toward himself.

In connection with the Council of Vesālî, which is roughly dated "one century after the death of the Blessed One" (i.e., *ca.* 380 B.C.), the question arose whether it was permissible for a *bhikkhu* to do anything adopted as a practice by his preceptor. This question, after due discussion, was answered in the negative.

V

In the scriptures of Chinese Buddhism, some of which were taken over from India, we obtain evidence of the moral discipline that went with the devout life. Samuel Beal quotes the celebrated *Sūtra of Forty-two Sections* which had reached China by A.D. 70. Section 5 of this series ascribes to the Buddha a list of ten things by which men become evil. Three of these, murder, theft and lust, belong to the body; four belong to the speech—equivocation, slandering, lying, flattery; and the remaining three, envy, anger and delusion, are vices of thought. Here we recognize the Ten Good Actions referred to above, with variations, and they are reflected again in the ten negative rules added in the Chinese document. In these rules the seeker of perfection is forbidden to kill, commit adultery, lie, drink intoxicants, eat after midday, attend dances or theaters, use perfumes or unguents, seek the better seats in company, covet or possess gold, silver or jewels. In these lists we recognize correspondences to the Second Table of the Ten Commandments and to the Seven Deadly Sins of medieval Christianity. Not to repent of these sins would postpone perfection to another stage of bodily life. For a wrong done, said Buddha, "I will return ungrudging love." A man who cherishes lust and desire is like a vase of dirty water; the mud in the water is removed and true knowledge attained by a gradual process of confession and penance. In another Chinese document, *The Daily Manual of a Shāmān* (ascetic), we find a series of short prayer-poems for forty-three daily acts or situations from rising in the morning to going to rest at night. These verses glow with benevolent and virtuous sentiments. They are, however, strangely punctuated by magic formulas for security against danger. For example, on drinking water one says seven times:

Om! fu - sih - po - lo - mo - ni. Svāh.

Such elements are marks of the popularization of the Mahāyāna Buddhism of the Far East.

The cult of Kwan-Yin appeared in China probably about the beginning of the Christian era. In a liturgy of this cult, translated by Dr. Beal, which took its extant form in A.D. 1412 and was in use in South China monasteries in the late nineteenth century, we find a remarkable formula for public repentance. Protracted and minute preparation is made privately by the worshipper, designed to purify the three faculties of thought, speech and action. Together they confess "the grievous sins we have committed in thought, word and deed" which have prevented advance in true knowledge. "With a loud voice," and for the sake of all sentient creatures, they confess their sins and repent. Making a complete prostration, they publicly acknowledge their love of outward things, sinful friendships, wicked hearts and continuous pursuit of evil. In fear and shame they renounce these offenses, turn to the pursuit of good, and ask the mercy of the great and compassionate Kwan-Yin. This document in its form suggests the influence of (Nestorian) Christianity, but its contents are in accord with much that appears elsewhere in the Buddhist scriptures. Not only monastics but also laymen were evidently admitted to participation in this penitential rite. A sixteenth century Chinese romantic writer, Wu-Cheng-en, in a book entitled *Shi Yeu Ki* that has been called "the Buddhist *Pilgrim's Progress*," sought to make Mahāyāna Buddhism attractive to the common people and to call attention to the virtues of lay adherents. It is based on the narrative of the seventh century Chinese traveler and observer of Buddhism in India, Hiuen Tsiang.

At its best the guidance of youth in Buddhism has invoked a happy association of master and pupil. R. Spence Hardy has translated from the Singhalese (or Cingalese, the language of Ceylon) a modern *Manual of Buddhism*. This interesting work presents in an attractive light these personal relations. The scholar is to honor his teacher by rising to meet him, carrying his packages, washing his feet, and by asking questions and trying to remember everything he has been taught. The teacher is to assist the scholar by teaching him how to behave, how to eat, and to keep only good companions. He should explain all things clearly, teach what his own teacher has taught, encourage the pupil, and induce him to please his parents by study. The teacher is given twenty-five rules with reference to the scholar: these require kindly oversight, patience, the use of endearments to encourage him to study, and kindly ministries when he is in trouble or in sickness.

In an unpublished Columbia University dissertation, *Beyond Philosophy, or, The Paradox of Nirvana*, Robert H. L. Slater has included an intimate account of the functions of the Burmese monks (*bhikkhus*) as teachers of youth and moral counselors of the people. He quotes a Buddhist layman's statement: "Of all charities, charity of learning is the noblest," and points to the expression of this virtue in the village schools conducted by the monks. There the boys learn to read, and are indoctrinated in the elements of Buddhist morality. In these schools Dr. Slater finds "a wholesome atmosphere of intimacy and understanding between the teacher and the taught." Most boys at the age of puberty spend a period in residence with the monks: some of them remain to join the order. Other services performed by monks for the community may include alms and hospitality to the needy and the rescue of condemned prisoners, who become their companions. Highly important, in Slater's opinion, is the monk's activity as counselor to laymen. "It is as the individual adviser of each villager that the monk's influence is most strongly felt." Slater's whole treatment stresses the extent to which the learned *bhikkhus* of Burma have made available to the people both their basic teachings and their moral help.

VI

Within the framework of a religion of rewards and punishments, and contemplating a series of incarnations that extended toward deliverance from the bondage of the body, both Hinduism and Buddhism found the answer to this life's problems in the progressive curbing of the passions and acquisition of the virtues which are their contraries.

We are not here engaged in a general critical evaluation of the Indian religions. In the phase of them here considered we see weaknesses and values. Their adherents possessed in unsurpassed degree a conception of the terrifying possibilities of human destiny, and intensely realized the importance of spiritual and moral training. But typical Hinduism is both too negative and too aristocratic, and the authority and veneration it has accorded the spiritual director has been excessive and unwholesome. The earnestness of its discipline failed to save it from its defects, and the more important of its modern revivals have been in large degree responses to Christian influence. Buddhism marked a distinct advance upon Hinduism in its moral perceptions and values. As compared with Jainism it greatly modified the doctrine of *ahimsa*. It quite disregarded the caste system and the notion of aristocratic privilege. Yet it failed in the end to gain control of the life of the common people, and suffered extinction in the land of its origin. Hīnayāna or primitive Buddhism survives in Ceylon, Burma and Siam; the Mahāyāna branch, with its greater altruism and tolerance of popular religion, has many adherents in China and Japan. These great Indian systems have by no means ceased to offer the guidance of souls with which they were originally so deeply concerned. Whether they can summon up energies to perform this task effectively under the impact of modern forces remains to be seen. But any religion dominant in Asia will have to reckon with centuries of established tradition in counseling the sinful and perplexed.

VII

The ancient sages of China summoned their countrymen to the cultivation of virtue. Lao-Tzu, who is supposed to have lived in the sixth century B.C., has been credited with the authorship of the *Tao-Teh-Ching* or Book of the Way and Its Manifestation, but this classic in its extant form may be from the period of Confucius. The writer expressed his thought in brief, paradoxical precepts which seem to have been ill-adapted to the minds of his contemporaries, since he lived to lament that they met with neglect. Taoism proved a very different thing from the moral philosophy of the *Tao-Teh-Ching*. But the little book was held in respect, and was doubtless not without influence. It teaches a doctrine of quietude and self-restraint—"the virtue of not striving."

There is no greater sin than ambition. "Desire not to desire; learn not to learn." True greatness is founded upon lowliness. The three most precious things are gentleness, frugality and humility. "Be gentle, and you can be bold; be frugal, and you can be liberal; be humble and you can be a leader." Such precepts represent profound insights; but they are among those salutary lessons which few have been willing to learn.

The teaching of Confucius (d. 478 B.C.) was more widely received. He is said to have had seventy disciples of special talent, and the impression made by the *Analects* is that the miscellaneous sayings there reported were uttered in conversations between him and his students. His method, however, differed widely from that of his Greek contemporary, Socrates, in the absence both of continuity of theme and of close analysis of the thoughts, and faults, of his pupils. The reader is impressed by the placidity and cheerfulness of the sage, his high estimate of human nature, his stress upon filial duties and traditional ceremonies, and the gentlemanly code of honorable behavior which he stresses. (When hunting, he would not shoot at a sitting bird.) Though the aristocratic note is strong in Confucius and he frankly disliked rustics, he was personally humble. As he traveled about with his disciples he induced them, on one occasion, to admit a raw village boy for an interview—having, characteristically, first ascertained that the lad had "purified" himself in order to be admitted. In Mencius (d. 289 B.C.), his loyal follower, we have a more strenuous personality. He evidently delighted in sharp repartee, and he dared to rebuke the great, including an Emperor. For Confucius, "the holy man," his admiration was unqualified. He shows, however, much less aristocratic aloofness, and interests himself in the affairs of the working class. The reports we have of his utterances show an ampler expression of the basic moral ideas of Confucius—love, or benevolence, righteousness, courtesy, wisdom and the obligations of kinship. Both philosophers magnify the duties that accord with these principles; they also present a pattern of happy, civilized living in which music and poetry play a constructive part.

Confucianist teaching dwells much upon government and the duties of rulers and subjects. But it is evident that the sages placed the personal and family virtues above the gifts of rulership and considered them fundamental to society and government. "The kingdom," says Mencius, "is rooted in the house, the house is rooted in the person" (Lyall's translation VII, v). He was a great believer in the transforming power of teaching, but this is by example quite as much as by words. Teaching, like rain, brings new life; it shapes the mind, calls forth talent, answers questions and secretly cleanses men (XIII, xli). He has many passages that stress the winning power of love. That every man is essentially merciful appears from the feelings men have on seeing a child in danger (III, vi). "The great man is he that does not lose his child heart" (VIII, xii). The loss of love is the straying of the heart; the scholar is one who goes seeking "our stray heart" (XI, xi). "To lack love is to lack wisdom," and "lacking love, wisdom, courtesy and righteousness, man is a slave" (III, iv). If men do not respond to our love and courtesy, we should examine ourselves for the cause (VII, iv; VIII, xxviii). But he disapproves of the teaching of his elder contemporary, the anti-Confucianist Mo-Ti (Mo-Tzu) who "loved all alike," not observing the special claims of relatives. His gentlemanly ideal involves also an element of stern self-discipline that resembles the Stoic practice. "Before a man can do things there must be things he will not do" (VIII, viii). The right is to be preferred to life, where we cannot have both (XI, 10). A man should hold himself to his principles by systematic self-examination. Master Tseng, a prominent disciple of Confucius, is reported in the *Analects* (I, 4), as saying:

Every day I examine myself on these three points: in acting on behalf of others, have I always been loyal to their interests? In intercourse with my friends, have I always been true to my word? Have I failed to repeat the precepts that have been handed down to me? (Waley's translation)

Such are the more obvious elements in the early direction of the Chinese mind, and they have permanently marked the character of the good man as understood in China. The sages admonished kings to be considerate of their people's security and peace; they urged their disciples to honorable, generous and kindly conduct, above the plane of crude economic striving and feudal violence. Confucianism did not rest upon clearly articulated religious beliefs, and did not examine closely man's inner problems and anxieties. It sought full happiness without entering these profounder realms. We may indicate the objectives of its guidance of the individual by these words of Mencius (VII, xxvii):

To serve our kin is love's core; to follow our elders is the core of right; to understand these two and not depart from them is the core of wisdom; to apportion them and adorn them is the core of courtesy; to delight in them is music's core. Delight is life; life cannot be held in; and as we cannot hold it in, our feet stamp and our hands dance, without our knowing it.

VIII

The guidance of souls in Islam offers an inviting field of study but can receive only brief and inexpert notice here. From the beginning lay Muslims were exhorted by preachers who sought "to thrill with hope and frighten with fear" (D. M. Donaldson), and to fix in the minds of their hearers the simple outlines of the faith. A prescribed exercise was the frequent recitation of the creed: "There is no deity but Allah and Muhammad is his prophet." They were encouraged to make pilgrimages to Mecca where they would hear preaching in abundance. In reply to an inquirer Muhammad (d. 632) is said to have defined faith as "believing in Allah, His angels, His book, His meeting, His apostles, and the final resurrection." When asked, "What is Islam?" his reply was: "Islam is serving God without associating anything with Him, performing the *salāt* (ritual prayer five times daily), paying the *zakāt* (the annual alms) and fasting during the month of Ramadān." To the question, "What is righteousness?" he responded: "Serving Allah as if He were before thine eyes. For if thou seest him not, He seeth thee." The Five Foundations of Islam are, accordingly: Bearing witness to Allah as the only deity; the *salāt*; the *zakāt*; the fast of Ramadān; and pilgrimage to Mecca. These are supposed to be observed by all the faithful. The believer was expected not only to cultivate an intense awareness of Allah, but to possess an elementary theology. Books were provided to aid him in this. A catechism of the eleventh century states that everyone mentally competent who has heard the preaching of Islam is bound to acquire a knowledge of Allah. A modern (*ca.* 1800) summary of theology for the common people requires a familiarity with, and ability to defend, a series of not less than fifty articles of belief.

But a great number of earnest Muslims have gone far beyond these elements, and obtained guidance from leaders of eminent piety. Despite the repudiation of asceticism in the Qur'ān ("Allah wishes you ease, but wishes you not discomfort"), there is a pronounced otherworldliness in Muhammad's utterances of the Mecca period, which Goldziher speaks of as an "ascetic tone." The period of conquest, with its experiences of power and possession, saw the decline of this spirit. But it was soon to be revived and cultivated, in various forms. Typical Muslim piety of later ages has been highly ascetic and mystical. Many religious orders have arisen, and their devotees, variously called *Faqīrs* (poor), *darwīshes* (or *dervishes* = mendicants), and *sūfīs* (wool-clad), have abounded since the ninth century. Asceticism marked by anxious penitence but without mysticism appeared in the seventh century. Sūfiism (or Sufism), the Muslim mystical asceticism, had its beginnings in a numerous group of saintly figures of the eighth century. Louis Massignon had named and characterized these early Muslim saints using a geographical classification. Most of the eminent ones were schooled at Basra in the lower section of the Mesopotamian plain. One of these was Ihrāhīm ben Adham (d. 783), Prince of Balkh, who renounced his kingship and possessions, adopted a life of extreme poverty, and held the spiritual reward "well worth the price." Another was Rābi'a (d. 802), an enslaved orphan girl of Basra who, freed by her master because of her disconcerting piety, attained the heights of disinterested love of God. She is said to have prayed:

O my Lord, if I worship Thee from fear of hell, burn me in hell, and if I worship Thee from hope of Paradise, exclude me thence; but if I worship Thee for Thine own sake, then withhold not from me Thine eternal beauty.

Another of the early Muslim mystics was Housayn ibn Mansūr Al-Hallāj (d. 922) whose utterances during imprisonment and torture, according to later legend, show the triumph of divine love. He is said to have been a missionary apostle of Islam in Khorasan, India and China. When about to be crucified at Bagdad, he pours forth an ecstatic prayer for his slayers. The story has apparently been shaped under the influence of Christianity, and the saint himself may have felt that influence. Massignon has devoted two ample volumes to the life and death of this "martyr mystic," and Reynold Alleyne Nicholson, making use of this work, has examined his mysticism. In his identification of the soul with God, Al-Hallāj approaches, but does not arrive at, complete pantheism:

I am He whom I love, and He whom I love is I.
We are two spirits dwelling in one body.

Muslim saints have habitually assumed the guidance of others on the heavenly way (tarīqa), and have been eagerly sought out by those conscious of the need of direction.

Authorities on Sufism stress the requirement of what is called in the Dictionary of Islam "absolute submission to the murshid or inspired guide." Murshid (one who guides aright) is the common word for the spiritual director. Another word employed is shaikh (literally, old man), a general name for one in authority, and applied to the head of a religious order. The Persian word *pīr* is used in the same sense: one twelfth century founder of an order was called *"Pīr of pīrs"* for his distinction in piety and leadership. The *shaikh* or *pīr* is always a *murshid* or personal director, though not all *murshids* are *shaikhs*, or rulers of organized communities of the devout.

The system of Sūfī direction seems to have been well established by the tenth century. This was the time of Al-Hujwiri (d. *ca.* 1087-91) whose book *The Unveiling of the Veiled* has been edited by Nicholson and forms the subject of an illuminating study by Joachim Wach. A section on "companionship" in this mystical work explains the relationship of the spiritual guide and his disciple. Three years of probationary training under a *pīr* must be spent before the novice is admitted to the path (*tarīqa*) and invested with the Sūfī garb. Al-Hujwiri refers to the skill of the Sūfī "physicians of souls" in discerning and prescribing for the inner needs of each disciple. He leaves the novice free, however, to seek aid from a succession of masters.

In the Sūfī discipline the aspirant, or disciple (*murīd*) takes a vow of obedience to his *shaikh*, and unreservedly follows his direction on the mystic way. By a metaphor familiar in Christianity, he is spoken of as a "traveller" (*sālik*). The studies and exercises prescribed are designed to lead the pupil through seven stages of experience. The list of these stages is variously given. John A. Subhan, in a book of popularization, has named and explained them in the following order: service (including repentance); love of God; renunciation; knowledge; ecstasy; reality; union. Other scholars present us with a more complicated arrangement. Complete absorption in God is the objective of the whole discipline. But the disciple is required to be "annihilated into" his guide, then into the Prophet, and finally into the Deity. Through all the way to this mystic union the guide is complete master of the "traveller," and his authority is not subject to question even though his commands may seem arbitrary and capricious or contrary to the Qur'ān. "Like a corpse in the hands of the washer" is a figure used in Sūfī writings to indicate the proper attitude of the disciple. This parallels closely the language employed by Francis of Assisi and by Ignatius Loyola—*"perinde ac cadaver."*

Some would attribute the unlimited authority of the *murshid* in Islamic sects to the influence of Vedanta Hinduism; others regard it as an adaptation of Christian medieval practice. Certainly Christian influences in Sūfī mysticism are clearly indicated. Neoplatonic elements are also strongly marked. In a section on "The Sūfī *Pīr* and the Hindu *Guru*," Subhan points out the "striking similarity" between these in modern India with respect to their control of their disciples, and to the doctrines imparted in each case. As in Hinduism, intimate companionship with the director commonly follows the commitment to his will. Although in Islam this companionship is designed to lead to absorption of the soul in Allah, it may become a substitute for this. Cases are reported in which a director is so revered that after his death his grave becomes a place of pilgrimage and worship—a practice deplored by orthodox Muslims as a lapse into idolatry. The Turkish order of dervishes known as the Bektashis from the name of its thirteenth century founder, exhibits a similar submission of the pupil to the guide (*mürşit*). Dr. Birge in his account of this order quotes examples of its numerous poetic scriptures. In one of these we read:

> If you have a mürşit you may become a human being.
> If you have no mürşit you will remain an animal.

IX

The great medieval mystic and reformer of Muslim piety, Al-Ghazzālī (d. 1111), recommended the confidential consultation of a *shaikh* or director, and submission to the penances he might impose for moral and spiritual healing. For his requirement of a daily examination of conscience Al-Ghazzālī has been likened to Ignatius Loyola; but the same method was practiced and enjoined by the Greek sages from Pythagoras to the later Stoics, and in Confucianism. Not only did the Muslim saint require that the acts of the day be critically conned over at nightfall, but that a record of the devotee's defects and achievements be kept in a notebook, in order to test his progress. Here is an anticipation of the pious and sometimes disconsolate diaries of the Puritans.

The ethical teaching of Al-Ghazzālī is impressive. His treatise, *Explanation of the Wonders of the Heart*, presents a catalogue of sins derived from the four classes of qualities—lordly, demonic, beastly and brutish—of which each of the last three causes "a dirty stain and a rust which is destructive and deadly." He urges the importance of a balanced attention to "the intellectual sciences" and the "religious law" of the Qur'ān and the Sunnah, or tradition:

For the intellectual sciences are like foods, and the sciences of religious law are as medicines. The sick person is harmed by food whenever he neglects the medicine. Thus the diseases of the heart can be treated only by the medicines derived from the religious law, which are the offices of the rites of worship and the works which the prophet set in order, for the reformation of hearts. So he who does not treat his sick heart by the use of ritual worship, but is content to use the intellectual sciences alone, is harmed thereby, even as the sick man is harmed by food.

In penitence, Al-Ghazzālī distinguishes three elements: knowledge (or belief that sin is deadly), remorse and resolve. No man is free from sin, and repentance is obligatory upon all, and at all times. He quotes the Prophet: "There is an oppression in my heart until I ask pardon of God seventy times every day and night." As a king would refuse a dirty garment, God will not accept a sinful heart: but repentance will cleanse the heart as soap a garment. Merely to say "I repent" would be like saying "I have washed the garment" without having done so. Death will not delay, and hell with its eternal fire is peopled with procrastinators who expected one day to repent.

Al-Ghazzālī had passed through a conversion experience of the greatest intensity. Having become a successful scholar he felt baffled by his temptations, and endured a period of great distress. His description of his confusion of mind and fluctuation of feeling is comparable to the record of mental tortures given by John Bunyan in *Grace Abounding*. He was unable to teach or utter his thoughts; of this he says vividly: "God locked my tongue." Relief was found when, with firm resolution, he took flight (*ca.* 1095) from the worldly environment of Bagdad which had become for him as a "City of Destruction." In Syria he placed himself for two years under Sūfī discipline, and by this his inner life was completely altered.

Many later instances are related of ecstatic conversion experiences associated with the direction of a *murshid*. "Filled with unspeakable happiness . . . I vowed a blind obedience to my master, and I chose him once for all as my spiritual guide," said a woman disciple of the seventeenth century director Mollā-Shāh. A greatly distressed nineteenth century seeker of guidance, having wandered widely in his quest, addressed a newly met venerable, white-bearded ascetic in the words: "I am seeking a spiritual guide and my heart tells me that thou art the guide I seek," and thus entered upon a lasting relationship.

There is a saying ascribed to Muhammad when he had returned from a battle: "We have returned from the lesser war to the greater war"— the struggle against self. The Muslim word for self-mortification is related to the word for war, and the Sūfī disciple enters on a lifelong conflict against his sinful nature. Fasting, trying postures, restraint of breathing, ablutions, intonations of complicated sequences of phrases and syllables including the ninety-nine names of Allah and the ninety-nine names of the Prophet, recitation of the Qur'ān, prescribed prayers and ejaculations, protracted meditations, veneration of saints and recounting of their miracles, are characteristic features of the rigorous course imposed on the learner by his *murshid*. Often the chief elements of the discipline required are on a low plane of ritual formalities and recitations. In some instances hypnotic methods have been employed by the director. In certain sects, however, the ethical element is stressed in the language of the rites. Thus the Bektashi, we are told by John P. Brown, employ an exercise of seven fastenings and unfastenings of the symbolic stone in the sacred girdle worn by them, uttering the words:

> I tie up greediness, and unbind generosity;
> I tie up anger, and unbind meekness;
> I tie up avarice, and unbind piety;
> I tie up ignorance, and unbind fear of God;
> I tie up passion, and unbind love of God;
> I tie up hunger, and unbind contentment;
> I tie up Satanism, and unbind Divineness.

It must be recognized that Western writers who describe the Muslim religious orders, in general, leave us with the impression that the piety cultivated in them, although sincerely ascetic, is greatly entangled in minute ritual requirements, and presents little evidence of high religious idealism or moral attainment.

X

Unless the present writer has been wholly misled in his explorations, no very favorable judgment can be rendered upon any of the systems discussed in this chapter with respect to the guidance of souls. Yet, in some measure, each has achieved its own ideals; and the representatives of each would dispute the presuppositions of a Western Christian. If abject obedience to a human superior is assumed to be a prime condition of the soul's deliverance, and if the end of human life is self-extinction, the Hindu has the advantage over us. If the world is explained as the scene of universal and irremediable suffering consequent upon self-assertion, where no God can help us, the Buddhist way of self-denial, contemplation and penitence may be the best course. If human nature is as good as Confucius thought, we may regard as adequate and admirable the cultivation of benevolence and the decencies of life which he prescribed. In fact, we Christians do not find ourselves satisfied with the generalizations on which these systems rest. But from them we have much to learn. Their historic disciplines have lessons for the Christian, and for the Christian counselor. Not least among these lessons is that which lies in their high seriousness in the face of life's problems and in the heroic earnestness and self-commitment they have often called forth.

Chapter IV

THE GUIDANCE OF SOULS IN THE NEW TESTAMENT

I

IN ANY review of great historical figures one must come to the one name that is above every name, Jesus of Nazareth. From the first century to the twentieth he has challenged the allegiance of the generations, and increasing numbers have called him Lord and Master. Yet, when investigation turns from the impression Jesus has made to the documentary records of his ministry, these appear surprisingly meager and fragmentary.

We have, of course, no genuine writing by Jesus himself, and it is unlikely that any part of his teaching was noted down at the time of its delivery. The treasure was entrusted to the fallible media of men's ears and memories. Until a century ago most Protestants were armed with a doctrine of miraculous verbal inspiration which ignored the hazards of transmission from uttered word to written page. We cannot recover certainty along that line. Recent approaches to the synoptic problem by the method of "form history" have perhaps done more to aggravate than to resolve the major difficulties. Some exponents of this method have become extremely skeptical of the possibility of any satisfactory knowledge of Jesus and of the words he uttered.

A similar problem arises with many other teachers of antiquity. If the problem is felt less keenly in their case than in the case of Jesus, it is because they and their teachings are a less vital factor in our lives. Even in Plato's version of Socrates, where there is no time gap, and no chain of intermediaries, scholars are uncertain regarding what the pupil did to the master's conversations. In other instances such as Buddhism, where the centuries in which the sacred books took shape are dark, the process almost wholly escapes the investigator, and with it the relation of the original utterance to its extant form. In the case of Christianity the lapse of time between the spoken word of the Founder and the written record is about half a century. The period was long enough to have witnessed the shaping and reshaping in manuscripts of what men remembered of his life and words. Certain reasons for the delay in the appearance of written Gospels have been set forth by Frederick C. Grant. In accord with his view we may say that the very idea of the utility of such records scarcely entered the minds of the first generation of Christians. But in order to perpetuate the authentic tradition the need of written memoranda was felt, and the task of writing undertaken.

The puzzling questions regarding the documents from which the Evangelists drew, and the sermons, paradigms, tales, legends, analogies, exhortations and other "forms" discovered, for example, by Martin Dibelius in the Gospels, and treated as clues to their development, cannot detain us here. While the process may in some degree be understood, the most expert study of it has not brought to recognition any large body of the teaching ascribed to Jesus that certainly remains in his *ipsissima verba*. The Gospel writers themselves make no secret of the fact that Jesus' teaching was often misunderstood: it is plain to us that it was imperfectly reported.

It is necessary to give due weight to these negative suggestions as we examine Jesus' ministry to individual persons. Yet complete skepticism is quite unjustifiable. It is one thing to admit: "Jesus may not have used these words," and quite another thing to regard his basic teaching as undiscoverable. Ernest F. Scott has remarked that "all our accounts of Jesus' ethics are in perfect harmony" and has objected to the assumption that unless we can ascertain the exact words of Jesus we have lost his message. He suggests that if the Evangelists could be recalled to earth they would answer without embarrassment modern questionings and justly claim that they had recorded faithfully what was vital. The soundness of this view will be apparent to habitual readers of the Gospels. Through the verbally imperfect record the vital substance of a unique message is conveyed, and the divergences in language are not contradictions in teaching. The unexhausted force of this teaching is well expressed by Chester Charlton McCown. Having examined the course of modern historical studies of Jesus he remarks:

In spite of all literary and preliterary criticism . . . there is still enough of the historical Jesus to stir the conscience and challenge the world. . . . The

Gospels contain, not merely the apostolic faith . . . but also a record, meager but vivid and vital, based upon authentic and largely trustworthy tradition, about a Jesus who actually lived in Palestine nineteen hundred years ago.

II

In the opening chapters of Mark's Gospel we see Jesus' early ministry calling forth wide popular response. Crowds press upon him, both to witness his miracles and to hear his teaching. A definite impression is conveyed, however, that he preferred not to be attended by great numbers, but to minister to a few. But this preference is repeatedly overborne by the demands of the situation. He goes before daybreak to pray in "a lonely place," but the message comes: "Everyone is searching for you" and he begins a preaching tour of Galilee (Mark 1:35-39). The leper he cleanses is charged to tell nobody; but he spreads the news, whereupon Jesus withdraws from towns to the countryside (Mark 1:40-45). When he enters a house in Capernaum, a crowd assembles, and when he goes to the seaside many throng about him once more (Mark 2:2, 13). When he again "withdraws" to the sea with his disciples, "a great multitude" follows out of Galilee, "also from Judea and Jerusalem and Idumea and from beyond Jordan and from about Tyre and Sidon, a great multitude," so that he orders a boat to be in readiness for his escape, "lest they should crush him" (Mark 3:7-9). Only when he goes up into the hills can he get his chosen disciples alone. Thereafter "he went home; and the crowd came together again, so that they could not even eat" (Mark 3:20). Matthew gives a similar impression of Jesus' inclination to withdraw from the throngs that congregated when he appeared. "Seeing the crowds he went up into the mountain and when he sat down his disciples came to him . . ." (Matt. 5:1).

Most of his recorded teaching is addressed to small groups or imparted in conversation with individuals. Sometimes, it is true, he addresses the massed multitude. From a boat he tells the parable of the sower to "the whole crowd" lining the shore (Mark 4:1-9): but the meaning of the parable is unfolded afterward to the twelve. To the assembled people themselves he speaks as to individuals: "He that hath ears to hear let him hear." The parable stresses the responsibility and destiny of each individual. In addressing assemblies, Jesus' method is far removed from that of the rabble-rousing demagogue who seeks to attract and sway masses and launch a political revolution. He preferred to instruct a few whom he could lead to a true understanding of his message.

It is increasingly recognized by scholars that most of the teachings of Jesus are substantially paralleled in the Wisdom and rabbinical literature. B. T. D. Smith, in a study of the parables of Jesus, points to many similarities of phrase and figure between the Talmud and the Gospels. In the parables of the Prodigal Son and the Barren Fig Tree, the resemblances extend to the book of Ahikar. The titles applied to Jesus in the Gospels include "Messiah," "prophet" and "rabbi." He is addressed as "rabbi" four times in Mark and seven times in John. Bultmann supposes that he would not have been so-called if he had not received formal scribal training. This scholar holds, too, that Jesus lived and taught as the rabbis, using the same methods of argument, and like them employing proverbs and parables. The word "disciple" applied to his followers is regarded as a technical term for the pupils of a rabbi. Gerhard Kittel had earlier remarked (in his study *Jesus als Seelsorger*): "He was not scribe and not rabbi, not teacher and master of wisdom; what men discovered in him was exactly this: healer of souls." We have seen in a previous chapter, however, that this term may in some sense be applied to the rabbis.

The evidence of Jesus' observance of the law, and his recognition of the authority of the scribes and pharisees (Matt. 23:2, 3) is to be weighed against his free approach to the former and his low opinion of the latter. The evangelists create an impression of harsh conflict with official Judaism; they may have exaggerated the hostility. Both Matthew and Mark call attention to the difference rather than the similarity of Jesus' teaching and that of the scribes: the crowd was astonished because "he taught them as one who had authority, and not as their scribes" (Matt. 7:29; cf. Mark 1:22). Bultmann recognizes, indeed, differences which many writers have noted. Unlike the rabbis Jesus had women among his disciples; unlike them also, he held conversations with publicans and moral outcasts. But Bultmann regards as common to him and them the unquestioning recognition of the authority of the Old Testament.

Yet his teachings do indicate a difference in the realm of authority, and Bultmann himself points out that the obedience he demanded was not finally to the written Law but to the will of God. The most remarkable example of this is where Jesus boldly amends the law of divorce

(Deut. 24:1-4). It was "for your hardness of heart," he states, that Moses permitted divorce. And against the Deuteronomic regulation he lays the weight of passages from the Creation narrative: "God made them male and female." "For this reason a man shall leave his father and mother and be joined to his wife, and the two shall become one" (Gen. 1:27, 2:24). This is a frank adoption of the more humane of two passages ascribed to Moses, and a frank annulment of the other. Jesus sees the will of God in the words, "the two shall become one," and adds: "What therefore God has joined together, let not man put asunder" (Mark 10:2-10).

This, indeed, was teaching as one that had authority and not as the scribes. Such a declaration, direct, decisive and free, marks a break with the traditionalism and caution of the rabbis and prepares us to read without astonishment the sharp words of condemnation: "Woe to you scribes and Pharisees, hypocrites! . . . You blind guides straining out a gnat and swallowing a camel!" If he came not to destroy but to fulfill the law, the fulfillment was to be bold and revolutionary, involving principles and actions at variance from those often discovered in the law by its official interpreters. G. Stanley Hall has written of the "supreme pedagogy" of Jesus. His arresting sureness and fearlessness carried home his message.

Sometimes Jesus finds in the plain meaning of a Scripture passage a clear, authoritative pronouncement against the ceremonialism he desires to combat. Thus Mark reports him quoting the passage from Isaiah 29 which we used in an earlier chapter as possibly a prophetic objection to the popular effect of the "precepts" of the wise man, and adding: "You leave the commandment of God, and hold fast the tradition of men." In the same chapter he vigorously condemns the nullifying of the commandment, "Honor thy father and thy mother," by the scribal casuistry that would permit men to shirk the duty of caring for parents by the declaration of Corban—"thus making void the word of God through your tradition" (Mark 7:1-13).

These condemnatory passages turn upon an axis that extends from the goodness of God to the needs of men. Jesus is equally impatient of every divergence from God's righteous will, and of every decision adverse to man's best life. He dissolves in a sentence the negative and oppressive elaboration of the sabbath law: "the sabbath was made for man and not man for the sabbath" (Mark 2:27). He reproaches the lawyers who "load men with burdens hard to bear" which they themselves will not touch with a finger (Luke 11:46). Obedience to God is not divorced from, but associated with, the freedom of the human person.

Much has been written of late years to modify the conception that is conveyed by the Gospels of the "scribes and pharisees" of Jesus' time. The conclusion is forced upon us, however, that he condemned them repeatedly and severely. He is frequently confronted by questioners who represent the pharisaic scribes and raise commonplace points of rabbinical discussion. "Is it lawful to heal on the sabbath?" they ask, in order to obtain an answer that could be used against him (Matt. 12:10). "Would you not rescue a sheep from a pit on the sabbath?" Jesus asks in reply and adds: "Of how much more value is a man than a sheep!" Again, in order "to entangle him in his talk" the question about paying taxes to Caesar is brought to him by Pharisees and Herodians. The latter are described by Dr. Finkelstein as "aristocratic adherents of the house of Herod," and as "assimilationists," i.e., submissive to Rome and tolerant of pagan culture. Their question to Jesus was probably familiar debating ground between them and the Pharisees. Jesus' answer: "Render to Caesar the things that are Caesar's and to God the things that are God's" (Matt. 22:21; Mark 12:17) is not, as sometimes supposed, an evasion. The image on the coin to which he calls attention would be a reminder of the familiar concept of the image of God in man. Jesus is saying: Pay your taxes, but do not fail to yield your soul to God.

While some of the scribes present casuistical questions only to embarrass or endanger Jesus, one of their number has a friendly exchange with him over the commandment of love. When this unnamed scribe affirms that love to God and neighbor is much more than ritual offerings, Jesus, seeing that he "answered wisely," responds: "You are not far from the Kingdom of God" (Mark 12:34). For the spiritual wisdom of the rabbis, as distinct from their casuistry, Jesus has no word of disapproval.

III

The conversations of Jesus as given in the Synoptic Gospels exhibit his method and power in the guidance of souls. Much of his teaching was uttered in dialogue. Apparently he preferred this personal and conversational method. Kittel asks us to "reflect on the very simple fact that he readily makes a conversation—a lively interchange—out of an instruction." A conversation is often so turned that it is the other person who voices the point to which it leads. In some instances, as in the case of Peter's declaration in Matthew 16:16, this result is obtained by direct questions.

It is of great interest to observe how freely the Gospel conversations are strewn with interrogation points. The frequent interchange of questions gives vividness to the narratives and creates a sense of the tremendous eagerness of Jesus and the impressiveness and challenge of his personality. At this point a comparison with Socrates can hardly escape the student. Yet the Gospels do not exhibit the Socratic method. Jesus did not hold with Socrates that the intellectual apprehension of truth is the chief end of man. Accordingly he does not probe the mental processes of his hearers in protracted inquisition. His questions bear upon central themes of religion and conduct. The transformation of lives he achieves is instituted not in the exposure of error and confusion of thought, but in inducing repentance and commitment to the Kingdom of God. "Repent for the kingdom of heaven is at hand" (Matt. 4:17) is the message with which his ministry begins. But the kingdom of heaven is a society of changed individuals who have become fit to enter it.

The importance of the conversion of one individual is the theme of the great parables in Luke 15. These parables are fraught with the gladness of redemption. We feel the exultant joy of the shepherd at the recovery of the one lost sheep, and the happiness of the woman who has found her one lost coin. "I tell you, there will be more joy in heaven over one sinner who repents than over ninety-nine righteous persons who need no repentance. . . . I tell you there is joy before the angels of God over one sinner who repents." The father celebrates with robe and ring and feast the return of the prodigal son from the far country—"for this my son was dead, and is alive again; he was lost and is found. And they began to make merry" (Luke 15:7, 10, 24).

If the restoration of the individual soul is so important as to be thought of as the occasion of celebration for angels in heaven, so also peril or damage to a soul is of the gravest concern. Jesus uses memorable and vivid imagery to stress the enormity of an offense against the soul of a convert. Better to be weighted with a millstone and thrown into the sea than to cause "one of these little [or humble] ones" to fall into sin (Mark 9:42). Mark does not make the word "little ones" (*mikroi*) refer to children. Matthew connects the saying with the child placed in the midst by Jesus as an example of the quality of spirit of those who enter the Kingdom (Matt. 18:1-6); but by "little ones who believe" he apparently understands unsophisticated disciples of any age.

We saw Mencius affirming that one must not "lose the child-heart." Jesus seems to have called attention repeatedly to the requirement of the childlike simplicity and unpretentiousness that keep open the way for grace, as against the pride and sophistication that block its course. How unteachable those tend to be who have to defend a reputation for knowledge! Jesus warmly appreciated the simple truth-seeking of the child, who instinctively knows that he has everything to learn.

IV

Numerous incidents are reported in which Jesus deals with individual spiritual needs. As he walks out of Capernaum a man comes running, and kneeling before him asks: "Good teacher, what must I do to inherit eternal life?" Jesus replies with a counter question: "Why do you call me good?" and adds, "No one is good but God alone." From what follows it is evident that the man has already thought himself "good": he claims to have kept the Commandments from his youth up. But the Kingdom is closed to the self-righteous who suppose they have fulfilled the requirements of God. "Jesus looking upon him loved him"; but the case was a grave one. It was the case of the wealthy man who wants a form of salvation that will not challenge his conscience or disturb his property. The heroic medicine of renunciation must be applied: "You lack one thing: go, sell all that you have, and give it to the poor." The inquirer's "countenance fell, and he went away sorrowful; for he had great possessions" (Mark 10:17-22; cf. Matt. 19:16-22). In the apocryphal *Gospel according to the Hebrews*, as A. E. J. Rawlinson notes, the passage is interestingly extended. Nonplussed, the inquirer scratches his head while

the Lord said to him, How canst thou say, I have fulfilled the Law and the Prophets? For it is written in the Law, Thou shalt love thy neighbor as thyself; and behold many of thy brethren, the sons of Abraham, are covered with filth and dying of hunger, and thy house is full of good things, and nothing goes from it to them.

In the canonical account Jesus uses the incident to call attention to the spiritual handicap of riches. It is easier for a camel to go through a needle's eye than for a rich man to enter the Kingdom! That he means this as a hyperbolic declaration of warning is apparent when he adds: "all things are possible with God."

Jesus' treatment of an unsocial and unintegrated individual in relation to the ethics of material gain is strikingly illustrated in the story of Zacchaeus (Luke 19:1-10). Here we are again made aware that, despite the predicament of the rich man indicated by the comparison of the camel and the needle's eye, "all things are possible with God," and even the rich wrongdoer is not beyond hope. Zacchaeus does not, like the rich young man of the previous story, go away sorrowful; he finds glad deliverance through renunciation. Luke leaves so much to the imagination that we cannot judge with certainty all that took place in the conversion of the greedy tax collector. His was the case of the rich man who is a social outcast. He has less worldly security than the rich young man. He has been looked upon by the good folk of Jericho perhaps as churchgoers today regard a wealthy gangster. Jesus shocks society, and takes off-guard the public enemy himself, by proposing to visit him. As if he had been pining for such recognition, Zacchaeus is most happy to receive him as his guest. Here Luke's silence baffles our curiosity. If the incident is historical, it is not remarkable that the matters discussed between the Master and the penitent remained undisclosed. We cannot know what confessions were made by this "malefactor of great wealth" in the liberating presence of Jesus, or how under his guidance a new course of action, the reverse of what had been habitual, was resolved upon. The private conference ends with Zacchaeus' declaration of intention to use his possessions for poor relief and in fourfold restitution of what he had fraudulently exacted. He who has been an exploiter becomes a benefactor of his fellow citizens, and realizes that he is identified with them. The healing of the publican's soul is bound up with this transformation. "Today salvation is come to this house, since he is also a son of Abraham. For the Son of man came to seek and to save that which was lost." Here we have in another form the theme of the lost sheep and the lost coin. The repentance of the sinner is the matter of importance.

Such instances may remind us that for the understanding of many of Jesus' oft-quoted teachings attention must be given to the persons to whom they were addressed and the personal problems they were designed to resolve. This point is approached from another angle by Amos N. Wilder in some remarks on Jesus' "so-called ethical absolutes." These he would regard neither as universally binding rules of life nor as fragments of an "interim-ethic," but as "occasional utterances to particular persons." We may not, of course, infer that they have for this reason no general instruction to furnish. For the rich man and for Zacchaeus alike, the obstacle to the soul's true attainment was a form of covetousness, and this is an evil that Jesus frequently condemns in more general discourses. Yet, we commit an error if we look upon every recorded word of Jesus as equally addressed to all men.

That Jesus was quick to discover spiritual qualities, is seen not only in instances in which the inquirers are Jews, but also where he is in contact with non-Jews. Such are the Syrophoenician woman, called a Greek by Mark and by Matthew a Canaanite, whose undiscouraged faith is rewarded by her daughter's recovery (Matt. 15:21-28; Mark 7: 24-30); and the Roman military officer who came to him with a plea that his servant might be healed by a word spoken in absence. Jesus is said to have "marvelled" at the centurion's faith: "I tell you, even in Israel I have not found such faith." In Matthew's account he is led by the incident to forecast an ingathering into the Kingdom from east and west, to sit at table with Abraham while Jews are thrust out.

V

In some of the incidents we have reviewed we are confronted with miracles of healing. In these cases healing of the body is frequently associated with the healing of the soul. "Take heart, my son, your sins are forgiven," is Jesus' greeting to a paralytic; charged with blasphemy for this, he effectively commands the invalid to take his bed and go home (Matt. 9:2-7; Mark 2:1-12; Luke 5:17-26). To the woman who has touched the fringe of his garment, he says: "Take heart, my daughter; your faith has made you well" (Matt. 9:22). "Go your way; your faith has made you well," is his parting word to Bartimaeus who has been given his sight (Mark 10:52). Ordinarily the faith referred to is evidently a belief in Jesus' ability to effect healing. "Do you believe that I am able to do this?" he asks two blind men, and touching their eyes pronounces the words: "According to your faith be it done unto you" (Matt. 9:27-29). As the healing of the body and of the soul are linked together, so it is impossible to separate from these utterances the consciousness of Jesus that he exercises a divine power in both spheres. Although he is seen declining to produce "a sign from heaven" on the demand of his opponents, except the "sign of Jonah," which Luke interprets as the "preaching" of the prophet (Luke 11:32), he very frequently appears not only working miracles but claiming a divine power to do this, and eliciting faith in himself on that ground. This emphasis in the Gospels is of course most pronounced in the Gospel of John, in which the miracles are few but impressively treated as a basis of faith rather than as conditional upon it.

We merely glance here at problems and mysteries that are attracting new attention in our century. We cannot dismiss the Gospel miracles as mere pious tributes to the unique and cosmic importance of Jesus by second generation admirers. Nor can we explain them away as cures of nervous disorders by the use of "suggestion." If, on other grounds, we are convinced of his uniqueness—if indeed he was, in a sense other than that in which it is true generally of prophets and saints, God incarnate —we need not be surprised if his acts exhibit a unique power in the realm of bodily health. On the other hand, modern knowledge of biology and psychology may help to make some of them explicable on natural grounds. In this realm we must for the present, however, be content with many uncertainties. Contemporary research and experience recognize unexplained case histories of healing that would be incredible if they were not well authenticated, and which make it difficult to deny to any powerful and benevolent person the possibility of seemingly miraculous cures. The range of this uncharted field is well suggested by the most striking miracle of mental healing in the Gospels, that of the insane man (demoniac) whose disease (a legion of demons) at Jesus' bidding passed from him to the Gadarene swine. In all the Synoptics the details of the incident accord with prevalent first century notions of demon possession, and the miracle is a dramatic act of exorcism. Selby McCasland points to the prevalence of exorcism in ancient Palestine, and remarks: "Regardless of the scientific standing of the theory of personality involved . . . many cures are well authenticated in both ancient and modern times." If any solution of the problem of Jesus' miracles is forthcoming, it will have to await further fundamental knowledge.

VI

Jesus made available two great boons which we humans ceaselessly crave, spiritual renewal and spiritual repose. The former of these is reflected in the Fourth Gospel incidents of Nicodemus (John 3:1-10) and the woman of Samaria (John 4:7-42). Jesus abruptly confronts the inquiring Nicodemus with the necessity of being "born anew." The new birth is not of the flesh but of the spirit. The author of the Fourth Gospel here reveals what was, on many testimonies, the experience of the first Christians, a sense of a personal new beginning so complete as to be best expressed in the analogy of birth. "He who loves is born of God," we read elsewhere in the Johannine writings (I John 4:7). The story of the woman at the well is rich with symbolism. The material well yields place to the unfailing spring of living water "welling up unto eternal life" within the soul. Both stories suggest the imparting of a divine life of inexhaustible resources—in the words of Henry Scougal's immortal title, "the life of God in the soul of man."

The other priceless boon we have mentioned is expressed in the closing verses of Matthew 11. It is held by many commentators that verse 27 (". . . no one knows the Father except the Son . . .") and the Great Invitation of verses 28 to 30 were originally unconnected. Both fragments express, however, an advanced Christology such as we should expect to find in John's Gospel rather than in the Synoptics. C. G. Montefiore and others see verses 28 to 30 as a call to Jews to escape the burdens of the law under which they "labor and are heavily-laden"; but these words well describe the plight of all men who are burdened and fatigued by care and toil. The reference to a yoke calls up the image of laboring oxen. The word "rest" (*anapausis*) seems to bear much the same variety of meanings that we give to the English word, including repose, relaxation and refreshment. This variety is well brought out in the Vulgate, which has for "I will give you rest" "*reficiam vos*" (I will refresh you), while for the noun in verse 29 it has "*requiem*" (repose). In the Sermon on the Mount there is insistent warning against anxiety regarding the necessities of life. Life is more than food, and the Father knows your needs; "seek first his Kingdom and his righteousness, and all these things shall be yours as well" (Matt. 6:25-33). The soul is healed by a trustful faith in God. In the Great Invitation Jesus is represented as calling for this trust in himself; in him the weary find rest and restoration. Theologically the claim implied in this reaches far. But both these Matthew passages have the same suggestion for the therapy of souls by means of an unquestioning trust in One who is wholly adequate.

Nor are the passages from the First and from the Fourth Gospel that have here been placed in contrast to be regarded as contradictory. Jesus in Matthew does not offer us Lao-Tzu's "wisdom of not striving," but a recovery of vitality and inner repose, an enrichment of the resources of personality that will enable us to press on untiringly as we "seek the Kingdom." The toil and discipline of life are not abolished, but through restored strength they become as an easy yoke. Jesus vividly impressed his hearers with the availability to harried people of repose and deliverance from anxiety, and of a divine energy that recreates the soul.

VII

When we move from the Gospels to the Epistles we pass from the inauguration of the Kingdom to the erection of the Church. The genuine epistles of St. Paul are all of earlier date than the earliest of the Gospels. They did not, like the Gospels, arise out of a long process of accumulation and sifting, but were written down substantially as we have them, by the Apostle or at his dictation. They make us, then, very intimate with those aspects of the Christian life to which they allude. We see pervading them an awareness of Christ glorified and ascended, and of the church and its communion sustained by the Holy Spirit here below, and expectant of the Lord's return.

The Church must have had to meet the problem of discipline almost at the very beginning. The standards of belief and behavior it required had to be maintained, and lapses from these standards treated under an authoritative discipline, if they were not to be surrendered. The Church must have the means of determining fitness for its fellowship, and of correcting its unsatisfactory members. This necessity would in time produce an intricate penitential discipline; in the New Testament we see its inception.

Some passages in the Gospels and in Acts have been repeatedly and minutely examined in this connection. They have been so often explained as offering support to some later ecclesiastical system, that it is still difficult to interpret them without suspicion of prejudice. Whatever the source and date of the language of commission in Matthew 16:16-19 (which has no parallel in the other Synoptic Gospels), it testifies to a high conception of disciplinary authority. Peter, on confessing that Jesus is the Christ, is authorized to remit or retain sins.

Jesus is represented by Matthew as giving direction for specific procedure where one brother has sinned against another. The injured brother first privately asks redress; if this is refused he interviews the offender again before witnesses. "If he refuses to listen to them tell it to the church; and if he refuses to listen even to the church, let him be to you as a Gentile and a tax collector" (Matt. 18:15-17). The form of this logion suggests a date after Church organization was well advanced. The admirably unhurried and considerate process of discipline here outlined, which gives the offender no less than three opportunities to correct his behavior before excommunication, may have been normal in such cases. With this direction, Matthew links a commission of authority: "Whatever you bind on earth will be bound in heaven, and whatever you loose on earth will be loosed in heaven" (Matt. 18:15-20).

In John's Gospel, in a scene immediately following the Resurrection, there is a commissioning of the ten Apostles present. "He breathed on them and said to them, Receive the Holy Spirit. If you forgive the sins of any, they are forgiven; if you retain the sins of any, they are retained" (John 20:22-23). These passages differ in the identification of the organ of authority in the Church, whether in St. Peter (Matthew 16), or in the whole group (Matthew 18), or in the body of living Apostles with the exception of Thomas the doubter (John 20). But they impress us alike with the consciousness of the importance of discipline, and of authoritative declarations of the pardon or rejection of offenders. What is declared by the Apostles on earth, is ratified in heaven.

What is probably the earliest general regulation of conduct in the expanding Church is connected with the Council at Jerusalem (A.D. 48 ?), reported by the writer of Acts as having been necessitated by the demand that Gentile converts must be circumcised. This requirement was rejected, but the council declared that the Gentile brethren should "abstain from what has been sacrificed to idols and from blood and from what is strangled and from unchastity" (Acts 15:29). The variation in manuscripts here makes it possible for some (e.g., Hugh J. Schonfield) to suppose that the prohibitions were of "idolatry, fornication and murder," a triad of major sins in the Mishnah. (Cf. Matt. 5: 21, 27, 33.) However we understand this passage, it presents the first Christian canonical list of grave sins. There would later be many catalogues of offenses to be avoided or penalized, including those designated by St. Paul in Galatians 5:19-21 as "the works of the flesh." We shall observe an increasing interest in the identification and detailed classification of the sins as we reach the Middle Ages.

In his study of Paul as a missionary Martin Schlunk states that the greatness of the Apostle derives from the fact that "he possessed the gift of the cure of souls (Seelsorge) in outstanding measure and employed the art with wonderful mastery." Paul was very conscious of his responsibility for the rising Christian communities. While filled with eagerness, he is also weighed down by what he calls "the daily pressure upon me of my anxiety for all the churches" (II Cor. 11:28). His letters show him alertly and imaginatively concerned for local church situations and the individuals associated with them.

The distasteful side of this service was the discipline of scandalous offenders. The loathsome offense of a Corinthian member, and the failure of the church to discipline him, call forth from Paul a peremptory demand for action: "When you are assembled, and my spirit is present, with the power of our Lord Jesus, you are to deliver this man to Satan for the destruction of the flesh, that his spirit may be saved in the day of the Lord Jesus." He points out that "a little leaven ferments the whole lump of dough"—the whole church may be corrupted if the offender is not removed (I Cor. 5:4-6). Excommunication and the imposition of the penalty are acts of the church "assembled." Paul's language of rebuke suggests that this should have been done without his intervention. If, as usually supposed, the case is the same as that referred to in II Corinthians 2:5-11, Paul was anxious that the offender, when properly penitent, should be received again and "comforted," that he might not be overwhelmed with sorrow. It would be perilous to infer from the language of the latter passage, "Whom you forgive, I also forgive," that either Paul or the Corinthian Christians felt it necessary for the validity of the reconciliation that his apostolic authority should seal it. If, in fact, the two passages have reference to the same offender, Paul, having demanded his punishment, would feel it important on other than official grounds to consent to his restoration when the punishment was completed. Yet if his intervention was not an assertion of apostolic authority, it was an assertion of the moral authority of an apostle, and may have been effective mainly for this reason.

Whether we link together the two passages or not, the first illustrates excommunication, the second reconciliation, at an early stage of the Church. In the first we see expressed the two constant valid motives of the corrective discipline, restoration of the sinner and protection of the Church's purity. "Delivering to Satan" probably means returning him to the kingdom of Satan (paganism) from which he came when he renounced Satan's "pomps" at his baptism, and "the destruction of the flesh" may refer to bodily austerities or penances imposed. (Joseph Klausner's suggestion that Paul here "approved the death sentence" appears ridiculous.) In the second passage, we are impressed by the note of considerateness and tenderness: "I beg you," says the Apostle, "to reaffirm your love for him." In view of the foulness of the offense, this was a good deal to ask; but in the Apostolic Church forgiveness was a reality. Similarly St. Paul writes to the Galatians: "Brethren, if a man be overtaken in any trespass, you who are spiritual should restore him in a spirit of gentleness" (Gal. 6:1). The Epistle to the Hebrews, on the other hand, appears to forbid the reconciliation of those once "enlightened" who have "committed apostasy" (Heb. 6:4-6). This was probably written against a background of persecution, when "apostasy" was a serious danger.

VIII

The guidance of Christians in day-to-day living is a prominent feature of the Pauline and other New Testament Epistles. Requests for such guidance were probably often made. Introducing a passage on sex ethics, St. Paul refers to "the matters about which you wrote" (I Cor. 7:1). Underlying all the advice of his letters is the concept of a new life which Christians know through faith in the risen and exalted Christ. They therefore "walk in newness of life"; they avoid sin and obey God "as men who have been brought from death to life" (Rom. 6:4, 13). "If anyone is in Christ he is a new creation" (I Cor. 5:17). Paul can combat sins of the body with such persuasions as: ". . . your bodies are members of Christ; . . . your body is a temple of the Holy Spirit. . . . So, glorify God in your body" (I Cor. 6:9-20). To the Roman Christians he writes: "Be transformed by the renewal of your mind" (Rom. 12:1). This principle of renewal, now supported by frequent reference to the Resurrection, is basically the same as in the Fourth Gospel. The motive of fellowship within the Church, the maintenance of the "one body in Christ" (Rom. 12:5) is also strong and commanding. In a truly great chapter of First Corinthians on the service of each Christian to his fellows in this common life, he affirms: "You are the body of Christ, and individually members of it" (I Cor. 12:27). From this passage he is carried on to his matchless commendation of Christian love. The expression of this concept reaches its culmination in Ephesians, which if not written by Paul is congruous with his thought. Within the fellowship men "bear one another's burdens" (Gal. 6:2).

In Romans we have not only a profound exposition of grace, but also a brief code of Christian behavior. The qualities commended are those which befit those within the fellowship of the Church. The Apostle is dealing with the conduct of individuals, but of individuals as mutually responsible and co-operative members of the "one body." St. Paul's brief, pointed injunctions closely resemble those of the Sermon on the Mount, but have more reference to mutual duties: "Let love be genuine . . . love one another with brotherly affection. . . . Contribute to the needs of the saints. . . . Live in harmony with one another" (Rom. 12:9, 12, 16). This is especially evident in the treatment of certain questions of conscience such as eating meat with pagans and the religious observance of special days (Rom. 14:2-6). Such matters are to be determined on the principle of fellowship and mutual forbearance. "None of us lives to himself, and none of us dies to himself": we live in Christ, and each is finally answerable to God. Hence we ought not to set ourselves up as judges of our brethren; but we must be always careful to avoid wounding the consciences of others. "Do not let what you eat cause the ruin of one for whom Christ died. . . . Let us then pursue what makes for peace and for mutual upbuilding" (Rom. 14:7, 15, 19). In these verses we see how completely Paul saw in the Gospel the solution of the problem of the relation of the individual to the society.

The intimacy of Paul's ministry to individuals is seen in many incidental references. His reported words to the Ephesian elders in Acts 20: 18-20 offer a suggestion of this. There is significance too in his frank admissions of his own weakness. "For we do not want you to be ignorant, brethren, of the affliction we experienced in Asia: for we were so utterly and unbearably crushed that we despaired of life itself." Though when he writes this he is triumphing in God's deliverance, he still pleads: "You also must help us by prayer" (II Cor. 1:8, 11). Thus he takes the new Christians of Corinth into his confidence. The father of a great mission church, he was no iron-hearted disciplinarian or bureaucratic official, but a brotherly Christian in need of the moral and spiritual support of the others. "His perception of himself corresponds to the perception of men that he shows in his relation with his church groups" (Heinrici). He observed and understood the persons with whom he came in contact, and was determined to meet them on common ground. "I have become all things to all men, that I might by all means save some" (I Cor. 9:22). He is so imaginatively sympathetic that he identifies himself with those who are undergoing personal crises: "Who is weak and I am not weak? Who is made to fall and I am not indignant?" (II Cor. 11:29).

Very striking, too, are the greetings to persons in Paul's letters. It is not merely that he gives them frank direction, as when he entreats two Philippian women to "agree in the Lord." Rather, it is the fact that he condenses into brief phrases much encouragement and commendation of individuals. These are not blanket phrases suitable to anybody, but are so specially applicable to the person concerned that they show evidence of personal attachment and appreciation: when "Prisca and Aquila . . . who risked their necks," "Epaenetus, the first convert in Asia," and "Mary, who worked hard" (Rom. 16:3, 5, 6) read or heard the chapter of greetings appended to the Letter to the Romans, they would be encouraged and rewarded, and filled with fresh enthusiasm. St. Paul had a keen memory of persons, and knew how to prompt others to their best effort by generous recognition. The delicacy of his touch in suggesting without demanding a course of action, is perhaps best seen in Philemon, a letter written in a difficult situation with great courtesy and kindness.

St. Paul's guidance of souls was enriched by a realization of the value of purposeful contemplation as a defense against passion and self-centered anxiety. He urges the Philippians to give their minds to the things that are true, honorable, pure, lovely, gracious, excellent and praiseworthy (Phil. 4:8). Scholars have pointed out that he here uses one of his favorite words, *logizesthe*—think appraisingly about, dwell thoughtfully upon, these things. Who has not felt a healing balm of the mind even in reading these elevated words? He dares here to present, as an example, his own manner of life: "What you have learned . . . and seen in me, do" (verse 9).

A list of virtues and good counsels may be framed—and the task has been done more than once—from the writings of St. Paul and the other epistolary literature of the New Testament, on the basis of which the early Christian ethic seems to parallel that of the late Stoics or other good pagans. Actually, however, the New Testament ethic is vitalized by a spiritual impulsion not known to them. The mystery cults offer some suggestion of the experience of a "new life," but hardly in a way comparable to this element in Christianity. When we read, in their several contexts phrases like these:

Let everyone speak truth to his neighbor, for we are members one of another . . . forgiving one another as God in Christ forgave you . . . and walk in love, as Christ loved us and gave himself up for us. . . . Be subject to one another out of reverence for Christ. . . . Husbands love your wives as Christ loved the church (Eph. 4:25, 32; 5:2, 21, 25). For the grace of God has appeared . . . training us . . . to live sober, upright and godly lives . . . awaiting our blessed hope (Tit. 2:11-13). As he who has called you is holy, be holy yourselves. . . . Having purified your souls . . . love one another earnestly from the heart (I Pet. 1:15, 22) . . . We know that we have passed out of death into life because we love the brethren (I Jn. 3:14)—

we become inescapably aware of the emergence in early Christianity of a new dynamic for personal moral living, the releasing of power for a new therapy of souls with which nothing else in the ancient world could compete.

IX

Lying deep in the experience and culture of the early Christian communities are the closely related practices of mutual edification (*aedificatio mutua*) and fraternal correction (*correptio fraterna*). Paul's rule for deciding on what meats are to be eaten is: "Let us then pursue what makes for peace and for mutual upbuilding" (Rom. 14:19). To the Thessalonians who were perturbed over the delay of Christ's return, he writes: "Encourage one another and build one another up" (I Thess. 5:11); and in the same connection: "admonish the idle; encourage the fainthearted" (5:14). He is happy to think that the Roman Christians are "able to instruct one another" (Rom. 15:14); and he prays for a rich endowment of the "word of Christ" for the Colossians as they "teach and admonish one another" (Col. 3:16). An offender under discipline is not to be treated as an enemy but warned as a brother (II Thess. 3:15). He would have the Corinthian Christians cultivate prophecy rather than speaking with tongues because "he who prophesies speaks to men for their upbuilding and encouragement and consolation. He who speaks in a tongue edifies himself, but he who prophesies edifies the church" (I Cor. 14:3-4). In such passages we cannot fail to see the Apostle's design to create an atmosphere in which the intimate exchange of spiritual help, the mutual guidance of souls, would be a normal feature of Christian behavior. The author of Hebrews, having quoted from the 95th Psalm, "harden not your heart," etc., warns his readers to guard against this peril by mutual exhortation: "But exhort one another every day, as long as it is called 'today,' that none of you may be hardened by the deceitfulness of sin" (Heb. 3:13). In the Epistle of James, which is now commonly regarded as a homiletic essay of the early second century, mutuality is again stressed: "Confess your sins to one another and pray for one another, that you may be healed" (James 5:16).

The last-quoted passage has a special relation to the bedside service in which the elders pray for the healing of the sick man, anointing him in the name of the Lord (5:14); though probably the healing here referred to is thought of as related to the "sins" as well as to the diseases of the body. As in Judaism and in the Gospels, so also in the early Church, these elements are closely related. Whereas the Stoics thought of disease as common to good as well as evil men, in the Bible it is usually implied that its cause is sin committed by the sufferer. In any case, it is an occasion of repentance and prayer. This passage in James is notable for its evidence on visitation of the sick and a ritual for bodily healing in the early Church. The vast development of healing arts and rites in the Hellenistic world would exhibit more contrast to, than similarity with, the simple act of prayer here prescribed. The passage vividly expresses the New Testament principle of intercessory prayer. Other striking passages in this connection appear in Ephesians: "For this reason I bow my knees before the Father . . . that Christ may dwell in your hearts through faith . . ." (Eph. 3:14-19); "Pray at all times in the Spirit, with all prayer and supplication . . . making supplication for all the saints" (6:18). In I Timothy 2:1-2, we see "all men" the objects of the Christians' "supplications, prayers, intercessions and thanksgivings."

The mutuality and brotherliness of the Christian life shine in these passages on prayer as in those on edification and correction. Men were to be spiritually available to one another for help and criticism. It is this underlying ideal that gives to the earnest ethical teaching of James its truly Christian character. The condemnation of the irresponsible and privilege-seeking rich, and the exaltation of humility, are prerequisites of Christian mutuality. The highest approval is bestowed upon the earnest believer who feels impelled to seek a lapsed and wandering member, and to bring him back from the error of his way, saving his soul from death (James 5:19).

X

In what degree these far-reaching religious concepts became vital for each individual within the Christian movement, we cannot be sure. The fact that they were stressed in the literature of exhortation may suggest that they were realized only in a disappointing degree. Christians possessed, indeed, principles which mere humans found exceptionally demanding. It is far easier to fast twice a week than to share with others life's highest treasures. Yet the apostolic apprehension of the Christian cure of souls was not a vain dream. It was because many

Christians—though perhaps a minority among them—faithfully adhered to these principles, that the Church emerged as a firmly knit organization. It was because they shared in these ways, and perpetuated by sharing, a new life in Christ, and effectively revealed it in their lives, that the Roman world failed to smother the Christian groups in its mass or crush them by its power, and that it finally turned to the Church for deliverance from its own political chaos. In later times the New Testament emphases sometimes became hidden in ecclesiastical routine, and were brought to light again by reforming teachers. Even today we have fresh practical lessons to learn from the Gospels and Epistles in the matter of the cure of souls. We see here more vividly than elsewhere that the cure of souls is never merely a method, even a method derived from a doctrine, or a task for certain hours in the week, but that it involves both the faith we live by and all our daily activities and contacts.

Chapter V

DISCIPLINE AND CONSOLATION IN THE AGE OF THE CHURCH FATHERS

I

THOUGH man is by nature a "social animal," he often neglects the obligations involved in being social. And while the early Christians by divine grace experienced a new spiritual life, some of them were not so controlled and empowered by it as to be steadfast in fulfillment of its high demands. They were urged and expected to live as those in whom Christ has wrought an inner transformation, and to expend their energies in service to their fellow men. But some were inconstant, and some lapsed entirely from the Christian way. Their failures were scandalous to the outside world, injurious to the Church and ruinous to themselves. Their offenses were committed against God and the Christian *koinōnia*. We have noted some evidence of measures taken both to purge the Church of evildoers and to correct and restore the offenders. Where grave offenses occurred, exclusion, discipline and restoration to membership status were necessary—in ecclesiastical terms excommunication, penance and reconciliation. With the growth of Church institutions, procedures for these ecclesiastical actions were gradually developed.

In cases of private conflict and injury there remained the opportunity (as in Matthew 18:15) of repentance and reconciliation without official action. Undoubtedly a continual play of mutual exhortation helped to keep individuals morally alert (cf. I Thess. 5:11; Rom. 14:19; James 5:16). But with expanding numbers the problems of discipline became more complicated. We see this in Revelation 2 and 3. Of the seven churches to whom letters of admonition are addressed five are urgently required to "repent" of some grave lapse into carelessness or some scandalous offense that has gone unchecked.

In documents of the second and third centuries we see evidence of divergence of opinion with respect to the discipline of offenders. The temper of the Church, confronted by the moral laxity of the contemporary pagan society, was stern toward those who violated Christian standards of behavior. There was much hesitation even about admitting to repentance and reconciliation those who had committed the grave sins of idolatry, unchastity and the shedding of blood. Some writers—remembering the language in Matthew (12:31-32), and Mark (3:28-30) about the sin for which there is no forgiveness, or the stern warning in Hebrews (12:15-17) concerning Esau who having sold his birthright "found no chance to repent, though he sought it with tears," or the reference in I John 5:16 to a sin unto death for which prayer is not recommended—held that these were unpardonable, or "irremissible," sins, for which the Church had no warrant to take any action leading to the sinner's restoration. But opinion varied. Tertullian, writing shortly before 200, and Origen (d. 253) are numbered among the rigorous disciplinarians, while Hermas (ca. 125) permits the restoration of an apostate and of an adulteress, and Clement of Alexandria (ca. 200) represents the Apostle John as pardoning a repentant bandit. The difference here is part of the whole problem of qualifications for church fellowship, aspects of which later gave rise to the Novationist and the Donatist schisms. The motive of protecting the fellowship from pollution was in tension with the motive of restoring the sinful brother. Gradually the more liberal interpretation prevailed, and as the penitential discipline was systematized it ultimately made provision for the reception of those guilty of the gravest offenses.

Since the Christian rite of baptism required earnest repentance and renunciation of sin, and baptismal repentance seemed decisive and final, the Church authorities were embarrassed by instances of serious misdemeanors by the baptized. Were the offenders to be simply and finally rejected, or were they, as St. Paul evidently held, to be encouraged to repent and return? The first stage was to permit a single act of post-baptismal penitence. The Angel of Repentance introduced by Hermas permits the restoration of an adulterous wife or husband, with the explicit statement: "There is but one repentance to the servants of God" (i.e., to the baptized). He explains that God, knowing the weakness of men and the wiles of the devil, has mercifully permitted this.

And therefore I say unto you that if after that great and holy calling anyone is tempted by the devil and sins, he has one repentance. But if thereupon he should sin, to such a man his repentance is of no benefit. (*Pastor* of Hermas, Commandments, iv, 1, 3)

Hermas treats these matters very gravely. Elsewhere he discusses the punishment of sin, which the penitent accepts rather than escapes. If he resolutely humbles himself under the divine affliction, God will have mercy and heal him (Similitudes, vii, 4). Hermas strangely fails to discuss the action of Church authorities in excommunicating and imposing penances. It is incredible that he was unfamiliar with this. But he is primarily concerned with repentance itself, as enabling the sinner to "live unto God." His interests are those of a spiritual monitor, not those of a canon lawyer. Repentance is a gift of God; but from some it is withheld, and they are not incorporated in the Church which God is building. Nevertheless, in one passage Hermas has the Angel of Repentance say: "Go and tell all men to repent, and they shall live unto God."

II

In the early centuries two Greek words stand out in the vocabulary of Church discipline: *metanoia*, repentance, and *exomologesis*, confession. *Metanoia* occurs in both noun and verb forms in the New Testament and means a change of mind in the sense of a conversion, or reversal of moral direction. In the Vulgate this word is rendered *"poenitentia,"* which basically means a contrite repentance; but the corresponding verb becomes *"agere poenitentiam"* usually understood "to do penance." Tertullian pointed out that the Greek had the sense of "a change of mind" (*Adv. Marc.* ii, 24); and Luther long afterward contended against the externalizing of the command *metanoeite* in the preaching of John the Baptist and Jesus (Matt. 3:2; 4:17) to make it refer to sacramental penances (*agite poenitentiam*). It was perhaps inevitable that repentance should in some contexts become indistinguishable from "the fruits meet for repentance," and that penalties ecclesiastically imposed should sometimes be regarded as the "fruits"; but the externalization was never theoretically complete.

The other comprehensive word, *exomologesis*, appears in the New Testament only in its verbal forms. When it has for its object "sins" it bears the simple meaning of a full confession: thus John the Baptist's converts "were baptized in the river Jordan confessing (*exomologoumenoi*) their sins" (Matt. 3:6; Mark 1:9) and James enjoins: "Confess your sins to one another" (James 5:16). But the application of *exomolo-*

gesis was early extended to cover overt acts of humiliation so dramatic and arresting as to "speak louder than words." The noun was taken over from the Greek by the Latin fathers, and used to signify both confession and penalty. Such terms change their meaning with use and with the change of the acts they refer to. In a Pseudo-Clementine homily of *ca.* 140 we are told that almsgiving is as good as repentance (*metanoia*) for sin. Later theology spoke of contrition, confession and satisfaction as the three parts of the penitential discipline, and connected these respectively with *poenitentia* (in its primary sense), *exomologesis* and *metanoia*. In our present period they did not assume this sequence.

As far as Church discipline is concerned, the word *exomologesis* is of first importance. Before the middle of the second century confession was a part of the Sunday services; whether this was a "general confession" or a personal confessing to one another as in James 5:16, is not indicated. In the *Didache* (*Teaching of the Twelve Apostles, ca.* 150) we read: "In church thou shalt confess thy transgressions, and thou shalt not betake thyself to prayer with an evil conscience. . . . On the Lord's day gather yourselves together and give thanks, having first confessed your transgressions . . ." (Did. iv, 14, xiv, 1). Irenaeus some decades later tells of a deacon's wife who, having been victimized "in mind and body" by a magician, and rescued from him, "spent her whole time in the exercise of confession (*exomologesis*) weeping over and lamenting the defilement she had undergone." This confession is evidently public; Irenaeus (*ca.* 180) explicitly refers to confessions made "openly" in similar cases (*Against Heresies*, i. 13).

Tertullian furnishes explicit information on the penitential discipline near the end of the second century. Like Hermas he permits one repentance after baptism, but unlike Hermas he does not extend this to the capital sins of idolatry, unchastity and homicide. He is hesitant about any concession to the sinner. When admitting "an opening for penitence" he disavows all thought of "an opening for sinning," and repeatedly stresses the limit of one repentance and no more. The shipwrecked man has one plank to support him, in baptism: one more is provided in the one act of repentance. These matters are set forth in his little book *On Repentance* (*ca.* 197), and there he has also an impressive description of exomologesis. He calls it "the discipline of the prostration and humiliation of a man, requiring a behavior conducive to mercy." We confess our sins to God, and repentance arises from confession. But the confession is made before men. The penitent appears in sackcloth and ashes; he mourns over his sins, weeping and moaning day and night. He bows at the feet of the presbyters, kneels to "those who are dear to God," and urges all the brethren to intercede for him in prayer. Tertullian stresses the necessity of this remedial humiliation which even "wipes out eternal penalties," and lays the sinner low only to raise him up again. It is not explicitly said that the sins are declared by the penitent in this public act, but the use of the one word which signifies an unreserved confession makes this the more likely. It is also implied in other sections of the same work. He deplores the fact that too many shun or postpone exomologesis as a public self-exposure. To conceal their sin from men is not to conceal it from God. "Is it better," he asks, "to be damned in secret than to be absolved in public?" The shame of the discipline is more forbidding than the bodily hardship. But harsh as the remedy seems, it is not comparable to the hell-fire which it quenches for the penitent.

Pope Calixtus I (218-23) drew upon himself the violent condemnation of Tertullian, and of his defeated rival Hippolytus, by an edict which admitted to repentance and reconciliation those guilty of the three capital sins. Tertullian had become a Montanist when he wrote On Modesty (ca. 220) against Calixtus. The book is a sarcastic and intemperate arraignment of the relaxed policy of the Roman bishop toward those guilty of "irremissible" sins. The commission to bind and loose, according to Tertullian, does not refer to these sins, and St. Paul does not in II Corinthians 2 sanction the restoration of the incestuous man of I Corinthians 5. As for Hermas, he is a lover of adulterers! Hippolytus shows no less severity, and even more of personal animus, in assailing Calixtus. Both writers refer especially to relaxation in the treatment of sexual offenders. The labor of scholars has not made clear the real content or the real purpose of the edict of Calixtus. But apparently it marked the official adoption at Rome of a less rigorous view than the prevailing one; while the protests against it show the outraged conscience of the rigorists.

There was difference of judgment in the East as well as in the West. Clement of Alexandria (ca. 200) follows Hermas in admitting one post-baptismal repentance and opening it to those guilty of the greater sins if these were not deliberate. Origen, on the other hand, refuses (ca. 230-35), as does Tertullian, to admit idolaters and adulterers to penance. His numerous references to the penitential discipline are not all consistently rigorous, however: in one homily he reverses Tertullian's view of the passages in First and Second Corinthians (Hom. 1 on Ps. 37).

In this debate the position of Pope Calixtus was probably in accord with that of St. Paul though not with that of some other New Testament writers. This humane position, in which the Church forgives the penitent offender and declares the forgiveness of God was to prevail in practice, if not in argument, against the rigorous party. It is not entirely clear how this victory came about. The considerable numbers who lapsed into "idolatry" in persecution, and afterward insistently sought restitution, the general let-down of discipline when persecution ceased, and the psychological analysis of sins by ascetic writers, were probably weighty factors in the process.

The first of these issues was faced by Cyprian (d. 258) in the Decian persecution. His approach to it was remarkably free from traditional presuppositions. He sought to restrain the clergy who had been too hasty in readmitting the lapsed, but he permitted the prompt restoration of the dying. Finally, those who from the first lapse had been lamenting their weakness were admitted "under compulsion of necessity" (Council of Carthage, 252, canon 1). In this Cyprian, as his letters show, was anxious not to reject any whose consciences drove them to repentance. The statesmanlike stand of the great lawyer-bishop did much to stabilize the Church, and set a precedent for moderation in discipline.

None of the third century Fathers authorized the repetition of the exomologesis; they are aware that this is sometimes asked for, but they allude only unfavorably to those who would permit it. The "iteration of penance" was an upgrowth of a later era, and, as Oscar D. Watkins has shown, is especially to be associated with St. John Chrysostom (d. 407). He was not followed in the West until much later. The traditional formula, "one baptism, one penance," was reaffirmed by St. Ambrose of Milan (d. 397) and favored in the West to the end of the sixth century. Pope Siricius (d. 398) permitted a deathbed repentance to those who had undergone an earlier penance. A sermon of Caesarius of Arles (d. 542) guardedly approves a second act of penitence. But a Spanish council of the year 589 sternly reaffirmed the earlier rigid standard (III Toledo canons 11, 12).

One of the most remarkable transformations in the history of Church discipline is the gradual admission, leading ultimately to the requirement, of the frequent penance which had long been earnestly rejected. We should remember, however, that there had always been recognized a class of minor sins that could be disposed of in mutual confession and forgiveness or in private prayer and alms. The medieval system included within it this class of faults with which the early exomologesis was not concerned. The obligation of frequently repeated acts of confession and penance, together with the vastly enlarged range of the sins· confessed, doubly enhanced the importance of the penitential discipline in the Church, both in the life of the lay people and in the functions of the clergy.

III

Another feature in which a fundamental change occurred was the public exposure and humiliation of exomologesis. Tertullian, Origen and Ambrose seem to regard the public humiliation as its most dreaded feature. The private and secret confession of later days is an entirely different thing. It is possible that at an early period a private interview normally preceded the public act: but this cannot be adequately proved. What is explicitly requisite is the penitent's submission to open shame and his overt appeal to church officers and fellow members. Among the earliest to suggest private confession is Origen who in his Homilies on Leviticus (ii), describing the laborious way of remission through penance, has the phrase: "When he does not blush to declare his sin to a priest of the Lord and to ask for the remedy." He cites the passage, "Let him call for the elders of the church . . . he will be forgiven" (James 5:14-15). But while apparently here the process is initiated in private, it is continued in public. Origen, in accord with others of the Fathers, definitely demands a public confession, even of secret sins:

For sins of every kind are to be confessed and everything we do is to be made public. If we do anything secretly, if we commit any sin in word alone, or in the secrets of our thoughts, all must be published, all brought to light.

The devil will reveal them otherwise: but if in this life we anticipate him and become our own accusers, we shall escape his wicked devices. "To utter forth our sin, merits the remission of sin" (Hom. iii on Leviticus, § 4: with reference to Leviticus 5:4-5).

Attempts have been made to show evidence of private penance in Origen's statements. These have apparently been sufficiently refuted by "A. Lagarde" (J. Turmel), B. Poschmann, R. C. Mortimer and others. But it cannot be doubted that he did authorize private confession. In a homily on Psalm 37 he warns of the error of burying sin in the heart. One should seek out a suitable person to whom to make confession, one "who knows the discipline of compassion and sympathy, . . . a learned and merciful physician." His advice is to be followed, and if he recommends a confession before the whole church—whether for the benefit of others or for one's own prompt healing—he is to be obeyed. Elsewhere Origen associates this function of physician of souls with the priests. They are to admonish, exhort and instruct the sinner, bring him to repentance and correct him of his faults and so fit him for the favor of God (Hom. v on Leviticus, § 4). This passage is reflected in many of the medieval penitential books. Father Ernest Latko, however, points out that such references in Origen imply not private penance but only spiritual direction, while Mortimer and some earlier writers observe that there is nothing here of private absolution. The priest is the sinner's friend and expert spiritual counselor. This private soul guidance, whether by a priest or by another qualified "physician," may have been increasingly common. Evidently it was often the prelude to the public ecclesiastical penance. The *Life of St. Ambrose* (d. 397) by Paulinus states that he wept with penitents when they confessed to him, and "never revealed to any but the Lord" what had been confided. In his treatise *On Repentance* (ii, 91 [*ca.* 380]) he urges sinners who are not ashamed to confess to "a man," that they should not shrink from confessing and pleading before the assembled church. Ambrose, like Origen, regards private confession as salutary and advisory rather than ecclesiastically authoritative. For reconciliation the further step of public confession must be taken. In the celebrated case of the exclusion by Ambrose of the emperor Theodosius after the massacre of Salonika, the restoration of the imperial sinner took place only after he had prostrated himself (as Theodoret reports), plucking at his hair and tearfully crying: "My soul cleaveth unto the dust; quicken thou me . . ."

It is probable that in early monasticism private confession and guidance were much in use. St. Basil of Caesarea (d. 479) in his *Shorter Rule* (129) prescribes confession to those who, like good physicians, have power to heal, and in his *Longer Rule* (26) he says that no one should keep secret, or declare incautiously, any agitation of his soul, but confess it to "trustworthy brethren" who are charged with sympathetic direction of the weak. Certain monks were given responsibility for this service by the head of the monastery (53). In other writings Basil gives his full sanction to the system of public penance, which in his province of the Church had now undergone a great change.

The numerous passages in the writings of St. Augustine (d. 430) which deal with confession and penance have been sifted and discussed by many twentieth century scholars. R. C. Mortimer in 1939 ably and patiently refuted the argument of P. Galtier, S.J., and reached the conclusion, as "A. Lagarde" and others had done earlier, that Augustine offers "no evidence for the existence of private penance with absolution." It is the old public discipline that the African father presupposes. However, he habitually made use of a private interview to receive confessions, and advised offenders to engage in prayer, almsgiving and fasting as corrective treatment for a wide range of minor sins. He also exhorts violators of the Decalogue not to delay public penance where it is called for, and so trespass on the patience of God. In one sermon (392) he bids his hearers: "Do penance [Agite poenitentiam] as it is done in the church, that the church may pray for you." He does, however, permit those whose sins are secret and without scandal to avoid public confession.

In the third century a plan by which the excommunicated are advanced through grades of penance to readmission, appeared in Asia Minor. St. Gregory the Wonder-Worker, bishop of Neo-Caesarea in Pontus, about A.D. 260, in a letter to another Pontic bishop, whose people had suffered morally and physically from war and invasion, indicates four grades or classes of penitents prior to their restoration to full communion. The "weepers" or "mourners" stand outside the door of the church, beseeching the faithful to intercede for them; the "hearers" are placed in the narthex; the "kneelers" kneel within the nave amid the standing congregation; the "co-standers" join normally in the services with others except that they may not take communion. Later writers and Church councils indicate the spread of this system in various provinces of Asia Minor. The system was one of public penance, giving great publicity to the penitent through his progressive return to communion. The stage of the mourners has the features of exomologesis, as earlier practiced. Sozomen, describing the penance of Theodosius, says that he was dressed "according to the usage of mourners." A synod held under Felix III of Rome in 487 or 488 to deal with apostates of the Vandal persecution in Africa, offers the only instance of specific Roman recognition of these stations of penance. It explicitly bases this procedure upon canon 11 of the Council of Nicea.

IV

Along with the local practice of these stations of penance went an increasing attention to assigned periods of time for the parts of the discipline. Similarly the specific duration of a penance is often laid down in the Indian codes; and we shall see the working out of this method with meticulous detail in the penitential books of the Celtic monks. The Council of Ancyra (314), seeking to meet disorders induced by the persecutions that had just ceased, required of those who had readily apostatized that they spend one year as hearers, three years as kneelers, and two years as co-standers (can. iv). Amid numerous similar canons, bestial sins are penalized by a period among the weepers, here called the "storm-harried" since they were exposed to the weather as they stood without, begging the prayers of the worshippers (can. xvii). The Council of Nicea (325), at this point more severe than Ancyra, decreed that apostates should be restored after two years among the hearers, seven among the kneelers, and two among the co-standers (can. xi). The Synod of Laodicea (of uncertain date 343-81) states the broad principle (can. ii) that sinners of various kinds who by "public confession and penance" have proved their repentance, shall, in consideration of the pity of God, be restored to communion "after a period of penance in proportion to their fall."

Not only bishops in council but individual writers ventured to compile codes on this principle of making the penalty proportionate to the crime. Celebrated among these is St. Basil of Caesarea (d. 379), whose three "canonical letters" were written about 374-76 to Amphilochius of Iconium. The letters contain 83 canons on a larger number of offenses, and are the fruit of thoughtful reflection upon the symptoms of human depravity. In some instances only the period of exclusion is indicated; in others it is divided among the several stations of penance. Thus for adultery the period is fifteen years, four with the weepers, five with the hearers, four with the kneelers and two with the standers excluded from communion (lviii). Perjurers are subjected to ten years of penance, two, three, four and one, respectively, in the series of grades.

Gregory of Nyssa (d. 398), a younger brother of Basil, also wrote to a fellow bishop a long canonical epistle in which he treats of the faculties of the soul and the sins that affect them, and makes some prescriptions of terms of penance. For homicide he commands a penance of twenty-seven years, nine years in each of the first three stations of penance; but the officer in charge of the discipline should have due regard to the penitent's behavior, and where contrition is manifest may shorten the nine year periods to eight, seven or five years. A similar discretion is accorded in some instances by Basil. Both these writers claim the authority of tradition.

The administration of discipline in a large church occupied much time, and an effort was made to shift the burden from the bishop and all clergy to a special officer. Thus in Constantinople from the middle of the third century to about 391 there was a "presbyter of penance" who received confessions. The office was abolished by the Patriarch Nectarius because of the scandalous offense of a deacon and a penitent woman. It is often assumed that the confession was secret, but, however we read the somewhat divergent accounts of the two historians (Socrates and Sozomen) who report the matter, it would appear that the deacon as well as the presbyter of penance had knowledge of what the lady confessed. It is possible that deacons were assessors with the presbyter during confessions. Apparently, when the office was abolished formal penance was for some time neglected at Constantinople, and everyone was left to his own conscience with regard to taking communion.

In Rome the discipline was public, but not graded as in Asia Minor. St. Jerome (d. 420) realistically describes the public penance of the Roman lady Fabiola (387) who on her second husband's death mourned, not for him, but for the sin of a second marriage. Bishop, presbyters and people wept with her as she made her lamentation. While Jerome regards her case as exceptional, his phrase, "in the order of penitents," suggests that numbers of penitents were to be observed at Rome, among whom Fabiola was distinguished by her aristocratic rank. Sozomen about 450 speaks of a place in Rome for penitents to stand mourning, and after services to prostrate themselves with groans and lamentations. After various self-imposed austerities they are absolved by the bishop. Both at the beginning and at the end of the penance the bishop identifies himself with the penitents, sharing their prostrations and tears.

Authorization of secret confession has been attributed to Pope Leo the Great (440-61), but his leadership in this direction is easily overstated. We have seen that Sozomen, writing in the same period, describes the dramatic scene of public penance at Rome. Leo himself assumes that penance is public, and that it is not repeated—as had his predecessors

Siricius and Innocent I. Innocent, however, gives large authority to priests to assign penance in accordance with the nature of the confession, and Leo similarly emphasizes the role of the priest in hearing confession and evaluating satisfactions. A letter which Leo wrote in 459 to the bishops of certain districts of Italy is his most striking utterance on the question. In this he condemns the practice—not otherwise attested and presumably local—of compelling penitents to read publicly a detailed confession. The use of this method he regards as an unauthorized innovation calculated to alienate penitents because it exposes them to danger from enemies who may seek to ruin them by legal action. It is sufficient to confess to God and to a priest who will intercede for them. Leo's indignation was perhaps as much due to the novel documentation of offenses, as to the publicity given to them in detail. It does not appear that Leo is forbidding all public confession, and the letter says nothing to alter the public character of penance itself as distinct from confession. Poschmann has shown that open confession even of secret sins was still the rule. A contemporary of Leo, Maximus of Turin, reproves the sinner who "like a fox" conceals his sin, blushing to confess his wickedness "in the midst of the church." Mortimer sees anticipations of the Celtic type of penance in the statements of Leo, and in a letter of Felix III on the discipline of boys and girls, of whom ordinary penance is "not to be expected."

If these popes favored a method of private confession and penance similar to that which was then being introduced in the Celtic churches, evidence that in their time this method was actually adopted in Rome is lacking. Gregory the Great (pope 590-604) appears to know nothing of it. In his time penance had fallen into neglect in Italy, and his effort was to revive it along the old lines of public penance preceded by public confession. Following Origen, he takes the command "Lazarus come forth!" allegorically as a summons to confession. It is only when God has first absolved the sinner that the absolution of the penitent is real (vera): Lazarus had already been restored to life before he was loosed. Repentance occurs "when the resolute mind begins to let loose against itself words of abhorrence which aforetime from a feeling of shame it kept to itself." Public confession of secret sins is a salutary exercise. Yet the impression of Gregory's Pastoral Care is that private confession of minor sins, followed by minor penitential satisfactions, was becoming more common.

V

Despite this disciplinary correction and the procedures of confession and penance, it would be highly erroneous to assume that the guidance of Christian souls in the Patristic Age was confined to these matters. The pastoral office was defined as including watchful care over all members of the flock, particularly those inclined to be disorderly. "Lest the undisciplined be consumed and perish," writes Cyprian to a bishop, "endeavor, beloved brother, that as far as you are able you govern the brotherhood by salutary advice and take counsel for the salvation of each" (Letter lxi). A sermon of Augustine (d. 430) contains a more extended list of the duties of pastoral guidance: "Disturbers are to be rebuked, the low-spirited to be encouraged, the infirm to be supported, objectors confuted, the treacherous guarded against, the unskilled taught, the lazy aroused, the contentious restrained, the haughty repressed, litigants pacified, the poor relieved, the oppressed liberated, the good approved, the evil borne with, and all are to be loved" (*Sermo* ccix). The pastoral writings of Chrysostom (d. 407) and Gregory the Great give a similar impression of the multiple task of the pastoral care of souls.

Part of this ministry consisted in a Christian continuation of the Consolation literature of the classical age, which has received attention in Chapter II. Cyprian was the earliest of the Christian masters of this type of writing. In the time of his episcopate (247-58) Christians suffered bitter persecution and many needed support and comfort. In numerous instances Cyprian reworked the old topics of the pagan treatises with which his studies had made him familiar, adding suitable affirmations of Christian doctrine. He was followed by Ambrose, Jerome, Paulinus of Nola (d. 451) and others. Charles Favez, in a close examination of the Christian Latin Consolation, has justly affirmed that it is the Christian element that predominates in this entire literature, dependent though it is for its form and much of its content upon pagan models. In the perilous and heroic days in which Cyprian lived it was natural that exhortations to faithfulness should be freely mingled with words of comfort. The time of Antichrist is at hand, he writes to the Christians of Thibaris, and the world is passing away: we must prepare for battle, thinking of nothing but the glory of eternal life. The unavoidable ills of life featured by Stoic consolers give place here to concrete, imminent persecutions. These should not surprise us: they were foretold in Scripture. The Lord would have us "leap for joy" in persecution, when the soldiers of God are proved and the heavens are opened to martyrs. Why fear to die, when the slain are to be crowned? Christ is the companion of his soldiers in flight and hardship and death. The examples of moral integrity used in the pagan consolations give place to Bible heroes and saints. The deeds of Abraham, Daniel and his companions, and the Maccabees, are vividly recalled. The discipline and courage of war are sublimated, with appropriate reference to "the whole armor of God." Death in this strife is entrance to a happy and immortal life with God (Epistle lv).

Many Christians were sent by the persecutors to the unspeakable cruelty of the mines. Cyprian wrote to these a moving letter, full of heartfelt admiration for their martyr spirit. The beatings, chains, filth, hunger and labor which they endure are severally contrasted with the heavenly rewards that await them. The body is captive, but the heart reigns with Christ.

In the year 252 plague added to the toll of suffering: "a pestilent disease took possession," says Eusebius, "of many provinces of the world." Many were stricken and many bereaved in Cyprian's province of North Africa. For the afflicted he wrote a celebrated treatise: On the Mortality, which bears the marks of the older consolation type more noticeably than the letters just referred to. He reproves those who seem to lack a steadfast mind and a firm faith. Storms, famines, earthquakes, pestilences should not affright us: Christ predicted them as signs of the end of the world. Who trembles then? Those who have no faith, who do not believe that they shall reign with Christ. The ordinary world offers us only a battle with sin: why wish it prolonged? For the believer, great is the advantage of leaving the world. But some are troubled because Christians suffer equally with heathens. In all matters we share the perils of life with them, as in famine or common diseases. The difference is the faith that steadies us. Job, the Apostles, Moses and Abraham, are examples of the faith in God that prepares us for everything. "The pilot is recognized in the tempest," and grain is separated from chaff in the wind. The terrible symptoms of the disease may be matched by the strength of a mind unshaken. Christians who die escape miseries, corruptions, and the fear of persecution. Men are tested by calamity, and it is discovered whether the healthy tend the sick, whether men love their kindred, whether masters pity their servants, whether physicians do not forsake their patients. But some lament that the pestilence robs them of the chance of martyrdom. God does not ask for our blood, but for our faith. When He calls us from the world, we may not resist His will. And we should not "sorrow as those without hope," for those who have been taken to their reward before us. The world hates the Christians: why should they linger with the world? Rather, "with a robust virtue, let us be prepared for the whole will of God," and welcome our departure to the delights of the heavenly kingdom.

VI

These consolation writings of Cyprian are addressed not to individuals but to groups undergoing a common experience of calamity. Others, like Seneca and Plutarch, write to individuals in bereavement or distress. Gregory Nazianzen (d. 390), for example, has a short but typical consolation letter (No. cxcvii) on the death of a "sister," who may have been a deaconess. It is addressed to a close friend who is himself a person "able to console others." Gregory is also the author of a number of funeral orations which contain similar materials.

St. Ambrose, too, composed letters of consolation. Some of these, such as those addressed to Faustinus (389) who was grieving for a sister, show strongly the influence of Cicero and the Stoics. The disinclination of the bereaved to be comforted, the fact that death is the common lot, the view that the departed one will be offended by her brother's tears, are old elements of this literature, here employed in a Christian context. The Christian faith, Ambrose notes, will only be discredited by excessive sorrow (Letter xxxix). When Valentinian II was murdered in 392, Ambrose wrote a letter of sympathy and consolation to the Emperor Theodosius, whom he had earlier subjected to penance (Letter liii) and delivered a funeral oration.

St. Jerome has a number of such letters. One written in 384 to Marcella is an example. Marcella was the head of a group of ascetic women, and her friend Lea of another such group. While Jerome was explaining a psalm to Marcella word came suddenly that Lea was dead, and she "turned deadly pale." Jerome took the earliest occasion to write a letter which is at once an encomium of Lea and a consolation for Marcella. He contrasts the dismal state in hell of a lately deceased rich and proud consul with the glorious happiness of Lea in heaven (Epistle xxiii). Five years later he wrote to Paula, whose daughter, Blaesilla, had been taken by death, a more extended and more typical letter of consolation. He extols the young widow's intellectual powers as rivaling those of Origen (!), and describes her devotion. While he deeply shares the mother's grief, he teaches from Scripture acquiescence in the will of God. In health or sickness he rejoices in God's will. We are not born to live forever here. We should mourn only for those of the dead who are in Gehenna, but rejoice that Blaesilla has passed to the realm of light. He seeks to dissuade Paula from fasting and mourning for her daughter: mourning is for those who wear silk, not for the religious. He goes to some pains to interpret Scripture passages on mourning as offering no pattern to be imitated by the bereaved Christian, and presents the example of a Christian lady bereaved of her husband and sons, who smilingly vowed herself to fuller service to Christ than before. Let Paula spare the feelings of Blaesilla in heaven, and of her young sister Eustochium who needs her mother's care. Jerome is manifestly anxious lest the heathen say that he has induced Blaesilla to kill herself by fasting, and he rather inhumanly scolds the weeping mother. Then, quite in the manner of Seneca, he puts a happy speech in the mouth of the departed, now in the company of the blest. The speech ends with a warning: "She is not my mother who displeases my Lord." He promises that in his writings the name of Blaesilla shall never die (Epistle xxxix). A letter. of 399 to Theodora on the death of her husband, Licinius, a man "holy and revered," mingles the consolation of an assured reunion in heaven with praise of the staunch orthodoxy of the deceased, his liberality to the poor, and his provision for the copying of Jerome's writings.

Favez especially praises among Jerome's consolatory letters that which he wrote to Eustochium on the death of Paula in Bethlehem, 404. I am unable to share the French scholar's enthusiasm. The letter is too long to be reviewed here, but may be briefly characterized. It contains much biographical material, written in a highly laudatory tone, especially concerning Paula's asceticism and charities. A long passage on her holy travels is adorned with Biblical and classical references. The author describes her tranquil death, and the thronging of monks and nuns, and of "the whole population of Palestine," at her funeral. Not less than in the pagan consolations and *epicedia* we observe a fulsome laudation of the departed. Jerome twice refers to the heavy debts incurred through Paula's benefactions and left to her daughter; he warmly applauds Paula for this shining evidence of renunciation. While he laments the rudeness of his style, the letter bears the marks of a conscious literary effort. He tells Eustochium that he has spent "the labor of two nights" dictating the "treatise" and that thereby, in the language of Horace, he has erected to Paula "a monument more enduring than bronze." In the laudatory characterization of Paula we discover the ascetic ideal of Jerome in all its ruthless intensity.

In this and other respects the Christian Fathers, though fully conserving their faith, freely utilized pagan elements in their guidance of souls. Yet possibly the later philosophers owed something to their Christian contemporaries in this matter. Adelaide Douglas Simpson has fruitfully compared the manner of life of Epicureans and Christians of the second century, with special reference to the dialogue *Octavius* of Minucius Felix (*ca.* 200). She shows reason for regarding this puzzling Christian writer as a former Epicurean. In a later study Miss Simpson points to evidence of the craving, among good pagans and thriving citizens of the second century, for *ataraxia*, or freedom from fear, and its pursuit by a specific method, especially among the Epicureans. Their character training involved what she calls "social adjustment through the practice of correction." The "frankness" they advocated had nothing in common with the "reviling" manner of the Cynics. The faults of friends were to be mutually criticized; those of beginners by "advanced members of the school," but always with kindness and courtesy. The corrector included himself in the admonition, and to avoid humiliating those under criticism, their faults were discussed with reference to the lives of others. Miss Simpson believes that the Epicureans in whose training "freedom from fear" was combined with frankness, were "persons characterized by good sense, good manners and good fellowship." She sees a fairly close parallel between their way of life and that of the Christians as described by Minucius Felix—men who lived quiet lives of mutual helpfulness. We may suspect that the disciples of Epicurus had learned something from the Christian practice of *correptio fraterna* (see above p. 85): numerous second century patristic references to this have been noted by Josef Hoh.

St. Ambrose in his book *On the Duties of the Clergy*, in which he is heavily indebted to Cicero, finds Scriptural examples of the four classical virtues, prudence or wisdom, justice, fortitude and temperance, and links them with the Christian virtues of faith, hope and love. This important treatise is a capital example of the integration of the loftiest elements in pagan ethics with the spirit of Christianity. The Seven Virtues here listed were to become stock material of later Christian ethics, and were habitually set over against the Seven Vices or capital sins as described by St. Gregory the Great. Here also Ambrose makes extensive application of moral principles to practical instances. In Ambrose casuistry becomes a noble ally of ethical idealism. He commends honesty in business and generosity in dealing with the poor and unprotected. He is sensitive especially to infringements of the rule of fair play, and takes from classical and biblical sources, as well as from life, numerous apt illustrations of fraud and trickery. He assails those who get wealth by the misery of others, and indeed seems to reject the profit motive entirely; while he warmly approves agriculture as supplying the needs of all. The treatise has been called (by Kenneth E. Kirk) "the first great Western textbook of Christian Ethics." The sharp reproofs of duplicity which it contains may be compared with Augustine's later discussion of the problem of lying (*Against Lying, ca.* 420), which, while distinguishing different gradations of falsehood, takes similarly rigorous ground. These earnest Fathers were awakeners of the Christian social conscience.

VII

The New Testament teaching had laid great emphasis on the virtues and attitudes that were associated with the communion of the faithful, and this element persisted in the teaching of the Fathers. Yet their writings contain a great amount of detailed doctrinal discussion and technically expository material, much of it highly controversial and remote from the warm piety of the apostolic founders. The cessation of persecution and the consequent secularization of church life led many of the more devout to take flight to desert retreats where they became associated in monastic communities and stimulated one another to pursue an ascetic and spiritual life. Among the leaders of this movement were some who gave fine expression to the aspirations which animated it, spiritual quests influenced by Neoplatonic mysticism and nursed in the Bible. While in its excesses this ascetic Christianity cannot be approved, in its spiritual devotion it enriched Christian experience. Some of the homilies, for example, which Macarius the Egyptian (d. *ca.* 388) addressed to his fellow monks offer inspiration and religious guidance to Christians of any period. The theological element in these spiritual talks—they are like chapel talks, though spoken in desert haunts —is simple and directly scriptural. But they are profusely sprinkled with illustrations from the common life of merchants, soldiers, countrymen and women. At the same time they show a mature experience of the struggles of the soul. Macarius has been, by his editor, A. J. Mason, likened to John Bunyan, and, in view of his conception of the Christian life as a warfare and a perilous pilgrimage unto the end, the comparison is aptly made. No writer, perhaps, has treated more feelingly the soul's experiences under the impulse of the Spirit (cf. Homily xviii). A few passages suggest the possibility of high attainment for a few who are "smitten with the heavenly longing" and, delivered from the passions, reach "the unspeakable mystic fellowship" of the Holy Spirit (x). But this he does not expect of many. Though himself an intense ascetic, he has no immoderate praise of the ascetic life, but offers counsel suitable for any who take Christ as the Great Physician of the soul. The virtues are linked together in a kind of spiritual chain—prayer, love, joy, meekness, humility, service, hope, faith, obedience, simplicity—and they are in conflict with a series of vices in the long battle in which only death brings full victory (xl). Macarius shows how a community of about thirty brethren may so dwell together that there is for all a beneficial sequence of prayer, reading and labor. One at work should not envy those at prayer, but say, "The service which I am doing is for the benefit of all" (iii). But most of the advice is for the individual in his private striving and heavenward journey.

John Cassian (d. ca. 435) having spent years as an observer of the monastic communities of Egypt, settled at Marseilles to imitate them in a monastery of his own foundation, and, after a lapse of twenty years or more, shaped into books his impressions of Egyptian asceticism. His *Institutes* and *Colloquies* supply a fund of information concerning the life of the desert monks. The former book was to become prescribed reading for the followers of St. Benedict whose *Rule for Monasteries* was written a century later. Cassian finds in monasticism the "way of perfection": it leads by steps of renunciation and devotion to the love that knows no fear (I John 4:18). In Book V of the *Institutes* Cassian lists the principal vices or deadly sins, eight in number: gluttony, fornication, avarice, anger, dejection (*tristitia*), languor (*acedia*), vainglory and pride. Through eight short "books" (V-XII) he discusses these in order, indicating the treatment for each. Gregory the Great was later to revise the order. Setting apart pride as the mother or "captain" of the others, he lists these as vainglory, envy, anger, dejection, avarice, gluttony and lust (Gregory: *Moralia* xxvi, 28). Gregory's list (of seven, with pride pushing vainglory into a subordinate category) was commonly used in the Middle Ages; but medieval literature has many references to Cassian's arrangement, and shows familiarity with his treatment of the sin of languor, or worldly weariness and revolt from spiritual effort.

Cassian has here provided a suggestive exposition of the conflict of the soul against the sins that beset it, with appropriate illustrations and exhortations to heroic endeavor.

The *Colloquies,* or *Conferences,* of Cassian consists of a series of twenty-four interviews with, and discourses by, abbots of the desert of Scete, each devoted to a special topic. Some of the topics are: contemplation; discretion; renunciation; prayer; spiritual knowledge; chastity; mortification; the eight principal sins. The book is well arranged to enlist interest, and the discourses usually rise above the level of monastic elements to set forth the ideals of the spiritual life. Thus Abbot Isaac summons to continual perseverance in prayer, the crown of all virtues, and presents a searching treatment of the conditions of true prayer. He regards the Lord's Prayer as delimiting the legitimate range of our petitions, and notes that it contains no petition for wealth or honor or power or health. Some people, he says, for lack of devotion omit the phrase "as we forgive our debtors." The highest prayer escapes our words, and even our thoughts; but few attain to this sublime height. Cassian's abbots have little to say of faith, or of the transforming grace of God. In one colloquy (xiii) Abbot Chaeremon seems to affirm the complete dependence of the soul upon divine grace, and its perpetual need of God's help and consolation; yet he raises without explicitly answering the question of the priority of grace to man's good will. In accordance with Cassian's opposition to Augustine's doctrine of grace (and also with the teaching of Macarius), man is held to be by nature capable of some good, and his good will is not always prompted by grace.

The practice of confessing sins and temptations to elder monks has frequent illustration in the *Conferences.* Abbot Moses contrasts the severity of an old monk who, when a young monk confessed his temptation of lust, merely reproached the youth as a miserable creature, with the helpful kindness of an abbot who, admitting his own assaults of lust, consoled and restored the same young man. The good abbot later visits the elder monk and severely rebukes him for his harshness and lack of sympathy.

St. Benedict of Nursia in the Prologue of his *Rule for Monasteries* (*ca.* 529) invites those who will undertake a warfare for Christ the true King —"that persevering in a monastery until death we may share through patience the sufferings of Christ and deserve (*mereamur*) to be partakers in his kingdom." With all its deep devotion, monasticism laid emphasis upon the soul's attainment of salvation by approved exercises rather than its acceptance by faith. The guidance of souls within Benedictinism was carefully provided for. The discipline is, however, naturally directed to the maintenance of an orderly and happy community. Monks who are stubbornly disobedient, after private warning and public reprimand, are to be excommunicated, and if still incorrigible, to be corporally punished. There are different conditions of excommunication for lighter and weightier offenses: for the latter Benedict requires penitential labor and meditation, and eating off-schedule and alone. But the abbot, as a wise physician, is to provide the excommunicated monk with counselors (Benedict uses a word which originally meant "playfellows") who will console and correct him, and all the monks are to pray for him. Benedict warns severely against any neglect of this ministry by the abbot, citing the Good Shepherd who left the ninety and nine for the one. The "wise physician" may have to proceed to the use of the "knife," the severe measure of expulsion; but the expelled may return, on repentance, even to the third time! Obedience is greatly emphasized: an attempt must be made even to obey impossible commands. The charming statement that monks are to obey not only the abbot but also one another, should not lead us to forget that ranks of seniority were rigidly maintained. One who fails to obey a superior must make amends by falling down before the offended official or senior, remaining in that posture until he is pardoned. Obedience is here called "a means of grace" (lxxi); it is also, as Tennyson says, "the bond of rule," of which fact monasticism could not be unmindful.

VIII

Gregory Nazianzen in his Second Oration (362) explaining his former flight to monastic retirement and his motives on becoming a priest and pastor, enlarges upon the high responsibilities of the pastoral office. A physician of souls, the pastor must prescribe medicines, or cautery, or the knife. Great is the difficulty of diagnosing and curing patients where habits and passions, lives and wills are involved, of turning the fierce to gentleness, and "arbitrating fairly between soul and body." This function is more difficult, and of more worth, than that of the healer of the body. The soul must be given wings to fly to God. The necessity of attentiveness and watchful devotion makes the task of the physician of souls an exacting one, and to Gregory almost terrifying. Evidently from thoughtful observation of human qualities, he recites in some detail the variety of treatments that are required for people of diverse temperaments and faults. Like Epictetus and other Stoics, Gregory believes that the director must sometimes feign emotions that he does not feel—anger, disdain or despair—in order to awaken a desired response. A feature of this eloquent address is the use ingeniously but not inappropriately made of many Scripture passages to reinforce the argument and furnish examples. The paragraphs on St. Paul's pastoral labors are particularly impressive. Gregory speaks as one about to undertake trying duties from which he shrinks, but surely with vivid realization of what they will involve. This brilliant oration was of use to St. Chrysostom in his treatise *On the Priesthood*, and, with more relation to our present interest, to St. Gregory the Great.

Of all the popes, none was more the pastor of the Western Church than Gregory the Great (590-604). His *Book of Pastoral Rule* (*Liber regulae pastoralis*), often called *Pastoral Care*, was written at the beginning of his pontificate. It sets forth the functions of priests so admirably as to give it a position of first rank in literature of this type. For Gregory the priestly office is one of authority over souls and "the government of souls is the art of arts." This control is to be exercised, however, in the greatest humility and with selfless devotion. Example, for Gregory, counts not less than precept. The guide of souls must be a compassionate neighbor to all, but superior in spiritual qualities. He should be a mother in tenderness, but a father in discipline.

It is from Part III of this work that the modern pastor will receive the most useful suggestions. Gregory here acknowledges an obvious debt to Gregory Nazianzen. He too would adapt admonitions to the needs of each individual. He lists a great many contrasted types of personality, such as: the joyful and the sad; the wise and the dull; the impudent and the bashful; the simple and the insincere; the slothful and the hasty; the meek and the passionate. Along with such variant types he takes into consideration variations and contrasts in life situations, which likewise demand the special concern of the counselor or preacher. Gregory's guide of souls must be a shrewd observer, and may have to employ an astute psychological strategy: the rich, he suggests, may have to be approached as the surgeon approaches a patient with the lancet concealed beneath his robe. The joyful and the sad should have their respective temperaments pointed out to them, with the peculiar sins (lust and wrath respectively) to which they are temperamentally prone. Servants are to be exhorted to humility and obedience, and masters to be reminded of their equality by nature with their servants. The impatient are to be warned of the confusion they create; the patient are urged to avoid malice against, and to learn to love, those whom they must bear with. The simple-minded are to be taught the value of prudence, and the insincere to be warned of the temporal burdens involved in duplicity and the divine penalties which it entails. Gregory habitually assails all forms of pride; but he notes that humility may be tainted by fear, and admits that in rebuking the haughty we may wisely employ "some poultices of praise." He has an appropriate word for the priest who has to direct the contentious and the peacemaker, the beginner in scripture knowledge and the proud scholar, the successful and the frustrated, the married and the unmarried, the incontinent and the innocent. Though virginity is better than marriage, virgins may not exalt themselves above the married.

In a series of chapters Gregory refines upon the different treatments for confessed sins of thought and of act, for sins of intention and of impulse, for those who abandon the sins they bewail and those who cling to them. He points out that sins may be abandoned while not lamented, and holds that in such case they are not remitted: a writer does not erase what he has written by ceasing to write. Care should be exercised with those who readily pass from one state of mind to another; the physician of souls must be watchful and discerning here, and like the physician of the body, have medicine "to meet moral diseases by a varied method." Gregory takes the view that a temporary toleration of lighter sins may be the necessary condition of victory over more dangerous vices.

IX

In teachings of this sort the bishops and monks of the Patristic Age instructed pastors in the cure of souls. While they present all too much evidence that the pastoral function of a personal ministry was widely neglected or attended by abuses, they made an earnest attempt to give it vigor and significance. They were careful students of human nature, and saw in it elements of moral confusion that it was necessary to expel. Somewhat experimentally, they employed in their curative work various types of discipline, admonition and consolation. While they developed these on a Christian basis, this did not exclude the free use of pagan aids. They would not question the New Testament affirmation of "newness of life" in Christ, but, living in an age in which Christianity was more often professed than inwardly embraced, they devised ways of penance and of soul care for people who exhibited little evidence of an inner transformation. They tended to rely rather upon the enlistment of the human will than upon the life-giving experience of which the early Christians were aware.

The pursuit of holiness took the form of ascetic discipline, wherein a few attained a high spirituality but the majority were earnestly engaged in a perpetual warfare with their besetting sins. The simple lists in the New Testament gave place to a detailed catalogue of sins which must be systematically checked and overcome. That reflection upon the soul's diseases which we observed in Cicero and Seneca appears here in new forms and results in a veritable science of the soul, an increasingly systematized psychology. The "disorders" of the soul are now "sins"; the guide, or physician, of souls diagnoses the patient's case in terms of sin, and applies the remedies in rebuke, counsel and penance.

Man is in the midst of a vast and frightful realm of sin, against which few prevail and still fewer gain a sure and lasting victory. Gregory Nazianzen, Chrysostom and Gregory the Great are aware of the need of a constant ministry to souls caught in this predicament. Preaching, sacraments and formal penance are not enough. The anxious and conscientious pastor must be a personal director, and, humbly conscious of his own unworthiness, must continually seek to help men in the toils of sin and temptation. The element of authority is enhanced; both the authority of the guide and that of Scripture come to recognition. Something had been lost of the liberating power of the Gospel, and medieval doctrines of sacramental grace were still not far developed. But men had before their eyes at least a trembling hope of heaven, and only the willfully unrepentant were utterly unhappy.

Chapter VI

THE CELTIC PENITENTIAL DISCIPLINE AND THE RISE OF THE CONFESSIONAL

I

BY THE thirteenth century a type of penitential discipline had come to prevail in the Western Church which was widely different from that of the Patristic Age. Instead of being public and unusual, confession and penance had become private, frequent and common to all. Whereas in the early period the offender was hesitantly admitted to one, or possibly a second, act of penance, every Christian was now under obligation to come to penance not less than once a year. The ancient exomologesis was no longer in use, and confession was made under seal of absolute secrecy. Formerly a public reconciliation normally followed the assigned period of penance: absolution was now commonly accorded in private when the penance was undertaken. The discipline was embraced within the sacramental system of the medieval Church, and priests rather than bishops were its principal administrators. How had this transformation come about? A variety of answers have been given.

The medieval penitential system constituted one of the most controverted issues in the Reformation era, and the contenders turned to the evidences of history. How and when had the medieval procedures in penance come to be adopted? The Reformers represented them as a tissue of relatively late innovations. Defenders of medievalism attempted to show scriptural and patristic authority for the system and to read back its various features to the early Church. In course of time serious historical research grew up on both sides of the controversy. It is instructive to compare the points of view of contending seventeenth century scholars. Jean Morin (d. 1659) an Oratorian and a convert from Protestantism, in a folio volume nearly three inches thick, *Historical*

Commentary on . . . the Administration of the Sacrament of Penance
(Paris, 1651, 2nd edition 1682), with prodigious labor and with honest
intent, sought to explain the steps by which new elements entered the
discipline. The Protestant pastor Jean Daillé (d. 1670), in a smaller yet
bulky tome, *Disputation on Sacramental or Auricular Confession* (1661)
made men wonder at his scholarship as he argued, in refutation of the
"crass errors" of Cardinal Bellarmino, that the ancients knew nothing of
the later practice. While he discovers in the ninth century certain de-
partures from the early discipline, Daillé regards the legislation of Innocent III in 1215 as the decisive change. After Daillé's death a Gallican
theologian, Jacques Boileau, arose to present a spirited reply entitled
History of Auricular Confession (1684) in which he offers contrary
interpretations of many passages adduced by Daillé, charges him with
neglect of Morin's evidence, and defends Pope Innocent from the charge
of innovation.

With all their formidable learning, these seventeenth century authors
appear to have been quite inadequately aware of the decisive historic role
played by the Penitential Books that were widely used by parish priests.
These manuals for confessors formed a long series. They were written by
British (Welsh) and Irish monks, and their English and Continental
imitators, from the sixth to the sixteenth century. Although the scholars
just named knew certain members of the series, they were unable to see
these in historic perspective or to appraise the cumulative influence of
this family of books. The critical study of the Celtic churches had
scarcely been begun, and it is only within the past hundred years that
their story, and that of the penitentials, has been substantially told.

In 1851 F. W. H. Wasserschleben published a careful edition of the
principal documents of the Celtic penitential series. Many scholars since
have enlarged our knowledge of these sources, and contributed to their
interpretation. Our present interest does not require a fresh examination
of the involved problems of authorship, dates and relationships among
the documents. It is sufficient here to illustrate certain characteristic
features of the discipline they exemplify, citing a few passages for this
purpose.

If we exclude two sets of canons attributed to St. Patrick (d. 461) the
earliest extant fragments are associated with the names of St. David
and St. Gildas, leaders of the sixth century Welsh Church. The earliest
document that can be thought of as a complete penitential book is
probably the work of St. Finnian of Clonard (d. *ca.* 550), though some

would say the "Vinniaus" named as author was Finnian of Moville, his younger contemporary. The reader of these elementary penitentials will at once recognize features not new or strange. We note, for example, the habitual measuring out of the duration of penance to match the sin. This, we have seen, is very common in Brahman codes, and is illustrated in the regulations of fourth century councils and in the Canons of St. Basil. The later penitentials were to carry to great detail these tariffs of offenses and penances.

Another marked element in Finnian's and in many other penitentials, is the method of contraries, and its application to the correction of offenders. The principle, "Contraries are cured by their contraries," can be discovered in many patristic treatises. It was apparently derived by the Fathers, who were fond of medical analogies in the cure of souls, from the teaching of the "methodist" school of physicians founded by Themison of Laodicea *ca.* 50 B.C., and widely approved in Cassian's time. To these medical men the principle of contraries was fundamental; and it had a natural and fairly obvious application in the religious life. Cassian (d. *ca.* 435) expounds it in his *Conferences* (xix) and keeps it in view in dealing with the correction of vices. Finnian takes it from Cassian: "But by contraries . . . let us make haste to cure contraries, and to cleanse away the faults from our hearts and introduce virtues in their places." Thus patience will take the place of wrathfulness, kindliness of envy, dejection will yield to spiritual joy and greed to liberality (92).[1] Similarly St. Columbanus, an Irish saint abroad, writes (*ca.* 600): "The talkative person is to be sentenced to silence, the disturber to gentleness, the gluttonous to fasting, the sleepy fellow to watchfulness, the proud to imprisonment, the deserter to expulsion" (251). Many instances might be given.

The Irish monks were indeed familiar with Cassian. We have a penitential much more ample than Finnian's, probably the work of Cummean the Long (*ca.* 650), which is subdivided in accordance with Cassian's organization of the Eight Sins. In his prologue Cummean also avails himself of a homily of Caesarius of Arles (d. 542) which is based upon one of Origen. A number of documents of the series make considerable use of various Church Fathers, such as Basil, Jerome, Chrysos-

---

[1] To avoid the necessity of labored references to the passages in the numerous documents cited, I am employing numbers in parentheses which represent pages in *Medieval Handbooks of Penance* by John T. McNeill and Helena M. Gamer (New York: Columbia University Press, 1938) where the documents are translated with notes.

tom, Augustine and Gregory the Great. Some of them follow Cummean in his appropriation of Cassian's classification of sins, notably the one known as the "Bigotian" (from the library which once contained the manuscript), and a related one written in the Old Irish language (*ca.* 800). Many canons of the ancient councils are cited. In general it may be said that the expositions of repentance and the remission of sins contained in these more expanded documents, are based upon the Fathers and the Bible. Their authors were not original thinkers, but thoughtful and discriminating legislators of penance and advisers to those charged with the guidance of souls. By their use of ancient materials they helped to maintain in some vigor, through times of violence and moral disorder, the moral force of historic Christianity.

II

For the development of penance, however, what is historically most significant about these Celtic manuals is that they replaced the ancient discipline by new procedures, and were highly conducive to the rise of the confessional as it is seen in the thirteenth century. To make their influence clear it is necessary to point to some factors in the culture of the Celtic peoples. The Welsh and Irish Churches of the sixth century were under the sway of monastic ideals. It is not possible to show institutional connection between pre-Christian and Christian ascetic communities in Ireland, but we know that the former existed, and we may suppose that familiarity with them enhanced the attraction of monasticism for the early Christian Irish. Most likely, too, the pagan Irish possessed a discipline for the correction of faults, and were familiar with the function of the spiritual and moral director.

The Irish had a word of their own for a guide of souls who hears confessions and gives authoritative counsel. The word is *anmchara,* often translated "soul-friend." Some have supposed it a derivation from the Latin *anima cara.* The latinized Greek word *anachoreta* has also been suggested, though there are texts in which Irish anchorites appear to have been so isolated as to be excluded from any function of guidance. An eminent Celtic philological scholar, Henri d'Arbois de Jubainville, has held that the word is not of Greek or Latin origin but (with its cognate *anmchairde* or *anmchairdine,* "spiritual direction") independently Irish, and that it represents an important functionary in pre-Christian Irish life. A word for penitence (*aithrige* or *athirgi* etc.) appears in Old Irish tales scarcely affected by Christianity. The Welsh language, too, has a word for confessor (*beriglour*). In both countries the function was prominent in the early stage of Christianity. A stern discipline involving a much dreaded excommunication, was practiced by the druids of Gaul and noted by Julius Caesar (*Gallic War* vi, 13). We are probably in touch here with an immemorial Celtic tradition of penance, in some ways comparable to that of ancient India. The pre-Christian Irish possessed a highly-trained professional class of *druids*, *brehons* (judges) and *file* (versifying wise men). Recruits to the order of *file* had to qualify by twelve years of adult instruction. The numerous kings in Ireland, including the High king who claimed sway over the others, had their "soul-friends" who belonged to this educated class. Legends of St. Patrick represent him as replacing Dubthach, High King Loeghaire's pagan adviser (the father of St. Brigid), and becoming the king's *anmchara*. Columba of Iona is reputed to have been *anmchara* to King Aidan of Dalriada.

Various scholars have shown remarkable parallels between ancient Irish and ancient Indian practice with respect to the spiritual director. Much is conjectural here, since the materials for Ireland were written within Christian times. We may not go so far as to say with Sir Henry Maine (1886) that the brehons "are the brahmans" with characteristics altered through the removal of their sacerdotal authority under the influence of Christianity. But it is hardly to be doubted that the pre-Christian Irish reverenced their judges and wise men, looked to them for personal guidance, and accepted the obligations they imposed.

That such authoritative counseling was widespread in early Irish Christianity may be inferred from various sources. The *Senchus Mór*, in the cómpilation of which Patrick is said to have collaborated with Dubthach and other pagans, is a large collection of legal decisions. It is extant only in mutilated and disorderly form, and parts of it are much later than the fifth century, but it undoubtedly preserves much evidence of early customs. It recognizes the *anmchara* in terms that suggest a general use of his services. In the early lives of saints the term appears with the same implications. The saying, "Anyone without an *anmchara* is like a body without a head," is attributed to two sixth century saints, Brigid (d. *ca.* 523) and Comgall (d. *ca.* 570), a teacher of Columbanus; it may have been a popular adage. It would appear that everybody was supposed to have his spiritual guide.

It is probable, too, that confession was ordinarily made in confidence and with the understanding that it would not be revealed. Bertrand

Kurtschied has examined in full detail the evolution of the doctrine and practice of the seal of confession. He finds no specific evidence in Church law of insistence upon secrecy before the middle of the ninth century, when Frankish councils introduced limited measures of the sort. We have seen that Ambrose felt obligated to "tell none but the Lord" the nature of the offenses revealed to him in private. No doubt at all stages there was a good deal of prudent and charitable concealment of confessions. Medical ethics may have offered (in the Hippocratic Oath) a helpful example to the clergy in this matter. Paulinus of Aquileia in 802 observes that a priest like a wise and perfect physician should know how to heal and cleanse wounds and not to talk about them *(non publicare)*. Some of the evidence cited by Kurtschied indicates peculiar sensitivity regarding the publication of clerical offenses. In connection with the undisclosed sin of a cleric Finnian writes: "Sins are to be absolved in secret by penance" (89). The Penitentials do not as a rule provide penalties for violation of secrecy. But, in one manual to be frequently cited below, Burchard of Worms, writing about 1008-12, sternly warns that a priest so offending is to be deposed and made to do penance in perpetual pilgrimage, deprived of all honor. The Old Irish *Speckled Book* which though a late formulation reflects usage, makes the divulgence of a confession one of the four offenses so grave that for them no penance is possible.

The "private" character of the Celtic penance appears in the fact that in general it is wholly dissociated from church assemblies. There is no public exposure except in cases in which the penance undertaken is such as to attract notice. And there is no provision, as in the "canonical" penance, for a public act of reconciliation. The Penitential connected with the name of Theodore of Tarsus (Archbishop of Canterbury 668-90) states concisely what is Greek and Roman practice in this matter, and adds: "Reconciliation is not publicly established in this province, for the reason that there is no public penance either" (195). Here, apparently (though the passage may have been inserted a generation later), the Greek archbishop of the English Church bids adieu to the ancient discipline, neglected as it is in England, and yields to the Irish practice.

Some of the early Christian Irish counselors were not in holy orders. Not only in Ireland, but elsewhere, as we have seen, confession was made by monks to their seniors. Confession to laymen was not uncommon in the Eastern Church and was occasional in the West; and there is evidence of confession to monks in both East and West. An Old Irish rule for monks, ascribed to an early sixth century saint, enjoins "resorting to a sage to guide thee." In Ireland women occasionally acted as confessors. Both St. Brendan of Clonfert and the great missionary saint, Columbanus of Bobbio, are reported in early lives to have confessed to women and acted on their advice. But the tendency to restrict the function to priests is manifest in Columbanus himself, whose Penitential requires laymen guilty of certain offenses to "confess to a priest." The Penitential of Theodore, in some of the manuscripts in which it is preserved, explicitly excludes women from prescribing penance, since this is a function of priests alone (205).

The last named penitential is an important one, especially as marking the expansion of Celtic influence in penance. It does not profess to be directly from Theodore's pen, but to have been edited later from notes taken at his dictation. Whether the Greek Theodore, or the first scribe, or the editor, is responsible for the Celtic element in this document of the Anglo-Saxon Church, we cannot be sure, but it reflects the principles and language of the Celtic books. By the time of its final compilation (*ca.* 700) some of the Irish documents had found circulation on the Continent and some had been written on the Continent by Irishmen. The eighth and ninth centuries saw the production of numerous anonymous or pseudonymous books prescribing penances in the Irish manner and with free quotation from the Irish documents. After a determined resistance to their inroads, the prelates of the Frankish Empire, following the example set in the Penitential of Theodore, began to sanction and imitate them.

III

The penitentials are practical manuals for the use of confessors and are designed to equip their users to deal with all sorts of persons in all moral and spiritual predicaments. The earlier ones are more concerned with monks and clerics than with laymen; in the later and fuller documents, written for parish priests, the reverse is true. But the layman is never forgotten. St. David and St. Finnian apply much heavier penalties to clerics than to laymen. Finnian puts a quarrelsome cleric on bread and water for half a year, and for a whole year requires him to abstain from wine and meat, while for the same offense a layman gets off with a week's penance. This is an unsual degree of variation, but the clergy regularly get the heavier penalties. There were reasons for this more obvious than that supplied by Finnian in this case. As "a man of this world," he observes, the layman's "guilt is lighter in this world and his reward less in the world to come." The penance for a layman's death or injury is also lighter than in the case of a cleric. An eighth century penitential ascribed by Dom Bruno Albers to the Venerable Bede (d. 735) has typical canons that illustrate this (224 f.). The slayer of a monk or cleric performs a seven year penance, of a layman only four years: for attempted murder the penalties are respectively three months and three weeks. In the so-called *Irish Canons* (*ca.* 675), a document which consists largely of penitential provisions and claims synodical authority, heavy payments are required for injuries to bishops, some of which show survivals of the primitive practice of retaliation. For every hair plucked from a bishop's head the assailant loses twelve. If a bishop is wounded so that blood flows and a bandage is required, "wise men judge that he who shed the blood be crucified or pay [the value of] three female slaves." Princes and scribes are given the same protective insurance (124). Such weighting of penalties helped toward security and the maintenance of rank and authority in Church and State.

"Diversity of guilt," says Columbanus, "occasions diversity of penalty," as physicians employ diverse remedies. Not only differences of clerics and laymen but variations of age, sex, economic status, education and disposition, as well as the circumstances attending each offense, were weighed by the physician of souls. In some penitentials there are introductory or concluding paragraphs that usefully explain the principles of the discipline. In these passages the medical analogy is a commonplace; the penitential discipline is called by Cummean (d. 662) "the health-giving medicine of souls," and Columban had earlier observed that spiritual physicians ought to follow the method of physicians of the body and heal with various treatments "the wounds, fevers, transgressions, sorrows, sicknesses and infirmities of souls" (251). Distinctions in the severity and duration of penance are made to accord with the diverse conditions of individual cases. If on many pages the mathematical equation between offense and penalty seems unrelieved, a reasonable discretion on the part of the confessor is generally implied.

Because of the range of offenses itemized in these booklets, they furnish an index to the censurable habits and dark misdeeds, the evil imaginings and intentions, of medieval people. The authors may not have known accurately the ancient canons but they knew the sinners to whom their clerical readers were to minister. The graver sins of homicide, adultery, sacrilege, theft and perjury are treated in their many varieties and circumstances, and there is much reference to gluttony, including drunkenness. Sexual offenses, even the most repulsive, are listed without apology. We are frequently reminded of the importance of the intention behind an act, and of the time during which an evil course has been pursued. The confessor must compute all such factors, including the guilt of one who "sins by planning to sin," though the plan be frustrated (250). We discover lurid offenses and queer offenders: one who "drinks holy oil to annul a judgment of God" (339); one who sets fire to a church (336); one who denies God (272); one who worships the moon or the sun or the stars (330); the woman who uses magical philters (246); the man who intends to hang himself (291); those who keep pagan customs for the dead such as the Irish "keening" dirge (121); and the wizard who conjures up storms (227). Among clerical offenders we find the priest who induces another to get drunk *humanitatis gratia*—for the sake of good fellowship (172); the habitually drunken bishop (153); the cleric who has stolen a horse (253); the monk who talks privately with a woman—for whose case Columban assigns a penalty of two hundred strokes (265). There are people who dance on the way to church, singing amatory songs (273), and women who, pretending to pray, engage in gossip and stories during worship (837). Such instances show how completely the correction of sins was adjusted to contemporary life and brought to the level of its cruder manifestations.

There is undeniably a good deal of crudity in some of the penances prescribed. The penalty of exile noted in ancient Gaul by Caesar, and well attested in early Irish tales and in Welsh law (375) appears to be reflected in the Penitential of Finnian (91), and in others of Irish origin (103, 158, 254). The Old Irish Penitential has some exceedingly harsh penances as alternatives for longer but milder ones. To sing the *Beati* (the 119th Psalm with its 176 verses) seven times with arms extended "in honest cross-vigil" (146) is a feat that would test the stamina of the most practiced ascetic. In a work ascribed by its editor to Bede, a monk who is dejected by bereavement or other sorrow is sent to another place and made to fast on bread and water "until he can be joyful" (168). A penalty of one hundred *palmatae*, apparently beating of the palms of the hand on a hard floor, is prescribed for contaminating liquid food with a dirty hand (231). Floggings are frequently referred to as regular or substitute penalties (145, 163, 265). A distinction is implied between *plagae* (blows) and *percussiones* (strokes), concerning which Raban Maur says that the former are more severe. A penance of "seven hundred blows of a lash" for lying seems inhumanly excessive (163). St. Charles Borromeo (d. 1584) sets a three year penance for a woman who paints herself with ceruse (367). Yet these extreme penalties tend to be replaced by more reasonable ones in the later books. The majority of the prescriptions are not of this type, but well designed to make the punishment fit the crime, to restrain the wicked, deliver the young from temptation, protect the weak, and reclaim the fallen.

We can easily imagine how a good, large penitential would be welcomed and prized by an active pastor, since it provided him with a valuable directory and a norm of judgment in his function as confessor and guide of consciences. It enabled the priest to administer penance efficiently without consulting his bishop. Whereas in the Patristic era penance had been controlled by bishops, the bishops of the Frankish church had failed to exercise this function. Even in the fifth century, as we may infer from Salvian (*ca.* 435) and other writers, penance had been widely neglected, and the *History of the Franks* (*ca.* 591) by Gregory of Tours presents a picture of extreme ill-discipline. Later attempts to restore the "canonical" penance of the Councils and Fathers were sporadic and largely fruitless. The legislation of Charlemagne enjoined the priests to give attention to penance and to bring their people to confession. In a wide diocese no bishop could journey through mud and snow to deal with offenders in the parishes. Yet bishops viewed with alarm the new situation in which any literate priest might provide himself with a manual to direct him in this work.

IV

Why, in view of their utility, did the prelates offer resistance to the circulation and use of these manuals? Episcopal opposition to them was in part justified by the wide variations of the penalties prescribed in different texts. Perhaps the penalty of three forty-day periods of fasting plus a fine of nine marks for intentional homicide (360), found in an Icelandic penitential (*ca.* 1300), should be regarded as a concession to a social condition in which homicide was not remarkable; but the common penalty is at least seven years, and for grave sexual offenses an earlier Icelandic penitential sets a term of fourteen years (358). This is an exaggerated instance of the typical confusing variety of penalties. It made a great difference to the penitent whether the confessor followed, for example, Cummean or the Pseudo-Roman manual of Halitgar (830). The former prescribes penance until death for premeditated murder (107), the latter, for murder to obtain property, a term of twenty-eight weeks and the restitution of the property to the victim's wife (310).

The series grew without ecclesiastical authorization or agreement, and each penitential had only the authority of its author. Of the authors themselves in most cases little was known. Provisions were almost recklessly copied, often with free alterations, from any document in which a compiler found them. The very numerous and very energetic Irishmen on the Continent were often regarded by the hierarchy as disturbing intruders, and now through the penitentials they were reviving penance on a new basis and with an appalling lack of uniformity.

Moreover, some provisions of the penitentials were open to serious moral objection. One element in the laws of Ireland and Wales, and no less of the English and Frankish kingdoms, was *composition*, or payment in satisfaction for personal injury or murder. This principle marked an advance upon the earlier permission of revenge, and was not morally questioned in secular cases. Many of the secular codes of the time are stuffed with detailed application of it. But, adopted in penitential provisions, it was dangerous and in some instances it became morally repugnant. The Old Irish Penitential explains that "if the offender can pay fines, his penance is less in proportion." The principle is well illustrated in the Canons attributed to St. Adamnan of Iona (*ca.* 697), where the payments are to be made "to Adamnan" or to the community of Iona, and are reckoned in *cumhals*, i.e., *ancillae*, female slaves. A cumhal was by Irish reckoning the equivalent of three cows (136 f.; cf. 118 f.). Incidentally, Adamnan's rules are remarkable for the protection they afford to women. In a set of canons erroneously ascribed to King Edgar (961-75) but really by some unknown cleric of the same period, penance is to be performed by gifts of land to a church, improvement of highways, building of bridges, and by the vicarious fasting of "seven times cxx men" which the offender may procure "in whatever manner he can." Gifts of property to monasteries and churches for the good of the donor's soul were an accepted feature of medieval life. Near the beginning of the thirteenth century Robert of Flamesbury in a penitential notes that authorities differ in their estimates of the value of church- and bridge-building for the remission of sins, but in a general way "commends such remissions" to all penitents (354). At a Council of Cloveshoe in England (747) the bishops, under the presidency of

Archbishop Cuthbert, commented 'in astonishment on the case of a rich man who boasted that by the penitential acts of others he had made satisfaction for his sins if he should live three hundred years. The bishops appropriately refer to the saying of Jesus about the camel and the needle's eye (394). A number of penitentials authorize less crass methods of vicarious penance. Thus the eighth century Pseudo-Cummean permits one who cannot fast or sing psalms to pay for the services of "a righteous man" who will perform his penance, and to give to the poor a denarius for every day of the penance assigned (269).

More common than composition and the employment of vicarious penitents was the commutation of penalties into briefer and more tolerable ones. In some documents commutations are genuine intensifications of the penitential austerities in order to shorten their duration. A long list of provisions of this sort is contained in an eighth century Old Irish catalogue of commutations (143 ff.). They involve floggings and protracted prayer and psalmody in "cross-vigil" (that is, standing with arms extended), genuflexions, sleeping in water, or on nettles or nutshells, or with a corpse. The document opens with an *arreum* (a word of Irish origin meaning commutation or equivalent) "for saving a soul out of hell." From the (supposed) number of joints and sinews in the human body, according to the author, though we might have thought from the calendar instead, the penalty consists of "three hundred and sixty-five paternosters, three hundred and sixty-five genuflexions and three hundred and sixty-five blows with a scourge" every day for a year, together with a fast every month. This is almost impossibly severe; but considering the fact that penances for great offenses lasted ordinarily for seven years or more, the alternative may have appealed to heroic sinners. The reduction of a year's penance to twelve three-day periods is recognized in the penitentials of Theodore and the Pseudo-Cummean, and the latter indicates how a seven-year period may be similarly reduced. The prescription involves some severity but is far from impossible, and the author makes further liberal concessions to those who are unable to perform a hard penance. This penitential is known to have enjoyed wide popularity, and may have given impetus to the process of relaxation of the discipline and helped to prepare the way for the abuses of the indulgence system of later times. The mingling of commutation and composition, especially in the form of a commutation of terms of penance into money payments, is not unusual. The Pseudo-Roman demands from a rich man twenty solidi instead of seven weeks of penance, and three solidi from the "very poor," stating in anticipation of protests that the larger payment is easier for the rich than the smaller for the poor. But the intention is to be considerate of the weak. Of slaves the author says, "You are not to be hard on them or compel them to fast as much as the rich" (299). Most authors of the penitentials show a commendable considerateness of the poor. The Icelandic bishop Thorlac (d. 1193) lays it down flatly that:

A rich man shall always be more severely punished than a poor man for the same sin; the hale than the sick; the learned than the unlearned; a man of superior, than a man of inferior rank; a fortunate man than an unfortunate; an adult, than one of minor age. (356)

The expression "redemption of penance" was commonly used for various types of commutation that involve mitigation of the penalties. Burchard of Worms (d. 1025) has a series of redemptions by which austerities are reduced to psalm-singing, e.g., "for one month in which he should fast on bread and water, he shall sing twelve hundred psalms kneeling. But if he cannot do this, he shall sing sixteen hundred and eighty psalms, sitting or standing . . ." (344).

By the tenth century commutation and composition were widely accepted as normal elements in penance. Regino, the learned abbot of Prüm, in Book II of his *Ecclesiastical Discipline* (*ca.* 906) has a series of lax provisions involving both principles, and in his conclusion frankly refers to "the lightening of penance" which these can effect. To cite one example: the first year's duties in a substitute penance of three years consist of a payment of twenty-six solidi in alms. The case of Zacchaeus is taken as an example of the proper penance for a rich man (320). But by comparison with Zacchaeus, Regino lets the rich offender off rather easily. In the opinion of Leclercq commutations and redemptions of penance were "the most effective causes of the debasement of *la pénitence tarifée* [quantitative penance] and . . . greatly favored the introduction of indulgences properly so-called."

V

In their alarmed resistance to the penitentials, the ninth century bishops denounced them on the ground both of their relaxation of penance and of their confusing discrepancies and lack of ecclesiastical authorization. Many of the bishops sincerely sought uniformity in the penitential discipline in the interests of authority and order in the

Church. The adoption in a council at Aachen in 802 of the old collection of canons made by Dionysius Exiguus (d. 556) did little to promote this end. These canons support the ancient public discipline, but this was not restored by their formal adoption. A capitulary of Charlemagne of 813 attempted to bring in one element of the older penance by requiring open confession for open sin. This was in accord with the second of the capitularies (ca. 798) of Theodulph, Bishop of Orleans (d. 821), who, however, seems to assume the use of a penitential book (397). Two councils of that year, at Arles and Chalon-sur-Saône, show an effort by the bishops to recover the vanished system. The latter of these launched an attack upon "the booklets which they call penitentials," demanding that they be "utterly cast out." "Their errors are obvious, their authors undetermined." They "inflict light and strange sentences for grave sins," and in the words of Ezekiel, "sew cushions under every elbow" (401). At Tours, however, in that year, the bishops, either more favorable or more prudent, decided to seek authorization of one selected penitential book, leaving the choice to a council soon to meet at Aachen (402).

Whatever the reason, Aachen did nothing about the matter. Dr. Watkins suggests that Charlemagne and his advisers may have been unwilling "either to condemn the penitentials or to authorize one of them." We may add that the selection of one among the many would have been difficult, and its imposition impossible. But there exists an uncompleted draft of a Capitulary of Charlemagne of about the same time, which has this sentence: "Concerning the determination of penance: we leave for inquiry by what penitential or in what manner penitents shall be judged" (391). Apparently the Emperor felt the need of further study of the problem. In 829 a council held at Paris denounced the books in severe language and demanded that they be wholly abolished. Many priests, the prelates complain, have used penitentials that are "written in opposition to canonical authority," to the deplorable ruin of souls. Each bishop must now diligently search out and burn "these erroneous booklets . . . that unskilled priests may no longer deceive men." Instead the priests are to be carefully instructed in their duties by the bishops (402-3).

These well-meant fulminations apparently went the way of many resolutions of church assemblies. It is hardly likely that many of the offending books were burned, and assuredly the canonical discipline was not restored. Some years later (857) in the province of Rheims, Hinkmar (d. 882) made a vigorous attempt to revive public penance with excommunication for murder, adultery, perjury and other crimes "openly committed" (408). Numerous eminent prelates thereafter took a similar stand, with varying degrees of temporary success. Public penance was never, of course, abolished. It was employed in celebrated cases where kings and rulers were involved. In the later Middle Ages it was occasionally practiced, though then chiefly in cases of heresy. Distinct from ordinary public penance was "solemn penance," which resembled the practice at Rome in the fifth century in its ceremonies of Ash Wednesday and Holy Thursday. Morinus (V, xxv, 31) shows that it could not be performed more than once. Robert of Flamesbury in his Penitential (*ca.* 1207-15) neatly distinguishes solemn, public and private penance. Solemn penance is enjoined only by a bishop, other public penance by a priest; "private penance is that which is done privately every day in the presence of a priest" (353).

With the prevalence of private penance and its integration in the sacramental system, these remnants of the old public discipline became, as Lea points out, anomalous and unusual. Public penance had never been stabilized or uniform. It could hardly have been authoritatively described, and it could not have been imposed, without much modification, on the tumultuous feudal society of the ninth century and the proud races that dominated it. A private treatment of sins was more possible, and the local priest was its natural administrator. Already by 813, as we saw, the bishops of one province were willing to have a single penitential officially adopted—a concession that was virtually a capitulation.

But the most dramatic act of surrender was concealed by a misrepresentation. Among the works of Halitgar bishop of Cambrai (d. 831) there occurs a penitential which Halitgar himself, or someone pretending to be he, claims at the beginning of the document that he has taken "from a book cabinet of the Roman Church" (297). The compilation of the book can hardly have been unconnected, however, with the fact that Halitgar's friend Ebbo of Rheims had urged upon him the duty, in view of the confused state of the existing manuals, of writing a penitential that would be based upon the Fathers and the canons. In reply Halitgar complained of the difficulty of the task, but did not flatly decline it. In its use of ancient canons the document shows some measure of attention to the purpose of Ebbo's request. But it is largely made up of Celtic materials, with some elements from Theodore, and with liturgical additions. The claim of Roman origin is quite unsubstantiated, and was probably a device, characteristic of the age of the Forged Decretals, to secure its wider acceptance and to allay the controversy which had come to a sharp point in 829. Halitgar is a fellow-traveler with the other mitigators of penance by commutations and money payments, and the book is an interesting member of the penitential series. It was respectfully received, but any hopes that it would prove the penitential to end penitentials were illusory. Other compilers followed, who simply cited and plundered it along with its rivals, in the old way. For the countries north of the Alps the battle had been lost and won, and the penitentials held the field.

Resistance would continue longer in Italy, which had known less of the invasion of insular clerics and their books. A council of Pavia of 850 reaffirms the old form of public reconciliation of penitents and strictly confines to the bishop the right to perform it. Two centuries later St. Peter Damian, cardinal bishop of Ostia, in his celebrated work of moral castigation, *The Book of Gomorrah* (1051), protests against the penitentials with indignation and sarcasm. They are spiny thorns and spurious sprouts; they have no ascertainable authors and no authority (411). But the tide could not be turned back until all Western Europe felt the effects of the penitentials. During the thousand years between Theodore of Tarsus (d. 690) and Cardinal Charles Borromeo (d. 1584) numbers of penitentials were produced in England, Germany, France, Iceland, Spain and Italy, all bearing, though with marked variations, the stamp of the early Celtic models.

VI

The response of the lay people to those with a reputation as confessors was often eager. In certain instances Irish saints, including Columba of Iona, turned away those who wished to confess to them. The early life of Columbanus of Bobbio by Jonas tells us that "the people flocked together from all sides for the medicine of penance." The compiler of the Penitential of Theodore says that men and women "with inextinguishable fervor . . . made haste in crowds to visit" the archbishop for this purpose. But some of the flock were indifferent and neglectful, and the good pastor would seek them out. Thus Halitgar observes that since we are members one of another it is needful to be solicitous for sinners, to call them to penance, and always to accompany advice by some assignment of penance (297). A few years later Hinkmar of Rheims states that any who refuse to come to penance are to be cut off from

the Church until they repent (408). The nineteenth book of the celebrated *Decretum* of Burchard, Bishop of Worms (d. 1025), consists of
a long penitential and is entitled "Corrector and Physician." In language
that parallels the earlier phraseology of penitentials written by monks
(223), Burchard states his aim to teach every priest "how he shall be
able to bring help to every person, ordained or unordained; poor or rich;
boy, youth or mature man; decrepit, healthy or infirm; of every age, and
of both sexes" (323). This clear determination to make confession and
penance as universal as possible is increasingly the conscious policy of
earnest churchmen.

The penitentials also provide for the reception of penitents to confession "as often as they come" (297). In view of the great variety of
sins for which penances were provided, and the variety of persons and
circumstances to be considered, the priest in a parish of awakened sinners would be very busy. His burden would be enhanced if, in accordance with the Pseudo-Roman, he joined the penitent in fasting "for
one or two weeks or as long as we are able" (297). The administration
of penance, if the penitentials were literally followed, was an exacting
labor. For convenience the penitentials were, in most cases, fairly well
classified, by use of the scheme of the Deadly Sins or of the Commandments (Borromeo) or by some other device. Halitgar, Burchard and
others provide specific direction on the procedure. In accord with some
of the Fathers, and in close imitation of the language of the St. Gall
Penitential (*ca.* 800) Halitgar stresses greatly the sympathetic treatment
of the penitent as a fellow sinner. The ministrant must not be as one
of the scribes who lay on others heavy burdens which they themselves
will not touch; he must familiarize himself (*particeps fuerit*) with the
sinner's foulness; he must humble himself and pray with moaning and
tears. The penitent will the more abhor his sins when he sees the priest
weeping (298). A series of finely phrased prayers are provided in the
forms for the admission and reconciliation of penitents which precede
this Pseudo-Roman Penitential of Halitgar. Some of these appear substantially in the Gelasian Sacramentary (*ca.* 725-850) where they fall in
the context of directions for the Maundy Thursday public ceremony for
penitents. One that may be from another source, or original here, is as
follows:

Almighty, everlasting God, in Thy compassion relieve this Thy confessing
servant of his sins, that the accusation of conscience may hurt him no more

unto punishment than the grace of Thy love [may admit him] to pardon. Through our Lord Jesus Christ. (301)

In some of the books—the best example is Burchard's *Corrector*—we find thoughtful suggestions for the interview with the confessant. He is to be tenderly led step by step. The priest "shall softly and gently question him first on the faith"; questions on the Trinity and the Resurrection follow. The next question is from the Lord's Prayer and is an element often stressed: "Wilt thou forgive those who have sinned against thee?" Is the penitent incestuous, or insubordinate: if so he may still obtain forgiveness. Then the priest is affectionately to exhort him, beginning: "Brother, do not blush to confess thy sins, for I also am a sinner, and perchance I have done worse deeds than thou hast." If he is still bashfully silent, the priest suggests that his memory needs prompting and proceeds to question him in detail, warning him against concealment (324 f.). Thus a cautious, gradual and sympathetic approach having been made, the confessant is confronted with the task of revealing his sins to the priest one by one. A minute interrogation follows. But in chapter vii, after a brief exhortation on the curing of the several Deadly Sins by their contrary virtues, the penitent prostrates himself on the ground with tears, confessing himself guilty of all the sins "either in thought or speech or deed or love or lust." The priest also prostrates himself, uttering psalms and prayers (342).

These ceremonies were well designed to make of the confession an experience of profound importance for the penitent. All was adapted to his own individual case. The personal quality of the discipline is further seen in many special provisions, of which those for the confession of the sick are among the most important. From early times there had been a considerate treatment of sick penitents, and the penitentials continued to provide for this. The Old Irish Penitential twice states that they may "eat at any hour of the day or night" (158-59). The book of Theodore urges the most careful attention to modification for sick persons (198). Halitgar authorizes a postponement of penance, with admission to communion, until the sick penitent recovers. In the Customs of the Irish monastery of Tallacht (*ca.* 831-40) we are told with approval of the addition by an Iona abbot of butter to the pottage of penitents who had lost their health through fasting (423). The ministry to the sick had its special problems. A penitential from the Spanish monastery at Silos (*ca.* 800) assigns a penance of thirty days for the watcher by a bedside who negligently leaves the patient if the latter grows worse or dies before he returns. The Penitential of Ciudad, a Spanish document of the fifteenth century, indicates the direction that might be given where recovery was doubtful:

And if the confessant is ill, then let the confessor be cautious . . . saying to him in effect: If thou wert well thou shouldst do such and such penance for thy sins, but since thou art ill I do not enjoin it upon thee; but when thou art recovered thou shalt do it, or thou shalt come to me or to another priest, and receive penance afresh; but if thou shalt die of this illness, make thy will and give so much alms, or cause so much to be given, for thy soul. (363)

Such provisions for the intimate personal direction of bedridden folk could not but render the system vulnerable to abuses. The spirit of the harpy-like legacy hunters of pagan antiquity has never been extinguished, and cupidity found various expression in the medieval confessor. The practice of payments exacted by the confessor was later to be a subject of legislation and a frequent theme of literary satire. As in the Brahman codes, the requirement was discouraged but voluntary payments were often so eagerly welcomed as to become other than voluntary. H. C. Lea, who gives evidence on this matter, points to the fact that the *Beichtpfennig*, or penitent's fee to the confessor, reappeared in the Lutheran Church and survived many regulations against it. In the Middle Ages it was not the gravest of the abuses that sprang from the conditions of penance. There is no escape from moral perils in the delicate relationship of the spiritual guide with his clients, save in his possession of the highest virtue.

Regino, Burchard and others adopt the method of interrogation, and the latter's book is essentially a detailed series of questions that search the joints and marrow of personality, and call to the foreground the habitual sins of medieval people. Theodulph had suggested that if the confessant hesitates he should be prompted with questions based on the penitential, yet with caution:

But, nevertheless, not all the offenses ought to be made known to him, since many faults are read in the penitential which it is not becoming for the man to know. Therefore the priest ought not to question him about them all, lest perchance when he has gone away from him, at the devil's persuasion he fall into some one of those offenses of which he previously did not know. (397)

Regino requires bishops to ask their priests whether they have "a Roman penitential, either the one put forth by Bishop Theodore or that by the Venerable Bede" so that from its contents they may question the confessant and assign the penance (217). The language is striking in its suggestion of the meaning of "Roman penitential," but also for its indication of the use of the tariffs of the penitential books as a basis for questioning the penitent as well as for determining the penalty. By some unnamed writer the step had already been taken early in the eighth century of setting down the provisions in question form (154). The Council of Paris which attacked the penitentials in 829 also urged that priests be taught how to "inquire discreetly" of the confessant (403). In the long interrogatories of certain later penitentials discretion on the part of the questioner was assumed. Not all the questions listed were, presumably, asked of each individual penitent. Such would have been a waste of time, and for many an instruction in sin. No confessor in his senses would read to men the numerous questions intended for women in the *Corrector*, or, from Regino's book, ask a tender maiden: "Hast thou cut off the hands or feet of a man, or gouged out his eyes?" (317).

There have been severe critics of the penitentials on the ground of their alleged incitement to sin. They may sometimes have been clumsily or willfully used with that effect. Though written with a high purpose, they had evil suggestions for evil minds. Dr. Kinsey is hardly better informed than Burchard on the sexual behavior of the human male—and female. The bishop enlarges on current superstitious practices and beliefs, which he condemns in an enlightened spirit, even if he describes them in a fascinating way. This element gives to Burchard's work, indeed, its greatest attraction to students of the pagan substratum of medieval life; and most other penitentials have similar features. Yet there is never a doubt that, like the preacher heard on one occasion by Calvin Coolidge, he is "against sin" in all its forms, and his book is to be read in that light. The writers of the penitentials probably never supposed that what they wrote was sensational or morally questionable. Their frankness in the description alike of the foul sins of the body and of the dark delusions of the mind flows from their essential honesty and earnestness of purpose. A judicious use of their materials would do no injury to the morals of their consultants. The worst effects of their work lay in their uncritical adoption of elements of common social custom. It would have been better, if possible, to have avoided all tabulations of equivalents which seemed to set an equation between sins and shillings.

The Christian Year provided special seasons of repentance. There is an eighth century text, apparently by Egbert of York, which contains an explanation of the four fasting seasons (*ca.* 750). An interesting feature of this is the December fast of twelve days, celebrated in England by the lay folk, who "come to their confessors and cleanse themselves" by tears and alms that they may be purer when they partake of the Christmas communion (243). But the opening of the Lenten fast was the chief season of confession. In language similar to that of Theodulph more than two centuries earlier, Burchard calls upon priests to assemble their people in the week preceding the beginning of Lent to reconcile their contentions and give penance to those who confess (323). The phrase used by Egbert is, "in the first week of Lent"; by Regino, "at the beginning of Lent." Probably what is meant is the same in these references: the Lenten period had been irregularly increased by four days, the beginning being pushed back from Sunday to Ash Wednesday. The preceding Tuesday was especially the time of confession and absolution. It came to be called "Shrove Tuesday" since on that day souls were shriven that they might enter the Lenten season in purity. Its "carnival" aspect was a later secular innovation.

VII

In the above treatment of the Penitential Books most of the typical features of medieval confession and penance have emerged to view. But we have withheld discussion of the sacramental aspect of penance, and to this attention must now be given. In the early period it was generally held that the passages, "Whose soever sins ye remit they are remitted . . ." (John 20:23) and "Whatsoever thou shalt bind on earth shall be bound in heaven" (Matt. 16:19) conveyed authority to the Apostles and their successors to "bind and loose" in such a way that the action was ratified in heaven. This view is strongly asserted in the *Didascalia,* a third century Syrian manual in which bishops are urged to use mercifully this divinely bestowed power. There were objectors to the full logical interpretation of this teaching. Origen called it "ridiculous" that bishops bound in the chains of sin should claim the power to bind and loose only because they were called bishops (Commentary on Matthew); and Cyprian wrote: "Let no one deceive himself: only the Lord can grant mercy" (*On the Lapsed,* 17). Yet the Gospel passages referred to greatly helped to promote sacramental as distinct from disciplinary ideas of penance.

The rite of reconciliation was then performed normally by bishops only: infringements of this were not infrequent but were defended only on grounds of necessity. The imposition of the bishop's hands upon each penitent's head was a feature of the ancient public reconciliation rite. No extant liturgical materials of the Patristic era indicate the words used in reconciliation. A letter of Innocent I of about 416 indicates that it was customary at Rome to "grant remission" to penitents on the Thursday before Easter. The reference is to a public reconciliation of numerous penitents following the public penance to which our attention has been called (p. 98 above). In the earliest extant formulations, absolution consists essentially of a prayer rather than a declaration, and scholars are agreed that this had been so from the first. "We gather," says Msgr. Duchesne, "from the Life of St. Hilary of Arles (d. 447), that the bishop gave an address, laid his hands on the penitents, and recited a prayer." The view that absolution is remission granted by the Church, and "the act of the priest whereby in the sacrament of penance he frees man from sin" (*Catholic Encyclopedia*) was not expressed through the use of this deprecatory form. Some would say that the original imposition of hands "aimed to say" what was later expressed in the declaratory form, "I absolve thee" (Jungmann). Some third century documents indicate that at the elevation of a bishop a prayer was offered that he might receive power to forgive sins. The prayers of reconciliation, however, imply no such power but appeal solely to the pardoning mercy of God. Morin (VIII, x, 1) found no exception to the "deprecative" type of absolution prayer before the twelfth century. Some texts have been noted that mark a transition stage, e.g.,

May God absolve thee . . . and mayest thou be absolved by the Father, the Son and the Holy Ghost . . . by the angels, by the saints and by me, a wretched sinner.

Gradually indicative forms were adopted. In the later Middle Ages the formulas included "I absolve thee," but this has regularly been preceded by a petition for divine absolution. The theological definition of the sacrament of penance advanced slowly, and was not completed until the Scholastic era.

"The twelfth century," says Kenneth E. Kirk, "witnessed the rapid development of a sacramental theory of absolution." With this change we at once observe increased attention to the circumstances of confession and its secrecy. About 1197, Odo, Bishop of Paris, issued regulations

that show this development. The priest is to be available in a place of easy access in a church, and not in another place unless by necessity. He may not look at the countenance of the confessant, especially of a woman. He must patiently seek an "integral" or complete confession. He shall absolve only on the confessant's promise to "refrain from every mortal sin." He shall not inquire the names of accomplices in the sins confessed, but rebuke confessants who mention them. "He shall not dare to reveal anybody's confession," from any motive, even fear of death, "by sign or word, generally or specially, as in saying: 'I know what kind of persons you are.'" If he does so, "he is to be degraded without mercy" (412). Hubert Walter of Canterbury (*ca.* 1200) requires that a wife's or a husband's penance shall be such that one partner in marriage shall not be led to suspect the other of heinous sin (413).

Such rules, adopted by provincial authorities, anticipated the well known legislation of Pope Innocent III at the Fourth Lateran Council of 1215 (Canon xxi). It bears within it the requirement "that this salutary enactment shall be frequently published in the churches"; and it is of such historic significance that every Christian minister should know its language. Yet its importance is not that of originality. Much of what we have been considering in this chapter is reflected in it. Even the requirement that every adult Christian "shall confess all his sins to his own priest" represents a long-time effort to render the local priest the principal administrator of penance. Innocent allows for the possibility of an exception where "his own priest" gives his consent. The demands made: that the priest be "discreet and cautious"; that he proceed "like a skillful physician"; that he "diligently search out the circumstances both of the sinner and of the sin"; that he employ "various measures in order to heal the sick," were all familiar from frequent repetition in the penitentials. And there was ample precedent for the essential matter of the final passage:

Further, he is to give earnest heed that he does not in any wise betray the sinner by word or sign or in any other way; but if he needs more prudent advice he shall seek this cautiously without any divulging of the person, since we decree that he who shall presume to reveal a sin made known to him in the adjudication of penance, is not only to be deposed from the priestly office but also to be thrust into a strict monastery to do perpetual penance. (413-14)

VIII

The Celtic penitential manuals, and many of the others prompted by them, poorly written and often wretchedly copied, are, with few exceptions, almost the rags and tatters of Church Latin literature. Their lists of sins, and of penalties, mark them as products, no less than correctors, of a primitive society. They came down the centuries little esteemed except by the humbler clergy, who, possessing no other practical directories for discipline, found them indispensable. In the hands of simple priests these booklets secured for themselves a functional place in the life of the Church while they were still despised and rejected by most churchmen of rank and learning. Their use was little affected by episcopal condemnation, and they went on silently remaking the penitential discipline until able bishops, recognizing a *fait accompli*, began to imitate and improve upon them. The improvements consisted largely in explanations of procedure and in the addition of valuable liturgical elements. The major moral weaknesses remained in the later exemplars of the series. There was a deplorable lack of watchful defense. against the commercialization of penance—later the occasion of scandalous abuses. It is truly regrettable that better books of direction were not provided for the discipline of the peoples of Europe in the age in which they were slowly appropriating the heritage of Christianity. Nevertheless the balance sheet adds up in their favor. We cannot doubt that they were instrumental in the recovery and rehabilitation of many who had made shipwreck of life, and in elevating and stabilizing the morals of many more. The experience of our ancestors under the guidance of confessors familiar with these manuals must have helped to redeem them from superstition, inhumanity and vice, and to set their feet on the pathway of spiritual and moral advance.

Chapter VII

THREE CENTURIES OF ENRICHMENT AND
DETERIORATION, FROM THE COMING
OF THE FRIARS TO THE RENAISSANCE

I

Our concentration upon the development of the confessional has precluded other aspects of soul guidance in the medieval period. The centuries between Gregory the Great and Innocent III offer much additional material that cannot be reviewed here. Much of it would be associated with the leaders of monastic reforming movements, who, through ages of feudal disorder, bore testimony to spiritual values and established rallying points for the cultivation of the soul. Their service was not entirely to the members of their own communities. The monasteries gave to the Church many of her best bishops and produced a fair number of books, other than penitentials, for the guidance of priests. Various treatises and letters of Isidore of Seville (d. 636), the Venerable Bede (d. 735), Alcuin of York (d. 804), Raban Maur (d. 856), Aelfric of Eynsham (d. *ca.* 1020), Anslem of Canterbury (d. 1109), Guibert of Nogent (d. 1129), Richard of St. Victor (d. 1142), and others, might be examined for the evidence they contain of care for the pastoral ministry. There is not much new thinking in all this, but a reliance upon the Fathers, with applications, of course, to conditions of the writer's time.

August Hardeland in his *Geschichte der speciellen Seelsorge* devotes an illuminating chapter to the great Cistercian saint, Bernhard of Clairvaux (d. 1153). We see here the rigor of Bernhard's asceticism tempered by a paternal tenderness. "Be mothers in cherishing, fathers in correcting," he advises, in phrases learned from Gregory the Great;

"withhold the strokes, reveal the breasts" (of compassion and encouragement). Hardeland has chiefly used Bernhard's sermons. His letters finely illustrate his work of guidance. Whether written to a king of France or a pope, to a troubled abbot or a runaway monk, to the distressed parents of a young convert to monasticism, or to a virgin of "extreme beauty" whose burning glances and showy dress belie her professed intention to be a religious, they contain earnest appeals, frank accusations, and incitements to holiness. In some he ardently craves consolation for himself; in all he writes from a heart aflame with the fervor of devotion. The writing of spiritual letters reached a new height in Bernhard. For him the way of spiritual attainment is the way of monastic separation from the world. The layman's hope is to become a monk, ascend the "twelve steps of humility" of Benedict's Rule, and aspire to the mystical union which is the ultimate happiness of the soul.

During the pontificate of Innocent the Great (1198-1216) new tides were stirring in Western Europe. The Crusades, begun a century earlier, were still a major interest. When in the end their military and religious objectives had failed they had broadened beyond measure the horizon of the European mind. The wide regions, vast populations, strange customs and beliefs, of a world beyond the area of Western Christendom would unceasingly haunt men's dreams and later command their energies in those secularized crusades, the explorations and conquests of the Renaissance. The transforming influence of the still young universities was beginning to be felt. With their growth there would presently come an era of genius in a few and of intellectual maturity in many. This educational revival would spread to the clergy more widely with the passing generations, and in the fifteenth century be shared by a class of privileged laymen. The rising towns gave to many an environment utterly different from that which their ancestors had known, and vastly more stimulating. In the fight of the towns for release from feudal and episcopal control, a spirit of liberty was engendered. Business life itself, with its opportunities of wealth and worldly comfort, tended to produce in the townsman a shrewd, self-sufficient, dominant and aggressive type of character not easily disciplined by his clerical monitor. The greatest imaginable contrast existed between the life of the masterful leaders of town society and that of their poor neighbors. As trade and commerce grew, with money-lending as their accompaniment, traditional and even Scholastic formulations of Christian duties were found inapplicable, and the fifteenth century challenged the ethics of the thirteenth. Practical secularism was enhanced by the rise of national states able to enforce some measure of peace within their borders and to attack their rivals on a new scale of power. The kings and rulers were hardly more hostile to the Church than their smaller feudal predecessors had been, but they were more difficult to deal with. The clergy themselves were deeply affected by the secular currents of the age, while from a faithful or censorious minority came forth frequent protests against, and exposures of, the prevalent abuses and deterioriation.

II

New spiritual forces arose to combat the secularist trend and call men to repentance. Monasticism had functioned as the corrective of feudal violence. It had supplied the pattern of piety, and produced those manuals on which the parish priest relied for his personal ministry. The spiritual counterforce to the headstrong burgher life resided not in the monks but in the friars. St. Francis and St. Dominic were contemporaries of Innocent III, and in his time the friar orders had their modest beginnings. The public mission of Francis opened in his defiance of the acquisitive ethics of business as exemplified in his father. Dominic's career began in his encounter with the free and heretical thinking of the townspeople of southern France. Both were earnest guides of souls, and their followers took upon themselves the tasks of the counselor and the confessor.

The sources for our knowledge of St. Francis (d. 1226) offer great difficulties which the labors of many scholars in the past half century have not fully resolved. Francis wrote little that has reached us. Most of his reported utterances have passed through a process of reconstruction by his disciples. But nothing is more constant in the tradition than the highly personal quality of his ministry. In the *Little Flowers of St. Francis* we do not read far without coming upon conversations and incidents that illustrate this. Often Francis is in a mood to receive rather than to give counsel. He engages in a contest of self-abnegation with Friar Bernard, each commanding the other to humiliate him: "I command thee by holy obedience," says Bernard, "that every time we are together thou rebuke and correct me harshly for my faults." Francis can find little in Bernard to rebuke, so conscious is he of his own inferiority. He holds an amusing all-night disputation with Friar Leo whom he cannot induce to declare him worthy of hell and damnation, but who disobediently praises him instead. He tells Friar Masseo with great fervor that it is by reason of his very vileness that God has chosen him to confound the might, beauty and wisdom of the world.

Yet he can rebuke and instruct with authority. Francis, we are told, as a good shepherd, knew the dispositions of the brethren, and how to prescribe remedies for their defects "by humbling the proud, exalting the humble, reproving vice and praising virtue." Fearing that Masseo by reason of his preaching talent should become vainglorious, Francis commands him to act as doorkeeper, almoner and cook, and keeps him at these humble duties until the other brethren enter a plea in his behalf. In the case of Friar Ruffino, Francis leads him out of depression caused by the fear that he is predestined to be damned. On Ruffino's plea to be excused from preaching Francis sends him to a church to preach clad only in shorts; then he relents for having so humiliated his brother, and follows him in similar attire into the church and the pulpit. He finds Ruffino discoursing on repentance, penance, and love of God and neighbor, and Francis follows with an exhortation on voluntary poverty and the shame of Christ's passion, until the hearers weep in contrition and repentance.

Francis won men as much by his deeds as by his words. There is a vivid story of Francis washing the repulsive body of a leper who has reviled the friars, and healing him thereby; whereupon the man loudly acknowledges his perversity, makes confession to a priest of all his sins, and having gone away, presently dies of another disease—but in his flight to heaven pauses to bless the holy friar. Numerous conversions involving nobles, scholars, and men of wealth are effected by Francis and his brethren by conversations, simple preaching, and convincing example. Many of their acts were dramatic illustrations of their principles of poverty and humility. The gifted Friar Giles distributes water and carries wood for fuel a distance of eight miles to sell it and buy bread; he would "do any honest work for hire." This "holy honesty" was encouraged by Francis; but there was no calculated attempt at economic provision that would make unnecessary the beneficially humbling task of "asking alms from door to door": this was "the table of Jesus Christ" for Friar Giles. Mendicancy was valued as a training in holy humility, and as identifying the friars with the indigent and dispossessed. But Francis had no tolerance for idleness, and Friar Giles voices a gospel of work. He dissuades a man from seeking the wisdom of the schools, with the words: "I say unto thee, the word of God is not in the speaker, nor in the hearer, but in the true worker." Thus the Franciscan mission to the townsfolk was to match the active life of gain by an activity on behalf of men's souls.

To make voluntary beggars of rich men was a great achievement. "If any man," says the "Primitive Rule" as reconstructed by John R. H. Moorman, "shall come to the brothers . . . he must sell all his goods and be careful to give everything to the poor." Thereafter he would wear shabby apparel, and, as we read in the *Mirror of Perfection*, "possess naught save a robe with a cord and breeches," and "if forced by necessity, sandals." Francis fought the early attempts of some friars to build and possess houses. He shrank from accepting more than a minimum of food in alms, and he "did above all things execrate money." A friar who had innocently lifted money left as an offering in a church was commanded to carry it in his mouth and drop it on a dunghill. So extreme was his repudiation of wealth and of the mores of the town. Finding a man who seemed poorer than the friars he was put to shame —"since I have chosen Lady Poverty for my lady." Thomas of Celano (writing about 1247) says that Francis pursued this course not from vainglory but from compassion. He dramatically prodded the rich with his exaltation of poverty. As guest of the Cardinal of Ostia (later Gregory IX) he brought to that prelate's amply supplied table a handful of scraps that he had obtained by begging, and reminded the embarrassed Cardinal that Christ "though he was rich, became poor."

The Franciscans were able to carry their mission alike to the rich and to the needy masses because they rejected the social barrier of wealth, and what Miss Vida Scudder calls "the passion for the Proprium" from which men generally suffer. They themselves, in many instances, had exchanged wealth for poverty. Francis called his brethren *Fratres Minores*, remembering the *minori*, the little people of the Tuscan towns. To shed their own property was to make possible an unhindered intercourse with these children of poverty. Nor did they desert the rich; on the contrary they gave the rich every opportunity to be charitable to the poor. From time to time friends continued to provide Francis with a mantle, but giving it away when he met a man or woman in greater need was a habit with him. "We received it as a loan," he would say, "until we should come upon one poorer than ourselves." The poor he regarded as coming in the name of Christ, who took our poverty upon Him. One friar who suggested that a poor, sick fellow whom Francis was comforting might be as greedy as anybody in the province, was commanded to put off his tunic, cast himself down at the stranger's feet, and beg his pardon.

Francis was distrustful of learning, and the possession of books was a temptation to be shunned. In answer to a Dominican who inquired of him the meaning of a passage in Ezekiel, he called himself a simpleton. Like other wealth, books and absorption in them would, he thought, hinder the mission to the people. He had a haunting fear that learning would ruin the order, relaxing its firm spirit in time of tribulation. It is easy, and was easy from the first, to be either contemptuous or romantic about these extreme attitudes to wealth and learning. Instead we should thank Francis for dramatizing the perils that lie in both these concerns if followed in an unsocial, irresponsible spirit. His study of the gospels was wholly practical and the lessons he drew from them utterly simple. His whole being was aroused to love of Christ, and his one consuming desire was to follow Him in His poverty, renunciation and suffering. The joyousness of Francis, so often superficially interpreted, was not derived from the external world but from the love of God that he found expressed alike in creation and in tragic sacrifice. He lived in constant emotional stimulation, and his tears were more often evoked than his laughter. The Christ he found in the Gospels was not a being subject to theological inquiry. If he had searched every verse he would have found (as Petry suggests) that Jesus had none of his own exaggerated horror of money. He simply yearned to follow the Christ who renounced all advantage and underwent all pain for the salvation of souls. "Zeal for souls according to the pattern of Christ was the ideal of the Franciscan apostolate" (Felder).

III

Francis was not a philosopher or a social radical with a new plan for the secular life, but a missionary prophet with zeal for souls. His attitude to the Church was respectful. He told certain friars that to convert the world they must win the prelates by humility and reverence; they would then be welcome to preach and convert the people, and to hear confessions. If such was his strategy, it was to have a real but limited success. The friars went forth through all Europe, and into distant lands, preaching repentance and brotherly love, persuading men and women to peace and charity, hearing their confessions and assigning their penances. All this involved, however, organization and the rapid institutionalizing of the movement, and, quite inevitably, concessions with respect to property and learning that were quite uncongenial to the founder's spirit.

Celano, in his *First Life of St. Francis*, tells of the saint's vision of a great multitude coming to him of Frenchmen, Spaniards, Germans and English. In the *Sacrum commercium*, an early Franciscan tract, Lady Poverty asks some friars to show her their cloister, and they lead her to the summit of a hill where she beholds the wide world. They took the world for their parish. Thomas of Eccleston, in his charming *Chronicle* (*ca.* 1258) tells of their early activity in England, where, under the instruction of Robert Grosseteste, scholar of Oxford and the Bishop of Lincoln, the friars became scholars. He tells us that many of them who were not preachers or lecturers were appointed to be confessors to clerics and lay people. Friar Solomon in London was confessor-general to citizens and courtiers. Geoffrey of Salisbury was skillful as a confessor: he prompted contrition by his own copious tears. Nicholas, who "learned to read in England" became confessor to Pope Innocent IV.

Innocent III had required, as we saw, that confession be made by each "to his own priest." But it was always possible to put different constructions upon this phrase. Only twelve years later Gregory IX accorded to both Dominicans and Franciscans the right to hear confessions and absolve, with or without consent of the bishop (1227). An unedifying contest of jurisdiction was to follow. A good idea of the issues can be readily obtained from the *Apology for the Religious Orders* by St. Thomas Aquinas. In chapter iv of that work the objections raised against the preaching of the "religious" and their hearing of confessions are stated at length, and, in the characteristic manner of Aquinas, disposed of one by one. The Dominican makes no express plea for his own order, but uses the words "monks" and "religious" to include friars and others under rule. His argument is such as to support the authority of bishops who make use of the friars' services, and of the pope and his plenipotentiaries who issue letters authorizing their activities. Pope Innocent's phrase, "his own priest," is actually interpreted to mean the bishop of the diocese, or the pope, and "vicegerents" appointed by them. Thus the parish priest has no case. It is assumed, of course, that the "monk" who hears confessions is in clerical orders.

The issue was being decided apart from scholastic argument. The people warmly favored the friars against the local clergy. Mathew Paris (d. 1259) says they would not confess to their own priests. "None of the faithful," says this chronicler, "any longer believe themselves to be saved unless they are guided by the counsels of the Preachers [Dominicans] and the Minorites [Franciscans]." Father Victor Green rates this aspect of the Franciscan work in England as more important than their preaching.

In dioceses whose bishops desired a revival of religion and a reformation of manners, the friars were welcomed and given that free access to the people which Francis had desired. The best known example is perhaps that of Lincoln after Grosseteste became its bishop (1235). Grosseteste (d. 1253) was unsurpassed as a scholar in his century, and at the same time a firm disciplinarian and an earnest reformer. He once said to Innocent IV in Rome: "The life of the pastors is the book of the laity"—it was, as matters were, an injurious book. Though he had been, at Oxford, specially associated with the Franciscans, he valued highly the services of the Dominicans also. He began a series of systematic visitations for reform in his diocese. In course of these he held assemblies of clergy and people, which he thus describes: "I preached to the clergy and some friar to the people. Four friars were employed at the same time in hearing confessions and enjoining penances."

The early Franciscans earned the love and gratitude of the townsfolk by a variety of services. They often showed the greatest personal kindness to people in trouble. Some condemned to die were rescued through their intervention. Even so industrious a scholar as Adam Marsh proved a friend to many whose only claim upon him was their need of counsel and help. There was a new spirit in this work. Eccleston has elements of the casualness, exuberance and humor that very often break into the early Franciscan literature. But this was the accompaniment of a deep, almost awe-stricken, sense of the value of human personality. The spirit of Francis was potent among his followers in their constant effort to allay quarrels, and, especially in the Lenten season, to bring about reconciliations between alienated and contentious people.

St. Francis awakened and guided the soul of Santa Clara, who at his direction founded the Second Franciscan Order, the Order of Poor Ladies. The holy affection between Francis and Clara may be said to have formed a pattern hardly discoverable since the first century, for the hallowing of the relations between men and women. The Franciscans had strict rules against worldly familiarity with women and were required to confine their services to "giving advice as the Spirit shall direct them." Francis also brought into existence the Third Order, which consisted of persons pledged to follow a spiritual discipline within lay society and family life. It was similar to certain already existing voluntary groups, but from the social rank of the many Franciscan converts, it grew to considerable importance and its membership included many distinguished names. The Tertiaries, or Brothers and Sisters of Penance, formed local groups, and gradually took on wider organization. In the modern *Penitentes* we see a specialized and fanatical expression of the Tertiary discipline. In the beginning they were chiefly different from others in their strictness of behavior, adherence to the "just price" in business, and avoidance of war and violence. Apparently St. Elizabeth of Thuringia (d. 1231), in the late years of her short life of amazing devotion to the poor and sick, was a Franciscan Tertiary.

IV

We have mentioned St. Dominic (d. 1221) and his Preaching Friars. Dominic's primary concern was to combat the spread of heresy. He assailed it in its stronghold in Southern France where the Albigensians were numerous and Waldenses and other sects mingled with them. We may accept the view of Angelus Walz, an authorized Dominican historian, that zeal for the salvation of souls was the great mark of his personality, even though the interests of ecclesiastical authority appear strongly in Dominican history. He disapproved of well-mounted monks and pompous bishops in the presence of heretics who practiced severe austerities, and determined to approach them with humility and patience, to surpass them in fasting and exposure, to labor with them personally and refute their arguments in public. A university alumnus, Dominic remained a constant reader of books, especially of the Bible, and this gave an intellectual character to his ministry, and to his order. The sources for his life are inadequate and in them miracle stories, often frivolous, are allowed to crowd out any extended record of his conversations. But early writers tell us that "he tried to talk of God to everyone he met on the highways," and that he was "a kindly consoler of everybody, especially of his own brethren." He was known to spend a whole night in argument in order to convince a heretic.

The Order of Preachers was also an order of confessors. Dominic's successor as Master General was Jordan of Saxony (1222-37). Marguerite Aron in her biographical study extols him as a director of souls above all else. His long journeys about Europe, his legislation, his educational labors, all turned upon this one aim, the collective and individual direction of souls. We find him bidding novices laugh aloud with joy because they have been delivered from the devil, even while he imposes an austere regime of study. "Be a man, my son," he said to a despondent recruit, "you have entered an order of strong men," and the boy was transported with courage and hope. His thirty-seven letters to Sister Diane d'Andalo remind his biographer of the spiritual bond between Francis and Clara, and of the correspondence of Francis de Sales with Madame Chantal. Diane's replies are not extant, but the consolation was mutual. The uses of tribulation, moderation in austerity, equilibrium of the spirit, humor and charity, go with the ardor of mystical devotion in these letters which Jordan wrote in eloquent Latin.

The intrusion of the friars into the parishes was hardly more resented than their intrusion into the universities. Shortly after the middle of the thirteenth century resistance by the older corps of university scholars was finally overcome at Paris and Oxford. Oxford Franciscans and Paris Dominicans were thereafter to dominate the thought of the age. Amid their theological interests were the problems of penance, left open by twelfth century writers such as Abailard, Richard of St. Victor, and Peter Lombard. In the writings of Alexander of Hales, Raymond of Penafort, Bonaventura, Albertus Magnus and Thomas Aquinas, definitions were now offered of the parts of penance (attrition, contrition, confession, satisfaction), and expositions of its sacramental character. A series of books of guidance for confessors began to appear, which are classified as *summae confessorum*, confessors' compendiums. These were learned theological treatises, very different indeed from the simple and untheological penitentials. They were a natural sequel to the legislation of 1215. They contained reasoned expositions and interpretations of all that relates to penance as a sacrament. Members of the Dominican Order excelled in these writings. Father Walz lists more than a score of Dominican contributions to the series, chiefly of the thirteenth century, while Dr. Lea has utilized many such books by Dominicans and other friars and clerics.

One of the earliest and most influential of these authors was Raymond of Penafort (Pennaforte, Penyafort) author of the treatise usually entitled *Summa casuum*. Amadeus Teetaert has devoted to it a long study (1928), and dates it about 1222-30. Raymond became in 1238 Master General of the order, and may have been a centenarian when he died after long retirement in 1275. His teaching is somewhat in contrast to that which prevailed in the twelfth century, in which the emphasis was laid upon the efficacy of contrition. He still regards contrition as important, but treats absolution as the definitive factor in penance. He also enlarges on the different kinds of satisfactions, which include "macerations of the flesh." The doctrine of the keys is expounded by Raymond in relation to penance. There are two keys: the knowledge (*scientia*) to discern the relative gravity of sins, and the power to bind and loose. He is obliged to report that "many simple priests have the power who have not the knowledge." But the authority of the priest is stated strongly: to do penance without the priest's decision is to frustrate the keys of the Church. Confession to a priest is necessary, and it contains the useful experience of "blushing" for one's sins.

While the Franciscan theologians St. Bonaventura and Alexander of Hales were still building on the doctrines of Abailard and Peter Lombard with respect to contrition, Dominican writers were moving to new ground. In this they felt the stimulus of the Paris Aristotelian, William of Auvergne (d. 1248), who turned from university teaching (1228) to become Bishop of Paris. William so defined attrition and contrition as to differentiate them clearly, and his views, along with those of Raymond of Penafort, are reflected in the work of St. Thomas Aquinas. Attrition is sorrow for sin not motivated by love and not completed by sanctifying grace; contrition is sorrow motivated by love and completed by sanctifying grace. There is no remission of sin, according to Aquinas, without the power of grace. Penance as a sacrament is a cause of grace, though as a virtue it is an effect of grace. Attrition cannot become contrition until grace is infused. Full and true contrition brings pardon: but who knows that his contrition is complete? The sacrament of penance is necessary either actually or, where this is impossible, by desire. Contrition involves the intention to make confession. Priests alone exercise the keys by which souls are bound and loosed: "Our Lord commanded none but the disciples to loose Lazarus; therefore confession should be made to a priest." These elements of the teaching of the Angelic Doctor bring to central importance the function of the priest in the sacrament of penance, and the obligation of all to confess all their sins and make satisfactions at the direction of priests.

Some of the popular literature of the time reflects the official emphasis on the necessity of sacramental penance. In the *Gesta Romanorum*, a collection of *exempla*, or illustrative stories, that took its extant form about 1300, several tales illustrate this. A woman in repentance tries to kiss the feet of a crucifix, but the crucifix "drew away his feet" and spoke commanding her: "Go as soon as thou mayest and be shriven, and then shalt thou be saved without any fail." In another tale, Mary Magdalene appears to a penitent woman who has fasted long, to say that Christ and she herself are not pleased with her fasting, and that she must go to a priest and do penance. The effect of this teaching was to assert for the Church and the priesthood a truly totalitarian control over the souls of the faithful. It would be difficult to find priests adequately qualified to exercise this control to edification; it would be difficult to maintain it at all. In the very next tale in the *Gesta* a wicked priest discloses a woman's lurid confession to her husband (nos. lxxv-lxxvii).

V

That the experts were at variance on many aspects of penance, and that many of them admitted equivocations and relaxations of a highly objectionable sort, are unavoidable conclusions from the evidence presented by Lea, and less fully by other historians. The seal of confession was violated in many instances. Raymond of Penafort authorized this in the case of heretics. Some argued that the seal should not be inviolate where confession involved facts that would disqualify persons from marriage or clerics from ordination. The sanctity of the seal in cases where some great wrong or crime could be avoided by exposing the knowledge gained, was debated in that and later ages. The Lateran regulation, as we saw, prohibited not only disclosing the matter of confession in words but revealing it by signs or in any other way. If a priest on journey hears in the confessional that he will be murdered by bandits unless he changes his course, ought he to go on to his death in order to avoid divulging by an act what he had learned under seal? Or if a confessant declares his intention to kill his father or his king, can he claim the privilege of the seal?

The dangers encountered where unworthy priests heard the confessions of women, were always recognized, and some writers of the thirteenth and subsequent centuries give the impression that solicitation in the confessional was shockingly frequent. Monks like Caesarius of Heisterbach (d. 1240) and friars like St. Bonaventura (d. 1274) believed that many parish priests were addicted to this perversion of the sacrament, which Alain de Lille had referred to as confusing the keys of heaven with the keys of hell. The difficulty of suppressing this evil was increased by the fact that if the woman did not continue to confess to and be absolved by her seducer, she might carry the information to another confessor, thus violating the seal and possibly spreading scandal. Variant opinions on the validity of such absolutions were exchanged among medieval casuists. Centuries later, after a variety of efforts to combat the abuse, absolutions so granted were declared invalid by Pope Benedict XIV (1741).

In this period the ordinary place of confession was in the open church where the parties could be seen but not heard, and the time between sunrise and sunset. The confessional box had not yet been introduced. The presence of observers was regarded as a safeguard. Jean Gerson (d. 1429) says: "Confession is to be made before the eyes of all in an open place," not to a rapacious wolf in corners. For confessions of women, the presence of others in the church was expressly required by Odo of Paris (ca. 1198) and by later councils and authorities, but some moralists continued to charge that "secret places" and "shadowy corners" were used by unscrupulous priests. It is not our task to determine how widespread the abuses of the confessional were. That they were serious no student can doubt. The possibility of exposing them comes, however, from the fact that they were denounced by men of high moral earnestness, and legislated against by responsible bishops.

The diseases of the physicians are always coming to light. The medieval priesthood was recruited without adequate sifting and training. It contained good and consecrated men, and some who were weak and bad. The latter abused their high office and made the means of grace a means of corruption. No doubt the whole system was open to criticism. The fact that confession was required brought many to it with unwilling and impenitent minds. Many others neglected it, despite ecclesiastical pressure and penalties. An increasing flood of satirical comment on the confessional can be seen in late medieval popular literature. The fact is easily overlooked that in any system the relationships established in the secret, confidential guidance of souls are always subject to perversion, and can achieve their proper ends only where the guide, confessor or counselor is highly qualified and of a character above reproach. If this is not assured, his authority may mean only an enhancement of mischief.

The progressive deterioration of the sacramental discipline in the Middle Ages is, however, associated less with the character of the confessors than with the practice of Indulgences which grew upon the Church from the beginning of the crusading era. A number of elements combined to produce the indulgence traffic. Behind all was the belief in a shared merit in the Church, a natural inference from the sharing of the members in communion. Elements of this doctrine appear early. Tribal ideas affected the interpretation of communion, and as we have seen in the penitentials, the sharing of penalties by relatives of the offender. So also participation in the good works of others is constantly presupposed. "The Church," says Harnack, "looked upon the Christians as forming a clan with the saints in heaven." The doctrine of the Treasury of Merits was sketched by Alexander of Hales (d. 1245) and expounded by Thomas Aquinas (d. 1274). It consists of the combined infinite merits of Christ, the Virgin, and the Saints, and is placed by Aquinas under the administration of the pope. Pope Clement VI in 1343 and 1350 affirmed the doctrine of the Treasury, explaining that it was not a treasure secluded in a strong room but was distributed by the Blessed Peter and his successors.

Indulgences, or remissions of penalty due for confessed sins, were granted from this store of merit not, as Aquinas observes, annulling the penalty but providing to the sinner the means of paying it. The habitual use of commutations and money compositions in the penitentials made all too easy the commercializing of indulgences. There was always a temptation on the part of the lower administrators of indulgences to play upon the credulity of the people and to claim for their indulgence certificates more than they were authorized to claim. At the lowest level we have a tribe of charlatan *quaestores* or "pardoners," despised and exposed by satirists and sometimes condemned by councils and popes for their unauthorized peddling of pardons, but driving a lucrative trade. They enjoyed the same reputation, says Jusserand, in every country in Europe; in England their shameful devices are immortalized by Chaucer and Langland. Langland in *Piers Plowman* (1362-90) says "the simple fools" believed a pardoner when, armed with papal bull and bishop's seal, he promised to assoil them all. After Conscience has aroused the king, who has sent Dread to frighten Liar, the pardoners take pity on Liar, wash him and put a gown on him, and send him out on Sundays "to give pardons by the pound"—for pennies. Chaucer's "gentil pardoner," straight from the Court of Rome, has a wallet full of pardons, and a bag full of diverting relics, from "oure lady veyl" to "pigges bones." With this equipment he gets more money in a day than the settled parson in two months. But even the more circumspent and fully authorized quaestors were often unscrupulous as they exchanged indulgences for money designated for the building of hospitals, churches or bridges. There is little thought of true penitence in all this, but a growing spirit of cupidity which reached to the highest circles in the Church. Many . of the popes had endeavored to resist the tide, but the Renaissance Papacy became immersed in it, and authorized papal agents contributed to the general deterioration and commercialization of indulgences, which, in the words of Gieseler, "completed the destruction of the ancient penitential system."

Langland says the friars were teaching the people "to profit of themselves," and adds bitterly: "God's love has turned trader." By his time the friars had lost their early reputation for unselfish service. They had suffered from success. Pope Martin IV in a bull of December, 1281, had enlarged their opportunities to hear confessions, and a great many of both principal orders of friars were so occupied. They pursued the task free from episcopal control and with little regard for church order. The bishops in France and England protested against the papal policy, and Boniface VIII in February, 1300, issued a bull designed to meet in some degree their objections. The friars were still licensed in large numbers, but most of them were placed under restriction (*limitacio*) as to territory. In England these were called *limitours*. Chaucer's "Frere" is "a lymytour, a ful solempne man"—in our lingo, a Very Important Person.

> Ful swetely herde he confessioun
> And pleasaunt was his absolucioun.
> He was an easy man to give penaunce
> Ther as he wiste to have a good pitaunce.

Even from the poorest widow,

> So pleasaunt was his *In principio*,
> Yet wolde he have a ferthyng er he wente,

and his income was far more than he paid as "rent" for the district. Langland is earnestly concerned over the mischief wrought by this commercialization of sacred things. In one biting passage a friar is confessor to Lady Mede (covetousness) who has been forty years mistress of Falsehood, and offers to assoil her for a horseload of wheat. She contributes to his church and will place in it her picture labeled "Meed—Sister of the Order." Langland's Liar becomes a friar, and we meet Friar Wrath and Friar Flattery.

The stern and inexorable figure of Conscience, already a stock allegorical character of the religious drama, enters Langland's visions, to accuse the guilty confessors and manipulators of penance for gain; yet in the end Conscience survives only as a pilgrim. When in the Vision of Antichrist all have turned against Conscience, the friars come to help her, but they know not how. When Friar Flattery talks with Contrition, who has been injured by the parson's plaster, he gives him another plaster made of private payment, and Contrition ceases to weep.

> The Friar with his physic this folk hath enchanted,
> And plastered them so pleasantly they dread no sin.

Conscience will start out on a world-wide pilgrimage to seek the common man—Piers Plowman—who earlier in the book obtained "God's bull of pardon" (Matt. 25:46).

> I think on Piers the Plowman, and the Pardon that he had,
> And how the priest attacked it and reasoned it away,
> But I deem that Do-well had no need of indulgence.

The rising indignation against these abuses found expression among the learned. In England John Grandisson of Exeter, John Wyclif and William Gascoigne of Oxford, and on the Continent John Huss, John of Wesel, Erasmus, his Franciscan friend John Vitrarius, and Jacques Lefèvre were among those who bore witness against the evils affecting the cure of souls.

VI

It is pleasing to turn from these depressing matters to the efforts of churchmen who brought to their ministry a fine sense of pastoral responsibility and sought to meet religious needs. The layman was advancing in literacy and mentality. There was some attempt to provide the better instructed layman with reading matter in the vernacular for the guidance of his mind and conscience, and by the end of the Middle Ages a good deal of this had been done. A closely related body of writing, also partly in the vernacular, was prepared for the use of priests in parish instruction. The development of the new literature of piety was not without plan. The Franciscan Archbishop of Canterbury, John Pecham (or Peckham), in 1381 laid down the requirement that priests should faithfully instruct their people in the Fourteen Articles of the Creed, the Ten Commandments, the two Evangelical Precepts ("the twins of charity"), the Seven Capital Sins "with their progeny," the Seven Principal Virtues and the Seven Sacraments of Grace. Later provisions encouraged the preparation of texts for such instruction by priests, and this naturally led to the circulation of handbooks that laymen could profitably use. In these the pastoral function is conceived on a broader basis than that of penance and the confessional. This literature is bewildering in extent, as is also the modern scholarly labor over it. A realm of delight to philologists, it has been all too little explored by historians of society and religion.

These books embrace hundreds of treatises generally designated as *artes praedicandi*, methods of preaching. Many of these are from the pens of renowned Dominican and Franciscan preachers, and many are anonymous or pseudonymous. They offer guidance in the preparation of sermons and in the art of illustrating them so as to bring the message to the level of the hearer. Many consist largely of stories or "examples" (*exempla*). The use of *exempla* had been recommended and practiced by Gregory the Great, and almost all homiletic or hortative material of the Middle Ages employs them. From the early thirteenth century, separate collections of these anecdotes, *libri exemplorum*, were compiled in increasing numbers. A variety of the *exemplum* was the *speculum* (mirror), so-called because the story is a mirror to humanity, showing in sharp contrast the good and evil behavior of men.

Well-worn before their appearance in these convenient books, most of the tales have an enduring interest. They were derived through intermediaries from classical, biblical, Talmudic, Arabian, Patristic and medieval sources, and from contemporary experience, rumor and gossip; and they were narrated with a charming indifference to the distinction between history and fiction. They include miraculous tales of saints, and equally marvelous animal fables, the latter from the *bestiaries*, collections of animal lore, widely circulated from the thirteenth century down. The *exempla*, however, were chosen to illustrate sins and virtues, and they were not marked by Victorian refinement. The writers knew well how to attach to a tale of blood or lust, by the device of allegory or otherwise, a pious word of instruction.

The fact that the stories were told over and over in the various collections did not render them stale. A classic does not become stale; and many of these were so good as to be almost imperishable. Chaucer's Pardoner explains his success by the fact that he makes use of many "examples," "for lewed [uneducated lay] peple loven tales olde." Perhaps the attraction of these anecdotes for the "lewed peple" lay in the bringing of distant times, far countries, and famous figures of history vividly to their consciousness, and the creation for them of a new world of imagination, romance and wonder. But the urgent and thrilling use of these by earnest friars, whose preaching stirred men to their depths with fear of hell and hope of heaven, ought not to be forgotten by the modern reader who finds them vastly entertaining. It was fully recognized by the clerical purveyors of these anecdotes that they were bait for the hook by which souls might be caught and drawn heavenward.

Much of this fluid material passed from the preacher's library into vernacular books of moral guidance which in growing numbers became available to laymen. They incorporated a generous selection of *exempla*. In England, most of them were translations, with or without additional material, from Latin or French. (It is remarkable how far the English language was shaped by translators, from Bede and Alfred to the King James Bible.)

A collection of *exempla* by Jacques de Vitry (d. *ca.* 1240), the *Dialogue on Miracles* of his contemporary Caesarius of Heisterbach, and the *Gesta Romanorum*, from which we have quoted above, were among the treasuries drawn upon by later compilers. But some of the later collections were much more ample. A popular one was the *Speculum laicorum* of about 1250-75, probably by a friar of Kent, which has 572 anecdotes arranged alphabetically under ninety-one topics. A century and a half after the Dominican Jordan of Saxony, his Augustinian namesake (d. *ca.* 1377) compiled the *Vitasfratrum* which assembled a goodly number of tales to be retailed in later books. John Bromyard (d. 1418), an eminent English Dominican preacher and writer, has more than one thousand *exempla* in his *Summa praedicantium*, a great preacher's cyclopedia.

It is out of the question to examine the range of this expanding literature of piety. Some of it centered around the imitation of Christ—worthiest of all "examples." In England we have in this class the fifteenth century *Myrour for Lewde Men and Wymmen*, but this is preceded by much in the writing of mystics, and of Wyclif. On the Continent a contemporary of Wyclif (d. 1384) and of Gerard Groote (d. 1380, the author of most of the *Imitation of Christ* often ascribed to its editor Thomas à Kempis), wrote the most popular *Life of Christ*. This was the Carthusian monk Ludolf of Saxony (d. 1377). Since the late Dr. Shirley Jackson Case has given twenty valuable pages to this treatise in his *Jesus through the Centuries*, not to mention more technical recent studies, it is unnecessary here to call attention to its special features. But an examination of the book will show how its recommendations on prayer appealed to Ignatius Loyola and are reflected in his *Spiritual*

Exercises. When St. Ignatius read the book (1521) he was but one of many thousands of laymen who sought guidance in its pages. The *Biblia pauperum* (Poor Men's Bibles) circulated widely in fifteenth century block books with profuse woodcut illustrations, were made up of Bible passages centered in the life of Jesus.

The number seven had a great attraction for medieval writers. Hugh of St. Victor (d. 1141) was the author of a Latin book called *The Five Sevens* in which he treated the Seven Vices, the Seven Petitions of the Lord's Prayer, the Seven Gifts of the Holy Spirit, the Seven Virtues and the Seven Beatitudes. Similar arrangements are found in many of the vernacular devotional books. One of the most important of these was William of Waddington's versified (French) *Manual of Sins* which is better known as translated and improved by Robert Mannyng of Brunne under the title *Handlyng Synne* (1303). The translator adds discourses on the fear and love of God, and on the too scrupulous conscience; also some vivid *exempla* from English life. At the outset he promises to give his reader "tales, chances and marvels, some that I found written, others seen and known." They come in irregularly, and with arresting realism, to illustrate the Commandments, Deadly Sins, Sacraments, and the "twelve points of shrift" (confession). For Pride we have the tale of the lady who because she was proud of her beauty must be repeatedly burned to ashes in hell. The treatment of Sloth is rather brightened than clarified by the story of Bishop Grosseteste who kept harpers near his bed and loved music because it "destroys the fiend's might." The section on Shrift ends on the point of an entire or integral confession ("thy shrift all whole shall be") with the alarming case of a woman who after concealment of her sins finally confesses them to a friar, who notes that each sin comes from her mouth in the form of a black fiend. (In so unusual a case the friar is presumably not to be blamed for looking.) In the *Ayenbite of Inwyt* (Remorse of Conscience) by Dan Michel (1340) we have a poetic translation of another French work, the *Summary of the Vices and Virtues,* prepared in 1279 for King Philip II of France by the Dominican Friar Lorens (Laurentius) of Orleans. The original title indicates the nature of its contents, in which again we have the typical number method.

In some popular books interest in the stories themselves becomes uppermost. Geoffrey de la Tour Landry in 1372 compiled a book for the instruction of his four daughters. Using two priests as his research assistants, and two secretaries, he gave these young women 144 chapters and 150 stories to read. Again the contrasted virtues and vices are illustrated by a great variety of *exempla*—some remarkably unedifying except as morally interpreted. In many such books for lay readers *exempla* were effectively drawn in to illustrate the Seven Virtues and Vices, the twice-Seven Works of Mercy, and other essential topics of instruction variously numbered; and sometimes the story runs away with the moral. With John Gower (d. 1408), who calls Chaucer his disciple and who wrote poems in Latin, French and English, we find ourselves in a more obviously secular atmosphere. In his *Confessio Amantis*, an English dialogue of Confessor and Lover, the Seven Deadly Sins form the framework of a profuse collection of stories written more for entertainment than for edification.

The Lay Folks' Catechism, attributed to John Thoresby, Archbishop of York (d. 1373), and suspected of Wycliffite revision, is a good example of an earnestly pious use of the same method. Besides the Fourteen Points of Faith (i.e., clauses of the Creed) and the Ten Commandments, the Catechism deals with

the Seven Sacraments that be in Holy Church, the Seven Deeds of Mercy of our even [fellow] Christian, the Seven Virtues that each man shall use, and the Seven Deadly Sins that each man shall refuse.

The sacraments are presented in the unusual order: Baptism, Confirmation, Penance, the Eucharist, Unction, Ordination and Matrimony. The Works of Mercy are, as usual, in two classifications, "corporal" and "spiritual." The former list is based upon Matthew 25, and consists of: feeding the hungry; giving drink to the thirsty; clothing the naked; harboring the houseless; visiting the sick; helping those imprisoned, and burying the dead. The "Works of Mercy spiritual" include: teaching the ignorant; counseling men in doubt; reproving the undisciplined; comforting those in sorrow; forgiving offenders; patience under adversity, and praying for our enemies. The Seven Virtues are those we have noted above (p. 104) with reference to St. Ambrose. The Deadly Sins follow the order: pride, envy, wrath, gluttony, covetousness, sloth, lechery. Wyclif himself wrote short essays in English on each of the topics of the *Lay Folks' Catechism*, including "the Seven Werkys of Mercy Bodyly and Gostly." These articles are marked by an appropriation of the prevalent ways of discussing lay morality together with a critical slant against the hierarchy and the friars. The *Summary* of Lorens of Orleans, which as we saw, was the basis of the *Ayenbite of Inwyt*, appeared in several other English versions, of which the late fourteenth century (prose) *Book of Vices and Virtues* was the finest. Here again we have the familiar number scheme, and the puritanic injunctions on the Sins and Virtues. "Myrthe and jollitie" are associated with evil company and intemperance. The tavern is the devil's schoolhouse in which he works his evil miracles in competition with the Church. In the section on confession we are told that "when a man repenteth of his synne, than mote he begynne to wrastle." Some freedom of conscience is encouraged by the injunction to examine the counsel one receives and follow only the good.

VII

Some parish priests were all the while giving devoted service according to their lights, and Langland's reprehensible Parson Sloth is matched by Chaucer's wholly admirable "poor parson of a town." This good man is loath to curse for unpaid tithes, visits his remotest parishioners in all weathers, and practices no less than he teaches "Christ's lore and His apostles twelve." In real life we have such pastors, though our historians point them out as exceptions. Gustav Schnürer names four zealous and dutiful German pastors at work about 1500, including John Geiler of Kaisersberg (d. 1510), the celebrated preacher of Strasbourg. But Geiler's biographers show that he was a bold and caustic critic of popes, clergy, monks and friars. Time had been when an earnest churchman like Grosseteste could rely on the friars for help; but the no less earnest Geiler had a low opinion of them, and said he would rather have his sister a harlot than a member of the Order of Poor Clares.

The attempt to provide priests with directions for the conduct of their pastoral duties had taken various forms in earlier treatises, penitentials and *summae*. It was now producing simple and practical manuals, some of them in the vernacular. A well-known English book of this type is the *Instructions for Parish Priests* (*ca.* 1440) of John Mirk (or Myrc), an Augustinian canon of Lilleshall in Shropshire. It is in English rhyme and is substantially taken from a Latin original, possibly written by Mirk's own prior. The author hopes that ignorant and careless priests will read it—as well they might, although Mirk's instructions are not baited with diverting stories. He lays severe demands upon priests, and warns that evil living will annul their preaching. But his main interest is to instruct them in their pastoral duties. They are not to neglect the shriving of pregnant women, or the instruction of the midwife, who must be prepared to baptize a half-born child, lest she lament her failure forever. There is instruction about marriage and certain duties of parents; about behavior in church, and the faithful paying of tithes. Witchcraft and usury are forbidden. The Lord's Prayer and the Creed are expounded briefly: the Trinity is illustrated by the unity of water, ice and snow. Then follow the Seven Sacraments. The treatment is interrupted by a form of excommunication for violators of the church, usurers, perjurers, "all that make experiments or witchcraft with ointments of holy church," exposers of children, withholders of tithes, etc. Chaucer's good parson notwithstanding, they are to be roundly cursed with cross, bell and candle. In confession and penance, moderation is enjoined. If the parish priest is garrulous or immoral, a confessant may go to another. The priest must not look at a woman in confession, and he must sit still as a stone. A penance for untaught parishioners is to learn the Lord's Prayer, the Ave and the Creed in English. A set of questions on infringements of the Commandments is provided.

Mirk uses a catalogue of the Seven Deadly Sins in which *accidia* comes second, here in the sense of "sloth." "Hast thou been slow to teach thy godchildren? . . . to help thy wife and family?" are among the questions that occur here. There are penetrating questions on the other capital sins, on venial sins of the five wits (senses), and on a few miscellaneous matters. Much is said of "the manner of enjoining penance," allowance being made for many circumstances. Mirk favors mildness, since it is better by light penance to send a man to purgatory than by overmuch penance to send him to the pit of hell. There are careful prescriptions of remedies for each of the Deadly Sins, based on the old principle of contraries. The book is an affirmation of traditional discipline, frankly defensive of the Church as an institution, but written with sincere concern for the guidance of souls.

VIII

Whether our life be long or short, we die. The thought of death intruded more constantly in the Middle Ages than in our time. Violence, disease, pestilence and hunger shortened many lives. The Black Death of 1349 swept away half the population of Europe, and undoubtedly left a stamp of "somber melancholy" (Huizinga) upon the European mind. This has its most extreme expression in the Dance of Death, a ghastly variation of the miracle play, which appeared in the wake of the plague in Germany, France and Spain, and received the attention of

Holbein and earlier artists. Men recognized death in all its horror as the inexorable reaper of the lives of all, from pope to peasant. The need of a more spiritual preparation for death was met in a series of booklets on the Art of Dying.

The essential materials of these guidebooks were not original, but were supplied from incidental treatments of the subject by earlier writers, chiefly classical and Patristic. Jean Gerson (d. 1429) was one of the first to give to this specialty of piety a specific form. As the last part of his *Three-fold Treatise* (*ca.* 1408 [the other sections being "On the Commandments" and "On Confession"]), he has a little essay under the title *De arte moriendi* (*On the Art of Dying*). This great Paris doctor wrote many more weighty works, some of which, did space permit, might well have been considered in this book. A minor one important in the history of religious education, and belonging to his old age when he devoted himself to pastoral duties, is entitled: *On Bringing the Little Ones to Christ*. His *Art of Dying* is somewhat dependent upon a section of the French *Sum of the Vices and Virtues* (1279) which we noted as the source of the *Ayenbite of Inwyt*. Gerson may have profited also by a chapter on death written by Henry Suso (d. 1366) which was later widely read; it was translated from the Latin by the poet Thomas Hoccleve (Occleve) shortly before his death in 1450. Gerson's aim was to provide material by which "one friend might support another in the article of death." The dying friend is first admonished to attend to the salvation of his soul. Six questions to be asked of him are then set down, with proper answers, including a promise to live better than before, should he recover. There follow prayers to God, Mary, his guardian angel and patron saints. The sick man is induced to take the Eucharist, and, if time permits, legends, histories and prayers are read to him. An image of the Crucified, or of a specially revered saint, is held over him. His wife, children, friends and household must not encourage him with false hopes of recovery.

Franz Falk and Sister Mary Catherine O'Connor have traced editions and variations of Gerson's fragment on Dying, to the end of the Middle Ages and beyond. The latter scholar has argued that the longer of two main Art of Dying documents later printed with variations, originated at the Council of Constance (1414-18) and is the work of a Dominican who cannot now be identified.

With the introduction of printing, these booklets had a wide circulation in various forms and in many languages. Woodcuts accompanied the meager texts, and no doubt explain their popularity. Even those who could not read could see a picture, and would not soon turn away from these vivid representations of Moriens, the dying man, tempted by hideous beak-mouthed, claw-footed demons and exhorted by winged angels and solemn, kindly saints. At first the shorter editions were circulated in block books. Many in various languages have a common set of eleven woodcuts. W. Harry Rylands in 1881 edited with facsimile reproduction what he called the First Edition of the block book *Ars moriendi* from a British Museum copy of about 1450, in which these eleven illustrations occupy pages opposite appropriate portions of the (Latin) text. George Bullen's introduction to this edition gives a substantial explanation of each of the woodcuts. Soon longer and shorter books of the series began to be issued in movable type. In 1490, William Caxton printed, without pictures, *The Arte and Crafte to Knowe Well to Dye*. In 1505 Wynkyn de Woorde used no less than eighty cuts in *The Crafte to Live Well and to Dye Well*. In most Continental countries the printing of the Art of Dying Well was earlier than in England. Caxton's is a translation from an unknown French original.

In these texts and illustrations death is not treated lightly. The deathbed is a battlefield on which malign and gracious spirits contend for the soul. Death is, indeed, commended in the manner of the old consolation literature; but the dying man has his "great and grievous temptations, greater than those he has met hitherto." And here the artist of the woodcuts has given full play to his talent for the grotesque. The devils seek to destroy the sufferer's faith and hope and patience, or to entrap him in vainglory. He is questioned on his faith, and instructed in repentance and in prayer for pardon and divine help. Some of the prayers supplied are to the Virgin, some to St. Michael and other angels.

Although the theological element is quite consistent with medieval orthodoxy, there is ordinarily no role for the priest to play. Even the allusion to the Eucharist does not mention the presence of a priest. Sister Mary O'Connor explains this on the ground that they were intended for use where "the ministrations of the clergy were not available," as in time of plague. However, they suggest no such restriction, and such phrases as "every good Christian man," "all sinful men," in the introductory sections seem to stamp them for unrestricted use. The same writer suggests that Caxton's attention to the Art of Dying was a part of his general interest (represented by various "books of codified manners" which he published), in the conduct becoming to a gentleman, who should combine urbanity with godliness. Others have pointed out that Caxton's *Arte and Crafte* was published shortly after his wife's death, which probably gave him a personal concern for the problem. In any case, death is not quite a matter of etiquette, and the Art of Dying handbooks made it much more than that. Yet, before modern hospitals and drugs, an edifying death was held in high importance, and the attitude of the dying was better observed and remembered than today. To "make a good end" was in some sense felt to be an "art" even in the modern sense of that word. In this respect the Art of Dying Well is a contradiction of all that was suggested in the Dance of Death. Despite death's horrors, the Christian man is taught to die with dignity. It may have been with some recollection of these medieval counsels for the dying that Francis Thompson, viewing the setting sun, was moved to write:

> Thou dost thy dying so triumphally.

We shall note later some post-Reformation developments of the theme of these strange books in which medieval writers and artists sought to show how death might be, for the believer, "swallowed up in victory."

IX

We have seen something of the gains and losses of the three centuries preceding the Reformation, with respect to the cure of souls. In the Art of Dying the Good Angel and the evil spirits are found contending for the soul of Moriens, the dying man. A comparable contest of good and evil forces was being waged for the soul of Europe. Devout and zealous men were doing what they could to avert disaster, and to guide the tempted and morally defeated to deliverance. The ecclesiastical life of the time shows a progressive deterioration, and this is illustrated in sacramental penance and its related practices. Yet in this respect efforts to assert sincere religion were unceasing.

Perhaps the more regrettable phases of the medieval man's religious experience were connected with his approach to the problem of sin. For long centuries the emphasis had been not on sin as a state of the soul from which repentance and divine grace would emancipate it, as upon sins in the plural that swarmed in great numbers and must be confessed in complete detail. The tendency to center religion about repeated clear-ances from innumerable and ever-returning sins, can hardly be whole-some. On the other hand, if sin is treated as a state and not a series of acts, laxity regarding sinful acts may arise where sin itself is repudiated. Jesus' words to the paralytic were: "Your *sins* are forgiven," and sin-ridden souls need this annihilation of specific sins. Yet the meticulous enumeration of detailed sins may set up an obsession and prove a hindrance to deliverance. Such a method, unless conducted with the greatest wisdom, tends to make the conscientious man or woman un-wholesomely scrupulous and introverted. The New Testament inner renovation of the soul gave place to an anxiously fulfilled routine of penances. The state of mind thus created found some relief in indulgences. The pressure of sin's everlasting detail is lifted when all the penalties due for sinful acts over a period of time are authoritatively expunged at once. Strictly, however, this referred to penalties and not to guilt; moreover, the behavior of the "pardoners," and the voices of sectaries and satirists, brought indulgences into contempt.

Despite a sad loss of discipline and growingly vocal distrust, there had come a marked enrichment of the literary materials available for the cure of souls, and this fact testifies to an improvement in practice within a limited range. Good clergymen have always realized the value of good reading in the guidance of souls. John Pecham's effort to equip the priests to give spiritual instruction was followed and accompanied by the circulation of a great variety of laymen's books of spiritual self-improvement; and something similar was happening in many areas of the Continent. In this new attention to lay instruction lies the one great redeeming feature of the situation.

Perhaps by 1500 about 50 per cent of the townsfolk, and some other layfolk, had learned to read. For these the Virtues and Vices, the Works of Mercy corporal and spiritual, the Commandments and the petitions of the Lord's Prayer, had been not only schematized but also vividly and clearly interpreted. Many others had caught from sermons and from the mystery and miracle plays essential fragments, at least, of this teaching. The revival of lay literacy, lost since the fifth century, opened the way to a new appropriation of neglected elements of Christianity. There was great promise in this; but the promise went largely unfulfilled in the Middle Ages, and has been only incompletely realized in modern Christianity. Laymen were now invited not only to learn, but to share with one another, the great concerns of the soul. August Hardeland has illustrated, but for the late medieval period inadequately, the continuing use of the New Testament principle of fraternal correction. Gerson taught that we must all, under peril of mortal sin, correct our neighbor when he does wrong. Mutual edification has a recognized place before the Reformation in which it was to receive fresh expression. In some of the pastoral manuals we have referred to there appears a tendency toward the revival of these functions of New Testament Christianity. (See above p. 85.) In Caxton's *Arte and Crafte to Knowe Well to Dye* is the suggestion that a man should choose in good time "a fellow and true friend devout and commendable," who will attend him and assist his soul at the approach of death. All the booklets of this class were manuals intended not for private reading but for the bedside ministry of "a fellow and true friend." This illustrates one aspect of what Luther meant by the priesthood of all Christians.

To say that every pastor should make haste to know the medieval books of pastoral theology, would be to prescribe the impossible. Yet any pastor or layman who will make the acquaintance of these manuals will find the efforts of his medieval predecessors in the cure of souls not only fascinating but inspiring and suggestive. A renewed interest in these books might serve a useful purpose in calling attention to the sharp distinction between the Vices and the Virtues—on which distinction we see a menacing confusion in much contemporary literature. They would also acquaint laymen with the ways in which pre-Reformation lay Christianity functioned at its best. The modern literature of pastoral theology is abundant and varied, but it might be difficult to find in it much that is comparable in vividness, simplicity and directness with these unpretentious compositions of the late Middle Ages.

Chapter VIII

THE CURE OF SOULS IN LUTHERANISM

I

IN MATTERS concerning the cure of souls the German Reformation had its inception. Luther was by no means the first to denounce indulgences, nor was he more emphatic than his predecessors. John Wyclif in his *Trialogus* (1382) called it blasphemy for Urban VI to pretend to grant indulgences for the crusade against his Avignon rival. John Huss, who had once spent his last coin to buy an indulgence, revolted from the similar policy of John XXIII, and boldly denounced it in Prague, June 7, 1412, with such effect that the aroused people and their leaders publicly burned the bull in which the indulgence was authorized. But Wyclif's bones, and Huss's living body, were burned for other heresies, and no general movement resulted from their teaching. By 1517 the situation had changed, and revolt could no longer be suppressed. That momentous invention, the printing press, provided the Reformer with a European public and continued for half a century to serve Protestant propaganda, to the disadvantage of the Roman Catholics whose books were in little demand.

The Ninety-five Theses which Luther posted on All Saints' Eve, 1517, began with these two propositions:

1. Our Lord Jesus Christ when he said "Repent" [*poenitentiam agite*] willed that the whole life of believers should be repentance.
2. This word cannot be understood as referring to sacramental penance, that is, confession and satisfaction, which is performed in the ministration of priests.

With these words was launched a controversy that shook Western Europe to its foundations. Their author knew well that his Theses, or *Disputation of the Power and Efficacy of Indulgences*, would prove

163

startling: for that reason he had long withheld the utterance. The circumstances of the indulgence sale then being promoted were peculiarly offensive to the moral sense—more so, perhaps, than Luther fully knew. What aroused him was that simple people were being deceived; they were led to believe that if they bought indulgence certificates they could be sure of salvation, and that when the coin clinked in the box the souls of their loved ones in purgatory flew up to heaven. Luther's statement of this is confirmed by hearers of the preaching of Friar John Tetzel, the indulgence salesman. A popular jingle parodied this selling talk:

> Sobald der Pfennig im Kasten klingt,
> Die Seele aus dem Fegfeuer springt.
>
> (When in the chest the penny rings,
> The soul from purgatory springs.)

Other fantastic claims were made, couched in the typical language of the quack advertiser, and calculated to attract the unwary. Like the pardoners of the fourteenth century, Tetzel no doubt made unauthorized exaggerations. Yet he was fully authorized by his employer, Albert, Archbishop of Mainz, to commend four principal graces attached to the indulgence, of which the first was "the plenary remission of all sins": By this remission the favor of God would be secured and the pains of purgatory avoided. In a letter Luther sent, with a copy of his Theses, to the archbishop, he pleads for the withdrawal of these instructions:

I grieve over the utterly false notions the people have conceived . . . unhappy souls. . . . O good God! I could keep silence no longer. . . . Works of piety and love are infinitely better than indulgences. . . . Christ never commanded that indulgences be preached, but he emphatically commanded that the Gospel be preached.

What, precisely, did Luther mean by the opening statements of his Theses? The question would not have embarrassed him, for he was not merely acting on impulse but from thought and experience, even though in some respects he was still feeling his way. He had passed through a deep personal conflict over repentance and justification, and had reached some lasting convictions. One who had counseled him in his inward distress had been his monastic senior, John Staupitz. In the letter that Luther wrote to Staupitz on Trinity Sunday 1518, we find a good deal of light upon our question. Here he states his interpretation of the passage cited in the first of the Theses (Matthew 4:17), and explains how he has reached it. He reminds Dr. Staupitz of a former conversation on the meaning of *poenitentia*, in which the senior monk had spoken "as with a voice from heaven" declaring that true penance must begin in love of righteousness and love of God. This, however, is only the beginning of it; repentance would thus be a lifetime matter. Awakened by this discourse, Luther had searched the Scripture, especially dwelling upon the passage in Matthew 4. The Greek word *metanoeite* is here represented in the Vulgate by *poenitentiam agite*, usually taken to mean "do penance." Luther had found that *metanoia* meant "coming to one's senses"; it involves "a change in our heart and our love" in response to God's grace. From being a word of bitterness, *poenitentia* had become to him a sweet and pleasing one. Going further, he had come to regard the word as including within its meaning not only the change but also the changing and transforming agency of God's grace. The prevalent exposition of penance, which in neglect of the Greek original took *poenitentiam agere* to indicate not an inner change but outward actions, he had come to regard as false. This thought was "boiling in his mind" when "suddenly new trumpets of indulgences and bugles of remissions began to peal and to bray all about us," and attention was drawn not even to satisfaction, the poorest part of penance, but to the remission of that part. Then, says Luther, "I determined to enter a moderate dissent." He thus interprets his protest as not against true penance (*poenitentia*) but against substituting for true penance the mere remission of a secondary element of it. The primary matter, a heartfelt penitence, was being quite lost sight of.

Shortly before writing this letter Luther had publicly explained the purpose of the Theses in a tract called *Resolutions of the Disputation on the Virtue of Indulgences*. One emphasis in this piece is his objection to the required recitation in the confessional of every offense, which is an impossible demand, and conducive to despair or delusion. Luther manifestly still hoped to obtain from the authorities redress of the features to which he objected. He said long afterwards that at this period he was a "raving papist." Yet he had freely suggested some restriction of the powers claimed for the pope by the champions of indulgences, and was increasingly stressing the Pauline doctrine of regeneration by the direct agency of grace.

This point of view led not only to his opposition to indulgences with their commercialization of grace. His emphasis upon an inner transformation brought into question the whole procedure in confession. Luther laid a double charge of perverse laxity in penance and oppressive rigidity in the hearing of confessions. Whereas indulgences meant an extreme relaxation of even the external demand of penance, the confessional method in which every sinful act and thought had to be recounted, seemed tyrannical and injurious. In 1520 he published his *Confitendi ratio* (Method of Confessing), a Latin revision of a German tract that he had written in 1519. The remission of sins is here made to rest not on formal confession but on the goodness of God. Confession should first be to God, on whose love and promises the soul must rely. While sacramental confession may help against the great offenses, there is a large class of venial sins and temptations from which we cannot wholly escape, in which the confessional only worries without helping people. Not all secret sins of the heart need be confessed to a priest, but only those clearly purposed against God's commandments.

Luther expressly rejects the Lateran canon of Innocent III, with its demand for a total confession once a year. An exhaustive confession is, in fact, a sheer impossibility. The decretal is unacceptable unless it is made to apply only to those sins of which a man is accused by others or by his conscience—a "right" conscience, not perverted by traditions. Luther would sweep away all hateful and wearisome catalogues of distinctions "of sins against the virtues, sins of the five senses, sins against the Beatitudes," etc., and "the troublesome business of 'circumstances.'"

We have seen in a more favorable light the early attempts to discriminate carefully the nature of the offense in relation to the person and his circumstances. Luther, who had much experience of the confessional both as priest and as confessant, had revolted against the multiplication and mechanical use of these distinctions. The penitent is so troubled by the strain of recalling every minute point, that he is diverted from his desire for a better life, and when the confession is ended, glad not that he is absolved but that the "laborious nuisance" is over with. It is sufficient to follow the order of the Commandments; and here the Ninth and Tenth Commandments are excluded, since they deal with evil inclinations from which even good men never escape. In practice Luther finds that great offenses against the Commandments, and neglect toward a neighbor, are more leniently treated than mishaps in ritual or slight violations of the fasts. In this connection, he exclaims:

I am disgusted, wearied, shamed, distressed at the endless chaos of superstitions which has been inflicted upon this most salutary sacrament of confession by the ignorance of true theology, which has been its own tyrant ever since the time that men have been making its laws.

With Gerson, Luther favors occasionally partaking of the Eucharist without confession, "that a man may learn to trust in the mercy of God" rather than in his own diligence. This is not despising the sacrament or tempting God, if it is done to "accustom a troubled conscience to trust in God and not to tremble at the rustling of every falling leaf." Pointing, finally, to objectionable features of penance for offenses connected with marriage, he charges that the salutary sacrament of penance has become tyrannous and conducive to sin.

II

Luther took a continuing interest in the reform of the penitential discipline and lost no opportunity to assail the practice of confession in the Roman Church. In the *Babylonian Captivity* (1520), he cries out against the "tyranny" by which that Church's authorities "have utterly abolished the sacrament of penance." True contrition, necessary to this sacrament, really arises only with "a lively faith in the promises and threats of God," and where this is lacking the sacrament is vain. Moreover, it is intolerable to demand that we "frame a contrition for every sin." Here he writes emphatically:

Of private confession I am heartily in favor. . . . It is a cure without an equal for distressed consciences. For when we have laid bare our conscience to our brother and privately made known to him the evil that lurked within, we receive from our brother's lips the word of comfort spoken by God himself; and if we accept it in faith, we find peace in the mercy of God speaking to us through our brother.

In this context, decrying the "despotism and extortion of the pontiffs" in reserved cases (cases in which absolution could be granted only by the pope or at his authorization) Luther interprets Matthew 18:15-20 as a unitary injunction "to each and every Christian." The binding and loosing passage of verse 18 had regularly been associated with the Apostles, but Luther would regard it as an authorization to all Christians to hear confessions and absolve.

In Luther's theology this is to be associated with his doctrine of the common priesthood shared by all Christians, whereby we pray for others and share with them our spiritual gifts. Christ is where two or three are gathered in His name, and he who has sought pardon and amended his ways before any brother, is truly absolved: for Christ has given to every believer power to absolve both open and secret sins. Luther would therefore have every Christian, man or woman, allowed to hear confessions and every sinner free to choose whom he will of his Christian neighbors to perform this service and absolve him in the word of Christ. All the minute particulars of a sin and its circumstances may be ignored. What matters is that a brother has sinned and needs help within the Christian brotherhood.

Failing to teach that true satisfaction is "the renewal of man's life," exponents of the old system "torture poor consciences to death" with scruples, and impose pilgrimages, scourgings and health-destroying fasts and vigils. Sins for which full satisfaction has not been made must be recited anew, in the erroneous belief that life is changed in the moment of confession, and that satisfactions must follow. It would be better to have absolution follow satisfaction, as in the ancient Church.

Also in 1520, Luther wrote a little manual on *The Ten Commandments, the Creed, and the Lord's Prayer* which shows the influence of the late medieval popular expositions. It is a very simple textbook of instruction for laymen, done in Luther's inimitable way. The Commandments help to diagnose the soul's sickness. Ten or a dozen offenses are listed in violation of each of Commandments i-viii. The ninth and tenth (which together correspond to the tenth in the enumeration of Reformed churches) are again excluded from the confessional. The Lord's Prayer is expounded in a series of prayers which utilize much medieval phraseology. There is nothing controversial in this devout little book. One of the prayers contains a petition for "all poor souls in purgatory" and another for the enlightenment of "all bishops, priests and clergy that are in authority." In the Eighth Sermon of the series preached at Wittenberg after his return from the Wartburg in 1522, he again speaks of the value of confession to a brother; but it is not to be made compulsory. "Yet," he says, "I would let no man take confession away from me, and I would not give it up for all the treasures of the world, since I know what comfort and strength it has given me." Those only who have struggled much against the devil, know its full value in resolving doubts; when we have firm faith it is sufficient to confess to God.

More controversial than these handbooks for laymen was his *Defense of All the Articles Wrongly Condemned in the Roman Bull* (1521) which constitutes a résumé of the early years of the controversy. Here he states that the "Three Parts of Penance" (contrition, confession and satisfaction) are not in Scripture or in the Fathers, and that no one can make satisfaction to God for daily sins. On the ground that "everything that is not of faith is sin" (Romans 14:23), contrition based on mere disgust of sin and fear of hell is hypocritical and a mere "gallows-contrition." Even attrition, "a half-gallows-repentance," the pope pretends to turn into salutary contrition by the power of the keys. Our sins cannot all be confessed: some are known only to God. We must rely not on a meticulously exhaustive confession, but on God's mercy. The effectual operation of faith is strongly asserted. There is no forgiveness in absolution without belief in its validity: with this belief, even though the absolution were uttered in jest, the sinner is surely absolved. Any priest can do what a bishop or pope can in confession; and just as a layman, a woman, or a child can in necessity baptize, so they can exercise the keys of penance.

III

In Luther's varied treatment of these themes, he viewed confession and absolution with a pastoral eye rather than from the point of view of ecclesiastical authority. His task is that of a deliverer of troubled consciences. In the *Resolutions* he stresses the necessity of absolution for the assurance of the penitent. But confession may be heard and absolution spoken by a lay Christian. Confession is recommended, but its regular performance may be undesirable if it implies reliance on one's own habitual acts rather than on the grace of God. Faith is the basis of contrition; in some of his writings it so absorbs contrition as almost to exclude its distinct role. The "renewal of man's life" by faith overshadows all mere acts of satisfaction.

In the *Formula Missae* of 1523 Luther clearly abandons the uniform requirement of confession. All that he demands is that notice of intention to commune be given to the minister, so that he may admit those only who show evidence of an understanding of faith, and may comfort and console those in trouble and temptation. Even this check on communicants is ordinarily to be required only once a year, and some may be "so understanding" that they need it only once in a lifetime, or not at all. Shameless offenders in conduct, such as adulterers, drunkards, gamblers, usurers and slanderers, are to be excluded from communion unless they give proof of repentance. Private confession, though not necessary, "is useful and not to be despised." After the Lord's Prayer the *Pax Domini* is used as "a public absolution of communicants from their sins, the Gospel voice announcing remission of sins, that unique and most worthy preparation for the Lord's table if it is apprehended by faith, not otherwise, and so from the mouth of Christ." In his exposition of Psalm 51 (1531) he stresses the point that particular sins are committed because of our sinful nature—a position which annuls the attempt to deal with separate sins listed and classified, and makes central the forgiveness of the sinner rather than his absolution from the sins.

In 1530 Luther wrote to the clergy assembled at Augsburg a statement of his position, and of his complaints against abuses. He charges them with having written on penance and confession without a word about faith, and with nothing of the "comfort of absolution" which is the main thing in confession.

For some years Luther still regarded penance as a sacrament, while he argued for the employment of lay confessors. By 1528, in a work on the Lord's Supper, he had changed his terminology and spoke of two sacraments only. He was not always consistent in this later position, however, and he always maintained a high regard for the ministry of confession. He consistently maintained the inviolability of the seal of confession, a fact which mitigates without removing his offense in connection with the bigamy of Philip of Hesse. Confession, he says in the *Table Talk*, "is made not to me but to Christ: since He keeps it secret, I keep it secret." Luther himself went to confession; he may have done so frequently before communion. This occurred more than once during his last public labor as a mediator between the Counts of Mansfeld.

IV

Luther was himself a guide of souls and a well-experienced confessor. At dawn on April 17, 1521, in Worms, he was at the bedside of Hans von Minckwitz, a dying knight, to hear his confession and administer the sacrament. He had gone to Worms the previous day, appeared before the Diet, and slept (?) in a crowded inn, in a room with two other men. In a few hours he was to make his second, and historic, appearance before the Diet. The knight lived to have Luther visit him ten days later, on the eve of his departure from Worms. In the extreme pressure of his situation Luther might have secured for Minckwitz the services of another priest. But it was his habit to counsel the sick and dying. In 1527, during a visitation of the plague, he was faithful in attendance on the plague-stricken. He practiced what he wrote to John Hess of Breslau, that pastors should no more take flight from pestilence than from a neighbor whose house is burning, or from one fallen into a pit.

In Luther's *Table Talk* we have vivid stories that illustrate his ministry to the sick. "He conversed in a very friendly way" asking questions about the state of the sick man's body and soul. He commended to him Christian resolution and steadfast faith, and in reply to expressions of gratitude explained that this was his office and duty. In bidding farewell he would remind the patient that God was a gracious Father, and that Christ had wrought our reconciliation. Amid such exhortations he counseled a man suffering from dropsy to do as his physicians ordered, that God's blessing might not be hindered by his anxiety. A woman showing violent symptoms of psychosis was led by his prayers to confess her sin of pride, and to pray for divine help, whereupon she was soothed to rest: after a relapse, she was ultimately cured.

Many there were who consulted Luther when in perplexity or trouble, and we have numerous letters of advice or consolation from his pen. (Representative selections from these will be found in English in August Nebe's *Luther as Spiritual Adviser* and in *Luther Speaks* by a group of Lutheran ministers.) An early letter of this type was sent to George Spenlein, a former fellow student, who was undergoing an experience like his own (April 8, 1516). "I would fain know the condition of thy soul," says the young Luther, tenderly exhorting his school friend to abandon his own righteousness, find the consolation of Christ, and make the sins of others his own.

Among his later consultants were some of the young women who had left the nunneries, and had to meet new and unfamiliar situations. One whom he addresses (December 14, 1523) as "Decorous and dear Maiden Hannah" had asked his judgment on whether she should marry a certain suitor. Luther would be glad to be of use but cannot advise definitely without adequate knowledge. He commends her own view, however, that marriage should not be hindered by distinction of rank: "One human being is worthy of another, if they only delight in and love one another." To Elsa von Canitz, who on leaving the nunnery had come to Wittenberg, and later lived with an aunt and became melancholic, Luther wrote (August 22, 1527) inviting her to be a teacher of girls at Wittenberg. The devil has prompted her unhappy state of mind. "O my dear woman, do not let him terrify you." If you suffer from him here you will escape him hereafter. Christ and the prophets had hours of depression. "If you come we shall talk further of this matter." Two months earlier (June 10) he had written to another disconsolate "Elsa," the wife of his friend John Agricola. She had already been invited to Wittenberg for a vacation. He here briefly urges prayer, in which he will join, that God will strengthen her in body and soul. An undated subsequent letter to her husband resumes the topic. She is now at Wittenberg for Luther's psychiatric treatment, and this is a brief report. Her illness is of the mind rather than of the body, and her disease is not for the apothecaries. It will not be cured by the salves of Hippocrates but by the Word of God. Agricola himself could have consoled her, except that wives refuse encouragement from their husbands, supposing it to be biased by love. Luther confides to Agricola his impression that the wives of ministers think the Word of God is not for them but for their husbands only. Luther wrote many intimate letters to Agricola, revealing his own cares or bearing the burden of his friend's.

Another incident shows an insubordinate and perhaps alcoholic wife who was started off by her husband, Stephen Roth, from Zwickau to Wittenberg for Luther's treatment, but avoided his house. Luther wrote the husband a rather sharp letter: "Grace and peace in Christ, and authority over your wife. . . . Be a man" (April 12, 1528). Luther demanded of his own wife Katie co-operation rather than mere obedience. His references to her as "my Lord Katie" are merely pleasant persiflage.

Many of Luther's letters are to long-absent friends. On June 29, 1534, he wrote to John Rühel of Mansfeld who was related to him by marriage, in "heartfelt sorrow" over some affliction reported to him by Rühel's son. His letters to his own parents are filled with the consolation of faith. When his father grew ill, Luther sent a nephew to see whether he would come to be nursed in Luther's home, "which my Katie also with tears desires," and wrote a long and gracious letter of spiritual comfort and filial affection (February 15, 1530). A month before his mother's death he sent her a similar letter. "All your children and my Katie are praying for you." Luther often wrote letters to the bereaved. Citing some of these, Hardeland remarks: "His letters of consolation [Trostbriefe] are true pearls in the copious mass of his correspondence." This writer regards Luther's gift of consolation as "a peculiar charisma of the Reformer." Nor did he fail to live by his own advice. When death struck his home, faith was victorious over grief. At the deathbed of his beloved daughter Magdalena, aged thirteen, he was the most effective of spiritual advisers. "I rejoice in the spirit, but sorrow in the flesh," he said, when she was gone.

Former monks as well as nuns contemplating marriage sought his advice. One of these was Wolfgang Reissenbusch, who had become a schoolmaster. Luther's reply was written March 27, 1525. Luther had opposed vows of celibacy; his own marriage was to follow on June 13. He advises his correspondent that the former vow of chastity should not be an obstacle to his marriage, since "we are made for marriage" and "chastity is not in our power." In Scripture marriage is represented to be God's ordinance; a vow against it contrary to God's Word. Furthermore, "it would be a fine, noble example if you married," encouraging to others in like case.

Grave decisions involving exposure to persecution or other personal risk had to be taken by many in the Reformation. By authority of Albert of Mainz many adherents of Luther were imprisoned at Miltenberg, in October, 1523, and some, apparently, were put to death. In the February following, Luther wrote to the prisoners and published a long letter of consolation and spiritual counsel, at the same time sending (February 14, 1524) a reproachful admonition to Albert. It is "a proud and blessed consolation," he tells the imprisoned evangelicals, to suffer for God's Word and for God's sake. They ought rather to pity their enemies than contemplate revenge upon them. True revenge is to thank God for suffering for His Word. He quotes "from the mouths of babes and sucklings" (Psalm 8:2) on the triumph of weak submissiveness over the devil's violence. They should pray for courage to speak of God's Word even though this is prohibited. He has taken upon himself to write because they are persecuted, much to his regret, as "Lutherans": "they slander God's Word by giving it my name." But they will not overthrow Luther and the Lutheran people.

The issue of the Christian and military service called forth in 1526 a tract from Luther, *Whether Soldiers too Can Be Saved*. About the end of that year he sent a copy of it with a personal letter to Assa von Kram, a soldier and counselor of the Duke of Brunswick-Lüneberg, whose earlier long conversation on points of conscience had given origin to the book. Luther believes that in certain circumstances a Christian's duty might be to fight in war, and states that he has written the book for the instruction of the soldier's conscience. In accordance with Deuteronomy 28:25, a bad conscience makes men cowardly. To another military officer, Christopher Jörger in Vienna, the point of conscience was attendance at Roman Catholic worship, unavoidable in his situation. This nobleman had been, we know, a protector of Protestants in some Austrian localities, and was a convinced Lutheran. Luther advises him no longer to live in such a way that his conscience is always biting and lashing him, but to leave the service of a king who in this respect is the devil's servant (January 1, 1533). After a two-year delay, Jörger took this advice.

Most of Luther's letters to those in temptation make use of his own early experience. Barbara Lisskirchen, a sister of his friend Jerome Weller, fell into great distress over predestination. "I myself," wrote Luther to her, "was brought to the verge of eternal death in this hospital. . . . I will tell you how God helped me." The devil prompts us to search out what is too high for us. Dwell rather on the thought of Christ. If you believe in him, you are called and predestinated. . . . But "it takes a struggle" to repel evil thoughts and keep before us the image of Christ (April 30, 1531).

The Christian life is strenuous, but Luther will not have it gloomy. We must recognize the devil's devices in melancholy thoughts, and counter them with innocent delights. Music is a God-given means of arousing gladness. When the devil makes you sad, say: "Away with you, devil. I must now sing and play to my Lord Christ." "Music is the best cordial to a person in sadness," he wrote; "it soothes, quickens and refreshes the heart." And again: "Satan is a great enemy of music. It is a good antidote against temptation and evil thoughts." John Walther, the musician with whom he co-operated, is quoted as testifying that he spent many delightful hours singing with Luther, who so enjoyed it that he could never get enough. He knew well how to utilize in small, intimate groups singing and the (scriptural) harp as means of spiritual refreshment and soul healing.

The attention given by eminent and busy men to the personal problems of others is often surprising. Luther exhibits human warmth and reality in these matters, the product of his own vivid experience and emotional force. We are struck by his deep and unwavering convictions, and by the unprofessional and casual way in which he applies them in the guidance of souls. He writes not as one conscious of superior attainment, or as the representative of a priestly caste, but as a sinful and tempted Christian who is glad to bring such spiritual remedies as he has learned from Scripture and experience to the aid of those who ask, or need, his brotherly help.

V

In the *Small Catechism* of 1529 Luther gives a short model form for confession: "How the simple folk should be taught to confess." We are to confess our sins to God, including, by implication, those we do not recognize. The Ten Commandments are to form the scheme for this. But to the priest, a very brief statement is suggested. The confessions of a servant and of a master or mistress, are used as examples. The former confesses that he has angered his master and prompted him to swear, neglected his work and caused damage, been sullen to his wife and sworn at her. The master states that he has failed to train his family to the glory of God, spoken profane or unchaste words, injured or cheated his neighbor, etc. If sins are forgotten, we are not to confess invented ones. Absolution, says Luther here, is bestowed by God himself—and to be so received, believingly. The words used in absolution are:

And by the command of the Lord Jesus Christ, I forgive thy sins, in the name of the Father and of the Son and of the Holy Ghost. Amen. Go in peace.

Those who are specially troubled in conscience, or grieved or tempted, the confessor will comfort.

The Lutheran confessions of faith reflect Luther's main emphases on confession and absolution. The Torgau Articles of 1530 contain a section on confession in which these views are in fact briefly summarized. In the *Augsburg Confession* (1530) three articles are devoted to these topics (xi, xii, xxv). The signers profess that they continue to practice confession and absolution, ordinarily in preparation for communion, but without requiring the enumeration of all sins: for in that case consciences would never find peace. Repentance (*Busse*) consists of contrition, or terrors smiting the conscience because of sin, and faith (which springs from the Gospel and the absolution) that the sins are forgiven. The people are taught to prize absolution as the voice of God and a great consolation to anxious consciences. Chrysostom is quoted as favoring confession to God rather than to man, and Gratian is cited as authority for the view that confession is of human, not divine, law: "Nevertheless, because of the great benefit of absolution, and because it is otherwise useful to the conscience, confession is retained among us." The "benefit of absolution" is prized for its importance in the reconstruction of personality: the implied reference to the supernatural realm is not such as to exalt the officiant as the bearer of divine pardon.

In the *Apology for the Augsburg Confession*, Melanchthon, who in *Loci communes* (1521) had already written to the same effect, supports these positions against the demand of the opposing theologians that Innocent III's canon on penance (Lateran Council, 1215, canon xxi)

be restored. The benefit of absolution is that Christians believe remission of sins to be "freely granted for Christ's sake." The fixed time
for this required in the canon has no authority, but it is alleged that
"most men in our churches use the sacraments, absolution and the
Lord's Supper, often in the year." The enumeration of sins is not required by divine law, and is abandoned in order not to ensnare consciences as has been done in the past. That faith is a part of repentance
is reaffirmed; and it is pointed out that the old method of detailed
interrogatories in confession has led to confusion. The doctrine of
penance has become "a doctrine of despair," while the Lutheran teaching is "more healthful to consciences." Absolution is retained "as being
the word of God which by divine authority the power of the keys pronounces upon each," and again: "as the voice of God remitting sins and
consoling consciences." The confession commanded in James 5:16 is a
mutual one, not the private enumeration of sins to a priest. Canonical
satisfactions are condemned: scriptural repentance implies newness of
life and entails the good works that are the fruits of this renewal.

The early Lutheran pastor counseled and absolved his parishioners
privately, but he was not encouraged to carry this ministry to homes
where his counsels were unwelcome. Bugenhagen's *Kirchenordnung* for
Brunswick (1528) advises against visiting the sick without request, and
the Wittenberg *Kirchenordnung* of 1533 forbids this. Similar regulations occur elsewhere. Olavus Petri's Swedish *Church Manual* (1529),
which has been rendered into English with an introduction by O. V.
Anderson, contains, however, an extended form for the visitation of the
sick. Here a long prayer of confession is recited by the sick man, and
the minister is instructed to "cheer and comfort him in this manner:
Dear brother (sister) as you have now made your confession before God
and me, I declare unto you (in accordance with God's command) the
full forgiveness of your sins." An address of exhortation and comfort
follows; the Lord's Supper is administered, after which there are prayers
for the recovery of the sick person and another exhortation beginning:
"Do not worry about anything but hold fast to Christ." In this manual
there is also a form "for ministering to those about to be executed,"
marked by carefully chosen expressions of consolation and admonition
and including a direction for "inquiry if his sins cause him any concern,
and if he has anything unsettled with anyone." For some informing
pages on "confession in the Swedish Lutheran Church" the reader is
referred to the article by Granger E. Westberg cited below, p. 347.

VI

The private cure of souls was actively pursued, and frequently discussed, by Luther's early followers. Hardeland explains in this connection the work of Jerome Weller (d. 1572) and Erasmus Sarcerius (d. 1559), the former stressing the comfort of the tempted, the latter seeking to strengthen church discipline. Handbooks for pastoral use, as in the Middle Ages, formed a special group of writings. The early ones were *Sterbebüchlein*, for the ministry to the sick and the dying. John Bugenhagen (1527), Urbanus Regius (1529) and Friedrich Myconius (1540) are among the more prominent of the writers of these. The anxieties of the dying are three, says Regius: sin, death and hell. "Let the sick man not think only of his sins: direct him to hold the crucified Christ alone before his eyes, and to fill his heart completely with Christ." For Protestantism the earliest piece of writing directly on the pastoral office was Zwingli's sermon, *The Pastor* (1524), which will call for notice in our next chapter. More formal treatises began to appear. Köstlin cites, but does not describe, a Lutheran work of 1537, *The Pastoral Office Cleansed of Superstition* . . . by Gerhard Lorich.

The most outstanding of such works came from the pen of the Strasbourg Reformer, Martin Bucer (Butzer [d. 1551]). His *On the True Cure of Souls* appeared in 1538 in German and Latin versions.[1] Historically, Bucer holds a position between the Lutherans and the Reformed. Although he probably exercised a greater influence upon the latter than upon the former, the fact that through the Wittenberg Concord of 1536 he and his South German followers became a part of the Lutheran unity, makes it preferable to refer to his work in the present chapter. In the book he classified himself among those called Lutherans. Besides, his influence was felt in the Lutheran Pietism of a later age, not least in its concern for the cure of souls.

Bucer rests his treatment upon the authority of Scripture. He provides a chain of well-selected passages with each section, and develops his argument with these in view. From Acts 4:32 and Ephesians 4:4, 15-16, he argues that we owe one another mutual care in things of the body

[1] I have used the Latin text contained in Bucer's *Scripta Anglicana*. The numbers inserted in parentheses refer to pages in this work. Köstlin has quoted the German (*Von der wahren Seelsorge*) at some length; Hardeland, briefly, and Courvoisier, amply, have analyzed the book, using the German version, which I was able to consult only after writing these pages.

as well as of the spirit (269). The passage of which he makes most fruit-ful use is Ezekiel 34:16:

> I will seek that which was lost, and bring again that which was driven away, and will bind up that which was broken, and will strengthen that which was sick: but I will destroy the fat and the strong; I will feed them with judgment.

So reads the American Revised version. But Bucer uses a text which has instead of "I will destroy," *conservabo*—"I will preserve." (The Vulgate rendering is similar, as are some modern translations.) This verse furnishes the scheme for his discussion of a fivefold ministry in the cure of souls: to draw to Christ those who are alienated; to lead back those who have been drawn away; to secure amendment of life in those who fall into sin; to strengthen weak and sickly Christians; to preserve Christians who are whole and strong, and urge them forward in all good (293 f.).

We need not here discuss Bucer's view of the functions and election of presbyters and bishops, and his high requirements for the ministers as *curatores animarum*. Incidentally, he argues that the marriage of ministers is a valuable aid in their pastoral work. In accordance with his well-known ecumenical outlook, he interprets the phrase "seek that which was lost" as authorizing not only a ministry to the baptized and negligent but also a mission to those "alienated from Christ our Lord by birth and education"—Jews, Turks and other races of mankind. This mission, however, is primarily the task of Christian rulers. Yet he holds that "no one can be forced to Christ against his will," and interprets the *compelle intrare* passage (Luke 14:23), cited by Augustine, as en-joining the use of spiritual, not as Augustine held, physical, compulsion. When magistrates and people have failed to seek the lost sheep, the presbyters must be diligent to seek them (301).

Those who have been scattered after being members of the "flock and fold" may be either not wholly alienated, or else, never sincere. Since we cannot at once discern the difference, we are to seek to reclaim all, leav-ing no means untried, until with great rejoicing we carry them on our shoulders back to the communion of Christ (302 f.). The "broken" in Ezekiel are those within the Christian community who are torn and wounded and inwardly suffering from their sins of body and mind. To whom, Bucer asks, belongs the duty of tending and healing them? Primarily, he answers, to all Christians. Every Christian is to exercise toward his neighbor, at the direction of the pastors, this "binding up" of the wounded. But the task devolves especially upon those ordained to the cure of souls and the medicine of sins (304 f.). The word *elegzein* (tell) in Matthew 18:15, in the sense "show clearly to another," indicates a frank revealing of sins. This is necessary that the sinner may profit by his penitence: he must be led to say: "I have sinned; I seek pardon; I will amend." Then is the wound bound up. As Paul directed in the case of the Corinthian offender, great gentleness and charity are required in the exposure of sinners. Nathan, having brought David to repentance, consoled him with the pardon of God. "For the health and life of the inner man consists in a true and living faith in the mercy of God and a sure trust in the remission of sins" (305 f.).

Some sins, however, require severe measures. Bucer goes briefly over incidents in the early Church, where faithful bishops required such discipline. He has in mind here a system of public penance for grave offenses, which he seeks to revive. Seven years earlier, he and his Strasbourg associates had tried to establish such a discipline, in which twenty-one elected lay officers (*Kirchenpfleger*) were to assist; but they were made responsible to the magistrates, and the outcome was disappointing. This book was written in the year in which Farel and Calvin were obliged to leave Geneva when they insisted on the exclusion of scandalous offenders from communion. To Bucer as well, communion in the Church was not for those who lived scandalously. For the Church as well as its members, discipline was a requisite of health. The discipline should be in accord with Scripture, and, as in the early Church, it must contain where necessary public exposure, humiliation and repentance. He points to abuses in medieval penance, ending in its "perversion" (317). The "satisfactions" he demands are not the basis of remission, which is by the blood of Christ alone; but they are medicinal in that they tend to make men avoid sinning and relapsing into sin. If we could revive this discipline of the ancient Church, the children of God would flee from sin and detest it. True penance "is not satisfaction for past sins, but medicine against those of the present and future," and it should be completed before readmission to communion (319 ff.). Bucer labors at length here to defend his views against numerous objections (319-35).

He then takes up his fourth topic, "how the weak may be made strong." Citing various weaknesses of Christians (these include reliance upon "ceremonies" in worship), he prescribes remedies. He would use more effectively the exercises of public worship so as to prompt eagerness and ardor in the Christian life. Special teachings appropriate to each type of weak Christian are indicated; disputation is to be avoided, and magistrates are enjoined to secure to the Church a diligent ministry (335 ff.). The last class to be considered consists of the healthy members —*oves sanae et robustae*, who are to be guarded and fed. This is not the work of pastors alone, but of every member. Fathers of families, teachers, and especially magistrates should apply themselves to it. And the Christian life is not only to be maintained but to be enhanced, as St. Paul's prayers and exhortations testify. The work of edification should not be left to assemblies of the Church, but should proceed "publicly and from house to house" (Acts 20:20). There will be plenty of resistance, prompted by our corrupted nature, to the discipline of Christ. The Holy Spirit is not content with a general proclamation: a faithful teacher will not cease until he leads his pupils into all truth. He will follow up the public message in homes and with individual persons. Anyone who objects to this does not want the Holy Spirit to be the Church's patron and teacher. We ought to pray the Lord for such ministers, and, to the best of our ability promote this home and private ministry (340 ff.).

Bucer reverts to the importance of protecting of the flock from false members. A section is devoted to "the exclusion and separation of the he-goats" who mingle with the sheep and are persistently incorrigible. Without the discipline of excommunication no community exists. Those excluded are to be prayed for and helped when in need, but socially avoided. A discriminating discussion of obedience to Christ is added (350 ff.). It is not obedience to teachers, pontiffs or ministers. We do not want to open again a window to tyranny, but to fortify pious souls against this stratagem of Satan. The minister must ever hearken to the word of Christ, "Repent, for the kingdom of heaven is at hand."

While this book enlarges on some elements of little concern today, most of it is of lasting value for Protestantism. It is comparable, though not similar in detail, to Baxter's *Reformed Pastor*, and must be regarded as the outstanding early Protestant text on the subject. While it is as thoroughly biblical as any Reformation treatise, it sets the personal ministry clearly in the center, and calls forth the maximum activity of every Christian in behalf of his fellows and of the Kingdom of God.

Werner Bellardi has called attention to the probability that Bucer in his later years at Strasbourg instituted groups under the name Christian Fellowship (*Gemeinschaft*), recognizably similar to the later Pietist *collegia* or associations for mutual religious interchange. In 1692 a book appeared in Frankfort which purported to be a defense by Bucer of these associations, and to have been discovered in 1691 by a Strasbourg professor, John Schilter, a friend of Spener, the Pietist leader, who regarded it as authentic. Its publication at a time when Pietism was under attack might suggest forgery; but Bellardi points out that Bucer's name was not in good standing with the orthodox Lutherans, a fact that might rather have led to its suppression. References to it have haunted writers on Bucer and Spener. If it was a genuine memorandum of Bucer, it adds testimony to his eager interest in cultivating a voluntary mutual lay activity in the cure of souls. An interesting letter (quoted by Paul Grünberg) from John Marbach in Strasbourg to Bucer in England, who, unknown to the writer, was already dead, describes the meetings in the celebrated Nicholas Church; after catechetical exercises questions raised by laymen are referred to the ministers, who give very simply their opinions; and mutual exhortations follow (March 8, 1551).

VII

We must avoid any attempt to write the history of pastoral literature in Lutheranism. After the work of John Rivius (1548) the titles multiply. Nicholas Hemming, a Danish Lutheran, in his *Pastor* (1562) illustrates the concern for the cure of souls in the Danish Reformation. Hardeland's remark that he is related to Rivius as Sarcerius to Weller may suggest his emphasis upon a firm discipline of offenders in the interests of the Church's purity. E. H. Dunkley has pointed to the teaching of an earlier Danish Lutheran, Peder Laurensson, who at Malmö in the 1530's took a position on confession similar to that of Luther, favoring confession to well-qualified priests "or other sensible men" when one is disturbed about his spiritual state.

For later contributors to this literature the reader may consult Köstlin's *Die Lehre von der Seelsorge*, pp. 59 ff. Even in the confused period of the Thirty Years' War (1618-48) such writing did not wholly cease. John Valentin Andreae in 1619 published in vigorous German verse *The Good Life of an Honest Servant of God*, and in the same year his celebrated utopian work *Christianopolis*, both of which contain elements of pastoral guidance and discipline of evildoers. John Gerhard in his *Loci communes* (1610-29), Paul Tarnov in *The Sacred Ministry* (1624), and John Andrew Quenstedt in *Pastor's Ethics and Pastoral Instruction* (1678) indicate that the subject was not overlooked by the reigning theologians of the seventeenth century. These writers, however, view the cure of souls more narrowly than Bucer had done, and lay the emphasis on confession.

Though manuals were sufficiently abundant, the age of German scholastic orthodoxy and political disorder appears to have been one of decline in this as in other aspects of the Church's life. Authority in ecclesiastical matters was too largely in the hands of the "Christian prince," who often showed himself in a rather unchristian light, and the ministry was in no position to assert ecclesiastical discipline. The cure of souls was much neglected and largely confined to a limited amount of visitation and the rather mechanical practice of private confession, on the basis of the catechism, and with one of the many absolution forms locally used, for which a fee (the *Beichtpfennig*) was paid to the pastor. Tholuck points to various abuses and criticisms of this procedure. Critics revived a saying of Sarcerius: "The binding key is quite rusted away while the loosing key is in full operation."

With the rise of Pietism under the leadership of Philipp Jakob Spener (d. 1705) there came a notable revival of activity in this field. Spener and his followers combined, like Luther, attention to personal religion with a strong emphasis upon communion and the mutual priesthood of all Christians. He turned away from the scholastic refinements of theology to bring Christianity within the grasp of the laymen and the young, and to call forth an emotional commitment to the Gospel. He laid a new stress upon the necessity of regeneration as well as upon the continuous cultivation of the religious life. About 1670 he began to hold conferences for mutual edification in his study in Frankfort. The materials for discussion were provided by the Bible and a variety of devotional books, some of which were translations from English and other languages. The practice spread widely, and was attended by some manifestations of wayward enthusiasm which he was able in time largely to check. A feature of his *Pia Desideria (Pious Longings)* of 1675, often regarded as the foundation book of the Pietist movement, was the stress laid on the spiritual priesthood of all believers, and the need of group participation by laymen in Bible reading and other means of mutual edification. Christianity for Spener, as for Bucer, demanded the acceptance of responsibility, and the pursuit of holiness, on the part of all members. This applies, more expressly than in Bucer's *True Cure of Souls*, to the missionary extension of the Church. Spener once said in a sermon: "The obligation rests upon the whole Church to have care as to how the gospel shall be preached in the whole world." The call to laymen is developed in his dialogue or catechism entitled *The Spiritual Priest-hood Briefly Set Forth according to the Word of God* (1677). Here at the outset he defines the term of his title: it is the right bestowed by Christ on all believers by virtue of which they bring a suitable offering to God, and pray for and edify themselves and their neighbors. Thus all possess a triple ministry of sacrifice, prayer and the Word. The first involves yielding themselves to their Redeemer, body and soul, property, desires and passions. The second implies intercession for their brethren. By the third they are empowered to teach, exhort, rebuke and console others, not only in the family, but in groups assembled for religious reading and mutual exhortation. Albrecht Stumpff has emphasized Spener's view that every individual requires a unique approach, in accord-ance with his psychological constitution.

Spener freely criticizes the current Lutheran practice of private con-fession: in large churches it had become a superficial and meaningless procedure in which, he alleges, from ten to twenty are confessed in an hour! An oft-told incident gives point to this shocking statement. John Winckler, chief pastor in Hamburg, inquired of the Leipzig theological faculty whether, with thirty thousand souls to care for whom he did not personally know, he could regard himself rightfully as a pastor at all (1688). The ingenious theologians offered reassurance from the case of the Prophet Jonah, who ministered effectively to four times the number of Winckler's parishioners. "Who will believe," they ask, "that Jonah undertook special and individual care of each of his hearers?" The most that could ordinarily be done was the hurried hearing of confessions. Even at the best Spener felt that confession could easily be overvalued; yet it had possibilities of beneficial use, and although he considered its abolition, he could not bring himself to advocate this. In the *Pia Desideria* he expresses the wish that each earnest Christian should stand in confidential friendship with his pastor as his father-confessor, or with another understanding and enlightened Christian to whom he would render an account.

Spener stressed other means, however, for that "particular dealing with people" or "application to the individual" which he constantly urged upon pastors. He strongly believed in the value of private conversations, and made much use of the visitation of homes, and of the sick and con-valescent. For these visits he practiced and advised a thorough prepara-tion, including a selection of Scripture passages and nonscriptural readings. He favored a public discipline of penance, but without compulsion and without excommunication.

Spener's contribution to the cure of souls was mainly by way of stimulation, not of restraint. He succeeded in setting on foot a movement that elevated the layman in his religious status and taught him to contribute to others by fraternal counsel and *"aedificatio mutua,"* mutual upbuilding. He also evoked a new diligence on the part of many ministers. In his *Theologische Bedenken (Theological Considerations* [1700-02, with posthumous additions, 1711]) he appears, says Paul Grünberg, as "the father-confessor of a congregation spread over all Germany." "The sum of Christianity," says Spener in this work (II, 685), "is penitence *(Busse)*, faith, and a new obedience"; "true, inner, spiritual peace" follows from these.

Spener's published writings mount to well over one hundred titles. He has suffered from undue neglect by editors and translators. He was called upon to write many letters of advice, and left a great quantity of this material. What has been said here is too brief and slight to convey more than the most elementary conception of the fertility of his thought on the guidance of souls.

With variations of emphasis, the cure of souls was actively promoted by August Hermann Francke (d. 1727) and his Pietist associates of the generation after Spener, and by their awakened orthodox opponents such as Valentin Ernst Loescher, who favored the appointment of deacons to assist in the task. Francke's views were affected by his own intense experience of anxiety and conversion, which led him to regard a conversion experience preceded by an agony of conviction of sin as marking the distinction between the regenerate and the unregenerate. Many Lutheran ministers under the influence of Francke and the Halle Pietists made themselves very busy with personal interviews. It was a common practice for them to keep a "record book of souls" in which they noted what they said and learned in these conversations (Drews).

Count Nikolaus Ludwig von Zinzendorf (d. 1760) was nearer than Francke to Spener, who had blessed him in his childhood, and for whom he had a deep personal admiration. Through the Moravian Brotherhood, in whose organization, out of a refugee remnant of the Bohemian Unity of Brethren, he took the leading part, the principle of "mutual edification" received new and fruitful expression. The life of the early Moravians was marked by a close brotherly intercourse in prayer, song, instruction, and daily work. Under the oversight of the elders, the communities were organized into groups of married persons, of the widowed, of bachelors, of maidens and children, in which each member was to confide to the others the concerns of his soul. The isolation of the Brethren from secular communities, the authority among them of laymen of narrow education, with the relative absence of any intellectual check upon wayward emotionalism, set limits to the fruitfulness of their methods. Yet the movement released a remarkable spiritual power which sent its lay missionaries in one generation to the ends of the earth.

VIII

Hardeland has recited the views of Lutherans of the Age of Enlightenment and given some evidence of the methods used in the private cure of souls. Private confession remained in considerable favor, but there were critics and opponents. John Frederick Jacobi of Celle objected to the tax on time and strength involved ("my head began to swim"); it weakened him for preaching and communion. It passed out of use first, however, in the rural communities, not in the larger churches. It had been almost wholly abandoned before the nineteenth century revival. The period witnessed however a good deal of humane effort for individuals, especially in prisons. The concern over sin gave place to the advocacy of social virtues. Clerical rationalists taught that the sick should have their consciences soothed, and the anxious be relieved of unpleasant thoughts.

Unique in the originality of his pastoral ministry was John Frederick Oberlin (d. 1826) who for fifty-nine years labored at Waldbach, a village of the Ban de la Roche (Steinthal) in the Vosges. Following the advice of Philip Doddridge in *The Rise and Progress of Religion in the Soul*, Oberlin, when a student at Strasbourg, solemnly dedicated himself without reservation to God. His piety took a philanthropic direction, and he went about doing good in countless ways in his village and its environs. The building of roads, the procuring of modern implements of agriculture and the introduction of potato cultivation, he felt were needed Christian services to a community so retarded and poor that people went to church by turns using the small available stock of decent clothes. As he led them from destitution to comfort, he kept up a constant guidance of all individuals, employing a set of twenty rigorous rules of conduct which combined religion, thrift, sanitation and charity. He maintained for some years a special group, the "Christian Society," for prayer and religious conversation. He was very attentive to children, and on his visits to homes made a point of interviewing every child separately. Few pastors of the time combined as he did the eighteenth century social benevolence with evangelical religion and austere morality. His work resulted in a fundamental transformation of the whole district of his parish.

The struggle against Napoleon was attended and followed in Germany by a religious revival. In 1811 Schleiermacher, in a short plan for the reform of the study of theology, gave discriminating attention to different aspects of the cure of souls. This is the activity in which the pastor directly confronts individuals. Without it a church cannot continue to exist. It operates upon those who are as yet incompletely identified with the church. Where a member of a parish is prevented from participating in the common religious life, this "identity" is violated, and the task of the "clerical nursing" is to restore it, without harm to the "inner identity" of the patient. The lay Christian, however, has a part to play in this restoration. Especially where alienation from the church has occurred over issues of progress and reaction, a lay friend or acquaintance may helpfully step in. If it is a matter of fitness to communicate, the clergyman must be the *Seelsorger*. Schleiermacher recognizes mutual cure of souls as belonging in the general field of Christian life and morals, but declines to present a special theory for this.

A revival of private confession was soon apparent. In 1814 Philipp K. Marheineke in *Aphorisms for the Renewing of Church Life* spoke of it as "a conversation with God in the presence of the minister," and declared it essential for a sound church. He urged visitation of families, at least annually, and maintaining close contact with them. The aggressive reviver of Lutheranism, Klaus Harms of Kiel (d. 1855), included in the ironic antirationalistic Ninety-five Theses with which he celebrated the three hundredth anniversary of Luther's, the statements that conscience cannot forgive sins and that whereas in the sixteenth century forgiveness cost money we now do it ourselves for nothing. He favored the restoration of private confession, but only as part of a wide-reaching activity in the cure of souls. While he does not approve the visiting which consists of "fishing expeditions," he proposes (what some large American churches practice) a pastor not charged with preaching who would devote himself to those who stay away from church. He proposes that courses of training for this ministry be given in the universities. Harms himself desired to be a "psychic physician," and to have ministers qualified in "psychiatry." As a narrow literalist Harms has been called reactionary, but in the field of personal guidance he was among the most progressive.

Other staunch Lutherans concerned in this reform were the founder of the Order of Deaconesses, Theodor Fliedner (d. 1864), and the compassionate J. H. Wichern (d. 1881), founder of the "Rough House" who was looked to by thousands as their spiritual father. In his ministry to the poor in Hamburg, Wichern utilized a volunteer "visiting society" whose members brought to the needy both material and spiritual help. Wilhelm Loehe (d. 1872), well known in America for the missionaries he sent to Missouri and Iowa, at Neuendettelsau worked out a system of the cure of souls, and after long preparation, introduced private confession. Homer Reginald Greenholt says that in his Saturday hours of hearing confession he "opened a rich source of pastoral advice and consolation to his parishioners." He imposed penances where he felt they were required, and if they were refused by the offenders, communion was denied. His efficient organization of hospitals and his establishment and management of a notable foreign mission; even his occasional use of exorcism and his undertaking to visit the sick in his village thrice daily, indicate that Loehe was an unusual minister. Never wavering in his Lutheran teaching, he was tolerant of medieval usages, and in his worship reforms stands in a position comparable to that of Pusey.

IX

Early Lutheranism in America presents a picture of diversity. The pastors were few and the congregations scattered. It was Henry Melchior Muhlenberg (d. 1787) who was chiefly instrumental in its general organization, which began about 1742. Muhlenberg brought the ideals of Halle Pietism to his work and tried to institute a firm discipline. We find him, for example, on a visit to York, Pennsylvania, privately examining and hearing the confessions of the candidates for communion. At New Hanover an old couple failed to satisfy him because though professing humble penitence they showed by their lives little evidence of a "thorough change of heart." His journals are filled with incidents of spiritual guidance in conversations with those he met in his travels, and at the bedsides of the sick. He insisted too, in serious cases, on a public declaration of guilt before the altar of the church. He also brought from Halle an elementary knowledge of medicine, and in course of his active personal religious ministry he did not hesitate to prescribe physical remedies.

His Halle training had involved a psychological approach to the cure of souls, and he was firmly convinced that "a sick body produces a sick soul." The articles by Carl Schindler and John N. Ritter cited below bring to light the evidence for this, and furnish instances of his co-operation with qualified physicians, and his complaints of the incompetence of others. In one instance, he got a medical doctor to visit a woman who had been led to think herself bewitched, and by his diagnosis to deliver her from this delusion. Ritter suggests that Muhlenberg anticipated modern psychosomatic medicine in his recognition of the interaction of mind and body and in his concern for the bodily disorders of those under his spiritual care. The principle involved hardly differed, however, from that earlier expressed by many Puritans and current in the previous century. Frontier conditions challenged Muhlenberg to bring medical relief where he could, just as in England a lack of competent medical care led Wesley to undertake certain medical services. Medical knowledge and skill were very elementary in the eighteenth century, and an educated clergyman could invade the field without very great effort and without being thought a quack. Muhlenberg evidently had considerable medical information; actually physicians consulted him with respect. The psychosomatic idea was probably much more definitely applied by him than by William Perkins or David Dickson a century earlier, but it was not a new idea in his time—or even in theirs.

The principal founder of the Missouri Lutheran Synod, Carl Ferdinand Wilhelm Walther, came to America with Saxon refugees in 1839. He, too, was a disciple of Pietists, and familiar as a Leipzig student with the works of Spener and Francke, but he drew away from contemporary Pietism and was meticulously orthodox in his belief in the Lutheran formulas. A firm congregational discipline was established in this conservative branch of Lutheranism. On the basis of Matthew 18, excommunication was made an act of the congregation. Walther was a competent scholar. Among his writings is a laborious work entitled *American Lutheran Pastoral Theology* (1872). Written in German, it is an impressive monument to the devotion of an expatriated missionary to orthodox Lutheran authors of three centuries; as such it has considerable historical value. Walther quotes extensively from a great array of authorities, and affirms traditional positions. He warmly approves the Lutheran private confession and absolution, and defends the seal of confession. Like Loehe, he would like to revive the use of exorcism. In his discussion of the topic of brotherly correction he is indebted to Hartmann's *Pastorale evangelicum*.

The liberal Lutheran scholar, Samuel Simon Schmucker, well known in other denominations for his appeal for church unity (1836), was also the leader of a small group of ministers who in 1855 circulated in the General Synod a surprising reform proposal entitled *Definite Synodical Platform*. In this document private confession and absolution were rejected on the basis of the Schmalkald Articles of 1537 as against the Augsburg Confession. Schmucker afterwards regretted this ill-considered utterance, which obtained little support. It does not appear, however, that private confession was widely practiced in the General Synod. G. H. Gerberding in *The Lutheran Pastor* (1902) while favoring brotherly correction where it is truly brotherly, surrounds formal private confession with so many "ifs" that he seems unwilling to recommend it. He earnestly commends, instead, faithful visitation and "a confidential interview with each communicant every three months."

Another of the eminent figures in American Lutheranism is William Alfred Passavant (d. 1894), a native of Zelienople, Pennsylvania. He moved from the position of his master, Dr. Schmucker, to a conservative and denominational Lutheranism, and became a strong builder of the General Synod. After a distinguished pastorate in Pittsburgh he became the founder of numerous hospitals, orphanages and schools. Perhaps the chief inspirer of his philanthropic enterprises was the founder of the Lutheran Deaconess Order, Theodor Fliedner, whose House of Deaconesses at Kaiserswerth he visited in 1846, and whom he induced later to visit America. The deaconess movement has since spread throughout American Lutheranism, and has had marked success; the (Swedish American) Augustana Synod, for example, maintains a number of efficient hospitals with deaconesses as nurses. Passavant's life was motivated by a truly pastoral spirit and great Christian compassion.

X

We have now followed the main lines of Lutheran thought and practice in the cure of souls. Our examination leads to three generalizations. In the first place the Lutheran tradition reflects a free revision of medieval methods, particularly in the retention of the confessional in altered form. The modification is substantial in removing the compulsory requirement of confession, and in freeing the confessant from the necessity of a full enumeration of sins. There followed such a feeling of the relative unimportance of the practice that it often became a mechanical and hastily performed routine, or else lapsed altogether. Another consequence has been the improved possibility of making confession a searching and helpful personal conversation on the religious problems of the penitent. With devout pastors this end has undoubtedly been often achieved.

Secondly, the earnest pastor has usually devoted much time to the visitation of his parishioners, holding interviews in which he has sought the healing of souls and the quickening of religious devotion. The part played by books of devotion in this ministry would offer too large a subject to be admitted here. But the printing press was an ally of the Reformation in this, hardly less than in its controversial and strictly educational aspects. We should not forget that the ministry to families was an ideal of the medieval pastor; but he was generally ill-provided with the means of extending such a ministry by reading matter, and was dealing with a much less literate laity than his Protestant successor. At all periods the Lutheran pastor was expected to attend the sick, the dying, and prisoners, though these functions were performed with varying degrees of constancy.

What is potentially the most important phase of the Lutheran personal ministry has been the cultivation, as urged by Luther, Bucer and Spener, and widely practiced under the influence of Pietism, of the mutual cure of souls on the part of laymen. Each man was his brother's keeper in a spiritual fellowship. "*Seelsorge aller an allen*" (the care of all for the souls of all), aptly expresses this principle. This is the implementation of the doctrine of the spiritual priesthood of all Christians— a doctrine often erroneously interpreted in an individualistic sense. There are still undisclosed possibilities in the application of this principle in the Church, both in the direction of brotherly correction and of mutual enrichment. The principle of mutual guidance and spiritual stimulation is as old as the New Testament; in some sense, as old as religion. It rests upon the belief that the gifts of the Spirit move through the whole membership of the Church, and that, in no merely theoretic sense, all Christians are functioning members of one living body, exercising toward one another a spiritual or priestly office. Luther's vigorous assertion of the mutual priesthood, by virtue of which the gifts of God "flow from one to the other" and we "do to our neighbor as Christ does to us," was a highly significant reaffirmation of a neglected element in New Testament teaching, and a reinforcement of the mutual cure of souls. For this reason, as well as others, the Reformation doctrine of the priesthood of believers constitutes one of the most important aspects of the whole movement. Yet the doctrine has sometimes been inadequately prized, and curiously misconstrued, so that its full significance has not been realized. It still calls for wider and freer application than it has received. Only in the Pietist period did it come at length to full recognition, deeply affecting the guidance of souls, and the lives of individual lay Christians; and then it was associated with a far-reaching revival. In modern Protestantism mutual edification and correction are, needless to say, by no means confined to Lutheranism. That they are still cultivated in Lutheran church life is a fact well illustrated by the rules of membership of the Augustana Synod in which we read:

Members shall lead a Christian life in charity, humility, and peace, endeavoring through admonition, consolation and encouragement to edify one another in the faith.

Chapter IX

THE CURE OF SOULS IN THE CONTINENTAL
REFORMED CHURCHES

I

THE Reformation in German Switzerland began with Huldreich
Zwingli (1484-1531), who entered upon his duties as "People's
Priest" and chief preacher in Zurich, January 1, 1519. At Glarus and at
Einsiedeln earlier, he had taken a firm stand against the trade in mercenary soldiers that plagued his country, and against indulgences and
superstition. Not less than in Germany the reform in Switzerland was
concerned with abuses affecting the pastoral office; and one of Zwingli's
early writings was specifically designed for the guidance of pastors. In
Der Hirt (The Pastor), which appeared in March, 1524, we have the
earliest of Protestant treatments of the topic. It grew out of a sermon
delivered at the Zurich Disputation in January, 1523. Zwingli had been
asked to publish it by one of his hearers, Jakob Schurtanner, pastor of a
village in Appenzel. It has all the warmth that characterized Zwingli's
preaching, and is addressed with great directness to priests who are in
the crisis of deciding to follow his leadership along the novel path of
reform. The title was chosen, as indicated in the dedication to Schurtanner, with a reference to the *Shepherd* of Hermas; but the address
bears no resemblance to that imaginative classic. It is divided into two
parts; the first describing, from the language of the prophets and
apostles, the true shepherd of God's people; the second attacking the
"false prophets" in clerical office, who must be recognized, and corrected or else expelled.

Zwingli stresses the faithful preaching of repentance from the Scripture. But proclamation must be followed up by instruction and devoted
service to the people. The shepherd must be alert to prevent the sheep

192

that is healed from falling again into sickness. As the Spartans had their ephors, the Romans their tribunes, and the German towns have their guild masters, with authority to check the higher rulers, so God has provided pastors to stand on guard for his people. God's shepherds must in love do everything toward the increase and upbuilding of the flock. They must be on fire with love. In Matthew 19:29 Christ has promised them a great reward, but this is not a "bodily" one. It is the increase of the Church, and so far as this life is concerned such a reward only increases the pastor's care and solicitude.

In the second part, besides reciting abuses and charges against the papacy, Zwingli briefly sets forth his view of the local autonomy of churches. At the end he eloquently appeals to the good shepherds to be courageous and faithful, and to pray that the work God has given them may be fruitful in making known His name and Word, and bringing back the wandering sheep. He also exhorts the false shepherds, if they care anything for God or man, to turn to their neglected task, warning them by the punishment of the prophets of Baal.

This brief exhortation is a crisis document, and was probably effective toward securing the commitment of the Swiss parish priests to the Reformation. It is not a systematic treatise on the cure of souls, but it shows an ardent concern over this matter, and brings it into the foreground in the propaganda of reform. It was translated into English by John Vernon Sinonoys in the reign of Edward VI (1550).

Roger Ley in his Zurich dissertation has fully expounded Zwingli's concepts and practice with respect to church discipline. He holds that neither Wittenberg nor Geneva in this matter joined practice to theory, and that Zwingli in maturity departed from the proposals he had espoused in youth. With respect to the authority of church and government he wavered, increasingly acknowledging the competence of the state in church discipline. It should be borne in mind here, however, that Zwingli never thinks of the Swiss state as merely secular. The government is bound by the Word of God. Faced by the confusions of the year 1525, which saw the Peasant Revolt in Germany and the agitations of Anabaptists in Zurich and St. Gall, Zwingli justified and invited the aid of the state. In this year he wrote his *Advice on Excluding Adulterers and Usurers from the Lord's Supper*. Incidentally, Zwingli sets the maximum permissible interest on loans at 5 per cent: one who charges more is to be excluded from communion.

Since, in distinction from the situation of the early Church, contemporary governments recognize a responsibility to maintain Christianity, Zwingli approves state co-operation in the punishment of offenders. When the Church denies them the sacrament, the state excludes them from living and eating with the faithful. His object was the peaceful reform of Church and society. For the individual he had in mind a salutary discipline involving spiritual and secular penalties. The notion of "binding and loosing" lost weight in Zwingli's thought, says Dr. Ley: the measures taken in discipline no longer seemed "from above." The welfare of souls was not neglected; but "pedagogical and prophylactic points of view were predominant."

Various special regulations were enacted to give vigor to the discipline, particularly against adultery and prostitution. The Marriage Ordinance of May 10, 1525, written by Zwingli and promulgated by the Council of Zurich, sets up a court of six judges, meeting twice a week, to establish regularity in procedures and to handle offenses and complaints, such as had formerly occasioned expensive litigation in the bishop's court in Constance. Ministers are to exclude adulterers from the Christian community, and temporal penalties are left to the civil government. (English text in Jackson: *Selected Works*.)

Ley finds a new phase in Zwingli's handling of church discipline beginning in 1527, in connection with his controversy with Luther over the Eucharist. Referring now to the Eucharist as an "action of grace," he must forbid gross sinners from participation. This is "minor excommunication" which excludes from the Eucharist but not from all Christian society. Thus the discipline is definitely bound up with the sacrament. This excommunication is, however, confined to known and scandalous offenders: others are to be forgiven to "seventy times seven." He suggests that Paul in "Drive out the wicked person" (I Cor. 5:13) has in mind not excommunication but an amicable avoidance of the wrongdoer. In any case, excommunication is rare on the part of the Apostles. At this point Zwingli strongly opposed the Anabaptists. He deplored their frequent resort to this measure, of which we have (at most) only one example in St. Paul, and warned of the danger of Pharisaism and loss of charity. Against Roman Catholics he objected to the use of unbiblical terms such as "church power" and "coercion." Excommunication is not a power which God has "given away" to men. He also differed from his friend Oecolampadius of Basel who in 1526 introduced rules involving excommunication and three years later secured an ordinance which gave the Church a large measure of autonomy in discipline, with excommunication after repeated admonitions. The Basel experiment, sabotaged by the magistrates, was soon abandoned. Zwingli's more realistic adjustments may be criticized from the standpoint of a biblical theology, but through them some standard of church behavior was maintained until Bullinger improved the system.

Dr. Ley gives the distinct impression that Zwingli, experimenting with methods of discipline, gave decreasing attention to the more positive and scriptural aspects of the cure of souls. Zwingli's own treatment of the topic, as was unavoidable in the circumstances, is not systematic. His writings often betray the haste and superficiality forced upon him by the circumstances of his brief and active life. He himself lamented this defect, though he accepted it as a security against literary pride. One of his strongest statements of the hurried inadequacy of his work has reference to *The Pastor*. He never gave to its subject the rich and full treatment it deserved. He never ceased, however, to feel the importance of personal guidance for the anxious, and of the promotion of individual piety and the Christian virtues.

In this connection perhaps the most illuminating of his treatises is the long one *On True and False Religion* (1525). A man must "go down into himself"; he must probe the reasons for his acts, concealments, pretenses, dissimulations. He will find a slough of wickedness, and turn to God, begging for mercy. A new life then begins. Sin centers in self-love (*philautia*), which resists love of neighbor, and expresses itself in such impiety as a usurer endowing a priest. So sin as disease gives rise to sin as transgression of the law. The keys of binding and loosing are not in the hands of priests but in the Gospel itself. They were promised not to Peter alone, but to all who recognize Christ as Son of God. They set free the captive conscience. This is a matter of faith, not of an absolution formula: the sacraments do not remit sin.

The Christian is by grace a "new man." He does not escape sin, but he does not surrender to it. His old and his new nature are compared to the grafted fruit-bearing branches on the trunk of a wild pear. The trunk puts forth vicious growths, but they are constantly cut away. Indeed we may, like David, profit by the realization of our sins. But "he that is born of God keeps himself" (I John 5:18), watchfully resisting sin, tearfully repenting of it, and trusting in the atonement of Christ.

How does Zwingli treat the question of confession? Since it is God who forgives, confession should be to God only: the wound is shown to the Physician. If you do not fully know the Physician, not comprehending the grace of God in Christ, you are not forbidden to unburden your conscience to a wise counselor, a minister of the Word. He will pour wine and oil (the sharpness of repentance and the sweetness of grace) into the soul's wound. "Auricular confession is nothing but a consultation, in which we receive from him whom God has appointed . . . advice as to how we can secure peace of mind." Formal absolution without faith will help no more than saying to a fly "you are an elephant" will make it such.

Let us, therefore, confess frequently to the Lord, let us begin a new life frequently, and if there is anything not clear let us go frequently to a wise scholar who looks not at the pocket-book but at the conscience!

II

Henry Bullinger (d. 1575), Zwingli's able successor in the leadership of the Church of Zurich, prudently and gradually advanced the liberty of the Church, maintaining harmonious relations with the government. In 1541 he and his colleagues lent support to Farel in his struggle against the Libertine party in Neuchâtel, and exhorted the people to be reconciled to their pastor. The Second Helvetic Confession (1566) is from Bullinger's pen. It contains ample sections on repentance and confession (xiv) and on the office of the ministry (xviii). Repentance (poenitentia) is "the change of mind induced by the Word of the gospel and by the Holy Spirit, and received by true faith." Confession may be made to God alone, or in the general confession of the service. There is no need or warrant for auricular confession. If any one is overwhelmed by his sins and temptations, he may take counsel of a minister "or any other brother learned in the law of God." The power of the keys lies in the preaching of the Gospel. The penitent must diligently pursue a new life and prayerfully subdue his sins.

While the priesthood is common to all Christians, the ministry of the Word and sacraments is a special office. The minister's duties include teaching, preaching and the sacraments, comforting the faint-hearted, rebuking offenders, restoring the wanderers, raising the fallen, catechizing the ignorant, providing for the poor, visiting the sick and those entangled in temptation. A short statement on catechizing and visitation (xxv) requires instruction of children in the rudiments of the faith, the Commandments, the Creed, the Lord's Prayer, and the sacraments. Pastors are urged to visit the sick promptly, to pray with them and for them, and to take care that the dying "pass happily from this world."

Bullinger's writings abound in matetial illustrative of his great attention to the cure of souls. His celebrated *Decades* (1550), (five sets of ten sermons) covering the whole realm of theology, offer a great deal of such material. He stresses the disciplinary character of the semi-annual synods as corrective of negligence among ministers (v, 10). His doctrine of the priesthood of believers and its consequence in the mutual obligation of admonition and comfort, is hardly distinguishable from that of Bucer and, like his, grows out of Luther's teaching. As (lay) priests "we teach, admonish, exhort and comfort all our brethren," in accordance with Hebrews 3:13: "But exhort one another every day" (iv, 7). To leave all this to the ministers is shirking a Christian duty. Bullinger's treatment of the Holy Ghost stresses the title, "the Comforter" (iv, 8). His biographers have described his personal ministry. "From early morning till night his house stood open to everybody," wrote Carl Pestalozzi; "it was a free city and a city of refuge for the helpless of all sorts—for the poor and weak, for widows and orphans, for the oppressed and defeated, for all who needed counsel and help." With great patience and attention he listened while young and old opened their hearts and told him their most secret sorrows, confident alike of his silence and of his heartfelt participation in their needs. The many foreign refugees from persecution whom he aided materially and spiritually felt for him both gratitude and high admiration. He found time to visit the sick and dying, and when the plague struck Zurich he redoubled these efforts, and wrote a book on preparation for death (*Bericht der krancken*, 1538) in fifteen short chapters; it reflects the "consolations" of the ancients and the Art of Dying booklets, but chiefly enforces an evangelical and scriptural piety. Nor did he fail to attend prisoners and minister to those condemned to die. Pestalozzi sees in Bullinger "the living picture of an evangelical healer of souls (*Seelsorger*) in the fullest sense of the word, an inspiring example to his brother pastors and to many in later days."

III

"The office of a true and faithful minister is not only publicly to teach the people over whom he is ordained pastor, but as far as may be, to admonish, exhort, rebuke and console each one in particular." So wrote John Calvin in a section on Visitation of the Sick in his Liturgy. This is traditional and scriptural language, but Calvin gave to it rare emphasis in many utterances, and in the organization of the Church in Geneva. Jean Daniel Benoit, the expert on Calvin's work in the cure of souls, states boldly that the Geneva Reformer was more pastor than theologian, that, to be exact, he was a theologian in order to be a better pastor. In his whole reforming work he was a shepherd of souls.

The theological topic which lies closest to this pastoral interest is his doctrine of repentance. This has been closely analyzed by Hermann Strothmann in two studies (1909). With earlier writers, Strothmann observes a change in Calvin's presentation of repentance with the 1539 edition of the *Institutes*. If we look at the texts we find that in 1536, following Melanchthon, he treated *penitentia* as consisting of "mortification" and "vivification." The first is commonly called "contrition," the second is the consolation born of faith. In 1539 he thinks more than this is involved in vivification. Repentance now becomes "a spiritual regeneration, the end of which is that the image of God, which was obscured and so to speak effaced in us by the transgression of Adam, be restored." Strothmann points to the association (in 1539) by Calvin of words for "conversion" with words for "recovery," and the words have an ethical content. "Repentance is a process of moral transformation, of moral renewal."

It is needless to follow Calvin's interpreters into theological minutiae, or to show his relations to other Reformers on this point. When Luther said "all our life should be repentance" he did not use the word so broadly as Calvin does. It embraces the soul's progressive appropriation of the obedience, holiness and goodness that mark the restoration of man's lost or obscured image of God. Many would call it "sanctification": Calvin prefers to identify it with "regeneration."

Theologically, then, Calvin provides a limitless province for the cure of souls. He treats the medieval system of confession and penance in a manner closely similar to that of Luther. His objection to Scholastic doctrines of penitence begins with their stress upon the retrospect on sin rather than upon the transformation of repentance (*Institutes*, 1559, III, iv, 1); and he points to divergences between canonists and theologians. He charges against the old system that consciences have been tortured by its doctrine of contrition, and invariably driven either to despair or to pretense (IV, iv, 2-3). The obligation of annual secret confession to a priest, he treats with sarcastic disapproval. It was unheard of in the early Church. He quotes Chrysostom's second homily on the 50th Psalm: "Recite them [sins] to God, who heals them. Confess your sins upon your bed, that there your conscience may daily acknowledge your misdeeds." God is our physician, and the searcher of our hearts. But if the heart is penitent, one will also wish to confess before men, both in the ordinary public worship, and in special circumstances when public calamity has called attention to a common guilt.

Furthermore, the Scripture authorizes two kinds of private confession: to one another (James 5:16), with mutual advice and consolation; and to a neighbor whom we have injured, in order to reconcile him (Matthew 23:24). The former may be made to any member of the Church, but the best choice ordinarily will be the pastor, to whom this ministry is specially confided. Calvin interprets Matthew 16:19 and John 20:23 as authorizing ministers "to remit sins and absolve souls." The penitent should take advantage of this. But there is no general obligation to make confession in private. It is for those who cannot find relief otherwise from the anguish of guilt. And ministers must lay no yoke upon conscience in the matter. It is recommended, not required. Nor is anyone bound to enumerate all his sins in such confession. The penitent is the judge of what he should reveal for the entire consolation (*solidum consolationis fructum* III, iv, 12) of his soul; and this liberty is to be stoutly defended by faithful pastors. Private confession of the second kind is also strongly recommended; and where the injury has been done to the whole Church it becomes still more necessary. Calvin urges that the pastor hold an interview with each communicant before communion. In these three kinds of confession the power of the Keys is exercised to the benefit of offenders or of those distressed in conscience, of for peace between Christians. The minister, as Christ's ambassador, in public or private absolution authoritatively exercises this power—no slight consolation to those who are reconciled. The grace of the Gospel is thus "confirmed and sealed . . . in the minds of the faithful." We need not follow Calvin's attack upon compulsory auricular confession and its abuses. He believes it to be attended by great anxiety on the part of the confessant, whereas what he proposes has the security of Scripture warrant and imparts true comfort (III, iv, 1-23).

The organization of ministers and elders in Geneva has been often described. The discipline was watchfully applied to all citizens, all being regarded as candidates for the communion, which was to be guarded against contamination by the unworthy. The lay elders observed the conduct of persons and families in their own districts and co-operated with the ministers in acts of correction. The ministers met weekly to stimulate one another in teaching, and quarterly to correct one another's faults and exchange "brotherly admonitions." Provision was made for the visitation of the sick and of prisoners, and for the catechizing of children. These arrangements were adopted in 1541. The principle of *correptio fraterna* (II Thess. 2:15; Heb. 3:13) was specifically carried into the realm of political organization. In 1557 Calvin induced the magistrates who formed the Little Council to hold a quarterly secret session for the sole purpose of mutual correction in Christian charity— a "unique attempt" says James Mackinnon, "to apply the Christian spirit to the art of politics."

IV

Benoit is chiefly concerned with another aspect of Calvin's service in the *cura animarum.* Calvin is treated by him as "director of souls." For many Protestants this expression has objectionable connotations. It has been, especially in France since the seventeenth century, so exclusively associated with Roman Catholicism that Benoit has to defend its application to Calvin and other Reformed leaders. In his Strasbourg thesis *Spiritual Direction and Protestantism* (1940) this scholar quotes definitions of spiritual direction from some of its Roman Catholic masters (Fénelon, Jean Grou, etc.) that would describe the guidance of many a Protestant. According to Fénelon, spiritual direction occurs when one "takes an advice that tends to perfection," and Benoit interprets this as not necessarily meaning a prior decision to follow the advice. Sixteenth century Protestantism would not favor the word "perfection" here, but speak of growth in grace or an advance in the Christian life. That is not, however, our present concern. The Protestant hesitation over, or repudiation of the notion of "direction" is of course due to the fear of adopting a principle of *control* by a cleric that would be the negation of the common sixteenth century Protestant view. Yet it cannot be denied that Luther, Bucer, Calvin, Spener and countless other Protestants have written in quantity letters of "advice that tends" to Christian living, and often offered spiritual direction in that sense. Between them and most Roman Catholic directors there are, however, marked differences that should not be overlooked. The Protestant director does not claim so much of authority; nor seek to make permanent the relationship in which he gives counsel. He is a physician for a crisis who expects his patient to recover and normally to control his own health; he does not expect to continue in attendance, examining and prescribing for the patient with every visit, over an indefinite period.

These differences are not always apparent, it is true. In a crisis the Protestant may give his advice with an authority hardly less absolute than that of the Roman Catholic director. Calvin himself submitted, awe-stricken, to Farel's thundering injunction to join him in Geneva, with a feeling that in it "God had stretched forth His hand from on high." And Calvin, in some instances, continued through many years to exhort his correspondents to faithfulness and direct their consciences by the Word of God. Perhaps a more constant difference lies in the fact that the Protestant writer of letters of direction does not assume the position of sole guide, as is normally the case with Roman Catholics. And there is usually a relative absence of intimacy with respect to the state of the soul and its experiences.

For the historical inquirer spiritual letters have the advantage of supplying documentary evidence of the content of the advice given. We have referred to the epistolary guidance of Stoics and Fathers, of St. Bernhard, Luther and others. The element of personal guidance or "direction" abounds in Calvin's correspondence, as doubtless every reader of it has observed. Professor Benoit, in his *Calvin Director of Souls* (1947), has treated the subject comprehensively and with fine discrimination. With some aid from his valuable study, we shall here illustrate our brief reference to this subject by a few examples of the letters themselves.

Calvin wrote a good many letters of advice to eminent persons—kings and queens, great lords and ladies. In some of these his design is mainly to aid the cause of the Reformation, so that the personal element is secondary. Yet it is noteworthy that in almost all such letters there is an attempt to reach the conscience of the man, while suggesting the policy of the ruler. Thus, in writing to Sigismund Augustus, King of Poland (December 5, 1554), he disavows, as a minister of the Gospel, the intention of "mere compliment" and urges him to rise to the "heroic virtue" necessary to the restoration of God's "ruined Church." Two months later (February 13, 1555) he writes to the Polish prince, Nicholas Radziwill to the same purpose, exhorting the prince to surpass himself in zeal for the cause, and be a fellow worker with the king. King Sigismund replied favorably to Calvin, who sent him a fresh exhortation (December 24, 1555). Soon after the accession of Queen Elizabeth he addresses a letter in similar terms to William Cecil, afterwards Lord Burleigh: "If hitherto you have been timid, you may now make up for your deficiency by the ardor of your zeal." His letters to

Antoine de Bourbon, King of Navarre, include one of December 14, 1557, in which with many warm exhortations, he asks the king to read a book he had fourteen years earlier addressed to the German Estates: "Not that I desire to lay down rules for you, but because I am confident that you will not disdain to be instructed." He later implores Antoine to declare himself and become "God's standard-bearer," though by so doing he should incur opprobrium, as did the Son of God (June 8, 1558). These are the counsels not of a diplomat but of a prophet.

The Queen of Navarre, Jeanne d'Albret, in 1560 experienced a profound conversion that made of her a faithful adherent of the Reformation. Calvin wrote to her feelingly of the "inquietude happier than all delights" attendant upon conversion, urging her to complete self-dedication (January 16, 1561). When her inconstant husband, Antoine, yielded to other persuasions and allied himself with the opponents of Protestantism, Calvin wrote again to the queen. She has requested the prayers of the ministers of Geneva: they will not fail in this. The theme is courage and constancy: "Knowing in Whom we have believed, let us persevere." Antoine died of battle wounds in November, 1562, and on the following January 20 Calvin advised the queen regarding her government. Every knee should bow, says Calvin, "under the empire of Christ," and kings must especially do Him homage. Situated between states hostile to her, she must arm herself with the promises of God— and proceed prudently with reform.

Admiral Coligny and his wife, who when others weakened remained steadfast Protestants, received numerous messages of encouragement from Calvin. A good example is one sent to Madame de Coligny, September 24, 1561. He thanks God for her perseverance amid temptations, and commends to her the words and example of St. Paul: "forgetting those things that are behind . . . I press on." "I pray you, whatever happens, never be weary of employing yourself in the service of so good a Father." During her convalescence from an illness, and after Calvin himself had been similarly afflicted, he sent with a letter to her husband one to herself in which he refers to the spiritual uses of our diseases— medicines against worldly affections, and reminders that we should be prepared for death.

To the cultured French princess, Renée Duchess of Ferrara, Calvin wrote occasionally over a period of twenty-three years (October, 1541, to April, 1564). As the wife of an Italian conformist to the old system, Renée was not, after 1536, able to assert her sympathy with the Reformation, but after her husband's death (1559) she resided at Montargis in France and lent her support to the Reformed. After Calvin's death, Beza said that he had held her in "reverence." He was more patient with her during her years of compromise than might have been expected, knowing that it cost her "anguish"; but he encouraged her to "watch for every opportunity which God shall afford of making further progress." "On my part I will also pray Him"—so, typically, Calvin closes a letter of June 10, 1555—"that He may always have you in His holy keeping, increase you in knowledge, zeal and constancy, and in all good, that you may contribute more and more to his glory." In the later stage he commends her warmly as "a nursing mother to those poor persecuted brethren" who knew not where to go but to her castle: it has become "God's hostelry." Characteristically, in the same letter, he calls her attention to the duty of dealing firmly with a young man in her service who has dismissed his wife and taken a mistress, and further reminds her of a promise she had made to a certain old scholar to try to find a husband for his daughter (May 10, 1663).

Calvin had frequent correspondence for some years with Monsieur and Madame de Falais who in 1544 removed from Brabant to Cologne, in the service of Charles V, and were later in Geneva. Falais became alienated from Calvin over the banishment of Jerome Bolsec from Geneva at the end of 1551. To Madame de Falais he wrote (October 14, 1543) commending her piety and remarking that much exhortation would be superfluous, but hoping, as always, that the Lord would give her grace to go forward despite all hindrances. Sometime in the same year he wrote to her husband, encouraging him to think of his trials as "a passing tempest" from which God gives a safe retreat. Both letters close with prayerful commendations, or benedictions, in a tone almost liturgical—a common feature of his intimate letters.

V

In Calvin's correspondence there are numerous letters of consolation in bereavement. It fell to him to inform his friend Farel, shortly after their enforced separation in 1538, of his nephew's death from the plague in Basel (August 20, 1538). But the letter contains little beyond information of the circumstances. Calvin had provided a nurse, and had paid frequent visits to the youth's bedside, and prayed with him. In April, 1541, he wrote from Regensburg a long letter to a certain Monsieur de Richebourg, whose student son, Louis, and the boy's tutor,

Claude Ferey, both beloved by Calvin, had died of the plague in Calvin's house in Strasbourg, where they resided. The letter in many respects conforms to the ancient consolation type, but at the same time it is full of warm personal feeling. Near the beginning Calvin says he "will not take advantage of the common topics of consolation," but he swerves from that intention and actually employs most of the traditional topics, as if with memories of Cicero or Seneca or Plutarch. But the use of these is humanized by a sincere affection for the dead student and, as in the Church Fathers, illuminated by Christian faith. He tells the stricken father that the lad had been teachable and obedient, if at times a little unruly, and had acquired a true piety, and prompts him to find consolation in inward piety and recognition of the goodness and providence of God. The humanity of the letter appears where he draws a comparison between the impetuous and brilliant Louis and his more restrained and scholarly surviving brother, Charles, who remains a comfort to his father. Calvin, like Cicero, puts no stoical restraint upon natural grief, while he disapproves irrational mourning, in which he knows his correspondent will not indulge.

When a sister of de Falais died we have letters of the same date (November 20, 1546) to both de Falais and his wife. The former is a brief and gracious example of the consolation type with Christian coloring. God has been kind, he explains, in sparing the departed the sorrows and dangers of a longer life; and we shall meet her again. When the numerous family of William Budé, the eminent scholar, were bereaved of a brother (1547), Calvin who was acquainted with several members of the family, wrote to two of them a letter "for the whole household." He has heard of the victorious death of "your good brother and mine," and he takes occasion to urge them to the piety the deceased has shown. This is less a consolation than a moral exhortation, prompted by some concern lest they are losing ground spiritually. "The death of your brother is God's trumpet, whereby He would call you to serve Him alone." Calvin here seems hesitant to utter the sympathy he evidently feels, so anxious is he to point the way to a fuller devotion.

Calvin often had occasion to sustain by comforting letters those who had met defeat in the cause of reform. Such a letter was addressed to the doughty Lutheran, John Brentz, who at this time was inclining to Calvinism, on his enforced flight from Würtemberg to Basel when Charles V's *Interim* was applied in 1548. Calvin encourages the displaced minister to hope that God has yet some work for him to do;

what has happened is not bringing the Reformation to an end. God would not have carried the restoration of the Church so far "merely to have inspired a fallacious hope." The sad experience of John à Lasco, when, fleeing from Queen Mary in England, he and his followers were intolerantly forced to leave Denmark by sea amid the storms of winter, called forth a letter of warm sympathy (May, 1554). Calvin expresses "poignant sorrow," praise for the Polish Reformer's steadfastness, and shocked surprise at the inhumanity with which he has been treated. (The subsequent controversy of Brentz with à Lasco is referred to in Calvin's letters of 1557.)

During the persecutions of Henry II of France Calvin was in touch with the French Protestant churches, and wrote frequently to prisoners soon to die. He sometimes sent messengers to learn their spiritual and temporal condition, and sought to institute through political agencies measures for their release. Along with the ministers of Lausanne, Calvin was chaplain by letter to five Lausanne students from France, who were arrested near Lyons, held for a year in prison, and burnt at the stake there, May 16, 1553, despite the attempted intervention of Geneva and Berne. Calvin wrote to them first on June 10, 1552, to clarify some points of belief they had inquired about. There is a letter of March 7, 1553, expressing confidence in their firmness and praying that God may "by the consolation of His Spirit glorify Himself" in their continued constancy. On May 15, too late for them to receive the letter, he wrote again, very earnestly, "knowing that our heavenly Father gives you experience how great his consolations are." Their death was an affecting scene of courageous martyrdom. To five other young men imprisoned at Chambéry he writes (September 5, 1555) acknowledging that worldly means to deliver them may fail: "But God urges us to look higher." Let them repose in His fatherly goodness who has chosen them to be His witnesses. They wrote back to say that his letter had "greatly consoled" them; in a reply he commends them to God's mercy and asks them to pray for him. After a long trial, they "died with singular constancy"— as did many others heartened by his exhortations. There is an interesting letter to women who were imprisoned in Paris, in which he contrasts the weakness of their sex with the spiritual strength to which women attain, and exhorts them by the constancy, superior to that of the Apostles, of the women present at the death of Christ (September, 1557).

The severity which Calvin showed in dealing with opponents in

Geneva is rarely reflected in his letters. But there are examples of direct rebuke, and others of pained remonstrance. The departure of Louis du Tillet, his former fellow student and companion, from Geneva, and his return to the Roman Church, called forth a letter of wounded friendship and startled disappointment, in which Calvin confesses some "rudeness and incivility" on his part, but affirms that he can only tolerate and in no sense approve the secession of his friend, and prayerfully commends him to God (January 31, 1538). Madame de Retigny had been imprisoned in Paris, and Calvin wrote to her to confirm her faithfulness, December 8, 1557, but on the following April 10, having learned that she had made concessions in order to conciliate her alienated husband and escape danger, he warned her not to make a divorce from God in order to be reconciled to her husband. He admits, however, some ignorance of the circumstances and prays that she may have the Holy Spirit's guidance. Similar was the case of d'Andelot, a nobleman of Brittany, imprisoned as a Huguenot. Having written an admiring and consoling letter to him on July 12, 1558, he learned that d'Andelot had yielded and written to the king in testimony of his submission. Within the same month Calvin wrote again reproaching him with troubling "many poor weak souls" by his example, and bidding him return to the course he had formerly well begun. Augustin Legrant, an elder of the French church in Frankfort, received a severe reprimand on his heretical views and hostility to his minister: "I desire you to feel the enormity of your fault" (February 23, 1559). Still more severe is his denunciation of Sartas, minister of Sauve, who has led iconoclastic attacks against Roman Catholic churches (July, 1561).

Calvin often had to deal with people who had to make important decisions in which points of conscience were involved. Sometime in 1547, Madame Budé, widow of the scholar, received from him a letter of advice. Like Renée in Ferrara, she had not ventured in Paris to declare her Protestant faith, and her conscience was greatly troubled. Calvin offers her residence in Geneva. He does so, however, with the frank statement that if God had given her constancy to face death, it would have been better for her to make her testimony in Paris. Even in Geneva she is not to expect assured repose, since in this world we should always be "like birds upon the branch." After these frank cautions, he definitely argues for her making her home in Geneva, particularly considering the question of her unmarried daughter who was especially in her mind. Three years later the lady came, with her daughter and four of her seven living sons; the daughter later married a French refugee. In several other instances Calvin unhesitatingly invited troubled converts to Protestantism to leave France and take refuge in Geneva. He advises Madame de Cany to remove to Geneva without longer indecision and delay (July 24, 1554). Another is addressed to an unknown French seigneur, who is advised to flee rather than to compromise with idolatry. In a series of brief opinions chiefly on cases of conscience (Consilia, in Calvini Opera, Corpus Reformatorum edition, Xa) Calvin treats the question of emigration on the part of a married man whose wife does not share his convictions, or of one who has children. He would conserve in such cases a maximum of family unity. If the man must go without his wife let it be understood as an enforced absence for his protection, and let both bless God together. Children, "God's best treasure," should not be left behind to a bitter fate when parents emigrate.

In a chapter on cases of conscience, Benoit includes a discussion of the Duchess Renée's oath, made under pressure at her husband's deathbed, that she would not correspond with Calvin. Having heard from her by messengers, Calvin wrote July 5, 1560, referring to Herod's wicked oath to Salome, and holding her absolved from the obligation, as equivalent to "a superstitious vow." Benoit points out that this accords with his view of monastic vows, in which he agreed with Luther. As a casuist, Calvin treats in the Consilia a number of questions of church discipline, of marriage, and of morals. Most celebrated is his discussion of usury (pp. 245 ff.), which is really a letter, and has been identified as the answer to an inquiry made at another's request by Claude de Sachins, September 7, 1545 (Calvini Opera, Xa, 210). He is hesitant to give judgment on this debatable question, anticipating (justifiably enough) that he will be misunderstood. This danger lay in the fact that Calvin's exegesis of the Scripture references to usury did not require its complete rejection, and he fears that his saying this may lead his correspondent's friend "to permit himself more than I intend." Only that usury is forbidden which is "contrary to justice and charity." Anxious to avoid authorizing the practices of loan sharks, he lays down seven carefully stated restrictions. These are such as to protect the poor and to limit only loans that are equitable and conducive to production. The Venerable Company of Geneva in February, 1547, implemented

Calvin's judgment by passing an ordinance that prohibited, on pain of confiscation, the taking of interest higher than 5 per cent. The rate is the same as that permitted by Zwingli (above p. 193).

Calvin sometimes found it necessary to be a peacemaker between alienated ministers and other leaders. In one letter he urgently admonishes Farel to restore to his good will a young colleague, Christopher Fabri, with whose headstrong behavior Farel has become impatient. Calvin points out Fabri's many good qualities, which outweigh his defects. "Let him only feel that you love him, and I will answer for it, you will find him tolerably docile" (July 19, 1553). Another example is his letter to the legal scholar Francis Hotman (May 27, 1559), then at Strasbourg, concerning his quarrel with Francis Baudouin who had removed from Strasbourg to Heidelberg. Calvin favors Hotman's position, but deplores his excessive anger. Very interestingly, he reminds Hotman that "these counsels are given by a man who, though he is conscious of possessing a more vehement temper than he could wish"— is yet daily bearing in patience much more severe attacks than Baudouin's. Thus he confesses that besetting sin, the evil temper which on his deathbed he would call the "untamed beast," and at the same moment sets up the example of his recent success against it.

Although when quoting and interpreting the Scriptures Calvin often speaks with the ring of authority, he often expresses too, in these letters, his sense of inadequacy, and he often asks for prayer and sometimes for reciprocal advice. In 1543 he notes in a letter to de Falais the benefit he has himself received from the exhortations of friends. When his own wife died, he wrote to his friends Viret and Farel letters that show how he prized both their sympathy and the "support" of present friends (April 7, and 11, 1549). A letter to Francis Dryander shows him at the receiving end of that Spanish scholar's corrective admonition (November, 1557). Calvin has been controlling himself amid stormy scenes and personal attacks in Geneva: "Still I take it kindly of you to exhort me to moderation. . . . I am perfectly aware that my own temper is naturally inclined to be rather violent." Dryander "would be surprised," however, if he could see with what composure Calvin has been enduring these tumults. This was evidently the point at which Calvin felt himself most open to criticism, and was most anxious to correct, and accredit, himself.

We may follow Benoit in his view that Calvin's direction of souls is essentially biblical in a threefold sense. First, he writes in an atmosphere totally impregnated by the Bible, and assumes an intimate knowledge of it on the part of the receivers of his letters. Secondly, he continually urges the reading of, and meditation on, the Scriptures. Thirdly, he dwells upon the doctrinal points of his biblical faith, writing on these with a certitude that leaves no place for doubt. The only sort of doubt he recognizes is hesitation or lack of assurance about one's own salvation, the anguish of truth-seekers who have not yet come to the full light. This biblical position cannot be better illustrated than in his first letter to the Duke of Somerset (October 22, 1548): "That we hold God to be the sole governor of our souls, that we hold His law to be the only rule and spiritual directory of our consciences, not serving Him according to the foolish inventions of men."

The evidence we have presented shows, too, that his counsels are a part of his reforming activity and reflect its atmosphere of controversy. He is enlisting and supporting soldiers in a war in which, as he wrote to Madame de Crussol at the court of France, "God cannot endure any neutrality" (May 8, 1563). He does not plot out ascetic or devotional exercises leading to a detached holiness, but asks for prompt, heroic devotion in a course beset with dangers, and seeks to fortify the souls of men for sacrifice and martyrdom.

VI

The Reformed churches provided, in their official documents, some direction on the ministry to individuals. The Discipline of the Reformed Church of France (1559 with later amendments) contains puritanic regulations for the lives of ministers, elders, deacons and members, and indicates procedures in suspension and excommunication—the latter for the obstinately impenitent "after many admonitions and entreaties." Records of faults are to be erased from the Consistory's books after repentance. The seal of confession is explicitly recognized in a synod of 1612, which states that, except in cases of *lèse majesté*, "ministers are forbidden to disclose to the magistrates crimes declared by those who come to him for counsel and consolation . . . lest sinners be hindered from coming to repentance, and from making a free confession of their faults." When after 1685 Protestants in France were subjected to severe persecutions, the few ministers remaining, and especially Claude Brousson, who died by torture in 1698, attempted to hold the people together, and to maintain discipline. They enjoined the elders and deacons to "teach, reprove and comfort." The Rules adopted in 1619 at the Synod of Dort give ministers of the Dutch Church (no. 16) the task of watching over elders, deacons and people, and require elders (no. 23) to assist in visitation of the parishes "in order particularly to instruct and comfort the members in full communion, as well as to exhort others to the regular profession of the Christian religion." This language is retained, with some amplification, in the Constitution of the Reformed Dutch Church of North America, 1792, and its revisions of 1833 and 1874.

The Reformed Church of the Netherlands was the nursery of a notable pietistic movement that preceded Spener, and to which the great Lutheran Pietist was indebted. This Dutch Pietism in turn felt the influence of English Puritanism as represented by William Perkins, John Preston, William Ames, John Downame, and Lewis Bayly (see below p. 229) and later of the erratic mystic Jean de Labadie, a native of Bordeaux. Jean Taffin's *Treatise on the Amendment of Life*, written in French, is one of the earliest expressions of this strain in the Netherlands. A strong English influence is seen in William Teelinck (d. 1629) who had spent a period in England and Scotland. For many years at Middelburg he engaged in an intensive labor, and was constantly attentive to the personal cure of souls. His numerous writings were chiefly exhortations to the devout life.

In Gijsbert Voet (d. 1676) who, after a pastorate became a professor in Utrecht, and was a friend of Teelinck, Pietism was combined with a learned scholastic theology of the strict Calvinist type. His *Ascetica, or Exercise of Piety* (1664), intended for students, shows his appropriation of medieval as well as Protestant materials. He prescribes mental in addition to vocal prayer, fasts, vigils, silence and solitary devotion, and proclaims the soul's warfare against the promptings of the world, the flesh and the devil. He has a chapter on "euthanasia, or the art of dying," and one on Christian visitation for teaching, admonition, discipline and consolation. Voet drew a strong bow in controversy against Arminians, Erastians, Jansenists and Anabaptists; but perhaps his greatest influence was in the realm of piety. His disciple Jodocus van Lodenstein, pastor at Sluys and Utrecht, is described by Heinrich Heppe as a truly apostolic preacher and *Seelsorger*. The highly gifted Anna Maria van Schürman, friend of numerous eminent scholars, became at Utrecht Voet's spiritual daughter, and thereafter followed a daily routine of prayer in accordance with his teaching, though she later moved into the more mystical atmosphere of Labadie's circle.

The three thick tomes of Voet's *Politicae ecclesiasticae* contain, espe-

cially in the third volume (1676), a labored treatment of church discipline. Voet indicates a procedure, under the presbyters, in accordance
with Matthew 18:15-18. He restricts suspension and excommunication
to the obstinately unrepentant, even where the sins have been the
gravest. Major excommunication, when applied, is, however, severe. It
involves exclusion from ordinary conversation, common prayer, and
table fellowship, as well as from the communion. The offender is restored when he repents "or rather comes to his senses," openly before
the church. Voet attacks the Dutch and English followers of Thomas
Erastus (d. 1583) who in his (seventy-five) *Theses on Excommunication,* published only after his death, had denied that excommunication
was divinely authorized. Voet in this work gives incidental attention to
the pastor's ordinary labors' with individuals. His treatment of "visitation" suggests many questions to be propounded to the officers of
churches "visited" by synodical authority; these include inquiries to be
made on faithfulness in visiting the sick and afflicted, and visiting homes
before communion. It was assumed that these were obligatory functions
of the Reformed minister.

The elaborate manual, *Practical Theology* (1878), by John Jacob
Van Oosterzee of Amsterdam shows wide acquaintance with the literature of pastoral care, including "individual poimenics" or the private
cure of souls. Here due attention is given to the pastor's duty to the
sick, and to those mentally distressed or disordered. Though the
terminology at this point is antiquated, the whole treatment is marked
by wisdom and insight, and by respect for what the author calls "the
domain of psychiatry."

John Henry Alsted (d. 1638) of Herborn, one of the ablest of the
German Reformed teachers of the period of the Thirty Years' War,
included among his extensive writings a detailed work of casuistry
(*Theology of Cases,* 1630) in which the cases of consciences are arranged in accordance with (1) the articles of the Creed and (2) the
Ten Commandments. There are bright spots in this wilderness of casuistry; for example, when, in a long list of contrasts between a "sinner"
and a "Christian," we are told that the former is "in life a hog, in death
a dog, after death a worm," while the latter is "in life a dove, in death
an eagle, after death a phoenix." Under the Eighth Commandment he
deals with usury, or interest, using many distinctions. "Usury is not
intrinsically and of its nature evil," says Alsted; "it is a thing indifferent."
"Moderate usury is taken lawfully from strangers, for example, from

infidels; also from our brethren who are rich; it is taken unlawfully from the poor," and "gnawing usury" is utterly forbidden.

The roll of the Dutch Reformed ministers in early America contains the names of Theodore Jacob Frelinghuysen (d. 1748) and John Henry Livingston (d. 1825), both of whom were revivers of personal religion. At Raritan, New Jersey, Frelinghuysen drew upon himself severe criticism and set on foot a widespread revival by his vigorous pietistic demand for repentance, and denunciation of secularity. He introduced special groups for mutual edification that resembled the *collegia pietatis* of Spener, and he utilized lay "helpers" who conducted meetings, visited and conversed with the anxious, and catechized the young. Livingston, a saint and a scholar, was, from student days in Utrecht, a master of persuasion, and in late years, as president of New Brunswick Theological Seminary (1810-25), he retained a facility of creative religious conversation, which he exercised in numerous reported instances with students, and traveling acquaintances.

The German Reformed in eighteenth century America benefitted greatly by the apostolic labors and journeys of Michael Schlatter (d. 1790) who came at the age of thirty from Switzerland to Philadelphia in 1746. He did for the Reformed something like what his friend Muhlenberg did for the Lutherans; but politically motivated opposition from his ministerial brethren militated against his full success. He visited German settlers and engaged in pastoral labors in many parts of the Eastern states and followed a German colony to Nova Scotia where he spent two years. He adopted the well-proved method that we have seen suggested in the writings of the Reformation, of helping members of the church to help each other. This is shown in the rules he drew up for many congregations, including that to which he ministered in Philadelphia. The first Friday of each month was a day of penitence and prayer, on which, after a sermon the people conversed "in an open-hearted manner," composing their differences and exchanging brotherly correction. They were not to separate till everything was "adjusted in a friendly way," and nothing left to rankle secretly.

VII

We turn to a few instances in later French and French-Swiss Protestantism. Charles Drelincourt (d. 1669), Huguenot scholar and minister of Charenton, wrote a substantial book entitled: *The Consolations of the Faithful Soul against the Terrors of Death* (1651). The titles of

English editions vary. The seventh American edition, by an undisclosed translator, is of 1836. The book may be compared with Jeremy Taylor's *Holy Dying* (below p. 233); it is of the same date, and is longer, and on the whole, inferior to the Anglican classic. It owes something to the "consolation" and "art of dying" themes of earlier literature; but Drelincourt holds that the heathen philosophers, not excepting the Stoics and Platonists, have offered no true comfort for the dying. What material he has in imitation of them is overlaid by Christian theology and faith. In his order of treatment he employs mainly a series of "remedies" against the fear of death, followed by a series of "consolations," of which the former are moral acts and attitudes, the latter reflections upon aspects of divine grace. The twenty-four chapters are accompanied by twenty-nine long prayers suitable for different classes of people, including kings, generals, fathers and ministers. We are told that the prayer for the use of the dying minister was of great value to the author as his own death drew near. It is not one of the best, however, since it mingles with devout faith an intrusive element of self-approval. The book contains much Scripture quotation and not a few classical illustrations of the *exempla* type. Like other seventeenth century religious men, Drelincourt stresses the fact that we live with the hand of death upon us; time, like a cancer, never ceases to consume us all. Drelincourt wrote also *Charitable Visits and Christian Consolations for all Persons Afflicted* (1667), based upon his long pastoral experience; and many letters of consolation.

One of the most authoritative, and unoriginal, of Reformed theologians of his time was François Turretini (d. 1687) who taught in Geneva for thirty-four years, and wrote the widely circulated three-volume textbook *Institutio theologicae elencticae* (1680-83), of which an edition (still in Latin) was published in New York as late as 1847. In the third volume of this work Turretini introduces topics of interest for us. The absolution spoken by an evangelical minister is not "judicial" but "ministerial"; he holds the keys not in the place of God, but as God's steward, or doorkeeper, under His command. Turretini finds scriptural authority for mutual confession to brethren to obtain mutual peace and pardon, and of confession to a believer in order that he may help us by counsel and prayers.

Jean Frédéric Ostervald (d. 1747) of Neuchâtel took a leading place among liberal Reformed teachers of the early eighteenth century, and obtained a wide influence. His *Lectures on the Exercise of the Sacred*

Ministry (French 1737, English 1781) sheds light on the Reformed discipline of his time. When he writes, "We have, in general, more discipline than other Protestant churches," he is contrasting the system at Neuchâtel with that of other Swiss communities, as well as with Protestantism elsewhere. In Neuchâtel, the president of the consistory (except in two instances) is a pastor, whereas elsewhere a magistrate presides. Yet he feels the pressure of state encroachment, the common condition of the period, as a peril to discipline.

> Our discipline is purely spiritual. We nevertheless sometimes make use of civil punishments, but then the magistrate inflicts them.
> We use suspension from the sacraments and public penance. These things are not practiced amongst our neighbors. (Lecture ix)

Ostervald would like to reform the discipline of his church so as to bring under it all those whom the word of God would subject to it, and to add to suspension excommunication, which the state does not permit. He would prefer not to resort to the secular power in church cases, but to rely on spiritual methods. He is glad that the magistrate is not free to use evidence given in a confession before the consistory. The stages in correction are (1) censure, (2) the requirement of repentance, (3) suspension, and (4) public penance, of which (3) and (4) are exceptional; but the churches exact public penance for adultery and murder regardless of the pardon of the prince. In this act the penitent is required to "ask pardon in a loud voice before the whole church," and the pastor declares him absolved "if his repentance be sincere." Ostervald presents some details of the treatment of types of offenders, the contentious, the lewd, the profane, drunkards, etc. He has thoughtful and useful advice for ministers on the exercise of discipline—advice still largely valid—stressing fairness, firmness, mildness and love—and the reading of ecclesiastical history (xi). In a section on private admonitions he earnestly upholds the secrecy of confession, approving in that connection the "maxims" of the Roman church. There is an extended discussion of the visitation of the sick, and the final chapter is on the ministry to condemned criminals.

The early nineteenth century saw a distinct revival of the personal ministry in French-speaking Protestantism. In Felix Neff (d. 1829) who gave himself during his short career to a mission in the High Alps, an intense zeal is combined with a keen sense of the practical. In this he reminds us of John Frederick Oberlin (for whom he expresses admiration); but his spirituality sprang out of his Genevan mother's instruction. Neff's letters report many personal conversations, and carry messages of exhortation and encouragement to many in his broad parish.

In Alexandre Vinet (d. 1847) of Lausanne, the French-Swiss Reformed possessed a liberal evangelical leader of high talent and deep spirituality. His books reveal a genuine interest in promoting the cure of souls, and his extensive correspondence contains many letters of spiritual counsel and consolation. Vinet identifies himself with his troubled friends. In a letter of January 16, 1846, to one bereaved, we read: "We travel with you step by step the narrow and dark valley, and count all your sad steps. . . . May God sustain you as he has your dear friend." The religious revival at Geneva, led by César Malan and the historian Merle d'Aubigné, was theologically too rigid to receive his full support, but he was on friendly terms with its leaders. A letter of April 10, 1835, tells of a visit to him of Malan and Louis Bonnet. As they sat smoking, Malan suddenly, taking Vinet by the hand, asked his usual question, "How is your soul?" The answer was of a generalizing sort, he reports: whereupon they engaged in prayer. Such was the intimacy of these religious men; but Vinet himself would be less abrupt. He is afraid, he says in substance, that the revival tends to set an artificial pattern: "the soul loses all naïveté."

Ill-health and bereavement may have rendered Vinet sensitive and at times timid, but his very sensitivity deepened his understanding, and he could be sufficiently downright where criticism was called for. He shared his religious struggles with his friends and his letters contain more of confession than of counsel. His outlook resembled that of Kierkegaard who, as Paul Fuhrmann points out, praises him warmly; and he is one of the most understanding interpreters of Pascal. A man of wide scholarship, he was sought out by workmen and farmers for advice. A peasant woman, whose pastor had rebuked her doubts but also lent her some books of Vinet, visited him and talked with him for a whole day. She testified that his humility had broken her pride. "You say good things but you say them as a director," she told her pastor; "you judge me from above, but he . . . as my equal."

Vinet's *Pastoral Theology* (1853) was a widely used manual and contains much that is still of value. The personal cure of souls is treated in three thoughtfully wrought-out chapters, marked by Vinet's characteristic wisdom and sympathy. The relief of the troubled conscience may require a sincere confession and this should be held inviolably secret, except in the case of criminal acts, when the confessant should be informed that secrecy is not undertaken. He discusses the word "direction" in the Protestant cure of souls, and cautions against violation of the principle of liberty and responsibility: "Let us not direct too much." With this may be associated his great emphasis upon the reality and rights of conscience. The point of initiation of God's work of inner renewal of the soul is when conscience is confronted by Christ (cf. Fuhrmann). That the pastor must not permit himself to enslave consciences is a recurring theme.

Adolphe Monod (d. 1856), well known as the ablest pulpit orator of the Evangelical Revival in France, is equally distinguished for his spiritual letters, which are direct and penetrating, and at the same time biblical. To a group of pastors associated for "fraternal correspondence" he writes (May 5, 1834): "Let us go to the quick, and speak to each one according to his need." To an unnamed correspondent he writes: "Do not examine yourself and describe yourself so much. . . . Do not let your books trouble you so much. There is only one book which is always right, the Book of God." Monod as a "director" speaks with a good deal of finality; but he always seeks to give a stimulus toward spiritual maturity. Benoit, in his *Direction spirituelle*, calls our attention to the specific points of view of some who definitely recoiled from the consequences of "direction." Tommy Fallot, for example, finding the experience conducive to wrong attitudes on the part of the director, renounced the function and burned his letters (1875). At the end of the nineteenth century direction by correspondence was exemplified by the Geneva professor Gaston Frommel (d. 1906). Frommel was confidential guide to many students, summoning them to unreserved devotion and self-renunciation, in which asceticism was given a restricted role as a temporary measure of self-discipline.

VIII

If we compare the Reformed tradition with the medieval, we see essentially the same contrasts as in Lutheranism. Both discard vigorously the medieval requirement of confession and affirm on scriptural grounds the sufficiency of unmediated confession to God by the penitent soul. On the other hand, both prize the value of mutual confession and exhortation, and of the private and secret confession to a trusted counselor, ordinarily the minister, but quite legitimately a layman. But a comparison of the Reformed with the Lutheran cure of souls reveals some differences in practice to which the "activism" of the Reformed furnishes a clue. On the whole the insistence on an effective discipline has been much more constant in Reformed than in Lutheran churches, and the communion has been more watchfully protected against scandalous offenders. Even Vinet, who recognizes the modern impossibility of what was earlier called major excommunication, in which state sanctions were invoked against the excluded sinner, recognizes the duty of the church to exclude the incorrigible from communion. Such an attitude is by no means absent from Lutheranism, but there less uniformly asserted. It is likely that visitation of families was usually more active in Reformed than in Lutheran churches, especially where the visitor was uninvited, since the Reformed books of discipline made the visitation of all explicitly the duty of ministers and lay officers of the local church.

In both great branches of Continental Protestantism, however, zealous spirits often felt impelled to rebuke their negligent brethren and call for a revival of discipline. Perhaps equally in both, criticism and revival of the guidance of souls produced from time to time fresh efforts of an experimental and somewhat original sort. The formalizing of the practice of the confessional in Lutheranism, as we saw, led to its neglect, and called forth the vigorous efforts of the Pietists to care for individual souls by other means. In Calvinism there were periods and areas of neglect of the discipline, particularly in the eighteenth century when Erastian control of the churches prevailed. Evangelicalism, with its tremendous sense of the alternatives of salvation and damnation for the individual, called forth, apart from the formal discipline, a revival of private exhortation, which often took epistolary form.

We have given some attention to Calvin's letters in this connection, and by reference to other Reformed writers of letters of religious advice have suggested the extent of this method. It is not difficult to distinguish broadly this type of guidance in Protestantism from direction by letter in Roman Catholicism. The use of the word "direction" is immaterial if the distinction is kept in mind. To generalize on differences between Lutheran and Calvinist spiritual letters would be more difficult, and would require much more exhaustive study than can here be attempted. There are instances in which strong moral pressure is applied by Calvin and his successors in the Reformed ministry, but in general they treat their correspondents as St. Paul did Philemon: "Though I am bold enough in Christ to command you to do what is required, yet for love's sake I prefer to appeal to you" (verse 8).

Chapter X

THE CURE OF SOULS IN THE
ANGLICAN COMMUNION

I

Years before Anne Boleyn gained the attention of Henry VIII the English Reformation had its beginnings in the work of Bilney, Latimer, Tyndale, Frith and other evangelical spirits, who lost, or risked, their lives for their faith. The English Bible, in Tyndale's and Coverdale's versions, gave strength to the cause of reform. Henry was induced to permit the circulation of Coverdale's Bible in 1535. Such was the popular effect of the new Bible reading that Edward Fox, Bishop of Hereford, was moved to declare in 1537:

Think ye not that we can by any sophistical subtleties steal out of the world again the light that every man doth see. Christ hath so lightened the world at this time that the light of the Gospel hath put to flight all misty darkness. . . . The lay people do now know the Holy Scriptures better than many of us.

The English Reformers, however, far from being content with the spread of the Bible to the laity, shaped, within the framework of Henry's politically motivated reforms, the outlines of a new ecclesiastical system. Taking their ground upon the Bible and the Fathers, they made explicit provision for the cure of souls, in a series of formularies appointed for use. Of these, three are of special interest for their interpretation of penance: The *Articles about Religion* (The Ten Articles), 1536; *The Institution of a Christian Man* (The Bishops' Book), 1537; and *A Necessary Doctrine and Erudition for Any Christian Man* (The King's Book), 1543. The first of these affirms (Art. 3) the requirement of penance and absolution, and includes under penance contrition, confession and amendment of life as fruits worthy of repentance (Luke 3:8). Along

218

with other abuses, "the Bishop of Rome's pardons" are repudiated. Similar language appears in the other documents named. In the *Institution* confession to a priest is called "a very expedient mean" to obtain absolution, but is not enjoined as always necessary. Although Christ's death is a sufficient satisfaction, yet suitable fruits of repentance are required—"fasting, almsdeed, with much mourning and lamenting," restitution, and the ordinary works of mercy. The *Erudition* states the matter somewhat more amply, but to the same effect. "Penance is an inward sorrow and grief of heart" for sins, with detestation of them and earnest desire to recover the favor of God. The penitent, "pricked and stirred in his heart," prostrates himself before God, confesses to the priest "all such sins in which his conscience telleth him that he hath grievously offended," and gladly submits to the discipline which the priest may impose "according to the Word of God." Thus confession of grievous sins, rather than of all, the authority of the Scripture in the prescription of acts of repentance, and the definition of penance itself as inward sorrow for sin and desire for restoration, are the emerging emphases in these early and experimental Anglican formularies.

The Communion Service adopted in 1548 and incorporated in the First Book of Common Prayer, 1549, has a rubric requiring the exclusion of any "notorious and evil liver" who has offended the congregation or wronged his neighbors, until he shall have shown true repentance, and recompensed those he has wronged, to the satisfaction of the people. The curate is charged to require those at variance to forgive each other before admission to communion: if one party remains obstinate while the other repents, the latter is to be admitted.

The Communion Office contains also a rigorous exhortation to those "minded to receive" the sacrament, in which impenitent sinners—including with blasphemers and adulterers those that "be in malice or envy"—are warned to bewail their sins and not come to the holy Table. Where the people are negligent, the priest is to give notice in advance of the next communion, and exhort them to prepare by asking pardon of God for their sins "with inward sorrow and tears." He is to urge them to be reconciled to their neighbors and forgive one another, as they would be forgiven, and to make restitution of anything wrongfully taken or withheld. Without these acts of charity, the priests' absolution will avail nothing, and receiving the sacrament will only confirm their damnation.

And if there be any of you whose conscience is troubled or grieved in anything, lacking comfort or counsel, let him come to me, or to some other discreet and learned priest, taught in the law of God, and confess and open his grief secretly, that he may receive such ghostly counsel, advice and comfort, that his conscience may be relieved, and that of us (as of the ministers of God and of the Church) he may receive comfort and absolution, to the satisfaction of his mind, and avoiding of all scruple or doubtfulness.

Those who are satisfied with a general confession are not to be offended at those who seek to satisfy themselves further in "the auricular and secret confession to the priest," nor are the latter to be offended at the former, none judging other men's consciences.

Private confession is retained in the Second Prayer Book (1552) in a passage to be sometimes used, at the discretion of the curate:

And because it is requisite that no man should come to Holy Communion but with a full trust of God's mercy, and with a quiet conscience, therefore if there be any of you who by the means aforesaid (self-examination, confession to God, and satisfaction to a wronged neighbor) cannot quiet his own conscience, but requireth further comfort or counsel; then let him come to me, or some other discreet and learned minister of God's Word, and open his grief, that he may receive such ghostly counsel, advice, and comfort, as his conscience may be relieved; and that by the ministry of God's Word he may receive comfort and the benefit of absolution, to the quieting of his conscience, and avoiding of all scruple and doubtfulness.

The changes here from the First Prayer Book are significant, and accord with other variations between the two Prayer Books of Edward VI. The private opening of griefs is a special provision for the relief of the consciences of those who remain in a state of anxiety after the ordinary means have been employed. Thus private confession is now considered exceptional rather than regular. It is possible to overstate the difference from the earlier document, however: it too contains a qualification in the words, "if there be any . . . lacking comfort and counsel" that seems to lead in the same direction. And the omission of the word "secretly" in 1552 can hardly have meant that there was no obligation of secrecy. Yet there is now apparent a desire to avoid the terms of the medieval system, and to rest upon the authority of Scripture. Thus absolution is "by the ministry of God's Word." But the procedures remain essentially unchanged. In both books private confession is prescribed for those troubled in conscience, and the curate assumes the functions of confessor and counselor. The passage quoted above from the Second Prayer Book has been retained with immaterial changes through the later revisions. It was repeated in the Communion Office of the Protestant Episcopal Church in 1789.

Somewhat greater liberty has been taken with the rubric on private confession in the Order for the Visitation of the Sick of the book of 1549:

> Here shall the sick person make a special confession, if he feel his conscience troubled with any weighty matter. After which confession the priest shall absolve him after this form, and the same form of absolution shall be used in all private confessions.

The form that follows, for use in absolving sick penitents and all others making private confession (following the medieval Sarum Office) contains the words: "I absolve thee from all thy sins." Undoubtedly, as Blunt and others state, this confession of the dying was thought of as private auricular confession, and the same is true of the confession provided for in the communion service, for which the same absolution formula was to be used. But the 1552 Prayer Book omits the last clause of the rubric quoted, thus leaving optional the form of absolution used for those in health; as does also the Elizabethan book of 1562. The latter goes further and substitutes for "after this form" the more elastic "after this sort," thus making it possible to vary the language of absolution for sick penitents also.

The place of private confession and absolution was not entirely clear in the sixteenth century Church of England. But there is no evidence of intention to abolish them. Even the most strongly Protestant of the archbishops, Edmund Grindal (1576-84), did not seek a change in the regulations. John Cosin (d. 1672) in his Latin treatise, *Religion and Ecclesiastical Government of the Kingdom of England under the Rule of Elizabeth*, states: "The Holy Communion is administered to those who have been previously examined, absolved, or found worthy." This indicates a personal examination, involving confession and absolution for those in grave sins, before each communion. This, at least, was the ideal procedure: we may hardly regard it as so general as Cosin's statement would imply.

The practice of private confession is attested by a notable provision in the Canons of 1604. Canon cxiii of this series authorizes ministers and parish officials to "present" offenders to ecclesiastical superiors for discipline:

> Provided always that if any man confess his secret and hidden sins to the minister for the unburdening of his conscience, and to receive spiritual con-

solation and ease of mind from him; we do not in any way bind the said minister by this our Constitution, but do straitly charge and admonish him, that he do not at any time reveal and make known to any person whatsoever any crime or offense so committed to his trust and secrecy, (except they be such crimes as by the laws of the realm his own life may be called in question for concealing the same), under pain of irregularity.

This may be compared with the declaration of the French Reformed Church made ten years later (above p. 209), where the exception is the crime of treason.

John Bramhall, Bishop of Derry, at the bidding of a synod of the Church of Ireland, condensed to 100 the 141 English Canons of 1604, and included as Canon xix a statement on preparation for communion. This regulation required every parish minister in the afternoon before communion to call, "by the tolling of the bell or otherwise," all who "have any scruple of conscience, or desire the special ministry of reconciliation," to come for consultation to him. The people were to be exhorted to examine their own souls, and, according to need, to resort to their ministers for advice and absolution "for the quieting of their consciences by the power of the keys which Christ hath committed to His ministers." These Canons were adopted in 1634.

A word may be said of the references to confession in the *Book of Homilies* of 1547 and the enlarged book of 1571. The attitude taken in the Homilies toward ecclesiastical penance is less positive than that of the documents we have been discussing. The homily "Of Repentance" attributes the doctrine of auricular confession to "our adversaries." Nevertheless it concedes that those whose consciences are troubled "may repair to their pastor or other godly or learned man" with their troubles, and "receive the comfortable salve of God's word."

II

The English Reformers speak in ways consonant with the Prayer Book statements on matters of repentance and discipline. William Tyndale (d. 1536) is perhaps the most severe in rejection of the abuses of the old system. In his *Obedience of a Christian Man* (1528) he goes so far as to condemn auricular confession ("shrift in the ear") as a work of Satan. In *The Practice of Prelates* (1530) he exposes the pre-Reformation violation of the seal in the delation to the king, by Archbishop Morton, acting "by authority of the pope," of sins confessed at certain places. It is the abuses of the system that Tyndale has chiefly in mind:

in his *Exposition of I John* (1531) he admits parenthetically that the tradition of private confession "restored to right use, were not damnable."

In the works of the English Reformers we frequently note the use of "penance" as equivalent to "repentance" and not with reference to sacramental penance. Miles Coverdale, who follows Tyndale in translating *metanoia* "repentance," remarks that the two terms penance and repentance differ no more than fourpence and a groat.

The sermons of Hugh Latimer (d. 1555) contain many references to our subject. Preaching in 1535 on Ephesians 6:10-20, he introduces the topic of binding and loosing. "Whatsoever thou bindest" was "spoken to the apostles and all true preachers, their successors," who teach the law of God and redemption through the blood of Christ. In his famous sermon before the Convocation of 1536, he assails "the forgiveness of sins purchased by money." In his third sermon before King Edward (1549), with an indelicate exuberance, he tells an anecdote of one of his adversaries who boasted that his mule had been absolved along with himself at Paul's Cross—having, no doubt, says Latimer, repented of her stumbling. But Latimer took both public and private absolution very seriously, as uttered with divine and scriptural authority. In his Sixth Sermon on the Lord's Prayer (1552), he says:

For I would have them that are grieved in conscience to go to some godly man, which is able to minister God's Word, and there to fetch his absolution, if he cannot be satisfied in the public sermon; it were truly a thing that would do much good.

A godly and well-instructed minister may absolve in public, not of his own authority but "as an officer of Christ." He here declares also that it is impossible to forgive one who has wronged us until he repent; in that case we must put away rancor and be ready to help him; but even God does not forgive where there is no repentance.

Latimer is often seen engaged in the personal cure of souls. In the fourth of his sermons before young Edward (1549) he pauses to appeal to the king, on the basis of his own experience in prisons: "to move your grace that such men as shall be put to death may have learned men to give them instruction and exhortation." He tells here of a woman to whom he ministered in Newgate, who after an evil life was to be executed for theft because good men had not helped her. Evidently Latimer was counselor to her and other fellow prisoners, as his martyred friend,

Thomas Bilney (d. 1531), had been to prisoners in Cambridge. In another sermon he introduces reminiscences of visits in the 1520's to prisoners there, shortly after "Saint Bilney" had confessed to him and thereby caused him "to begin to smell the Word of God." (First Sermon on the Lord's Prayer, 1552.) Bilney "was ever visiting prisoners and sick folk. So we went together, and exhorted them as well as we were able." Latimer had there interested himself in the case of a woman condemned for the murder of her child whom he believed, and produced evidence to prove, innocent, and for whom he obtained a pardon from the king.

Another of Mary's victims, the able and noble-spirited John Bradford (d. 1555), in a sermon on Repentance (1553) discusses the "parts of penance," using the untechnical terms, "sorrow, good hope, and newness of life." He holds with the Reformers generally that a recitation of all sins in confession is impossible. Bradford wrote numerous spiritual letters, most of them from prison, marked by unswerving faith and conviction. Facing death, he yet thinks of the needs of others rather than his own. "Be merry, be merry, dear heart," he exclaims in the last of these, to Mrs. Joyce Hales; "God give us to meet in his kingdom."

Thomas Becon (d. ca. 1564), author of many popular books of piety in Edward's time, discusses penance in his *Potacion for Lent* (1542). He would retain auricular confession, discarding its abuses. Confessors should be "men of gravity, sagacity, integrity" and other high qualities. He furnishes six arguments for "confession to our ghostly fathers," the last of which is that the ignorant are through it "brought to knowledge, the blind to sight, the desperate to salvation, the presumptuous to humility, the troubled unto quietness, the sorrowful unto joy, the sick unto health, the dead to life." In a late work, often reprinted, *The Sick Man's Salve*, he gives a long but animated dialogue at a deathbed. Here Epiphanius, the dying man, begins by cursing the day of his birth, but on the persuasion of his friends he "makes a godly end," commending his spirit to God, and holding up a finger in token of his joyous faith. This is one of the most remarkable of the books of the expanded Art of Dying type.

Thomas Cranmer (d. 1556), the principal compiler of the Book of Common Prayer, expressed himself in accordance with its provisions on penance and confession. We have his notes on *The Institution of a Christian Man*: they contain an endorsement of the statement quoted above from that document. His Injunctions of 1538 require of the clergy that they enjoin good works both in preaching and in secret confession (No. v). In the same year he co-operated in shaping the Thirteen Articles which were intended as a basis of agreement with the Lutheran theologians then in England as emissaries of German Lutheranism. Article viii of this series is on penitence (*De poenitentia*), and is mainly an expansion of the Augsburg Confession xi and xii. God has instituted penance as an antidote and effective remedy against desperation and death. The confession called auricular and made privately to ministers, is to be retained and magnified for its many benefits, especially for that of absolution; which is the voice of the Gospel by which the minister announces and offers remission of sins, not of his own word but on the authority of Christ. Where the document states that auricular confession is "extremely useful and highly necessary," in one manuscript Cranmer's hand has stricken out "*summe necessariam*" and substituted "*commodissimam*"—very appropriate or satisfactory.

Private confession is not for Cranmer a matter of obligation on scriptural authority. In 1540 the King sent a questionnaire to the bishops on points connected with the sacraments, in order to obtain materials for a statement on the subject. The King's Book of 1543 reflected the replies. Cranmer gave a negative answer to the question of obligation, on the basis of John 20:23, to confess secret deadly sins to a priest. He added, however, that this must be done if absolution is to be granted. A number of the others consulted answered this question similarly, making absolution dependent on confession, but not declaring confession to be a scriptural requirement. One, Dr. Leighton, would make confession in such case requisite for those "who have not a knowledge of Scripture whereby they may quiet their consciences."

John Jewel (d. 1571) in his *Defense of an Apology* (1564) against Harding, deals at some length with the question of binding and loosing, and the power of the keys. The keys are "instruction and correction" (the preaching of the word and the discipline of offenders). To Harding's charges that Anglicans have abandoned confession, Jewel enters a denial and an explanation. If abuses are removed, and if the priest is competent, he says:

> We mislike no manner of confession whether it be private or public. For as we think it not unlawful to make open confession before many, so we think it not unlawful (abuses always excepted) to make the like confession in private, either before a few or before one alone.

He names, in Calvin's manner, the three kinds of confession that are scriptural—confession made secretly to God, openly before the congregation, and privately to our brother. "The abuses and errors set apart, we no more mislike a 'private confession' than a 'private sermon.'" But that it be made to a minister is not commanded, nor necessary to salvation. Jewel thus seems to place little store in confession to the minister, while he is entirely in favor of that confession which takes place in private intimate spiritual counseling between brethren. In *Of Private Mass* (1570) he observes that many have used private confession "as a rack of men's consciences to the maintenance of their tyranny"; and he cites St. Chrysostom on the sufficiency of confession to God. In his *Treatise on the Sacraments*, however, he states that confession to a brother "may do much good if it is well used."

Every Christian may do this help unto another, to take knowledge of the secret and inner grief of his heart, to look upon the wound which sin and wickedness hath made, and by godly advice and earnest prayer for him, to recover his brother.

In his posthumous *Exposition of Second Thessalonians* (3:14-15) he expounds excommunication in severe terms. But there must be no bitterness against those cast out of the Church: "Kill the sin . . . but recover the man."

Other anti-Roman controversialists, in their treatment of these points are chiefly concerned to refute the Roman doctrine of sacramental penance. Thomas Rogers in *The Catholic Doctrine of the Church of England* (1579-85) argues that the Roman sacrament of penance is wholly unbiblical, and that the enumeration of all sins is impossible. William Fulke, in his reply to Thomas Stapleton (*An Overthrow . . . to the Feeble Fortress*, 1580) accuses his opponent of misrepresenting passages from Bede's *Ecclesiastical History* (IV, xxv, xxvii), denying that Bede has there any reference to sacramental private confession. Fulke takes occasion in his *Defence of the English Translation of the Bible* (1583) to explain the New Testament words *metanoia* and *exomologesis* (repentance and confession) in refutation of Gregory Martin's argument for the confessional.

Richard Hooker (d. 1600), the most scholarly theologian of sixteenth century Anglicanism, in Book VI of *The Laws of Ecclesiastical Polity* assails the Puritan, and still more the Roman, teaching on church disci-

pline and expounds the Anglican position.[1] He weights his argument
with quotations from the Fathers to confute Bellarmin and Baronius,
and other Roman Catholic interpreters. To their views of the necessity
of secret confession to a priest, Hooker replies: "No, no; these opinions
have youth in their countenance; antiquity knew them not" (VI, iv,
137). He defends the general confession in the Anglican rite, noting
that in it every man may apply it to "his own particulars." Thus "the
difference between general and particular forms of confession and absolution is not so material, that any man's safety or ghostly good should
depend upon it." He has only incidental reference to secret confession
as an Anglican practice, and that chiefly in connection with the visitation of the sick. The Church of England has held it "the safer way to
refer men's hidden crimes to themselves and God only," while it provides for a "fearful admonition" before communion. Those who are
"culpable by their own confession," or convicted of crimes in secular or
church courts, are not permitted to communicate (VI, iv, 15). Satisfaction he takes to "include the whole work of penitency." The only adequate satisfaction for sins is that made by Christ, which faith alone
makes ours. Our works satisfy God only as evidence of repentance, and
in that sense change his wrath to mercy. The wrath of God, he affirms
with Augustine, is not like wrath in man, a passion, but a just assignment of penalty, "which God doth no where threaten but with purpose
of revocation if men repent" (VI, v, 4).

Repentance consists of "the pensive meditations of contrition," the
humility of confession, and the deeds that mark amendment of life. It
is the recovery of the soul—"a spiritual nativity." Where the sins repented are wrongs done to others restitution and recompense are inescapably entailed, a point well illustrated from Leviticus 6 and other Old
Testament passages.

We hold not Christian people tied unto Jewish orders for the matter of
restitution; but surely restitution we must hold necessary, as well in our own
repentance as in theirs, for sins of wilful oppression and wrong. (VI, v, 7)

[1] Book VI did not appear in print until 1648, and it is evident that a section of
it dealing with the lay eldership has been lost. John Keble in his edition of Hooker
published what we have of the book, in the belief that it was Hooker's work but not
originally a part of the *Ecclesiastical Polity*, and that the true Book VI is entirely lost,
although we have textual comments on it by two of Hooker's friends. On the whole it
is convincingly in Hooker's style, though it contains some paragraphs that lack his
usual high degree of clarity, and which, apparently, death prevented him from revising.

Hooker regards the types of vicarious penance that we have seen illustrated above (Chapter V) as "the postern-gate" by which "cometh in the whole mart of papal indulgences . . . a scorn both to God and man." In a list of differences of Anglican from Roman practice in the penitential discipline he states what Lutherans and Calvinists would equally claim:

We labor to instruct men in such sort, that every soul which is wounded with sin may learn the way how to cure itself; they, clean contrary, would make all sores seem incurable, unless the priest have a hand in them. (VI, vi, 4)

While Hooker affirms that in the Church of England "the priest's power to absolve is publicly taught and professed" (VI, iv, 14), he describes absolution as "ministerial," and declares that it does not take away sin but rather "ascertain [assure] us of God's most gracious and merciful pardon." This "ministerial absolution" both declares us restored to God's favor and readmits us to the divine mysteries, loosing the chains by which we were tied, so that we are as if we "never had gone astray" (VI, vi, 5). Here Hooker enters upon a discussion of the Scholastic theology of penance, criticizing both Aquinas and his pretended disciples who differ from him. Izaak Walton in his *Life of Hooker* tells us that he and Adrian Saravia "were supposed to be confessors to each other" and that Saravia attended Hooker at death, and gave him absolution.

We may see from the evidence presented above that the English Reformation fathers gave no little attention to the confessional and its reform. After the Second Prayer Book, there appears a fairly uniform body of opinion among them. Certain typical features of the medieval confessional, especially its necessity for all, and the requirement of total confession, were repudiated, and absolution was made to rest mainly on the authority of Scripture. Writers like Fulke and Jewel tended to reduce still further the unique place of the minister in hearing confessions, but even they were content not to challenge the authorization given for this in the Prayer Book. The frequent affirmation on the one hand, of the utility of confession "unto our brother," and on the other the superior emphasis often given (for example, by Hooker) to the general confession in Morning Prayer, weighed against any possible drift back to the medieval system. Most of what Anglicans wrote about confession was highly tinged by anti-Roman polemic.

III

Seventeenth century Anglican writers have a wealth of material on the cure of souls. On private confession they are usually, like their sixteenth century predecessors, concerned to assert their differences from Roman Catholics. Francis White, in A *Reply to Jesuit Fisher's Answer* (1624), an item in a tract controversy with the Jesuits of the late years of King James, combats the Roman requirement of private confession and the sacramental view that penance has "an operative virtue to confer grace." At the same time he approves private confession as useful for counsel, reproof of delinquents, comfort of the truly penitent, and preparation for Holy Communion. So used, it is "a work of godly discipline" agreeing with Scripture and the early Church. Ministers have received the keys, and have power to direct "the whole flock and every sheep and member of the same," in matters of salvation.

The High Church emphasis on the obligation of private confession appears in Bishop John Overall of Norwich (d. 1619), who in his Notes on the Book of Common Prayer, makes it a requirement in cases of mortal sin: "If he have committed a mortal sin, then we require confession of it to a priest." Launcelot Andrewes in 1600 occasioned some surprise by a sermon at Court in which he argued that contrition is insufficient without confession and absolution. In his Visitation Articles as Bishop of Ely, 1625, he employs the terms of the Prayer Book and of the canon of secrecy. Lewis Bayly, Bishop of Bangor, author of the enormously popular *Practice of Pietie* (ca. 1610), takes other ground. He stresses the value of confession for the discipline of humility, but calls it a "spiritual conference." Absolution is "ministerial," as in Hooker. It should be such as to leave no doubt that the sin is forgiven. Bayly's manual contains long sections on "how to behave thyself in time of sickness," "consolations against the fear of death," and related topics. Similarly Joseph Hall, Bishop of Exeter, in *The Old Religion . . . the Difference betwixt the Reformed and Roman Church . . .* (1628), approves private confession as "of singular use and behoof," but condemns the Roman view of its uniform obligation. Our Saviour, he points out, "many a time gave absolution where was no particular confession of sins." On the "basis of divine reason," says Hall, "this supposed duty is needless, dangerous and impossible."

Hall's admission of private absolution without particular confession is unusual in Anglicanism. In contrast we may note the high-church position of Peter Heylin (d. 1662), who in his *Theology of the Ancients* observes that confession to a priest is "agreeable both to the doctrine and intent of the Church of England, though not so much in practice as it ought to be." Heylin disagrees with the Romans who hold it to be universally obligatory and equally with "the grandees of the puritan faction" who neglect it. In absolution the priest exercises "a delegated, ministerial power, which, however, is not therefore "less judicial." Heylin holds emphatically that "no man not in priestly order can absolve from sin."

The poems of George Herbert (d. 1633) would furnish much to our purpose. In *The Church Porch*, a long poem of prudential morals, he versifies and modernizes an old injunction (lxxvi):

> Summe up at night what thou hast done by day:
>   And in the morning what thou hast to do.
> Dresse and undresse thy soul: mark the decay
>   And growth of it; if with thy watch, that too
> Be down, then winde up both.

But it is his subjective and devotional poems rather than those of moral counsel that are most distinctive of his genius. Herbert mingles startling conceits with edifying thoughts, as in this handling of a favorite theme (*On Death*):

> Death, thou wast once an uncouth, hideous thing,
>   Nothing but bones . . . ,
> But since our saviour's death did put some blood
>   Into thy face,
> Thou art grown fair and full of grace.

or in the well-known bold stanzas on *Discipline*, beginning with the line, "Throw away thy rod."

In a prose work, A *Priest to the Temple or, the Countrey Parson* (1632), Herbert presents the ideal village pastor, devout, competent and gracious, and "not witty or eloquent, but holy" (vii). After his Sunday morning services and afternoon catechizing:

> The rest of the day he spends either in reconciling neighbors who are at variance, or in visiting the sick, or in exhortations to some of the flock by themselves, whom his sermons cannot or doe not reach. (viii)

In his household he observes Friday as a day of abstinence and confession of sins: fasting is, however, adapted to the requirements of health (x). He is alert to visit the afflicted, and "hath thoroughly digested all the points of consolation." On visiting the sick he persuades them to particular confession (xv). When anyone in the parish sins, "he hateth him not as an officer but pityes him as a father" (xvi). When called to travel, he has prayers with the guests in the inn where he takes lodging, and as occasion offers, visits families to examine and advise them (xvii). Herbert would use the Catechism as the basis of a free Socratic dialogue. Questions compel alertness, even in those who would sleep during sermon and prayer (xxi). He supplies advice to the pastor for the direction of those in a good spiritual condition, and of those inclined to atheism, or to despair of God's favor (xxxiv). The "procession" or annual perambulation of the parish, is valued as an occasion of neighborly intercourse and reconciling of differences. The parson should encourage mutual visits between families, and where there is misunderstanding, take one of the parties to dine with the other (xxxv). Such are some of the practical suggestions of this classic, a book as practical as it is quaint. Herbert is well aware of the problem of contention in the rural parish; but he regards idleness as the prevailing vice—possibly because he knew it to be his own chief temptation.

Herbert's friend, Nicholas Ferrar (d. 1637), instituted at Little Gidding in Huntingdonshire a unique religious community, the members of which were mostly his relatives, men, women and children. Their leader kept a watchful eye upon all, enjoining ascetic austerities and spiritual exercises, including vigils, meditations and study of the Scriptures and other devotional books. The Psalms were recited and sung much as in monasticism. Instruction of the children, beginning at four o'clock on weekdays, and five on Sundays, involved much memorization. On Sundays it was extended to the children of neighboring villages, who were induced to come by the payment of a penny for every psalm or other assigned passage memorized, and by the dinner for all that followed. John Ferrar in his *Life of Nicholas Ferrar* describes this admiringly and recommends the method of "hiring children to learn psalms and chapters" as "a thing good, profitable to all." Ferrar's writings contain many short moral tales of the *exemplum* type. Both Herbert and Ferrar have left a few letters, of no great importance for spiritual guidance. Ferrar's letter to his parents of April 10, 1613, may be contrasted with Herbert's to his mother of May 29, 1622. The former is written in prospect of the writer's own death; the latter to an aged and sick mother. Ferrar repents his former indifference to death, prays with great earnestness for pardon, and provides for some minor debts. Herbert's is a somewhat formal consolation; much of it might have been written to a stranger. Herbert was not yet thirty, and perhaps here merely puts into impressive rhetoric what his excellent mother had herself taught him:

Madam, as the earth is but a point in respect of the heavens, so are earthly troubles compar'd to heavenly joys. . . . I have always observed the thred of life to be like other threds or skenes of silk, full of snarlls and incumbrances.

Archbishop William Laud (d. 1645), accused of importing "popish confession" because he proposed for the Scottish Church a rule similar to that of the Canons of 1604, claimed the support of "the learned of the Reformed Churches through Christendom" for voluntary confession which, he says, "Calvin commends exceedingly" (1645). A learned layman, Hamon L'Estrange, in a liturgical compilation entitled *The Alliance of Divine Offices* (1659), observes that the Church of England "approveth of, though she doth not command, auricular confession." He enlarges on the usefulness of private absolution to poor souls laboring under their sins, and points to three current views of it among Anglicans, that it is precatory, that it is declaratory and that it is authoritative. For each of these views he finds some support in the liturgy. The "I absolve thee" formula is "fitly applicable" only when the priest is assured of the sinner's sincere repentance. *The Cause and Cure of a Wounded Conscience* (1647) is a typical work of the brilliant Thomas Fuller (d. 1661). Confession to a "godly minister" is enjoined by the authoritative speaker in this dialogue, though with denunciation of its Roman form.

We omitted above one minor but significant alteration in the Visitation Office made in the 1662 revision of the Prayer Book, the insertion in parentheses of the clause "if he humbly and heartily desire it" after the words "the priest shall absolve him." The change is held to have been suggested by Bishop John Cosin of Durham, who in his early years had written a *Collection of Private Devotions* (1627). In this book he recommends preparation for the Blessed Sacrament by confession "to a learned and discreet priest," to receive advice and absolution. The effect of the inserted words in the Visitation Office is to restrict the use of absolution of the dying to those who earnestly wish it. Probably, however, Cosin would favor some such procedure as that of Laud, who in his *Private Devotions* indicates that he was accustomed to ask whether the sick man felt the need to confess and receive the "benefit of absolution." Thus the initiative would not be wholly left to the penitent, but the office would not be performed without his hearty desire for it.

IV

The celebrated Jeremy Taylor (d. 1667) in his *Unum necessarium or Doctrine of Repentance* (1655) warmly approves confession to a priest as of great profit to those "heavy-laden with their sins." He treats the matter with acute discernment. Though not necessary by scriptural command, confession is for some persons "a necessary charity": "it hath not an absolute, but may have a relative and superinduced necessity." He would have the confessant carefully avoid the accusation of another. For example, if he has committed incest he should confess only to a priest who is not acquainted with the other party in the offense. He would so guard the seal required in Canon cxiii of the 1604 series, that confession of treason should be withheld entirely rather than be divulged under the exception in the canon. He points to the value to the confessant of the mortifying shame of confession. The priest should not "lessen the shame" lest he also lessen the hatred of the sin. Confession should be such as to "express all the great lines of his folly and calamity," so that the confessor "may make a competent judgment of the state of his soul."

Taylor's *Holy Dying* (1651) merits special attention. Sister Mary O'Connor has called attention to the difference between this book and the medieval *Artes moriendi*, in the fact that Taylor makes the whole course of life a school for dying well. In this respect we may note a contrast also with Becon's *The Sick Man's Salve*, which, like the early books, is confined to the ministry of the deathbed. Taylor has, however, certain features of the Art of Dying literature, including temptations, devils and angels. Dedicating the book to the Earl of Carberry, he remarks: "I shall entertain you in a charnel house." Taylor reflects with a sad beauty on the brevity of life, in which "every contingency doth preach our funeral sermon," and depicts both the symptoms of slow bodily decay, and the startling suddenness with which death may strike. A well-disciplined life leading to a religious old age is desirable, but some short lives have been fruitful. The example of St. Ambrose is commended, who gave eight hours of the day to sleep and recreation, eight hours to work for others, and eight hours to study and prayer. Life is as miserable as it is short; and sadness sweetens the bitter cup of death.

Taylor's eloquence in describing man's woes on earth is superb, but the stuff is old.

Preparation for death involves the daily scrutiny of our actions. (The learned author naturally cites Pythagoras.) This is to be done in detail, and with full purpose of amendment—"that we may go to God, and to a spiritual guide, and search for remedies, and apply them." Men who have not done this, die timorously, as, too late, they examine their lives. Taylor contrasts the desperation of the reckless sinner at death with the good man's joy in passing, assured of pardon, into liberty and glory. "In sickness," he remarks later (III, vi), "the soul begins to dress herself for immortality." As a man who plans a noble life for his son "loves to see him pale with study or panting with labor," so God "dresses us for heaven" by our struggle with disease in which faith triumphs over pain.

Taylor provides a rich fare of high counsels, with many classical and biblical examples, designed to fortify the soul against temptation. He gives directions for prayer at stages of the sick man's experience, e.g., "a prayer to be said when a sick man takes physic," which may be compared with a corresponding one in Bayly's *Practice of Pietie*. He gives rules for repentance in sickness, including restitution of "all unjust possessions." But he has, after all, little faith in mere deathbed repentance. He supplies also a set of rules for the priest's visitation of the sick; this should not be delayed until "his reason is useless." While James (5:14) speaks of visitation by the "elders," Taylor would make sure that the sick man's curate or confessor attend him, "to set his soul in order." He gives no less than twenty-four arguments by which the confessor may move him to confession, and another long series of considerations to awaken a "stupid conscience." Confession should be ample and contrite, and the communion should be administered only when repentance is complete, and before reason is gone.

This is a truly great book, but no man in immediate prospect of death would have the strength to read or even to listen to it. It is written for "dying men" still in normal health. Many of the counsels to the sick call for choices open only to the active. It is a book of Christian moral philosophy, the product of a mind that exudes classical commonplaces of learning, and at the same time feels the awful alternative of man's destiny in heaven or hell. The latter gives intensity to Taylor's writing, as it does to Baxter's. In the companion volume *Holy Living* (1650) we see its fruits in an almost merciless emphasis upon the preciousness of time, and condemnation of idleness, "the greatest prodigality." For seventeenth century religion, Puritan or Anglican, the soul must never loiter, but press with vigor on.

In his *Dissuasive from Popery* (1664-67) Taylor holds that confession is to be "commanded to all to whom it is needful or profitable," and opposes the Roman view that full confession is required of all. He here makes the point that in John 20:23 we read "whose sins," not "what sins ye remit"; the judgment is of persons, not primarily of sins. "And therefore it becomes the minister of souls to know the state of the penitent rather than the nature and number of his sins."

Taylor left unpublished a slight book called *Christian Consolations*, written for a hypochondriac lady, and stressing Christ's "redemption for every sinner that repents and believes." Original sin remains with us, he here affirms, but he would have the penitent not fail to repent daily of "the multitudes of sins of under size." The book is a document in soul guidance, as are also his spiritual letters. Some of those written to John Evelyn, the diarist, a great Anglican layman, are of special interest. On March 31, 1654, Evelyn notes a conference with Taylor "about some spiritual matters," and states his intention to "use him thenceforward as my ghostly father." In February, 1658, Taylor wrote to console Evelyn on the death of his two sons. (The younger of these was a prodigy of early mental powers.) Taylor at the time was imprisoned in the Tower of London (on account of an innocent indiscretion on the part of his printer) but soon to be freed. Reminded of his own similar bereavement not long before, he feels the more deeply his friend's loss.

> But, Sir, I cannot choose, but I must hold another and a brighter flame to you; it is already burning in your heart; and if I can but remove the dark side of the lanthorne you have enoughe within you to warme yourself, and to shine on others.

The dead sons are now bright stars: "heaven is given them on very easy terms." Evelyn's grief has a reasonable cause, yet it is more reasonable to master it. Taylor's encouragements include the incautious statement that "the Apostles had no children": the story of Domitian and the grandsons of St. Jude has been overlooked. He undertakes to visit his friend "next week" in order to witness his Christian courage, and prays that he may be comforted. Three months after he writes with satisfaction commending Evelyn's piety and hoping that he will become immersed in the delights of religion. On the whole, however, this correspondence with Evelyn discloses more of mutual, equal friendship than of spiritual direction as ordinarily understood.

The Oxford royalist, Richard Allestree, has the best claim to the authorship of *The Whole Duty of Man,* the first edition of which is of 1658. It contains earnest recommendations of private confession on the basis of the Prayer Book. He would be a fool who would not seek healing for bodily disease, and the folly is greater where the soul is involved. The author warns those who miss this remedy because their very confidence is their disease. Since we are apt to favor ourselves, it might be very useful, especially for the ignorant, "sometimes to advise with a spiritual guide" so as to learn their true state and receive direction for subduing their sins. The book is packed with moral advice and casuistic solutions. The works of John Kettlewell (d. 1695), on the other hand, combine devotion with spiritual counsel. His *Companion for the Penitent and for Persons Troubled in Mind* (1693) and *Death Made Comfortable, or the Way to Die Well* (1694) enforce the requirements of the Prayer Book and supply copious scriptural passages for hours of devotion. The demand for such literature is more significant to the historian than its contents.

V

Despite all the competent Anglican writing on the cure of souls, Anglicanism lacked a general treatise on the work of the pastor. Baxter's *Reformed Pastor* is less an Anglican than a Puritan work. A year after Baxter's death this lack was supplied by Gilbert Burnet, Bishop of Salisbury (d. 1715), the well-known historian of the Reformation in England. His *Discourse of Pastoral Care* (1692, third enlarged edition 1713) was written in order "to raise the sense of the obligation of the clergy" in pastoral duties, which Burnet believed to be very low. He reviews the New Testament passages of special bearing on his subject, and with extensive quotation, the works of St. Gregory Nazianzen, St. Chrysostom, St. Gregory the Great, and St. Bernhard. Canons of various councils, including the Council of Trent, are also recited and interpreted. "Such examples," he observes, "are indeed reproaches to us." Much of his material on the Church of England is concerned with other matters, but the personal ministry receives thoughtful attention, chiefly in Chapter viii. While we neglect "the godly discipline that was in the primitive Church," he notes, we have authority for "much more than we practice."

Besides the disciplinary censures, there should be private labors of a personal sort, such as the discreet reconciling of differences, and tactful admonition of men of rank who set an evil example. Here "it may often be the best way to do it by letter." Visiting the sick is one of the pastor's chief duties; and this ministry involves a searching consideration of their course of life, with counsel to repentance and the restoration of unjust gains. It is "treachery to souls" to accept an inadequate deathbed repentance, leading not only to the loss of the dying man's soul, but also to the ruin of observers who see how slight a repentance is needed for assurance of salvation. The sick should make solemn vows of amendment in case of recovery, and thereafter be reminded of these engagements. He finds, in towns more than in the country, sick persons deeply troubled either because of evil deeds or because physical inactivity has induced hypochondria. The former must be assigned appropriate acts of penance; the latter "a little humored in their distemper" and not allowed to be too much alone with their depressing thoughts. Burnet holds that those who become unhealthily scrupulous from physical causes should have their condition frankly explained to them, and be directed to the principles of living rather than to their fluctuating humors. He also exhorts the clergy to visit their parishioners from house to house, for "an hour a day, twice or thrice a week." These visits may be brief, involving mainly "a short word for stirring them up to mind their souls, to make conscience of their ways, and to pray earnestly to God," with inquiries into the peace of the neighborhood and "their necessities, if they seem very poor."

It is probable that John Dryden's banal imitation of Chaucer, *The Character of a Good Parson* (1700) is based upon the pastorate of Bishop Thomas Ken (d. 1711):

> The proud he tamed, the penitent he cheered;
> Nor to rebuke the rich offenders feared.

We have already made use of Nathanael Marshall's historical and practical treatise: *The Penitential Discipline of the Primitive Church* (1714). In his fourth chapter Marshall pleads for a revival of features of the ancient public discipline. These include the use of the stations of penance, and the employment of suffragans who like the ancient "presbyter of penance" would each have charge of discipline for a district centering in a market town. He also suggests the addition to the liturgy of "a penitential office, explained by a proper rubric."

Anglican testimony on the cure of souls in the eighteenth century is almost as abundant as in the seventeenth. There is in it very little of material importance that is at all new. Perhaps the most noteworthy statements are found in the saintly and courageous Bishop Thomas Wilson's *Instructions for the Clergy* (1708) and *Sermons* which set a high standard of pastoral duty toward sinners and the sick, and offer many suggestions for the confessor. His interpretation of the clause which sets the condition of absolution in the 1662 Prayer Book, "if he shall humbly and heartily desire it," may be understood from his urgent language:

Every Christian . . . ought not to leave the world without the benefit of absolution, which he should be earnestly pressed to desire, and exhorted to dispose himself to receive.

The Nonjurors included numerous writers of distinction such as George Hickes (d. 1715) and Jeremy Collier (d. 1726) who take high ground on the authority of priests in the power of the keys and absolution. To their ranks belongs also the great devotional writer William Law (d. 1761), one of the most distinguished guides of conscience of the century. Much of his work is associated with personal consultations of which we have scant record. His spiritual letters that have been published are characteristically pithy and searching (*Works* edited by "G. Moreton," Volume IX). He regards the functions of the guide of souls as a useful "contrivance for human help." Yet he warns a correspondent ("a person of quality") that just as "to be always tampering with physicians and probing one's condition is the way to lose all true judgment," so we may do much hurt to our spiritual health "by running after spiritual advice on every occasion" (Letter vii, January 10, 1754). One who is "burdened with troubles" is advised that "the state of absolute resignation, naked faith, and pure love of God, is the highest perfection" (xi, undated). A zealous writer of letters of advice is rebuked: "Have a care of too much eagerness to set other people right" (xvi, August 4, 1753). It is notable that in his *Spiritual Call to a Devout and Holy Life* (1728) Law lays great stress upon daily self-examination and confession of sins to God, without enjoining confession to a priest or to a spiritual adviser. Ten years earlier he had defended the authority of absolution against Bishop Hoadly (*Works*, I, 47 ff.); but this churchly emphasis was abandoned. The cultivation of the soul, and the practice of repentance, are for Law primarily each man's duty to himself—with the aid of such plans of devotional routine as he provides in his *Christian Perfection* and *Spiritual Call*.

VI

The Evangelical Revival released new energies in Anglicanism, that found expression in foreign missions, emancipation of slaves, and a new devotion to pastoral labors. George Whitefield (d. 1770) in his preaching tours was privately consulted by many thousands, and once received in a single week one thousand letters of inquiry. Some fifteen hundred of his letters are preserved, a considerable number of which are definitely written for personal guidance. William Romaine (d. 1782), one of the earlier Evangelicals, deserves mention too for his religious correspondence. His letters have a fresh evangelical fervor and appeal, and stress the gladness of salvation against the background of natural depravity. Romaine shows impatience only with people who mourn their lack of holiness instead of receiving thankfully the pardoning grace of Christ. Rowland Hill (d. 1833), another Evangelical, who early felt the influence of the writings of the devout Scottish Episcopalian, Robert Leighton, archbishop of Glasgow (d. 1684), and was associated with Whitefield, was distinguished for his pastoral care of condemned prisoners and the poor.

Outstanding among the leaders of the movement was Charles Simeon (d. 1836) of Cambridge. His range of interest was wide and for half a century he exercised an increasing influence upon ministers and laymen. His correspondence contains numerous excellent examples of the letter of guidance, and his *Memoir* reports many a situation in which he provides direction. For example, when a young minister (1783), while waiting in a graveyard for a funeral procession to arrive, he brought religious consolation to a poor, discouraged woman who came to the place planning suicide. But his letters show that with all his zeal, Simeon is more often than not hesitant in giving spiritual advice. Look, for example, at three letters of 1817 that appear in sequence in the *Memoirs* edited by William Carus. The first is a rebuke to a young minister who has spoken the truth without love and driven away his curate, in which the writer is obviously afraid of alienating the receiver's affection by his frank criticism. The second is to a young woman whose evangelical views have aroused her father's displeasure. Simeon somewhat discounts his own seemingly very wise advice by emphasizing his lack of adequate knowledge of the case. The third is to a lady regarding difficulties with her husband: he likes plays and operas which she regards as vanities. The advice given is to comply with the husband's wishes without concealing her distress; but again with some hesitancy. "It is easy enough to lay down general principles, but to modify them to existing circumstances is extremely difficult." Simeon shrinks from the decisions of a casuist, and prefers to dwell upon principles, leaving to his correspondents a large choice in applying them. Occasionally, however, he is forthright enough, e.g., in rebuking a minister's unwise zeal or prejudiced opinions that drive people from church. On March 8, 1829, he wrote to a ministerial friend: "Against the Methodists you have taken up a very unwarrantable prejudice. . . . What would you think of a person who would speak in the same acrimonious way of you? . . . It is not easy for a person, noticed and caressed as you are, to preserve an humble spirit."

Simeon's later letters are increasingly rich in warm friendship and Christian sympathy. From a short letter of consolation to a minister on the death of his wife (June 8, 1833) we quote a characteristic sentence in which he almost apologetically acknowledges the danger of ill-chosen counsel:

> I do not mean to sing songs to a heavy heart, but to bind up, as God may enable me, and to heal a broken spirit: and if I have erred, impute it to nothing but misdirected love.

While a good many of his letters are somewhat didactic, they are informed with evangelical warmth, personal experience, and essential humility. There is little of authoritarian direction and technical churchmanship, but often he writes with authentic spiritual wisdom.

Evangelicalism did not favor the practice of private confession, and did nothing to restore it. On the other hand, Edward Bouverie Pusey (d. 1882), standard-bearer of the Oxford Movement, actively sought a revival of the cure of souls through the restoration of the confessional. His *Entire Absolution of the Penitent* (1846) lays emphasis on the authorization of confession in the Prayer Book, where, as he says, the Church speaks of "the benefit of absolution" as distinct from "ghostly advice and counsel"—both being needed. In 1877, after much debate and a widespread revival of confession, Pusey published in English, with a long argumentative and historical introduction, an adaptation of the Abbé Jean Joseph Gaume's *Manual for Confessors* (1854), a compilation from Roman Catholic authors. Pusey and his associates desired to establish private confession as normal practices, and interpreted penance as a sacrament. A large measure of success attended their efforts; the controversy that accompanied the change has hardly yet reached an end. It is impossible here to go over this relatively recent story, and the materials are available to the reader. It will be more to the point to examine some of the letters of guidance written by Pusey and his friend John Keble (d. 1866), an important part of their ministry of the cure of souls.

Pusey's spiritual letters extend in date from 1838 to 1882. The decision of their editors to conceal the names and circumstances of the recipients offers a handicap to their adequate interpretation. Most of the persons addressed have evidently placed themselves in Pusey's spiritual care and are professing to pursue the path of devotion. He is often very authoritative, and is inclined to lay down rules and schedules of prayer and discipline. Thus he advises a young woman to follow a plan of self-examination twice daily, with the use of a written list of sins (Section I, letter xx). He looks for progress in the replies to his letters. "I almost hope that you are improving," he writes doubtfully to another, "notwithstanding all you complain of, and some bad overt faults." He recommends in this case meditation on the privations of Christ, or of His Holy Mother. The habit of laughing—the result of former levity— is often a disease: "Think what Hell is." At a meal, a little hunger should be left; as for dress: "Try to recall in what Dives was drest" (I, xxvi). Apparently to a young divinity scholar he writes in 1838 condemning certain alleged views of Methodists and of Dr. Arnold, and recommending mental prayer at nine, twelve and three daily. As the young man's spiritual adviser, he raises two points of detected weakness in him, the danger of vanity, and that latitudinarianism which expresses itself in an offhand way of speaking of the symbols of the Four Evangelists (I, xxii). It would be well "to make vanity the subject of humiliation," he writes in 1844, and recommends against it seven acts of humility a day, such as reflecting: "Servants obey us, we disobey God."

There is a fairly strong urge to asceticism in the earlier letters: this becomes increasingly an asceticism of the mind rather than of the body. Disapproving in one woman's case "increased fasting," he remarks: "I doubt whether this would promote what I wish, the mind of a little child in you." Something that would check overactivity of mind would be a greater self-denial, and more beneficial (I, xxx). To another he writes bluntly, "The centre of your faults is self-conceit. . . . I do not know how it is that your manners are so unrefined. . . . Do you remember contradicting everything I said, until, at last, I required you to listen and contradict no more?" (I, xxxvii). Another, whose defects he observes, is advised, in one of his latest letters, September, 1881 (I, xli): "I dare not think of bodily penances. They fall so unevenly on different frames. Better, I think, pray for true repentance."

Some of the letters are addressed to opponents and are sharply critical. To an "unbeliever" he responds: "Writers of the class to whom I fear you belong decry dogmatism, yet none are more dogmatic" (II, ii). What may have been his last letter, of August 5, 1882, contains the sentence: "But you worship this deity that you have made for yourself" (II, xii). The Third Section of the letters has two on confession, of 1870 and about 1874. The second of these (xxxiii) contains a characteristic statement:

> Practically it is found that confession is a means of grace and not a snare to people's consciences. It is not necessary to the validity of a confession that a person should enumerate all sins, but only that he should not wilfully keep back any because he is ashamed to own them.

The letters of Pusey offer considerable range and variety of religious thought, and are marked by frequent arresting injunctions, such as: "Rouse yourself in the midst of doing things, in order to do them better, and to God" (I, xxiii); "The poor, as a matter of course, are our superiors. We cannot reach their self-denial when they give a penny" (I, xxv). His quotations, too, are often brilliantly chosen: "It is a deep saying of Pascal, 'To love man, we must know him; to know God, we must love Him'" (II, ii).

The contents of John Keble's *Letters of Spiritual Counsel and Guidance* reveal less austerity than does Pusey. Their editor observes in them a resemblance to Fénelon, and still more to St. Francis de Sales. Keble may occasionally recommend such devices as keeping "a register of your advances or relapses," preferably "in cypher" (No. xli); but there is not much suggestion of a scheduled and exacting discipline. As early as 1817 he wrote: "I do not think the glory of God best promoted by a rigid abstinence from amusements" (xii), and in 1860 he states that he is among those who take a "laxer" view of common recreations (xiii). In letters of consolation (xxiii, xxvi) he approves prayers for the departed, holding that they also intercede for us (xxvi, xxvii).

Keble, of course, practiced the confessional, and he gives some attention to its importance in the letters. In one instance he says that "the naming of crimes and bad habits" will be a sufficient confession (xxvii). To a correspondent who is under carnal temptation in London, he recommends regular, and not only occasional, confession. Here also he proposes that "a discreet and charitable director" of his acquaintance be consulted, but he will not decline to serve in that role (xlv-xlix). In reply to another's inquiry he discusses obedience to one's confessor. If an absolute, unquestioning obedience is demanded, he observes:

> I could not myself make such a demand unless, from previous knowledge of the case, I was tolerably sure it was necessary, e.g., to prevent a Romanizing conscience from trifling with me, and with the ordinance (xcv).

When his advice is sought by one who finds reason to change his confessor, Keble suggests, to avoid embarrassment, a period without confession: "Let it lapse for a while" (lxxviii). Another is advised to write a confession if it cannot be given directly, and either send it or lay it before God in prayer (lxxxvii). In one letter (cxxxvi) he refers to an unsatisfactory consultant, a lady who has shown herself to be "one of those who seek direction with the instinctive purpose of directing the director."

In these and other instances we get an impression of a gentle but watchful guide of souls, advising still sinful candidates for holiness with a fine personal considerateness, always within the framework of ideas of the Oxford Revival.

VII

The divergence of modern Anglican viewpoints on confession and absolution finds expression in the report of a conference of clerical scholars invited by the Bishop of London, held at Fulham Palace December 29 to January 1, 1901-2. The discussion covers much historical ground, but leaves the basic differences unresolved. Some strongly testify to the value of confession, others feel that it should be exceptional and that the highest Christian life would have no need of it. An independent liberal view of the matter is set forth by H. Hensley Henson, (later Bishop successively of Hereford and Durham) in the valuable long preface of his *Moral Discipline in the Christian Church* (1905). He is highly critical of the pressure to confess that arises where a priest really believes himself vested with the power of absolution and points to the dangers that inhere in the confessional of a tyrannous sacerdotalism and of an unwholesome casuistry. At the same time he recognizes the naturalness and moral necessity of confession of sins in repentance, though "there is no inherent necessity which ties the practice of confession to the Christian ministry." Henson's idea of a revision of the Prayer Book involves a complete rewriting of the passages on confession to guard against sacerdotalism.

The main trunk of Anglicanism has remained in England, but it has vigorous branches in Scotland, Ireland, Canada and other British dominions, and the United States—from all of which extensive materials might be drawn. The life of Philips Brooks (d. 1893) abounds in evidence of personal pastoral guidance. His Sermon on the Christian Ministry (1893) stresses the spiritual intimacy of the minister with his people: "The dramas of his people's lives are all replayed on the stage of his sympathies. . . . Their temptations and victories are his." Another Protestant Episcopal churchman whose gifts of guidance and consolation were distinguished was the Canadian-born Charles Henry Brent (d. 1929), a figure of world significance for his leadership in the Ecumenical Movement.

One of the best American exemplars of the High Church movement is James Otis Sargent Huntington (d. 1935), founder of the Order of the Holy Cross. The Harvard-trained son of a Protestant-minded Bishop of Central New York, Father Huntington became the inspirer of Catholic piety within the Protestant Episcopal Church, with an influence far beyond the small religious order of which he was head. From the beginning of his priesthood he practiced the confessional, and through many years he wrote letters of counsel to a variety of persons in need of it. Miss Scudder's biography contains a classified selection of these letters. The reader of Pusey's and Keble's letters will find himself here on familiar ground; but Huntington perhaps surpasses both of them in the way in which he enters imaginatively into the situations of his correspondents. Thus advising a young mother to make a self-examination twice a day, he suggests the time when her baby has gone to sleep in the morning, and when she is washing her hands before supper. He frequently urges the importance of confession and penance—"the *special, normal, appointed* remedy for mortal sin." There is no sentimentality in his consolation: "Try," he writes, "to live up to the dignity of this suffering." In one letter he confesses his sense of inability to meet the sufferer's hard case, but ends with a word of deep wisdom: "I have found people who could pray only with great difficulty, but to whom a new world seemed to open as they began to praise."

The rising importance of casuistry, which Henson deplored, is manifest both in England and in America. William Walter Webb, Bishop of Milwaukee, was the author of a scholarly book, *The Cure of Souls* (1892 and 1910), which supplies detailed rules for confessors, supported by extensive quotations from the Fathers and Anglican divines. There is a comparable English book by Watkin Williams, *The Moral Theology of the Sacrament of Penance* (1917) which, however, makes large use of Roman Catholic authorities. The Bishop of Oxford, Kenneth E. Kirk, has treated the subject historically and practically in his *Conscience and Its Problems* (1927).

VIII

We have sought to illustrate the salient features of the history of the cure of souls in Anglicanism from a literature that is vast in extent. In this material, with all its variety, interpretations of a few passages in the New Testament, and in the Prayer Book and supporting documents of Anglicanism, bulk very large. The element of tradition tends to overshadow that of immediate experience. The chief exceptions to this are in Evangelicals as represented by Romaine and Simeon, and in the impatient liberal churchman, H. Hensley Henson. But the appeal to the documents has involved a sometimes concealed and sometimes overt debate between those who would apply the directions for confession and absolution as widely as possible, and those who would treat them as provisions for exceptional cases. Since the beginning of the Oxford Movement the advocates of a wide use of the confessional have been more vocal and persuasive than their opponents. While sincerely opposing the Papacy, they have been in no small degree inspired by Roman Catholic models. This can be ascertained by even a casual perusal of the writings of Pusey, Keble, Huntington and others of the school.

While the cure of souls is a field of controversy in Anglicanism, this has led rather to its cultivation than to its neglect. In her praise of Father Huntington and the ascetic guides of souls, Miss Scudder pauses to charge that "Protestant churches tend to ignore the more intimate phases of human fellowship," and to neglect the needs of stumbling individuals, isolated by "the dignified decencies of good taste." William Cunningham in *The Cure of Souls* (1908) makes the claim:

The importance attached to this aspect of the ministerial office has been and is a special characteristic of the Anglican communion; every age and every school of thought in the English Church has done much to insist on and to illustrate the sense of pastoral responsibility.

These comparisons may be made without full consideration of other than Anglican practice. But it is probably safe to say that no other great communion has given more attention to the cure of souls, either in theory or in practice.

One element that stands out prominently in this chapter is that of spiritual direction by letter. We have seen parallels to this in Lutheran and Reformed, as well as in medieval, churches. The guide or director is ordinarily not the confessor of his correspondent. This is natural since confession is under the seal and its content could not be referred to in a letter that might, accidentally or otherwise, become known. Unless there is violation of the seal, we cannot know anything of what is said in private confession, and its real inner history can never be written. From the letters of directors, however, we obtain knowledge of the actual materials of guidance. Ministers and laymen might profitably make a habit of reading the letters of spiritual men that have been useful to perplexed and aspiring souls.

Chapter XI

DISCIPLINE AND GUIDANCE IN PRESBYTERIANISM AND PURITANISM

I

No ATTENTION has so far been given to the non-Anglican British churches and their daughter communions. The list of these is a long one, and some that have their own importance will have to be omitted. The present chapter is a rapid survey of the cure of souls in Presbyterianism and Puritanism. The Congregational and Baptist churches, Quakerism and Methodism will be treated in the next.

The Reformed Church of Scotland provided in its first constitutional documents for a close supervision of all its members. The Book of Discipline, prepared by John Knox and five associates and presented to the Council of the Realm in 1560, contains (Section vii) an explicit statement on ecclesiastical discipline. Despite the refusal of the Parliament to ratify this book (because of its liberal provision for education) its regulations were largely followed in the parishes. The authors hold that certain crimes worthy of death ought not properly to fall under censure of the Church, but be punished by the civil sword: these include blasphemy, adultery and perjury, as well as murder. Among offenses subject to church discipline are drunkenness, excess in apparel or at table, fornication, oppression of the poor by exactions or cheating with false weights, and "wanton words and licentious living tending to slander." The present neglect of civil punishments renders it necessary, however, to excommunicate those who ought to be subjected to them until the offenders openly repent. Excommunication ought to be decided on only by a "grave and slow" process, but once declared should be adhered to "with all severity" since "laws made and not kept engender contempt of virtue."

Procedures in dealing with offenders are carefully outlined with appropriate differentiations. A private warning is to be given to those whose offenses are not scandalous, and if the offender promises amendment no further censure is required. But if he is contemptuous, or unimproved in behavior, he must be admonished by the minister, and if still recalcitrant, subjected to further discipline. For publicly known crimes of a heinous nature, such as fornication, drunkenness, fighting and swearing, the offender is brought before the Kirk session (consisting of the minister, elders and deacons), and required to confess "so that his conscience may feel how far he hath offended God and what scandal he hath raised in the Church." If repentant, he is to confess his offense before the congregation, pleading for their prayers and for restoration to membership. The Church ought not to be more severe than God, who when the sinner unfeignedly repents will not remember one of his iniquities.

If secret offenders once admonished by the ministers continue stubborn, they are once more warned and given a little time before further action. This failing to move them, their offenses are to be made known to the Sunday congregation, the names being withheld, and prayer is to be offered for their speedy repentance. Only after these measures have been unavailing is the name of such an offender made known. The congregation then determines whether such acts as he has committed are to be punished. His relatives and friends are urged to travail with him privately, to bring him to a repentant mind. On the third Sunday the minister inquires whether he has shown signs of repentance; if so, he is examined by the officers, led to make public confession, and restored to full standing. Otherwise he is solemnly excommunicated, and his excommunication published "throughout the realm." None but his own family may then have any dealings with him, except by appointment of the church authorities and with a view to his conversion. No child of his can be baptized while he is under sentence, unless the mother or the culprit's friends present the child, condemning the father's sin and obstinacy. Murderers and adulterers who escape the legal death penalty are to be excommunicated, but may be restored, on evidence of unfeigned repentance, with the intercession of the Church, a humble public confession and appeal by the offender, and the favorable decision of the congregation. The penitent is reinstated with solemn prayer, the elders taking him by the hand, one or two embracing him "with all reverence and gravity." The minister completes the act of reconciliation with admonition and thanksgiving. All persons are subject to these regulations, rulers as well as subjects, preachers not less than the humblest members of the Church. The "greater excommunication," involving the civil and social penalties was rarely used.

The elders are elected annually by the people, and are to assist the minister in judgment and personal admonition of delinquents. The minister himself is subject to the admonition and correction of his elders, and with the consent of the Church and the superintendent, they may bring about his deposition. For great offenses, and for heresy, he is to be permanently expelled from the ministry; for minor misdemeanors he is suspended until he repents.

The authority of the elders was high in the Scottish Kirk. In John Knox's Liturgy (1564) there was provision for a weekly (Thursday) meeting of ministers and elders chiefly for mutual criticism, but also for consideration of the faults of the members. Ministers were subjected to the "brotherly admonition" of this assembly. The kirk session of Aberdeen in 1568 ordered a mutual "trial and examination" of the minister, elders, deacons and reader four times a year, and before each communion their trial "by the whole Church." Such meetings were held by presbyteries as well as kirk sessions to a much later time: the term often used in the records is "privy censure." The principle of "fraternal correction," exemplified in the Continental Reformed churches, had ample play in the Kirk. In practice, however, it was often not sufficiently "fraternal." Dr. Ivo Macnaughton Clark, in his *History of Church Discipline in Scotland,* holds that it encouraged men to show up one another's faults. The elder's office was redefined in the Second Book of Discipline (adopted 1581) where elders were to assist in the examination of communicants and in visiting the sick, as well as to give "private admonitions" and to join with pastors and "doctors" in "establishing good order and execution of discipline."

II

Knox in his Liturgy treats thoughtfully "the order of ecclesiastical discipline," in the interests of the purity of the congregation and the true repentance of the guilty. He indicates the function of private brotherly admonition, and the public discipline of grave offenders. The former requires "godly zeal and conscience," so that we "seek rather to win our brother than to slander him." Admonition should be given in the presence of any who know the fault committed, and if it concerns the whole Church, the case should be brought before the ministers and elders. Where excommunication is necessary, care should be taken, when the fruits of repentance appear, to restore the expelled member without delay.

The Form of Excommunication and Repentance (1567), inserted in Knox's Liturgy, provides rules of procedure for excommunication and restoration. The low state of public law in cases of murder is reflected in these provisions. The Church must act where the magistrate has failed to act, by excommunication, exhorting the criminal to consider "how precious is the life of man before God," and laboring to call forth from him unfeigned repentance. If he is convicted in law, he is, if possible, to be led to repentance, then to receive consolation and absolution. If he escapes trial but is known to be guilty, he is excommunicated, and prayed for. The restoration is delayed until the culprit has stood three Sundays in front of the church, barefooted and bareheaded and in base apparel, bearing the weapon used in his crime, and pleading for reconciliation. Procedures for other sorts of offenders are indicated in the section entitled, "the form of public repentance"—a solemn and truly moving act of penitence. The absolution here is declaratory and conditional:

If thou unfeignedly repentest thy former iniquity, and believest in the Lord Jesus, then I, in his name, pronounce and affirm that thy sins are forgiven, not only on earth but also in heaven. . . .

The absolution formula for the restoration of the excommunicated implies a claim of ministerial authority not elsewhere matched in the Reformation:

In the name and authority of Jesus Christ, I . . . absolve thee from the sentence of excommunication, from the sin by thee committed, and from all censures . . . according to thy repentance, and pronounce thy sin to be loosed in heaven. . . .

Such, in outline, were the provisions by which the Scottish discipline was regulated. The system mingles watchful firmness with patient considerateness, and attempts to follow New Testament practice. So far as the documents indicate, it was not (as often supposed) a system of barren legalism. The language used implies the greatest concern to keep the procedure on a high religious level, and to invite repentance rather than to exact punishment.

But its application to all sorts of people, the religiously indifferent

included, made the high level difficult to maintain. Its ideal working
would have required a wider spread of piety and wisdom, than the times
afforded. Deterioration into one or other of the alternatives of mere
legalism and of indifference and neglect could not but follow. The
Second Book of Discipline made the status of elder permanent through
life. The authority vested in the elders called for the finest qualities, and
these were not always present. Some of the methods of discipline involved trivial forms of public humiliation injurious to the dignity of a
worshiping assembly.

Although the Form of Process adopted in 1707 exempted the minister
from censure by the kirk session, the elders sometimes evaded this rule
and took a high-handed course with their pastor. Professor G. D. Henderson's admirable study, *The Scottish Ruling Elder*, shows, by many
citations of parish records, the lights and shadows of the history of this
office. "Elders" he observes, "have not always been all that they might
have been." Yet on the whole he believes that the office has justified
itself: "It is a great institution, worth preserving, worth promoting,
worth improving." The evidence of the sources which Professor Henderson has amply reported and conscientiously evaluated substantially
exculpates the Scottish kirk sessions from Buckle's charge of arbitrariness and irresponsibility. Yet it shows frequent instances of crude penalties that cannot have contributed to anybody's edification. The Church
employed some physical penalties such as the "jougs" or iron collar
chained to the wall, and the "branks" or bridle for scolding women. The
stool of repentance was set in a prominent place in the church and
offenders were often made to stand on it during the sermon.

In the controversy over episcopacy, every action favoring an episcopal
order and its liturgical trend was subject to penalty. Thus in Aberdeen
craftsmen were called to answer for laying off work on Christmas day
(1575), and a man was accused for painting a crucifix to be used at a
funeral (1618). Adherence to "papistry" is a frequent charge before the
session: abjuration was required and usually but not always obtained.
In some such instances we have no record of further action; in others
excommunication was ordered. Church attendance was insisted upon,
and observers sometimes sent about during services to note the absentees.
Witchcraft and other superstitious practices, drunkenness, slander,
Sabbath-breaking and fornication were common offenses. Vagabonds
and harlots were alike arrested and banished; both types of offender had
a habit of returning. An Aberdeen piper was threatened with banishment in order to stop his Sunday bagpipe-playing (1609).

The parishes were divided into elders' districts, in which each elder was to examine communicants privately before each communion service, and to bring about reconciliations between neighbors found to be at variance. Metal tokens were distributed to those qualified to take communion, and were presented for admission to the communion table. Knox includes in his Liturgy an office in which the minister alone is made responsible for the visitation of the sick, but this was also, through the subsequent period, a function shared by his elders. Large responsibilities for poor relief devolved upon the session. Some of the records show remarkable and well considered liberality in gifts for the sick and poor, and in the distribution of Bibles and other books. In this matter the functions of elders and deacons were not clearly separated; the deacons also met with the session, though they were not always voting members. Collections were taken for distressed foreign churches, for prisoners of the Turks, and other causes abroad.

By catechizing of the young and by sundry regulations, the sessions sought to maintain an austere religious temper in the families. Thus by Aberdeen regulations of 1604 families were to keep the Sabbath without play or labor, attending the services and learning to sing God's praise. Heads of families were to attend sermons on weekdays, and, when required, the catechism exercises. Twice daily families were enjoined to observe periods of prayer. Swearing and filthy language in family life were to be corporally punished.

There is no reason to suppose that the adoption by the Scottish Church of the documents of the Westminster Assembly made any appreciable difference in its pastoral discipline. *The Directory for the Worship of God* (1644) states that the minister's duties include private as well as public teaching; he is required "to admonish, exhort, reprove and comfort" his people "upon all seasonable occasions."

He is to admonish them in time of health to prepare for death; and for that purpose they are often to confer with their minister about the estate of their souls; and in times of sickness to desire his advice and help timely and seasonably, before their strength and understanding fail them.

The Form of Church Government (1645) claims scriptural authority for those officers "commonly called elders," and regards them as representatives of the people—a point strongly emphasized by Charles Hodge and many other competent interpreters. They are authorized to make inquiry after the spiritual estate of members, and to admonish and rebuke the wayward. The Confession of Faith (1647) succinctly explains the purposes of the discipline, but nothing except the phraseology is new.

However, about the time of the Assembly there began to prevail a more legalistic and punitive purpose in disciplinary procedures. The Form of Process (1707) marks this change at a somewhat advanced stage. Dr. Clark finds in this period a loss of the earlier ideal of the reclamation of delinquents. He connects this deterioration of the discipline with the influence of English Puritanism, and with an increasing dependence upon the authority of the state. In the eighteenth century the Church courts were less attentive to discipline than formerly, and were content to deal mainly with sexual offenses. Steuart of Pardovan, however, in his *Collections and Observations* (1709) still represents the labor of pastors, following the Westminster Standards and acts of the General Assembly, as rich in duties connected with the cure of souls. The terms we have quoted from the Directory are treated as indicative of actual practice. Ministry to the sick is emphasized: this should lead the sick man to examine himself and repent; care should be taken that he be not cast into despair. An annual visitation of families is required, and the minister is to be accompanied by the elder of the district. The minister speaks separately with the servants and the children, and privately with the heads of families on the care of their souls, and their religious duties in the household. Family worship it to be enjoined, and Bibles and catechisms to be provided where the people are unable to buy them. Such is the picture of the faithful pastor of the eighteenth century as he seeks the welfare of souls and the ordering of home life. The extent and success of these labors would be hard to estimate. Of a home so ruled, Burns wrote: "From scenes like these, old Scotia's grandeur springs."

III

In the devotional literature of Scottish Presbyterianism spiritual letters have a considerable place. John Knox wrote a fair number of such letters. These are chiefly addressed in 1553 and 1554 to his English mother-in-law, Mrs. Richard Bowes who was later to reside with him in Geneva. "My mind was seldom quiet" he wrote frankly later, "for doing somewhat for the comfort of her troubled conscience." Mrs. Bowes was a hypochondriac. Robert Louis Stevenson, in a brilliant early essay on *John Knox and Women*, calls her a "weariful woman." Doubtless her alienation from her husband on religious grounds had helped to bring

on her state of depression. She clung to Knox for reassurance and consolation, reporting to him her religious worries. Freely confessing his
own sinful nature, "wretched infirmity," and strong temptations, he
nevertheless constantly affirms his faith in the mercy of God. He attributes to Satan's promptings her terror over the unpardonable sin
(Letters i, xiv, in Laing's edition, Vol. III) and when she charges herself
with the sins of Sodom and Gomorrah, he gently rebukes her obsession,
pointing out that she knows not what these sins were (xx). One is reminded of Fénelon's treatment of Madame de Montberon's distractions
(below p. 301); but Knox quotes passages of evangelical assurance from
St. Paul, while Fénelon urges humility and surrender of the will. Knox
addressed to Mrs. Bowes in 1554 on the eve of his flight from England,
his *Exposition of the Sixth Psalm of David*. Much of this fervent treatise
is directly designed to heal the distressed state of mind of his "Dear
Mother." The goodness of God, he affirms,

as it is infinite, so can it not be defiled by our iniquity; but it pierceth
through the same, and will show itself to our consolation, even as the
beams of the bright sun pierce through the mists and thick clouds . . . O,
Beloved! when thy afflicted soul . . . can stay itself upon God's infinite goodness, then are all the fiery darts of the devil quenched. (Laing, III, 147-49)

Samuel Rutherford (d. 1661) had been for nine years the zealous
pastor of Anwoth in Kirkudbrightshire when in connection with the
royal pressure to make the Church of Scotland episcopal, he was forced
out of the parish, forbidden to preach, and "banished" to Aberdeen
(1636). He had been a learned defender of high Calvinism against
Arminianism and was to be a prominent figure in the Westminster Assembly and to write *Lex Rex* (1644), a political classic, against royal
absolutism. Much of his writing is controversial and closely argumentative; but his spiritual letters with their lavish poetical imagery and
mystical exaltation exhibit a totally different aspect of his mind. Most
of his 352 extant letters were written in the two years of his confinement
within Aberdeen (1636-38), and are the fruit of his enforced separation
from former parishioners and friends: a few, however, are of earlier or of
later date. As is usually the case with spiritual letters, more of Rutherford's were addressed to women than to men. These letters reveal rather
more of the writer's religious moods than of direction for the receiver.
They also have frequent allusions to Church and State affairs, marked
by Rutherford's uncompromising Presbyterianism. In many of them,
the mystical espousal of the soul by Christ the Bridegroom is elaborated

upon with a variety and boldness of expression worthy of St. Bernhard of Clairvaux. As in St. Bernhard's discourses on the Song of Songs, the sexual imagery is wholly sublimated, but its excessive use becomes a little repellent to the sensitive reader. Equally bold and often highly impressive are the expressions of identification with Christ in His sufferings and heavenly reign. Rutherford's pithy and arresting sentences, his surprising metaphors, and the hyperbole with which he gives utterance to his fervor, make the letters a book of unique literary interest.

Marion Macknaught, the wife of Provost William Fullerton of Kirkudbright, received more of Rutherford's letters than any other correspondent. When he was at Anwoth he sometimes visited the Fullerton home and some of the letters are written to the husband. The Fullertons were of Rutherford's mind in matters ecclesiastical, and he could assume, even as he sought to confirm, their active loyalty to the Kirk. In letters of 1634 (xxxiv, xxxvi in Andrew Bonar's edition) he desires William to stand for Parliament against an unsatisfactory candidate, and assures Marion "that our Lord is heating a furnace for the enemies of his Kirk in Scotland." To Lady Kenmure, whose husband had placed himself under Rutherford's guidance and died a pious death, he also wrote many times. The letter of consolation (xxxv) written shortly after Lord Kenmure's death recalls his own wife's departure four years earlier as a wound not yet healed, treats with great boldness the theme of the heavenly Bridegroom, and assures the widow that "the star which shined in Galloway is now shining in another world." To these two loyal women Rutherford revealed the depressions and elevations of his spirit, as he sought consolation in Christ while witnessing what he esteemed the subversion of the true Kirk. Generally he writes in high hope of a divine reversal of the course of things.

Lift up your head. He is coming to save. . . . Oh, such wide steps Christ taketh! Three or four hills are but a step to Him. . . . I tell you, Christ will make new work out of old, for-casten [forsaken] Scotland.   *

He continues in this letter to Marion Macknaught (clxxvii: June 15, 1537) to tell "what lovely Jesus, fair Jesus, King Jesus, has done to my soul." The most difficult experience for him to accept was the silencing of his preaching, yet he appears never to have violated the command.

His letters to his fellow ministers similarly combine with personal testimony the note of courageous expectation. Even in letters of stern correction to men of the world there is much self-revealing:

Misspend not your short sand-glass, which runneth very fast; seek your Lord in time. Let me obtain of you a letter under your hand, for a promise to God, by his grace, to take a new course of walking with God. Heaven is not at the next door; I find it hard to be a Christian; there is no little thrusting and thringing to thrust in at Heaven's gates.

Thus he writes to John Gordon of Anwoth, March 14, 1637 (clii) rebuking him for swearing, anger, drinking, Sabbath-breaking, and hatred of enemies. He then adds:

Brother, I may, from new experience, speak of Christ to you—A river of God's unseen joys has flowed from bank to brae over my soul since I parted with you.

To another former parishioner, James Macadam, he had written a day earlier:

It will be a joy to my heart to hear that ye hold your face up the brae, and wade through temptations without fearing what man can do. . . . I was swimming in the depths, but Christ had his hand under my chin all the time; and now I have gotten to my feet again, and there are love-pearls of joy and springtides of consolation between Christ and me (cxlvi).

For Rutherford this fleeting life is a brief opportunity to lay hold of salvation. Mere superficial acknowledgment of the faith is utterly futile. Again and again he calls for the strenuous pursuit of holiness in a hostile world. To his Anwoth flock he wrote from Aberdeen:

Sew no clouts on Christ's robe. Take Christ in his rags and losses, and as persecuted by men, and be content to sigh and pant up the mountain with Christ's cross on your back (ccxxv).

The "clouts," it is true, are the vestments of the unwelcome Scottish Prayer Book of 1637; but the passage suggests that spiritual urgency that runs through Rutherford's whole view of personal religion.

The sixth part of your span-length and hand-breadth of days is scarcely before you; haste, haste, for the tide will not bide.

He writes to John Gordon (June 16, 1637, clxxx):

I cannot tell you what sweet pain and delightsome torments are in Christ's love . . . while I be head and ears in love's ocean.

IV

The Scottish Church possessed in the seventeenth century numerous ministers whose pastoral labors rose far above the level of a negative discipline. Such men were James Durham of Glasgow (d. 1658), David Dickson of Irvine (d. 1662) and William Guthrie of Fenwick (d. 1665). The first two were authors of some eminence. Dickson's works include a notable treatise on guidance, *Therapeutica sacra* (1656), published in Latin and later (1664 and 1694) in the author's own translation, which shows variants from the Latin text. Theologically the work rests upon a doctrine of the Covenants; but its significance for us lies in its extended treatment of the cure of souls and of cases of conscience. The latter are mainly not specific issues of conduct but the states of mind of weak Christians—their doubts, apprehensions, depressions and temptations. He would have the theological principles so interpreted as to lead to repentance, but never to despair (I, xi), and would have the pastor or "prudent friend" carefully distinguish between hypochondriac symptoms and genuine cases of conscience. Where needed, the pastor or counselor should co-operate with the physician (II, i), Dickson's whole conception of pastoral care is one of kindly persuasion rather than of compulsory discipline. The treatise grew out of his pastoral experience. John Howie in *The Scots Worthies* tells how scores of persons in distress of soul resorted to his house for counsel and consolation after the Sunday services, and of his usefulness to many in determining cases of conscience and in advising students looking toward the ministry.

Guthrie found his Fenwick parishioners at first so hostile to religion that he sometimes disguised himself as a traveler to gain admission to their homes; he even paid a man to desist from Sunday bowling and attend church. He engaged in outdoor recreations not only for his health but to meet negligent parishioners, draw them into religious conversation, and win their friendship. He won his way to the warm esteem of the parish, and many came from other parishes to spend the weekend in Fenwick for his preaching and counsel. In an unacknowledged quotation from Thomas Fuller, Howie notes that "he was an eminent surgeon at the jointing of a broken soul and at the stating of a doubtful conscience."

Another great pastor was Andrew Donaldson, minister of Dalgety, Fifeshire, 1644-62. The session here was very active in such matters as providing Bibles for the poor—some of which in 1654 cost 40 shillings apiece—, teaching the Catechism, assisting the minister in examinations before communion, and reconciliation of persons at enmity. Public acts of repentance were required in the usual way for numerous cases of Sabbath-breaking, non-attendance at Church, and various superstitious practices. In the same area, for cases of confessed witchcraft, the presbytery obtained the intervention of a commission of the Privy Council which proceeded in the barbaric way then generally approved by public opinion.

In the Highlands there are also many instances of pastors who gave zealous labor to the reclamation of souls and the cultivation of personal religion. John Balfour of Nigg, John MacKay of Lairg, Alexander Pope of Reay, and other Gaelic-speaking spiritual guides of Highland parishes of the early eighteenth century, leavened the northern communities by faithful preaching and private counsel.

In the roll of eighteenth century Scottish ministers there were, despite the secular trend of the age, numerous other exemplary pastors devoted to the cure of souls. Thomas Boston of Ettrick (d. 1732), author of *The Four-fold State of Man* and other influential books of devotion, takes a noteworthy place in this company. Ebenezer Erskine (d. 1754) of Stirling, leader, with his brother Ralph of Dunfermline (d. 1752), of the First Secession, organized societies for prayer and edification in his parish. John Erskine (d. 1803), many years in Greyfriars, Edinburgh, published (1797) a set of letters of consolation for those who (like himself) had been bereaved of children.

The dynamic personality of Thomas Chalmers (d. 1847) is associated with an invigoration of the parish ministry in nineteenth century Scotland. In his two pastorates in Glasgow (1815-23) he found time amid many public activities to visit his people faithfully and to consult with them privately before communion. His numerous letters, some of them hastily written in minutes snatched between pastoral interviews, are replete with religious testimony and exhortation. The ministry of Robert Murray McCheyne (d. 1843) of Dundee was distinguished for peculiar devotion. We have his own record of numerous pastoral visits during a period of epidemic influenza when many of his parishioners were dying. The brief, terse notes indicate an intense and prayerful concern for each individual. He wrote also numerous letters of counsel, marked by evangelical spirituality. Nor should we omit to mention the well-traveled and warm-hearted Scottish layman, Thomas Erskine of Linlathen (d. 1870), who wrote theological treatises, formed friendships with many Continental and British persons of eminence, and wrote to them letters of spiritual consolation, doctrinal discussion and religious advice. His correspondents included Dr. Chalmers, Frederick Dennison Maurice, Alexandre Vinet, and Mme. de Broglie. He adhered to the main doctrines of Calvinism, but stoutly opposed their illiberal interpretation, and defended John McLeod Campbell and other representatives of the more liberal theology. Vinet and Erskine exchanged writings and opinions, and Erskine possessed gifts not dissimilar to Vinet's for the guidance of souls. "My dear friend," he writes to Mme. de Stael (the younger [September 4, 1829]), "we may speak to each other about God's love, God's forgiving love. . . . If a soul is not at peace, the only reason is because it does not know God."

In the century and a half from Ebenezer Erskine to Henry Drummond (d. 1897) Scotland was frequently stirred by evangelical revival movements, some of which affected all branches of the Church. These movements, especially in the nineteenth century, were not anti-intellectual, but were embraced by scholarly men, many of whom added lustre to the annals of the Scottish pulpit. They also called forth an extraordinary amount of lay activity in personal evangelism. Where there had been neglect and indifference these movements often brought about a new spirit in the eldership. Dr. Henderson cites evidence from the 1830's of efforts to improve the parochial activities of elders. He gives instances of fresh zeal on their part in care of the poor and prayer with the afflicted. The Poor Law of 1845, however, largely secularized poor relief. The old methods of discipline were no longer practiced, and the place of the penitent stool was utilized for pews. Discipline was restricted to sexual sins, drunkenness and profanity among church members; other persons and other offenses were left to the state courts. Increasing decency of behavior, and the relaxing of church authority, alike tended to make acts of discipline less common. The poems of Burns and the novels of Scott (who was himself an elder) cast discredit upon the harsh, and the insincere, elements of the older discipline. John Galt in his charming fictional representation of Scottish Church life, *Annals of the Parish* (1821), shows the minister, Micah Balquidder, acquiescing in the kindlier trend of the time. It is sometimes said that the Papacy's loss of temporal power in the nineteenth century rendered it a greater spiritual force. The same may be said of the Scottish eldership.

John Watson ("Ian Maclaren") (d. 1907) in *Beside the Bonnie Briar Bush* (1894) movingly presented the interaction of religious personalities in Scottish parish life. His Yale Lectures, *The Cure of Souls* (1896), is a book of true insight, though not of great originality. The chapter on "the work of a pastor" lays emphasis upon visitation and private consolation and is written out of rich experience. Good rules are laid down for personal interviews. The pastor is to avoid every temptation to mere curiosity and meddlesomeness, and to treat confidences as inviolably sacred. The book shows not a distinctively Presbyterian but an undenominational approach to the problems of pastoral care.

Among books for the guidance of ministers by Presbyterian authors William Garden Blaikie's *For the Work of the Ministry* (1873) and Patrick Fairbairn's *Pastoral Theology* (1875) take prominent places. Both are, however, primarily concerned with preaching and treat the private cure of souls as secondary. In his second edition (1878) Dr. Blaikie inserted an appendix containing a short and elementary statement on spiritual counsel. The Protestant pastor's duty in cases of conscience, he holds, is not to prescribe, but only to give guidance to enable people to resolve these issues for themselves. Principal Fairbairn's final chapter is on the administration of discipline; in it he points to the necessity of "a solid groundwork of spiritual enlightenment and conviction" to give meaning to disciplinary measures. He notes, too, how some types of offenses are complicated by circumstances and admit of so many degrees of culpability that it is difficult to know where corrective discipline should begin. He virtually bids adieu to the old Presbyterian discipline with its public repentance and rebuke, and argues that the minister's private dealing with the offender is something "really done by the church, and, one may say, in its presence."

For Free Churchmen and Kirkmen alike, public discipline had become virtually extinct by the end of the nineteenth century. The fact was recognized in an act of assembly in the established Church in 1902, which left the correction of offenders largely to private inquiry and decision by the minister. Dr. Clark in discussing this measure points to the parallel change from the public penance of the ancient Church to the private confession and absolution of the Middle Ages. Save for the continued activity of elders, which was less and less in a judiciary capacity, the Scottish Reformed Church had passed through a similar cycle.

Yet many faithful ministers continued to devote a large share of their energies to the private guidance of souls. A fine example is the highly talented George Matheson (d. 1906) whose pastorates at Innellan and St. Bernard's, Edinburgh were (despite his blindness) marked by intensive visitation of his parish, close attention to the poor, the sick and the aged, and a genial spirituality. "Every new person whom he met," says his biographer, "drew, so to speak, virtue out of him."

V

In early America, Presbyterian missionary pastors, like those of other denominations, had to adapt their methods to conditions very different from those of the mother churches with long established parish organization. Their contacts with individuals were often brief, but none the less vital. Thus we read of the "constant endeavor" of Gilbert Tennent (d. 1764) "to do good by his conversation" while on preaching tours in Pennsylvania and New Jersey, and of his "watching for opportunities of speaking for God" with those he met. His brother, William Tennent, Junior (d. 1777), in using the superior speed of his horse to overtake a lad in flight from his minister and his conscience, symbolizes the urgency of these spiritual encounters. Like the Tennents, Samuel Blair (d. 1751) lost no opportunity of giving private instruction and counsel, and his admiring follower, the eloquent Samuel Davies (d. 1761), was not less attentive to this duty.

The convictions by which the labors of these men were supported may be seen in Leonard J. Trinterud's admirable study *The Forming of an American Tradition*. Professor Trinterud shows the reliance of the Log College evangelists upon the works of their Puritan and Scottish predecessors, such as John Preston, Baxter, Dickson and Doddridge, from whom they learned "experimental" religion. They dwelt not so much on feeling as on duty. The term "happiness," freely used by the Old Side Presbyterians, had a somewhat hesitant use on the part of Gilbert Tennent and his fellows. "Sanctification," "holiness," "renovation" and "repentance" are among the commonplaces of their vocabulary. Interpreting Tennent's language, Trinterud notes that "a continual renewal of repentance was . . . utterly essential" for the Christian life. Good works are a part of sanctification, and these appear in "the duties of social life" and the pursuit of the common good.

In the nineteenth century Gideon Blackburn (d. 1858) in Kentucky and Tennessee, and Thomas Clelland (d. 1858) in Kentucky, are examples of those who followed in the footsteps of the devoted Log College ministers mentioned above. There was a great insistence upon dutiful pastoral guidance and these men made exacting demands. Blackburn, at the deathbed of a slave owner converted under his ministry, wrote his will, in which he provided for the emancipation of his slaves and their removal to Africa. (Relatives obtained its annulment.)

Clelland had undergone severe struggles of soul in his youth, which "enabled him to interpret," says his biographer, "the spiritual struggles of both sinner and saint at every stage of religious anxiety."

Among the early Canadian settlements a similar type appears. The life of James MacGregor (d. 1830), Presbyterian apostle of the Maritime Provinces, is replete with evidences of his constant ministering to individuals. During his arduous travels we find him dealing effectively with crude sinners of many sorts, with people in distress of mind, with quarreling cousins, with a sailor who had turned his back upon the piety of his childhood, with a woman who believed herself more sinful than Satan. The Anti-Burgher synod had commissioned MacGregor "not to make seceders but Christians" and he faithfully sought this end.

The pioneer missionary of 150 to 250 years ago gave place to a different type, the home-keeping pastor with one charge. The Westminster Assembly documents were adopted, with alterations, in America. But the Scottish parish discipline could not be fully duplicated in American Presbyterianism. Individual congregations sometimes made special rules of their own for applying censures, and types of offenses differed from those prevalent in Scottish society. Thus in the volume devoted to the Presbyterians in William Warren Sweet's series, *Religion on the American Frontier*, we find a Kentucky minister, William Mahon of New Providence, charged before his presbytery with "whipping unmercifully" his Negro woman slave. In view of the evidence at the trial, he got off lightly, with "a friendly admonition," while his accuser was rebuked "in brotherly love" for failing to confer with him in private at the outset (1798). There are a good many cases of disreputable behavior among ministers, including sex offenses, intemperance and fraudulent business transactions. Trials were conducted with impressive formality and with every appearance of justice. In some instances exoneration follows, in some repentance and reinstatement, and in others suspension or deposition from the sacred office. Dr. Sweet gives records of numerous session trials of lay offenders, which afford vivid illustration of the struggle to maintain moral standards in frontier society.

We may obtain a glimpse of the routine work of guidance in an early nineteenth century Presbyterian pastorate from Ichabod G. Spencer's book, *A Pastor's Sketches, or Conversations with Anxious Inquirers* (1850), which gives actual interviews with more than forty consultants in his Brooklyn charge. They are men and women of different ages and types, and the pastor shows great versatility in his approach. His aim is to lead the anxious to wholehearted repentance and faith. In some instances he breaks through reticence and proud resistance; in a few he confesses failure. His presuppositions are those of a scriptural and somewhat Calvinistic evangelicalism, without denominational narrowness. In some instances a number of meetings with the same person are recorded, and we get something like a spiritual biography of the person. Mr. Spencer met his consultants with a gentle urgency that arose from confidence in his message and a genuine sympathy for mental suffering. The book had wide circulation and I have found it quoted by British writers.

The works of the distinguished Southern Presbyterian, Thomas Smyth (d. 1873) contain an interesting treatise entitled *Solace for Bereaved Parents* (1848) which utilizes much early modern material of the consolatory type, including some from Roman Catholics. William Greenough Thayer Shedd's *Homiletics and Pastoral Theology* (1867) may be compared with Dr. Blaikie's work referred to above. Shedd gives very limited attention to the private ministry, yet values it highly. He urges systematic regularity in visiting, with a quickening of activity when there are signs of an awakening in the congregation. He insists, too, upon making every visit a sincere confrontation of souls, with no timid approach by way of secular talk, which only affords opportunity for evasion:

When, therefore, a parochial call is made, let the pastor plunge *in medias sacras res.* Let him not attempt to bridge over the chasm between secularities and spiritualities, but let him leap over.

Shedd evidently felt with his Episcopalian contemporary, Phillips Brooks, that "most pastoral guidance is pitched in too low a key." The Congregationalist, Washington Gladden, approved, however (in 1898) of bridging rather than leaping the chasm.

VI

The contribution of English Puritanism to the cure of souls is abundant and varied, and many of the Puritan ministers set an example of devotion in the personal ministry. Most of their preaching was aimed at the awakening and guidance of the conscience, and conscience was for them a tremendous and inescapable reality. This fact is well expressed by the Cambridge Puritan, William Perkins (d. 1602) in his posthumous work, *The Whole Treatise of Cases of Conscience:*

Let a man commit any trespass or offense, though it be done in secret and concealed from the knowledge of any person living; yet conscience, that knoweth it, will accuse him and terrify him, cite him before God and give him no rest.

Thomas Fuller in his celebrated *Holy State* (1642) takes Perkins as the model of a good minister, and remarks of him: "An excellent chirurgeon [surgeon] he was at the jointing of a broken soul and at stating of a doubtful conscience." Puritan pastoral experience flowered in many a treatise of casuistry of which the one by Perkins is a good instance. Perkins began his ministry in a remarkable mission to prisoners, and his treatment of cases acquires depth from experience in dealing with disordered souls. The comforter must, he notes, bear with the peevishness and "distempered and disordered affections and actions" of those whom he would help. He must identify himself with them, assume their sorrows and share their tears; and he must not be dismayed by seeming failure. Perkins vividly depicts the physical agony that accompanies the inward struggles of the soul dreading the wrath of God. The sufferer must be reminded that through these agonies God works by contraries, and in His wrath remembers mercy. Like many another guide of souls of his age, he recognizes the reactions between body and mind. If, as physicians say, "the mind follows the temperature of the body," he will affirm that "the body doth often follow the state and condition of the mind."

Somewhat after the manner of the medieval Art of Dying booklets, Perkins shows how the dying are to be prepared. They are chiefly to be taught to "set before their eyes the promise of remission of sins . . . wrapping and infolding themselves in it as in a close and warm garment that will keep them safe and sure amidst the wind and weather of temptation." But he is mainly concerned with the consciences of those in health and activity. His counsel on recreation is typical of Puritan casuistry. Recreation has a definite place in the Christian life; it is required for refreshment of mind and body. But certain recreations are condemned. Theatrical plays are unlawful because they portray sin and are against Scripture and the law of nature. Dancing "in these days" he observes, "is the very bellows of lust." Gambling and games of chance are also excluded. But shooting, running, wrestling, fencing, music and chess are "very commendable." Perkins, indeed, censures the rigor of some of the Church Fathers in these matters.

If we may judge from statements of Fuller, Jeremy Taylor and others, the demand for books of casuistry exceeded the supply in seventeenth century England, and Roman Catholic, Lutheran, and other foreign treatises were frequently consulted. Consciences were aroused by vigorous preaching, and troubled over new issues connected with cultural and ecclesiastical changes and the expansion of business. Despite the alleged lack of casuistic writing, treatises were fairly numerous. Anglicanism produced such weighty works as Robert Sanderson's book on promissory oaths, *De juramenti promissori obligatione* (1647), Joseph Hall's *Resolutions and Decisions of Divers Cases of Conscience in Continual Use Among Men* (1650), and Jeremy Taylor's *Ductor Dubitantium* (1660). Hall selects a list of topics on which he has found the most frequent inquiry, beginning with "cases of profit and traffic." Taylor's great work covers a very wide range, and makes critical use of materials from classical, Roman Catholic, Lutheran and Reformed casuists, as well as from British writers. The Puritan works of this class include: Immanuel Bourne's *The Godly Man's Guide, with a Direction for all, Especially Merchants and Tradesmen* (1620); William Goudge's *Of Domestical Duties* (1623) and *A Guide to go to God* (1626); the *De Conscientia* (1631) of William Ames—translated (1639) under the title *Of Conscience, with the Power and Cases Thereof*—a fundamental work; and Richard Baxter's huge compilation, *A Christian Directory* (1673). John Dury (d. 1680), the celebrated advocate of Christian reunion, in 1633, fresh from contacts with continental theologians, stirred up Archbishop Usher and other British scholars to seek the production of works of casuistry, and in his own writings treated some cases of conscience connected with ecclesiastical matters. (See Dr. Batten's list of Dury's titles.)

An examination of this extensive field is excluded here: I have given a brief introduction to it in an article: "Casuistry in the Puritan Age" (*Religion in Life*, XII). The treatises of Ames, Taylor and Baxter are deservedly the best known; of these the work of Ames is the most philosophical, Taylor's the most learned, and Baxter's the most directly practical. Baxter's casuistry extends to many other titles; but the *Directory* covers a vast number of the moral problems and religious concerns of his age. In some respects Baxter is more liberal than Perkins: he permits betting "for sport and not for covetousness." But he is severe on all "time-wasting sins," among them the reading of fiction, and many amusements. In economic matters he never strays from his principle of "the public good of Church and Commonwealth"—to take a phrase from one of his later writings—and he has this in mind in his permission of interest on money turned to productive use no less than when he condemns the oppression of greedy landlords.

But Baxter's greatest contribution in our field is his *Gildas Salvianus, the Reformed Pastor* (1656), which grew out of an address prepared for, but because of ill health not delivered to, a meeting of ministers. His citation in the title of those austere moralists, Salvian of Marseilles and Gildas of Wales, is a suggestion of the severity of his criticisms of the current neglect of the pastoral office. He has exacting demands for the minister, and is particularly concerned with personal counsel and discipline. In an introductory section he explains his own method. He spent Mondays and Tuesdays with the families of the parish, not in their houses, but in his. They were notified in advance by the parish clerk when to come. Fifteen or sixteen families were interviewed each week, so that each of the eight hundred families in his parish of Kidderminster was brought in for an unhurried spiritual review once a year. The pastor, he says, must not "slightly slubber over" his work of counseling but "do it vigorously."

Baxter has a bold and vital chapter of exhortation to ministers with regard to their own spiritual lives. His urgency resembles that of Gregory Nazianzen. "A holy calling will not save an unholy man." The minister has more temptations than others; and when he falls the world rings with the report. But it is his treatment of "the oversight of the flock" that is most to our purpose. He strongly stresses the need of a ministry to individuals. If anyone is neglected it should not be the unconverted: a man with a mortal disease should call for more compassion than a man with a toothache. The minister should make himself available to "those in doubts and straits," and publicly invite them to personal conference. Those already converted should be led from strength to strength as they become "inflamed by the love of God" and inspired by "a lively and working faith." Christians still affected by some unconquered sin, or who lose diligence and love, and backsliders in danger of apostasy, are to be specially counseled according to their needs, and brought to repentance and a fresh start. Baxter, who at the time was still a bachelor, lays great stress upon the promotion of religious observances and discipline in the family. "You are like to see no general reformation," he remarks, "till you procure family reformation."

His treatment of visitation of the sick is marked by pastoral wisdom and human sympathy. Visits to the dying should begin well before death approaches. A deathbed repentance may be deceptive; but it may be genuine. If the sick recover, they should be held to the good resolutions made during illness.

Baxter's discipline of serious offenders is that of the Reformed tradition and of the Westminster Directory. The features of this are a private admonition, where necessary, the further step of conference with chosen persons, and, if this is insufficient, a fully public reproof, with prayer for the offender. Repentance is earnestly sought at every step, and restoration follows repentance; but the persistently impenitent must be excluded, for the health of the congregation. Baxter would prefer that many vicious persons escape discipline that that one be unjustly judged.

The Reformed Pastor called forth the plaudits and gratitude of many ministers of the time, and has been much used since. It affected the view of the pastor's task held by such leaders as Spener, Doddridge, Wesley and Spurgeon. For Protestant ministers, no other book quite ranks with it: its appeal and influence are due alike to its originality, its tone of urgency, and its skillful use of traditional stuff.

VII

It is obvious that there exists a basic common ground between Scottish Presbyterian and English Puritan practice in the cure of souls. Both confronted the individual with an exacting code of behavior and treated infringements with grave concern. The differences in the sixteenth and seventeenth centuries, are largely due to the fact that in Scotland Presbyterianism was the form of religion sanctioned by the state and that accordingly the Church regarded itself as responsible for all the people, while Puritanism in England never attained the organization of a single Church that could be described as national and established. This holds even for the Cromwellian era, since a great variety of religious organization was then prevalent, despite the oversight of Cromwell's Triers and Ejectors. The unsettled state of the Church in the age of Puritanism probably conduced to the more active thought of the Puritans than of the Scots on our subject. Not possessing, as their Scottish allies possessed, a relatively inflexible authorized system of discipline, Puritan guides of souls were led to frame for their brethren elaborate codes of casuistry. There is more that is legal and compulsory in the Scottish system, and despite its full recognition of persuasion and fraternal charity, its tendency was toward an increasing reliance upon mechanical procedures. I fail to see the evidence that this increasing legalism in the late seventeenth century was, as some Scottish writers have argued, something taken over by the Kirk from the Puritans. Many of the Puritans, no doubt, would have welcomed a similar established and enforceable regularity, but they were not in a position to secure it. It seems better to regard the change in Scotland as the result of a very natural tendency toward such institutionalism and routine as will produce an economy of effort. The change took place when controversies over other matters absorbed much of the energy of the leading ministers.

The Scottish polity, however, offered a realm of service to lay elders in which they often labored fruitfully in private counseling. The very fact that it has survived the operation of the old discipline is a valid testimony to the values inherent in the office. With adaptations to greatly changed conditions, it remained, and remains everywhere in Presbyterian churches, capable of an indispensable contribution in the cure of souls. Vested in the authority of the congregation that has elected them, elders who possess the requisite gifts may be trusted counselors in times of personal trial and anxiety and in cases of defection, a sustaining and guiding force in the private lives of the members.

Seventeenth century English Puritanism was the parent of the churches that will be under review in the next chapter, even, in some sense, of Methodism, which was indebted also to Anglicanism and to German Pietism. Its experience in the field of pastoral guidance was of value to these churches and to later Presbyterianism as well. By precept and example the English Puritans placed all later English-speaking Protestantism in debt to them, and they have still much to teach us in this field.

Attention has been called in this chapter to the exemplary devotion of a number of pastors in their parochial labors with families and persons. Extended studies in this field are lacking and it is difficult to generalize on the available data. Considerable variety of method is indicated, but the main variations have parallels elsewhere than in Presbyterianism and Puritanism. The rebuke of sinners, the private interview with the anxious, and letters of religious guidance are common features of the cure of souls in all eras of Christian history. The practice indicated in the present chapter, by its nonsacramental character differs basically from that of the medieval Church, and has a close affinity with that of the Continental Reformed. Private guidance has here been related to the Eucharist as preparation for that sacrament, and has not itself involved a sacramental act. It has been in some degree an extension of preaching, a private application, in view of the state of the individual, of what has been more generally spoken from the pulpit. On this presupposition Presbyterian and Puritan writers on the functions of the minister have usually insisted that the true preacher is one who also gives his energies to the personal ministry. Persuasion to repentance and conversion, the relief of religious anxiety, and the awakening of conscience in the affairs of daily living, have been the ends of both. While not sacramental this guidance has involved a genuine religious experience, often a transforming one, redirecting the whole course of life. Its defects and failures have arisen from the inadequacies of many of those engaged in it—always the great limiting factor in the guidance of souls.

Chapter XII

THE CURE OF SOULS IN CONGREGATIONALISM, THE BAPTIST CHURCHES, QUAKERISM AND METHODISM

I

IN THE struggles of the Puritan era in England, the main contestants were the Presbyterians and Independents. In addition to these a variety of sects arose, many of which did not survive the century of their origin. Whatever their historical importance, their peculiarities were not rendered permanent by an enduring organization, and their testimony was to have only a limited influence upon more tenacious movements. Among them all, the Baptists and the Quakers alone succeeded in perpetuating themselves in considerable force, and they have since formed important units in the ecclesiastical complex of Protestantism. Both movements drew from Continental sources; but they grew up in the milieu of Puritanism, and reflect its common ideas and code of behavior.

The modern English Baptists may be said to have taken their origin in 1612 when Thomas Helwys, returning to England from Amsterdam, established a "General" (or Arminian) Baptist congregation in London. The "Particular" (or Calvinist) Baptists soon afterwards appeared: these two branches were united only in the nineteenth century. The early Baptists had severe standards of membership and their small congregations shared an intimate community life from which alien elements were excluded, and in which they felt the watchful care of pastors and leaders. Despite the disabilities entailed in their dissent from the establishment, they maintained themselves through the early seventeenth century, and under Cromwell exhibited both strength and variety.

The problems of discipline and guidance in Baptist churches were complicated by the persecuting laws of the late Stuart period. Many of the cases of discipline in John Bunyan's church at Bedford were of people who had left off attendance from loss of courage. The standards of conduct were strict, and withdrawal was sometimes associated with card-playing, "immodest company keeping," and other marks of worldliness. Persons who had withdrawn, and others who misbehaved, were repeatedly admonished, and final cancellation of membership was made only when hope of recovery was past, and by action of the assembled congregation. Thus, on January 14, 1670:

It was agreed that Humphrey Merrill (still refusing admonition) should the next church meeting be cut off from this congregation of God, if repentance prevent not.

A solemn act of exclusion followed a week later, effected in a document signed by Bunyan and six others. Bunyan had earlier written (in *Grace Abounding*) that he suffered more from the backsliding of his converts than if his own children had been carried to the grave.

The Act of Toleration of 1689 gave Baptists the same rights as other dissenters, and they shared with these the laxer trend of the eighteenth century. The Evangelical Revival brought new vigor. Among its early Baptist representatives were Andrew Fuller (d. 1815) of Kettering and William Carey (d. 1834) the eminent missionary. The selections from Fuller's correspondence published by Rylands contain a number of letters of spiritual counsel and consolation written with solicitude and sympathy. The brilliant and highly individualized Baptist leader, Charles Haddon Spurgeon (d. 1892), whose preaching long filled a tabernacle in Southwark containing six thousand seats, was a counselor of many, in person and by letter. He was constant in visitation during a cholera epidemic, and later obtained an embarrassing reputation for the healing of hundreds of sick folk through his bedside prayers.

The rapid spread of Baptist congregations in America was connected with frontier revivalism and the labors of devoted itinerant missionaries, some of whom ultimately became settled pastors. The Separate Baptist, John Taylor (d. 1832) of Kentucky is a good example of this type. His *History of Ten Baptist Churches* is autobiographical. Instances in it of personal spiritual counsel are not infrequent, but they are subordinated to preaching. The vivid journal of John Colby (d. 1817) a Baptist missionary in New England, gives more information on the ministry to individuals. Colby records many interviews with repentant sinners, old and young.

But one gets the impression that the cure of souls among the early American Baptists was largely a process within the ongoing groups and rising congregations. The local churches probably varied their practice considerably. The covenant embodied in the constitution of Buck Run Church, one of Taylor's foundations (1818), states: "That we will watch over each other in brotherly tenderness, each endeavoring to edify his brother." In discipline the basis of procedure is that of Matthew 18. A majority of the congregation could suspend an erring brother; for expulsion unanimity was required.

Dr. Sweet's documents in *Religion on the American Frontier: The Baptists*, give abundant evidence of corrective discipline. If members were involved in the fights and frolics of the frontier, or fell into dishonesty or property disputes, or intemperance or immorality, the churches had effective ways of dealing with them. Penalties were inflicted more in sorrow than in anger. No doubt that good disciplinarian, William Hickman of Elkhorn, Kentucky, was happy to note (in his hilarious spelling) on the second Saturday of January, 1819, that Samuel Gravett, who had been excluded on a charge of "pilfering a pair of gloves" in January, 1802, having been later proved innocent, was restored. Mr. Gravett secured this action in 1819 evidently in order to obtain a letter of dismission to another congregation. The practice was that persons excluded from one church on removal elsewhere could be admitted to membership only after information from the former congregation had been obtained.

We cannot fail to be impressed by the social impact of these small churches on the frontier in their careful attention to the behavior of every member and avoidance of slipshod admissions to membership. The churches of various denominations boldly set standards of morals far different from those of their communities, and the code covered all prevailing violations of the Ten Commandments. Their primary object was rather to save and educate souls than to improve community life; but the rise of social morality was a valuable by-product of the discipline of souls. (See Dr. Sweet's article, "The Churches as Moral Courts . . . ," cited below, p. 354.)

II

Even more than other denominations of Puritan parentage, the Quaker societies featured mutual admonition and correction. Their Discipline is the growth of three centuries' application of these principles. In 1696 they determined that those attending meetings for discipline should "labor to know that their own spirits are subjected to the spirit of truth." In 1833 they declared that the Christian cure of souls is not to cease with the disownment of delinquents.

At the same time real disciplinary authority is provided for. It is especially lodged in the elders and overseers appointed by the monthly meetings. The overseers especially, in modern American Quakerism, are commissioned to visit those in trouble, bringing them spiritual support, and to maintain a general supervision of the "walk and conversation" of members. The Quakers have borne faithful testimony to the rights of conscience, and their leaders have sometimes peculiarly felt a compelling responsibility to enlighten and guide the weak consciences of others. If this guidance has made too much of trivial matters of dress and recreation, it has also assailed slavery, racial discrimination, and dishonesty with uncompromising insistence. The Journal of John Woolman (d. 1772) well illustrates the Quaker conscience in these respects, and affords many illustrations of the gentle reproof, characteristic of Quakerism at its best.

III

The successors of the Independents of the seventeenth century were those nonconformists who, in the readjustments of the ecclesiastical parties after the Act of Toleration (1689), embraced a congregationalist polity. These possessed in Isaac Watts (d. 1748) and Philip Doddridge (d. 1751) two eminent leaders. Watts is best known for his religious poetry; but he was a prolific and scholarly author in many fields, and his extensive published correspondence includes a fair number of letters of spiritual guidance. A letter addressed February 8, 1702, to the congregation of Mark Lane, London, of which he was soon to become pastor, shows his zeal to promote personal and family religion. Impaired health forced his retirement from this pastorate (1712), but his interest in pastoral care is revealed in his later writings. Among these may be mentioned *An Humble Attempt Toward the Revival of Practical Re-*

ligion (1731). In this set of addresses he advises ministers how they may prepare themselves to "convince, direct and comfort others." They are so to rebuke men "that even your anger has something divine and holy in it," so to make inquiries as to avoid "prying curiosity," and in peacemaking efforts to beware of becoming involved in the quarrel. "Parlour [conversational] preaching" may, he thinks, prove far more effective than pulpit sermons (*Works*, 1800, Volume IV).

Doddridge was less talented than Watts, but he was an industrious reader in the classics and theology, and a popular writer on devotional and practical themes. His *Rise and Progress of Religion in the Soul* (1744) (undertaken at the request of Watts) was a classic still familiar to our grandfathers. The book aims to make adult converts; but in the preface to the second edition the author introduces with emphasis the possibility that grace may be at work in the heart "almost from the first dawning of reason" and may advance by imperceptible degrees. An important chapter (xix) consists of a long letter he had written in 1727 to a young friend, which contains an outline of private religious exercises for a day. Topics of prayer and reflection, and scripture readings are detailed here, and a place is made for recreations, which are to be entered upon with prayer. In the morning the day's activities are to be planned in a religious spirit, and the evening devotions include self-examination, for which a set of probing questions is provided. These include references to the daily series of devotional exercises, and such other self-interrogations as the following:

Have I pursued the common business of the day with diligence and spirituality, doing everything in season, and with all convenient despatch, and as "unto the Lord"? . . . Did I say nothing passionate, mischievous, slanderous, imprudent, impertinent? Has my heart this day been full of love to God, and to all mankind? and have I sought, found, and improved, opportunities of doing and of getting good?

Doddridge's voluminous correspondence contains many letters, most of which suggest no such regimen of devotion as this one, but offer more general directions for the spiritual life. We find him counseling the young son of Colonel Gardiner, a Scottish officer who had been converted under his ministry and had become his friend. The young man, recovering from a grave illness, is thus exhorted:

Thank God and take courage. In His name and strength set out on your heavenly pilgrimage with the word of God in your hand and heart.

When necessary he could write in terms of vigorous rebuke: witness his frank and biting, if meticulously courteous note to Sir John R . . . on that nobleman's profanity (December 8, 1742). Although some of his religious letters are not very rewarding—especially where he indulges in a rather humorless facetiousness—one might gather from them an anthology of fine examples.

His long pastorate in Northampton, where he conducted a famous academy, was rich in the labor of private guidance. His visits to prisoners in 1741 produced evidence of the innocence of a man condemned for murder: the law took its unjust course, and the victim at his death thanked Doddridge warmly for his compassionate efforts, and obtained permission to kneel and pray on the minister's doorstep. But he set his elders also to work at this personal ministry, and in 1747 presented to them an exacting scheme of visitation. They were, indeed, charged with many pastoral duties, and explicitly directed to meet the needs of those in spiritual distress. They were also to remonstrate with wrongdoers, at first privately, then if necessary with other good men. Scandalous offenders were to be publicly admonished and to be brought to such confession and humiliation as would satisfy the church. Characteristically Doddridge urges the elders not to hesitate to reprove their pastor for anything offensive in his temper and conduct.

IV

The cure of souls was the primary concern of early American Puritanism. Conscience was the theme of preaching, conversation and meditation. Within the soul there was waged a battle of the spiritual and the carnal; and Puritans were not strangers to the heights of spirituality. Roger Williams, unlike most of the others, carried over his sense of the profound reality of conscience into a demand that the varying consciences of all men be respected. In 1651 he thus admonished Governor Endicot to cease from intolerance:

Are all the thousands of millions of consciences at home and abroad fuel only for a prison, for a whip, for a stake, for a gallows? . . . It is a dreadful voice from the King of Kings, and Lord of Lords, Endicot, Endicot, why huntest thou me?

The horizon of most of the Puritan Fathers was narrower than this; but even where they favored persecution this was not without consulting their consciences. And they were ever active in stirring up and guiding the consciences of others.

The guidance of souls in old New England was not confined to the clergy. The leader of the Plymouth colony, William Brewster, performed, apart from the sacraments, most of the functions of a pastor, including personal counsel. During the first trying winter he ministered with the utmost devotion to the sick and dying. William Bradford praises highly these labors of Brewster, and notes that: "He had a singular good gift of prayer, both public and private; in ripping up the heart and conscience before God." When Mrs. Anne Hutchinson began to propound her antinomian doctrines, "she had," according to John Winthrop, the Younger, "more resort to her for counsel about matters of conscience than to any minister in the country."

The great ministerial guides of conscience such as Thomas Hooker, Increase and Cotton Mather, and Jonathan Edwards, strongly encouraged lay Christians to give themselves to mutual admonition as well as to the cultivation of their own souls. This statement is well illustrated in a long sermon by Edwards (d. 1742) on self-examination (from Ps. 89:23-24). Edwards urges his hearers not only to watchful defense against the subtle entry of sin, but also to care for one's neighbor in his moral and spiritual perils. Hatred and covetousness toward others are not more severely judged than failure to reprove a neighbor where he needs reproof. Such neglect is "a failure of our duty of love and charity" —a point for which Edwards appropriately cites Leviticus 19:17: "Thou shalt not hate thy brother in thy heart; thou shalt in any wise rebuke thy neighbor, and not suffer sin upon him."

The vast writings of Cotton Mather (d. 1728) "Keeper of the Puritan Conscience" (as he has been called by Ralph and Louise Boas) contain limitless data on the same theme. His Diary is a book hardly surpassed for intensity of religious experience and self-admonition. It is also a record of his pastoral work and of the affairs of his time. His attitude, like that of his father, Increase Mather, on New England witchcraft, was not enlightened, but at least it was less credulous and misguided than that of many others. Evil spirits and their disconcerting ways enter into the Diary, and mingle strangely with Mather's sensitive moral judgment and prodigious knowledge. Through its pages we see evidence that his sense of responsibility for the souls of his people was not less marked than concern for his own. Mather's *Manuductio ad Ministerium* (1726), a guidebook for ministerial students, and his *Essays to Do Good* (1710), contain numerous urgent passages on this theme. He feels that the personal cure of souls has suffered some neglect from his fellow ministers: but his standards are exacting. Visiting, catechizing, distributing books of piety, and faithfulness in reproof and consolation are recommended by Mather; but his treatment of these commonplaces is often far from commonplace. His familiarity with old books such as Gregory's *Pastoral Care* and Gerson's *On Bringing the Little Ones to Christ*, and with contemporary foreign authors, and his own unfailing vivacity of mind, render him readable and suggestive. Like English Puritans, he urges in some cases the co-operation of pastor and physician, and sees the need of what today would be called psychosomatic therapy. Disorders of the mind bring diseases of the stomach. In such cases physicians should present to the patient thoughts that are "anodynes," and endeavor to "scatter the clouds and remove the loads with which his mind is oppressed." The physician ought to seek the patient's spiritual health, though "without indecent intrusion into the office of the minister" (*Essays to Do Good*).

The New England ministers seem to have laid due emphasis upon the mutuality of congregational life and the reconciliation of quarreling members. We may cite an incident at Middleborough, Massachusetts, recorded by Waddington. The church there had been in angry controversy, but the parties were brought together by the pastor, Peter Thacher, who had them sign a solemn mutual declaration of humble repentance for their strife, and of desire to pledge peace and unity in a service of communion (April 10, 1738).

The later history of congregationalism in England and America alike abounds in material that is excluded from this chapter only for reasons of space. Spiritual letters might be illustrated by the once popular collection of Samuel Eyles Pierce, which appeared in sections between 1809 and 1835. The letter written by Henry Robert Reynolds on resigning his charge at Leeds (June 25, 1860) is such as Watts might have written. There is a wealth of suggestion in the *Familiar Talks* of Henry Ward Beecher (1870) such as the one "On the Duty of Conversing with Impenitent Sinners." Beecher here warns against "religious chatterers," but holds that there are many "unordained men ordained of God" whose gifts for this service should be fully utilized.

Among the worth-while books written for ministers of a generation ago is *The Pastor Amidst His Flock* (1890) by G. B. Willcox of Chicago. Dr. Willcox lays great emphasis upon the personal acquaintance of the minister with all his people, and upon the necessity of completely private interviews. He writes in brief, crisp sentences, which invite quotation. Here are examples from his chapter on "pastoral calls."

Never employ the supposed nearness of death to lead anyone to repentance. . . . A man needs Christ whether he is to live or to die. . . . Never betray any secret.

Of the ministry to those who appear ignorant and mediocre, he enjoins the pastor: "Throw your soul into the care and culture of such beings as these."

At the end of the nineteenth century Washington Gladden, in *The Christian Pastor and the Working Church* (1898), carefully examines the work of visitation in the light of the conditions of the time. He favors co-operation with neighboring churches of other denominations in parochial visitation, and advocates the use of the voluntary services of lay visitors. In contrast with the Presbyterians Blaikie and Shedd, he holds that the purpose of the pastor's visits to homes is to put himself in good relations with his flock. "The one thing needful is for them to know that he loves them and wants to do them good." Beyond this, he would, of course, wish the pastor to be alert to use occasions for religious counseling; but he seems almost to substitute a mere secular friendliness for the devout labor traditionally demanded. At the sickbed, he recommends "a few pleasant and sympathetic words with the patient," and the simple advice to rely on the "Infinite Care-taker." There should be readiness to hear the sick person's anxieties, but no "inquisition" into the secrets of his heart. Gladden is throughout anxious to avoid a sacerdotal assumption of spiritual authority. Nevertheless, in disagreement with Van Oosterzee, the Dutch writer cited above (p. 211), he admits as "a concession" to the desires of the sick, the celebration of communion at the bedside—there being no longer among American Protestants any danger of a superstitious view of this action. He also requires the pastor not to conceal from patients the approach of death, yet leaves the reader uncertain about what he regards as an appropriate ministry to the dying. Gladden represents the point of view of the liberal Protestantism of half a century ago, of which he was a distinguished leader. In this book, as the title implies, he is in fact less concerned with the cure of souls than with the harmonious operation of the Church in its local units.

V

The earliest units of organization of the People called Methodists consisted of the "bands," or groups for mutual confession and discipline. Wesley gives the rules for these groups under date of December 25, 1738. The "classes" and "societies" were forming in the following year; and from these some members were taken into the "bands," which had a more strictly remedial discipline. They were people who especially "needed to pour out their hearts" to one another. As a safeguard, bands were formed for married men, single men, married and single women. Each member, beginning with the leader, was to confess his faults and temptations and the state of his soul, and to accept criticism. In order to be admitted to the group each had to declare his desire to be told all his faults, even if this should "cut to the quick." Further regulations regarding conduct and devotions were later added, which resemble closely the rules of the "societies" given about the same time (1743).

The societies were subdivided into classes of about twelve members each, men and women, under a class leader. The members were to "help each other to work out their salvation." Wesley testifies that they obtained what was to them a totally new experience of Christian fellowship, and began to bear one another's burdens. The rules forbade not only profanity, drunkenness and quarreling, but also smuggling, usury, extravagant dress and worldly amusements. The members were to "do good of every possible sort," to feed the hungry, clothe the naked, visit or help those sick or in prison, and also to "instruct, reprove and exhort" those they should meet; to do business preferably with one another; to be diligent and frugal, and to attend worship and practice prayer and abstemious habits. The rules read like a description of the life of the early Christians: there is a suggestion, too, of the medieval "Works of Mercy" and of Puritan ideals of conduct. The bands, classes and societies constituted a structure of active groups engaged in the mutual cure of souls in a way that would have delighted Bucer or Spener.

Wesley in his apostolate managed to confer personally with an uncounted number of awakened and anxious souls, to pay many visits to the sick, and sometimes to talk with prisoners condemned to die. Among these was the pathetic case of Robert Ramsay who wished to make a confession to Wesley, but because of the jailer's refusal could not be reached after repeated efforts (January 11, 1742). Wesley, like Luther and Calvin and in accordance with the Book of Common Prayer, approved confession of sins "to a spiritual guide for the disburdening of the conscience." But he held that to make it obligatory for all "is to make, of what may be a useful means, a dangerous snare" (*Roman Catechism . . . with a Reply*). Under this limitation he was, in effect, father-confessor to very many.

"It was pleasant work," he writes of his visits to the sick at Kingswood and Bristol (October 24, 1741), "for I found none of them sorrowing as men without hope." Many entries in his Journal note such visits, but some of them cost trying spiritual labor. Two days before the above reference he found Edward W... dying in deep despair: "We cried unto God and his soul revived. A little light shone upon him and . . . his spirit returned to God." Wesley had a way of improving every occasion for religious conversation. When he was flung to the ground over the head of his horse, and the beast was caught and brought to him by some lads with an outpouring of profanity, he "turned to one and the other and spoke in love," and gave them religious books "which they promised to read" (August 22, 1743). This "turning to one and the other" is characteristic of his method of establishing personal relations in the presence of numbers: it was a method often brilliantly employed when he faced excited mobs. Between journeys he held interviews, or paid visits to homes for prayer and conference. Rarely did these efforts result as in the case recorded January 3, 1771: "Spent half an hour with an infidel, beating the air." John Wesley, as Richard Watson Guilder wrote of him, was a man

> Driven on forever, back and forth the world,
> By that divine, omnipotent desire . . .
> The hunger and the passion of men's souls.

His letters are the epistles of an apostle. Even where he writes of administrative problems, the dominant note is that of meeting the spiritual needs of men and women. This meant not merely bringing them into a religious life by the experience of conversion, but also holding them on the right way and reclaiming those who lapsed from it. Thus, during the crucial year 1775, in a number of letters to Thomas Rankin in America, he remembers a convert who has been overtaken by his old sin of drunkenness. "Your point is, first, save him from the occasions of sin; then incite him not to cast away hope. Nothing but his despair of conquering can totally destroy him." Nor is the apostolic and pastoral concern lacking in his letters to bishops and political personages. In 1745 he wrote to the Mayor of Newcastle, in deep concern for the soldiers stationed there and the negligence that left them without religious guides.

> My soul has been pained day by day even in walking the streets of Newcastle. . . . Can any that fear God and love their neighbor, hear this without concern? . . . Is there no man that careth for these souls?

Wesley had a gift for knowing people, beyond merely remembering names and faces. He wrote to many, and about many, with a keen realization of their qualities and possibilities, and in replying to personal inquiries he was prompt, direct and searching. To some he was for considerable time a spiritual guide. One of these was Samuel Furley, to whom he wrote occasionally over a period of ten years (1754-64). Furley was a Cambridge student, who became a minister, turned from Wesley's theology, and remained his friend. He sternly warns the young man to avoid the conversation of "good-natured triflers" that will stifle the grace of God in his soul, and advises rising "not later than five" and giving an hour morning and evening to his devotions. He is not to dispute with his tutor but to give him a tract, and to be ready to visit any poor, sick townsman. Furley meets temptation in female form, and fears for his constancy.

> Conquer desire [writes Wesley February 21, 1756] and you will conquer fear. But as long as you are a slave you must be a coward. . . . Cut off the right hand and cast it from you: otherwise you will be a poor dastardly wretch all your days.

Furley's reading habits do not please Wesley: he must read better authors, and Wesley's favorites on ethics and philosophy are prescribed. "Fight, Sammy, fight," says the anxious mentor evidently fearing an intellectual deterioration in the student. When Sammy plans to go to London, he exclaims in consternation: "Are you stark, staring mad? . . . fly for your life, for your salvation." If he cannot stick to his studies, let him leave college, and "come away to me. . . . You are on the brink of the pit." Furley must "stop the leak" in his character. Grace is 99 per cent of a minister's equipment: after grace comes learning. Perhaps Wesley was unduly alarmed about the young man's impatience. In 1762 Furley is a parish minister. Wesley now cautions him to use mildness in reproof of his people's failings: "The longer I live, the larger allowances I make for human infirmities."

An eminent pastor among Wesley's fellow workers was John William

Fletcher (d. 1785), for twenty-five years vicar of Madeley. A Swiss, trained in Geneva, Fletcher had become a Methodist in London, and while deciding on the ministry as his calling, had taken Wesley as his spiritual guide. In the beginning of his pastorate, his insistent personal attention to the irreligious and reproof of their behavior aroused violent resentment. Some instances given indicate a rather excessive severity. But his quiet courage, abounding charity, and saintly devotion in the end made a deep impression. The sight of a stranger in need, the news of a miner hurt in a pit, or of someone likely to die, was a summons to instant action. An able scholar and a wise counselor, he was Wesley's choice of a successor: but Wesley had the sad task of preaching at his funeral. The text was: "Mark the perfect man," for he exemplified Wesley's doctrine of perfection.

A very different ministry, and more like Wesley's own, was that of Francis Asbury (d. 1816), who rode nearly 300,000 miles to build and organize Methodism in America. His Journal records a prodigious activity; but not less striking is its evidence of his daily seasons of prayer and his constant readiness to minister to individuals, even when he felt exhausted or unwell. Apparently he had to overcome some diffidence. On April 11, 1772, he reproaches himself for having failed to be specific in talking with a sick man and having left without a prayer. But there are countless brief notes of visits to persons, homes, and afflicted folk, which bear the stamp of faithful evangelical guidance. Wherever possible, he seems to have made a point of seeing condemned prisoners. Shortly after the above incident he relates (May 26):

Found myself very ill but visited a prisoner under sentence of death, and strove much to fasten conviction in his heart. Through the mercy of God I hope the poor man was humbled.

Three days later he attended him again, at his execution.

Asbury was insistent upon the standards of the Discipline, and did not shrink from the exclusion of "disorderly members." To join the societies often meant a basic change in the pattern of conduct. He tells casually how he rode home with one who had been converted suddenly while reading the Prayer Book, and who now "had a stud of race-horses to part with" (January 17, 1809). He wrote thousands of letters, many designed to sustain the pattern of a dedicated life in converts exposed to the temptations of the frontier.

Professor Sweet's volume on the Methodists in his Frontier series reveals an amazing panorama of expansion, under the leadership of devoted saddlebag preachers. He gives a lucid explanation of the code of discipline, and of procedures in dealing with its violators, both ministers and laymen. In addition to the grosser offenses, the sins of private dishonesty and the acceptance of bribes and "treats" from political candidates, were watchfully suppressed. We obtain from the documents in this book an impression that every Methodist was made aware of his participation in an order of life morally distinct from that of the society around him, and that his defection from the Methodist standards left him the alternatives of repentance or exclusion with the attendant disgrace.

Revisions of the Discipline in the various branches of Methodism have retained the essentials of its original provisions. The procedure in trials of ministers and lay members is still described in detail with little variation from that of a century and a half ago. Yet, as in other denominations, these legal processes have largely fallen into disuse.

Other special features of the ministry received less emphasis as time passed, and the "methods of Methodism" became more nearly similar to those of other leading Protestant denominations, as the latter also were subjected to modern trends. Daniel P. Kidder of Evanston in *The Christian Pastorate* (1841) laments the decline of the class meeting and of the class leader. This ample book, abounding in detailed advice on pastoral duties, proposes a serious attempt to promote the training and revive the services of class leaders in what the author calls "sub-pastoral" activities. We learn that where classes are maintained they are inadequately supplied with leaders and too large for effective functioning in the old intimate way. Many members are habitually inactive or absent, and the leader alone cannot overtake his task of reintegrating the groups. He suggests that leaders call upon the services of their active members to extend his "sub-pastoral" work by visiting and reclaiming the negligent. Each class would then "become a miniature church" and the measure would "go far to re-invest class meetings with their original interest and power." He regrets, too, the failure to retain the separation of the sexes earlier practiced in the bands. Pastoral visitation, he urges, should involve from time to time "a thorough religious conversation" with each person, old and young, and where required, attention to measures of economic relief.

VI

In this chapter it has been convenient to treat the methods of guidance practiced in churches of divergent polities. Baptists and Congregationalists have stressed the autonomy of the congregation and recognized a realm of option with respect to local practice, while the Quakers and Methodists have followed a system prescribed with some minuteness and authoritative for the whole denomination. Yet when we compare the actual procedures there are many similarities. Fundamental in all four traditions is the stress laid upon mutual responsibility among members for one another's welfare of body and soul. We have noted different forms in which this principle has been expressed in the Lutheran and Reformed churches of Europe, and in other denominations of the English-speaking world. "Mutual edification" and "fraternal correction" have thus found general recognition in the Protestant churches as a whole, regardless of the relation of congregations to the wider communion.

This characteristic of Protestantism has often been erroneously interpreted as religious individualism. The spiritual care of the individual has been, to be sure, an intense concern of Protestant churches; but the priesthood of every Christian involves his attention to the care of others, and his profit by their care of him. In so far as Protestantism has revived this emphasis, it has revived the spirit of New Testament Christianity. Any Christian communion that would neglect this would abandon an essential of Christianity itself, and any communion in which it is cultivated gives proof of its truly Christian existence. It is thus appropriate to ask whether Protestantism in its recent trends has departed from tradition in this matter. An active mutual cure of souls is difficult to maintain in present conditions. It has always been difficult to maintain. But our generation operates on a vast scale and is disposed to treat human beings in the mass rather than as persons, while too many are apparently content to be so treated. There are, and always have been, too few qualified ministers to do the labor of guidance without the active co-operation of members, and indeed if ministers alone were the counselors of souls, the priesthood of believers would lack reality. Mutual counseling has been done through various forms of organization, and new methods have to be invented to maintain it in changing times.

We are confronted here with the modern decline in importance of the forms of corrective discipline that were formerly employed. It would be presuming too much to suppose that church members of today are uniformly free from the offenses for which their ancestors blushed, and made amends. Yet undoubtedly in the nineteenth century, before dis- integrating forces became apparent, there was established a pattern of behavior in substantial accord with the externals at least of the older codes of discipline. Moreover, this stabilized standard went far to deter- mine what in the common mind were the marks of a "respectable" man.

To say that this result was superficial is not to say that it was futile or deplorable. Yet it must be emphasized that in the past century the codes of Presbyterians, Methodists, Baptists and others were becoming alike somewhat antiquated and irrelevant, through the industrial revo- lution and the growth of business and urban life. It is difficult to tabulate offenses where actions involve a great chain of causes and circumstances, as is the case in our present-day economic order. Church courts would often not be competent to judge of the personal guilt or innocence of men suspected of dishonesty who are entangled in the modern web of business and industry. If it was possible to decide wrongly in 1802 in a case of "pilfering a pair of gloves," it would ordinarily be out of the question now for churches to censure people concerned with the devices of a corporation in acquiring a competitor's.glove factory.

Another reason for this change is that the churches have largely lost contact with the class of people most subject to the cruder types of temptation. Some of these folk have found in small, enthusiastic sects, the supporting fellowship and stimulating discipline which formerly characterized our now flourishing denominations but which have given place in them to patterns of church life suggestive of a moral and spiritual security such people do not share. Many, in disloyalty or need, have drifted from Protestantism altogether.

The difficulties of discipline have led to its too easy surrender by the churches. No church has ever ideally solved the problem of maintaining standards and correcting the shortcomings of its members without in- fringing the law of charity. But if discipline should disappear to the point at which the manner of life of church people is not distinguishable from that of persons who make no religious profession, the Church would have lost her significance. Despite some cynical judgments, this stage has certainly not been reached. Yet, in late decades, what insistence there has been upon standards of conduct for Christians has been expressed from the pulpit and in the persuasions of the counselor with little support from the old disciplinary mechanisms provided for it. This has probably brought more gain than loss. But it is not all gain. The guide of souls ought not to be left in a position in which he is unsupported by his Church when he is convinced that he ought to be firm. The old-time discipline of the frontier ought to give us a genuine respect for what it sought to accomplish, and make us a little impatient with those who would ridicule or decry it.

Chapter XIII

THE CURE OF SOULS IN ROMAN CATHOLICISM

I

WE HAVE seen something of the medieval system of penitential discipline with its variations and abuses. When in the pontificate of Paul III (1534-49) the recovery of the Roman Church began, serious attention was turned to this aspect of church life, which had attracted severe criticism from supporters as well as opponents. In the reforms that ensued the attempt was rather to rid the old system of abuses than to alter it in principle. The Council of Trent, in its Fourteenth Session (1552) presented a defensive exposition of the traditional doctrine of penance, with repudiation of Protestant criticisms. Penance is held to be a sacrament, but only for the baptized. It was instituted in Christ's post-Resurrection commission, of John 20:23. For those who have fallen after baptism, penance is necessary to salvation, just as baptism itself is necessary for those not yet regenerated. Contrition, confession and satisfaction together constitute the matter of the sacrament. Contrition, which is necessary to obtain pardon, contains the loathing of past sin as well as the purpose to abandon it. If perfect contrition reconciles man with God before confession, this is not to be claimed for contrition without desire of the sacrament. Attrition is imperfect contrition, arising from thoughts of the baseness of sin or the fear of hell, and has the virtue of disposing men to seek the benefit of the sacrament.

The Tridentine fathers take the ground that the universal Church has always held the entire (*integram*) confession of sins to have been "instituted by the Lord," and to be "by divine right necessary for all who have fallen after baptism." It is declared:

that all the mortal sins of which, after diligent self-examination, they are conscious, must be recounted in confession even if these sins be entirely hidden, and committed only against the last two commandments of the Decalog, for such sins sometimes very grievously wound the soul and are more dangerous than those which are committed openly.

The confession of venial sins is also commended on the basis of pious custom, but not required as a necessary part of confession. Importance is laid on the necessity of exposing all remembered mortal sins. Circumstances which may change venial to mortal sins must be indicated, that just penalties may be assigned. It is unreasonable to say that these circumstances are mere invention, and that one need confess only that he has "sinned against a brother" (cf. Luther's view, pp. 167 f.). It is also impious to assert that such integral confession is impossible. What is required is that, after search of "all the folds and hiding places" (*sinus et latebras*) of his conscience, one should confess all remembered sins that have offended God.

Despite the general practice of public confession in the ancient Church, we read here only that such confession is not forbidden, while the secret sacramental confession "has always been commended" with "unanimous agreement" by the ancient Fathers. Our examination of the ancient practice has led us to conclusions entirely at variance with this.

Confession is to be made to priests and bishops only, and priests in mortal sin exercise full authority in the office of remitting sins. Faith without penance affords no remission. Exceptionally heinous crimes are to be reserved to the judgment of the Supreme Pontiff, and bishops may in their own dioceses reserve to their judgment offenses requiring excommunication. Unless the penitent is at the point of death, ordinary priests have no power in reserved cases, except to urge the offender to seek the judgment of the higher prelate.

With regard to satisfactions, the Synod denies that when guilt is forgiven all penalty is thereby removed. The remaining satisfactory penalties check the sinner from new offenses, act as remedies for habitual sin, and make us comformable to Christ who made satisfaction for our sins. Despite the recognition of Christ's satisfaction, it is stated that the satisfactions imposed in penance are not only remedies but *vindicta et castigatio*, an avenging and chastisement, of past sins. The "innovators," by their teaching that a new life is the best penance, "take away the whole force and use of satisfaction."

II

When the Council of Trent closed (December, 1563), a commission was preparing a catechism to embody its decisions. This was completed at the end of 1564 and with minor revisions promulgated by Pius V in 1566, under the title: *Catechism for Parish Priests by Decree of the Council of Trent.* Its section on the sacrament of penance is much ampler than the statement of the council itself. The treatment is scholastic, and elaborates distinctions that we have briefly indicated. The high Roman Catholic view of the authority of the priest in absolution is affirmed. The words, "I absolve thee," signify "that remission of sins is effected by the administration of this sacrament." How thankful should sinners be that God has bestowed on priests this power! Penance restores us to the grace of God. There is no hope for remission by any other means: "Unless ye do penance, ye shall all likewise perish" (Luke 13:3).

Pastors are to excite people to contrition, and admonish them to examine their consciences. Few attain to contrition so complete as to blot out sins; therefore the Lord provides "easier means" of salvation through the use of the keys of the Church. Confession is succinctly defined as "a sacramental accusation of one's sins, made to obtain pardon by virtue of the keys." As no one can enter a place without the help of him who has the keys, "so no one is admitted to heaven unless its gates be unlocked by the priests to whose custody the Lord gave the keys." Children at the age "when they are able to discern good from evil, and are capable of malice" are bound to go to confession. The "once a year" requirement of Innocent III is supplemented for the cases of danger of death, of receiving the sacrament, and of "apprehension of forgetting some sin" that must be confessed if pardon is to follow. Frequent confession is urged, on the analogy of physical cleanliness. Sins forgotten in confession should be promptly confessed when they come to memory. All the circumstances that aggravate or extenuate sins are to be revealed in confessing them. The intentional suppression of sins in confession involves fresh guilt. It is stated that:

Secrecy as regards confession should be strictly observed, as well by the penitent as by the priest. Hence no one can, on any account, confess by messenger or letter.

Many directions are supplied for the conduct of the confessional with respect to various types of penitents. There follows an exposition of satisfactions, which are fundamentally of three kinds: prayer, fasting and almsdeeds. God "has granted to our frailty the privilege that one may satisfy for another." Indulgences are not here specially mentioned, but their validity is obviously implied.

In Session XXI (1562), the Council took up the problem of the abuses of indulgences and decreed the abolition of the office of *quaestor*, or itinerant pardon-seller. In its last Session (XXV, 1563), it reverted to this thorny question, and declared that the power to grant indulgences had been conferred by Christ, that its use was ancient, and is highly salutary, and approved by sacred councils. This unequivocal affirmation is accompanied by a resolve to remove the abuses that have given heretics occasion to blaspheme against the ordinance.

The attempt to exclude the pardoner's traffic met with much resistance. A further blow against this old abuse was struck by Pius V in a vigorous *motu proprio* of 1567. Spain continued to resist this reform, but elsewhere it was in time effective. Payments for indulgences were left untouched in principle by the abolition of the hawker: they simply passed through other channels, where, presumably, self-interest was not involved. "The seventeenth century," writes Lea, "witnessed a marked improvement in these matters." The new Canon Law of 1918 recognizes indulgences, including 'those for the dead "by way of suffrage," and explains their conditions, one of which is previous absolution. An unforgiven sin, even venial, may be an obstacle to a plenary indulgence, in effect converting it into a partial one.

III

Sacramental penance was thus carefully defined in the Counter-Reformation. It was at the same time vigorously revived. The great saints of the era such as Philip Neri (d. 1595) and Charles Borromeo (d. 1584) were extraordinarily zealous in its promotion. The Jesuit movement in its early growth, devoted much of its abounding energy to the confessional. Many of the Jesuits also became directors of conscience to persons of eminence and influence.

In the development of the casuistry of the confessional Jesuits took the leading part. They explored a very wide range of problems of conscience, and compiled great compendia in which countless cases were described and solved. A mere list of the titles would fill many pages. Their opinions have attracted much criticism; some of it undiscriminating and unjust. It is fair to recognize with their defenders that their object was "to determine the existence or non-existence of a strict obligation of conscience" (Brucker), and that this naturally led to a statement of minimum obligation, rather than of ideal conduct for saints. Some of the Jesuit teachers were undoubtedly lax, others more severe.

Early in the seventeenth century criticisms of a lax tendency were frequently expressed. André Mater, in a well-balanced book on the Jésuits, notes that by 1614 people spoke of *artes jesuiticae* (Jesuitical devices). The great literary attack upon them by Blaise Pascal in his *Provincial Letters* (1656-57) has left an unduly unfavorable impression. From this work it has been assumed that the members of the Order set out recklessly to lower moral standards. Whatever their lapses, this was not their purpose. Pascal cannot be convicted of serious misquotation, but he was animated by hostility to the Jesuits as the chief enemies of Jansenism, and was not careful to explain the contexts of his excerpts, which would often have produced a much less damaging effect. In a far more substantially annotated work—a dull and neglected treatise—David Clarkson presented Jesuit casuistry in an equally unfavorable light: *The Practical Divinity of the Papists Destructive of Christianity* (1676).

These controversial works must be cautiously read. Yet the lax decisions of some moralists, chiefly Jesuits, called forth from Pope Alexander VII in 1665-66, and from Innocent XI in 1649, condemnations of this dangerous tendency in many specific opinions then current, most of which were, indeed, morally (or ecclesiastically) subversive.

The principal moral danger arose from the method of *probabilism*. This is the determination of freedom from obligation of conscience on the basis of a "probable" opinion—one which has support from some authority, even where a contrary opinion is "more probable," i.e., has fuller support from authorities. The probabilist thus charted what was morally the easier way. The Jesuits were not the inventors of probabilism, but they made large use of it. The Dominicans had favored it, but when Alexander VII referred to "the arbitrariness of extravagant minds" in its lax employment, they somewhat abruptly gave up the method for the safer casuistry of *probabiliorism*, or reliance upon the "more probable" of competing opinions. The Jesuits continued to follow their favorite method and have not ceased to defend it. Innocent XI's condemnation of the "laxism" of "slightly probable" opinions, led, however, to greater caution.

The great Jesuit casuists include the Westphalian Hermann Busenbaum (d. 1668), author of the widely circulated *Marrow of Moral Theology* (1645), who though somewhat lax was not included among those assailed by Pascal. In the eighteenth century he was twice condemned by the Parliament of Paris for his judgment that one who is a subject in the family, in a religious community, or in the state may in self-defense slay his father, abbot or king. The doctrine of tyrannicide was of course not new. Whether Brutus justly slew Caesar was already an old debating theme when the Jesuit order began. The alleged connection of Jesuit directors with plots to slay rulers is a difficult topic which hardly lies within our interest here; but it was a charge from which their reputation suffered.

Antonio Escobar-y-Mendoza (d. 1669) of Valladolid was another well-known Jesuit casuist of the same period. His *Moral Theology* (1644) was frequently reprinted. Pascal's many references to Escobar have made his name a by-word for equivocation and prevarication; the word *escobarderie* entered the French language in this sense. Yet he has been much more generously judged by modern readers, and a contemporary English Jesuit, James Brodrick, has come gallantly to the defense of his economic ethics. Brodrick's explanations go far to exculpate Escobar; but readers of the quotations he gives may still smell an unpleasant odor of equivocation, especially in a passage permitting false witness.

The great Roman Catholic casuist of the eighteenth century was the Neapolitan Alfonso de Liguori (d. 1787) who devoted a long life to moral theology and the revival of ascetic piety. He was the founder of the Redemptorists (1733) an order which took up some of the tasks of the Jesuits when the latter were suppressed, 1774-1814. He was the great inheritor and reinterpreter of Jesuit casuistry, and he has exerted a dominant influence upon later casuists. In his *Moral Theology* (1749) he represents the confessor as father, physician, teacher and judge. He had recoiled from an early rigorism to a probabilist position. In later editions of his work he becomes more cautious and favors the position known as "equiprobabilism"—which relieves the conscience only where authorities are either favorable or at least equally divided. He insists upon the necessity of casuistry in the instruction and equipment of a confessor, especially in view of the many modern positive laws, bulls and decrees that are to be borne in mind. He presents a high and rigid standard on the part of confessors, warning them that one who hears confessions without sufficient knowledge is in a state of damnation, regardless of his bishop's approval. In these matters Liguori is still a rigorist. In another long work, *The Apostolic Man Instructed . . .* or *the Practice and Instruction of Confessors*, the same exacting standards are asserted, and detailed guidance for confessors is provided. Confession must be: vocal; secret; true, and integral (XVI, iii). In his statement and exposition of the principle: "particular remedies for diversity of faults" he reminds us of passages in the Penitentials. He frequently recommends·prayer to the Virgin (he wrote a celebrated book on *The Glories of Mary*)as a remedial penance. Liguori's labored texts are strewn with the (abbreviated) names of authorities; but to say that he makes his judgments by balancing their weight would hardly be true. It is unusual for him to disagree with Busenbaum, but he does this, on other authority, where Busenbaum says that a penitent can be absolved even though he will accept only a light penance when he deserves a heavy one. Here Liguori takes firm ground against yielding to the penitent's demands (XVI, iv). In his recognition of the value of attrition (the imperfect contrition of fear) he merely follows the Tridentine interpretation.

With virtual unanimity modern Roman Catholics accept the system and authority of Liguori. In 1831 all confessors were permitted by Gregory XVI to follow his opinions without the obligation to consult other authorities. In 1839 he was canonized, and in 1871 Pius IX declared him a doctor of the Church. The admired writers on confession and direction of later times, such as Jean-Nicholas Grou (d. 1803), Jean Pierre Gury (d. 1866), and Jean Joseph Gaume (d. 1879), have been his disciples. Thomas Slater, S.J., in his *Manual of Moral Theology for English-Speaking Countries* (1928), regards Liguori as his master. These authors guard their probabilism from laxity by use of the phrase "solidly probable," which avoids dependence on the "slightly probable" opinions condemned by Innocent XI.

IV

The art of spiritual direction reached a high level in seventeenth century French Catholicism. We must here again recall the distinction between the director and the confessor. It is true that the roles were often combined. Liguori's treatment of the duties of the confessor gives to the latter responsibility for guidance as well as for sacramental penance. Yet he adds to his *Instruction* an appendix on "how the confessor ought to conduct himself in directing spiritual souls." Direction has to do with the pursuit of higher spiritual attainment rather than with the sacramental pardon of sins. In most instances the director is not the confessor of his consultant. He often gives advice with respect to the latter's confession, or on the choice of a confessor. A study of biographies and other personal data would reveal a great deal of such direction. We can discover the advice of directors who have used letters where these have been preserved. No such light can be shed upon confession, which is necessarily, by the decision of Trent, unwritten, and is given under seal. There exists, however, a limitless quantity of spiritual correspondence of the period with which we are now concerned, the product of many pens. The art of direction was occasionally treated also in manuals for priests. One by the Jesuit François Guilloré (d. 1689), *The Way to Guide Souls*, which grew out of his experience in direction, appears to have been widely used. But the great spiritual personalities which we must mention here, hardly needed help from a textbook.

In the letters of the Savoyard Francis de Sales (d. 1622), Bishop of Geneva, of Vincent de Paul (d. 1660), celebrated for his works of charity, of Jacques Bénigne Bossuet (d. 1704), the eminent Bishop of Meaux, and of François de la Mothe Fénelon (d. 1715), Bishop of Cambrai, we have a fund of spiritual correspondence that would probably be impossible to match in any other era. These were all men of intellectual distinction who wrote with elegance and power, and they all held the work of direction to be an important part of their devoted service to the Church.

In a previous chapter we have seen the application of the term "director" to Protestant guides of souls criticized on the ground that the word implies too much of paternalistic control. Jules Michelet in his book, *The Priest, the Woman and the Family* (published in English as *Spiritual Direction and Auricular Confession*, 1845), made a passionate attack upon the confessional, and the direction of women by priests. He thus describes the tyranny of the director:

The patient and wary man . . . day by day depriving you of a little of yourself, substituting a little of himself . . . this is a thing different from royalty; it is divinity. It is to be the God of another.

This is the perverse and overbearing spiritual direction in which one person's will and conscience are yielded to another's. We have seen something of this sort in the Hindu's reverence for his *guru*, and in Islamic piety. That it has occurred in Christianity cannot be questioned. The relations of Conrad of Marburg and St. Elizabeth of Thuringia in the early thirteenth century indicate just such malign domination. But the description would be highly exaggerated if applied to any of those just named as revealed in their letters. The Abbé Moïse Cagnac regards Michelet's book as a mediocre and quite misleading pamphlet. He flatly denies, with reference to the seventeenth century directors, Michelet's characterization of direction, and the statement of another critic that it destroys responsibility. This is the view of an advocate, and it tends to minimize the element of mastery discernible in some of the letters.

In St. Francis de Sales we discover a spirit aflame with the love of God, and of his spiritual charges. His ardor calls for the fullest confidence in response. "Indeed, my dear daughter, you must make no difference between your soul and mine in the confidence that you must have in me" he writes to a superior of nuns. In the same letter (III, x, in Father Mackey's translation) he refers to a recalcitrant sister. Her desire to have control of her own will in order better to follow the will of God is a "chimera." "Often give commands to her, and impose upon her mortifications opposed to her inclinations." One begins to remember in such passages that the saint was a supporter of persecution. He treats with a complete lack of sympathy the case of a young novice who is pining for her lover. Her parents' decision is "worth a hundred thousand times more than the free use of her own will" (III, xxi). He has a fixed idea that women especially require supervision. "Your sex needs to be led, and never did it succeed in anything except by submission," he writes to a Benedictine abbess (IV, xxvii). In requiring of a mother superior some act of reformation of a nunnery he can be, properly enough, exacting. But most of his letters are free from asperity, and breathe a spirit of spiritual affection for his "dear daughters" in religion, to whom he is constantly opening vistas of devotion, and pouring out his heart. In one instance he pleads (quoting Philemon) for consideration of an impetuous novice who has exhausted the patience of her abbess (IV, xix).

St. Francis has stated a high view of the authority of the director of souls. In the *Introduction to the Devout Life* (1609), which was addressed to Mme. de Chantal ("Philothée") he has a chapter on "the necessity of a guide in order to enter the path of devotion" (I, iv). He cites historic cases, including that of Conrad and St. Elizabeth:

And indeed the guide should always be an angel in your eyes: that is to say, when you have found him, do not look upon him as a mere man, nor trust in him as such, nor in his human knowledge, but in God who will favor you and speak to you by means of this man. . . . Have the greatest confidence in him, mingled with a holy reverence.

Improving on the advice of Avila who said: Choose a director among a thousand, Francis writes: "I say, among ten thousand; for they are fewer than can be imagined who are fitted for this office." (One finds the last sentence often quoted, in the seventeenth century and later.)

The celebrated series of letters of Francis to Mme. Jeanne Chantal, the widow of a French baron, and chief co-founder with him of the Order of the Visitation, crowns his spiritual correspondence. The Order itself was busy with the sick and needy, an activity in which Francis had set an example. In the letters to St. Chantal he reaches the heights of mystical love and the depths of ascetic renunciation. During a retreat in which with other religious women she joined him, he wrote to her and received letters from her day by day. All our self-esteem, all of self, must, he says, "be buried in eternal abandonment." The correspondence at this point is extremely intimate. In one letter she wishes him "a thousand goodnights," adding: "I think I see the two portions of our united soul made one, abandoned and given over to God alone." His ardor had evoked this response; but he replies a day later: "Think no more about the friendship, the unity, which God has made in us . . . for you have given up all to God" (III, i-vi). Yet he frequently associates his own mystical abandonment to God with a boundless and very personal love of the souls under guidance. While devotion knows no limitation and "human prudence" is set at naught, Francis frequently calls for restraint in asceticism and checks the scrupulosity of anxious self-examination. He urges, too, the common virtues of affability, humility and courage. "Be humble," he writes to an unnamed lady "and God will be on your side. . . . Give yourself to him without concealment and without reserve." And to a mother superior of the Carmelites: "It is necessary that your humility be courageous."

V

Pierre de Bérulle, through his foundation of the French congregation of the Oratory (1611), his contacts, books and letters, gave a great impetus to the cultivation of the life of devotion, especially among priests. His 250 extant letters have not been estimated so highly as those of the others mentioned. He is a little ponderous and though sometimes sublime, is more often obscure (Cagnac). But he made directors of many of his young disciples, of whom the most celebrated is St. Vincent de Paul. Vincent's was a life of prodigious activity in service to prisoners and to the poverty-stricken of many communities, and in the promotion and supervision of missions to Poland, Algiers, Madagascar, and elsewhere. He is credited with writing about thirty thousand letters, most of which remain unpublished. A relatively small proportion of those pub-

lished are strictly letters of direction. Henri Brémond testifies to the
high literary quality of his spiritual letters; he finds in them "not a banal
line—a thing unique in collections of this type." This author holds
strongly that Vincent was more mystic than philanthropist. Like John
Wesley, he combined the life of religion with vast external labors and
maintained amid criticism a spirit of good will. Almost unique among
Gallican churchmen, he stoutly affirmed the legal rights of Protestants,
believing that the reform of the clergy and charitable persuasion would
avail more than harsh methods to win them.

Vincent in his early years rigidly obeyed Bérulle as his director; later
he was greatly drawn to Francis de Sales, whose successor he became in
the guidance of the Sisters of the Visitation. Madame de Chantal was
among his correspondents. His skill was called forth in the direction
of Louise de Marillac, the widow of Antoine le Gras, whose agitated
soul another director, Camus, a friend and disciple of Francis, had failed
to help. Vincent's direction, says J. Calvet, "was so simple that it is difficult to indicate its principles." One must simply and faithfully turn to
God, and, without waste of time in mystical analyses, labor for God. To
love God in the poor is so important that one should even leave the Mass
in order to help them. Brémond stresses the "theocentrism" of his
master, Bérulle, and its recurrence in Vincent. But the word is a very
general one, and would certainly apply to the direction of many others,
notably Bossuet. The quality in Vincent that Bossuet seems most to
have admired was simplicity. "Do not charge yourself," Vincent writes
in an early letter to Louise de Marillac, "with too many rules and practices, but confirm and perform well those you have—your daily acts and
employments, in short, that everything may tend to the doing well what
you are doing." Thoughts of some singular devotion are to be resisted,
as prompted by the spirit of evil. He prescribes for her reading the devotional books of Francis de Sales, and the New Testament, and makes
this requirement:

Write me briefly every two days what takes place, and your disposition of
body and spirit, and try above all not to strain (empresser) yourself but do
everything gently as you might imagine the good Monsieur [de Sales] of
Geneva did.

The lady was a prey to worries. One of these was her son's unwillingness
to become a priest. She thought this a judgment of God upon her. Even
Vincent shows impatience at this point. "I never saw such a woman as

you. . . . In God's name correct yourself, and know once for all that these thoughts are of the evil one, and that those of Our Savior are sweet and gracious" (1636?). We find him later rebuking her maternal possessiveness. "Leave his guidance to God," he tells her. He urges her to make her prayer with reference to Zebedee's sons, to whom, with their ambitious mother, Christ said: "Ye know not what ye ask" (1639). In the end, under Vincent's guidance, she escaped from the misery of her anxieties and found peace of mind in private devotions and charitable labors.

VI

The extant correspondence of Bossuet, who found time for an astounding variety of literary and administrative activities, fills fifteen large volumes. In an appendix to Volume IV the editors treat at length Bossuet's principles of direction. In his high view of the function, he held that the director has "the place of God" toward his charges. Yet in practice we find him habitually urging them to seek God's will for themselves. He emphasized, as his editors state, "that each soul should examine with application and with holy intention the ways in which God would have him walk." The director should inspire holy love, and induce the consultant to "taste of God and His holy truth." He is stern in rebuking directors who by compliance with triflers turn direction of souls into "mere amusement" (Bossuet was an opponent of probabilism). In one instance he thus turns aside unimportant inquiries: "My daughter, God has not given me anything on your questions; when He gives it to me, I will give it to you."

His letters to laymen and to religious women alike keep in the foreground the will of God; and for this reason one reader at least, in examining a fair number of them, has been reminded frequently of the counsels of another Frenchman for whom Bossuet had little admiration, John Calvin. Note, for example, the series written to the Maréchal de Bellefonds and his aunt, Agnès de Bellefonds, between April 25 and June 30, 1672. His friend Bellefonds has been thwarted in his political career, and is in deep distress. "How profound and terrible is God!" exclaims Bossuet. "Regard with the eyes of faith His guidance of you (*la conduite de Dieu sur vous*: Bossuet is fond of this phrase or variants of it). Adore the dispositions of divine providence, impenetrable to human judgment." And again: "All will go well, for God is in it. . . . Read the Gospel and hearken to God as you read it."

The letters to women in religious orders, or contemplating vows of religion, are very numerous. Most important here is the series written to sister Cornuau (Marie Dumoustrier, widow [1681?]) of Philippe Cornuau. She was a member of the Daughters of Charity, an order founded by St. Vincent de Paul, and she wished to become a nun. Bossuet withstood this desire, but finally consented (1697). In the first of this series (October 15, 1689) he gives her directions on the use of exclamatory prayers taken from the Psalms. He prescribes an exercise of consideration of the beauty of the works of God in the seven days of creation, and in the 148th Psalm, "Praise ye the Lord from the heavens. . . ." God is to be praised for light, for rain and sunshine, for fire and ice: and more for one's own eyes, speech, mouth, hands, feet and whole body; still more for the soul, with its intelligence and will. There are in all twenty-five letters written to this lady. It is thought that she retouched them, adding sentences from letters written to others. This literary offense has made them even more revealing of Bossuet's teaching in his guidance of ascetic women. With those who were essentially devout he, like Francis de Sales, was inclined to discountenance anxious self-discipline. He would have Madame Cornuau "not torment the head nor too much excite the heart, but take what presents itself to the soul, and without these violent efforts allow herself sweetly to draw nigh to God" (September 17, 1690). He supports by a reference to Francis de Sales his view that "surrender to the will of God is a more efficacious means than all extraordinary austerities": St. Francis, he notes, "appears far from approving these" (October 10, 1694).

Bossuet does, of course, sometimes prescribe routines of devotion, and he prizes the traditional devotions of his Church. He was active in the conversion of Protestants. After the Revocation of the Edict of Nantes (1685), when Protestant worship was ruthlessly suppressed, the Daughters of Charity of La Ferté-sous-Jouarre were engaged in the conversion of some Protestant women. Bossuet wrote (January 13, 1686) to advise them on how they should instruct the converts. They are not only to receive them when they come, but to seek them out in their homes and teach them the common devotions of the Church, leaving details for later attention. The acts of devotion he prescribes for individuals are simple. When Madame Cornuau was setting out for Jouarre, he prescribed for her a week's exercises, consisting of a list of Psalms to be recited, with selections from Isaiah, John and Romans, and with themes of meditation to accompany them (May 27, 1693).

VII

As a director of souls Fénelon is probably the best known of these great Frenchmen. His approbation of the somewhat reckless quietist, Madame Guyon, and the papal condemnation (1699), to which his one-time friend Bossuet was a party, of his *Maxims of the Saints on the Interior Life* (1697), written in her defense, are facts well known. In 1688 she had professedly come under his direction, and promised obedience to him. But she prayed that he would be converted to her opinions, and soon undertook to direct her director. She led him to assert doctrines that proved unacceptable. In the *Maxims* Fénelon cited authorities for the doctrine of "pure" or "disinterested" love. Cagnac shows that he was here anticipated by Francis de Sales, who, with similar meaning, spoke of "the state of resignation" and "holy indifference." Even the statement that the soul should be prepared to accept damnation and make to God a sacrifice of its eternal welfare, is paralleled in Francis. For Bossuet, this idea was intolerable. Piety must, he believed, always seek beatitude, the state of eternal blessedness. Morality, too, would suffer, under the impact of this doctrine. Fénelon accepted the papal condemnation, but he continued to express himself in language affected by quietism. He frequently warns against anxiety over the absence of inner peace: "this is to love our consolation, when we wish to love God." We must resign ourselves to the discipline of periods of dispeace.

Another element, easily associated with this piety of indifference and resignation, is a strain of Stoicism. Fénelon does not ask for reforming activity. "Let men be men. . . . Let the world be the world; you cannot help it." He disliked excess in everything from architecture to asceticism; he Christianized the "golden mean."

While Fénelon was at the Court of France he was busy with the direction of numerous high-born ladies and military men. Relatively few of his letters are written to persons in ascetic communities. The failure of wealth and worldly security to bring happiness is well illustrated in the states of mind to which Fénelon has to minister. The most distinguished of those he directed was Madame de Maintenon, who in 1685 was secretly married to Louis XIV. At the outset he urges her to confide in her director and in no one else. This is accompanied by frank reproof of her misguided piety. "You are seeking yourself when you think you are seeking God only." He wrote similarly, and repeatedly, to many others, with a subtle knowledge of the self-deceptions we are prone to. He calls for total abandonment of the will to God's will. When Madame de Maintenon has toothache, he writes, "God be praised": by being happy in suffering she can edify the King, and "pain will give you more authority" (Letters of 1690). She complains of weariness and disgust with court life. The faults of men, he says, serve to make us feel the greatness of God. "Do not try to force yourself by great efforts of courage." What is unavoidable is not to be resisted, either through haughtiness or through fastidiousness. She must reserve time for devotion. Fénelon advises her, as he does other court ladies, if necessary to resort to deceptions (such as pretending to rise late) in order to do this without embarrassment. He paraphrases I Corinthians 13, to warn against mere activity. "He who loves not does nothing though he may seem to do all. Strive only to love." He leads the great lady along the path of self-renunciation and childlike simplicity. The sin of Lucifer consisted in his delight at seeing himself perfect (May, 1699).

Among the best of his letters are those written to Elizabeth Hamilton, Countess of Gramont (1684-97). The faults he chiefly contends with, in this court lady of Scottish background, are worldliness, a taste for luxury, haughtiness and frivolous habits. He urges her to take half an hour for prayer each morning, and such other times as may be snatched during the day. As with Madame de Maintenon, he authorizes the prevarication of pretending to rise late or to have a letter to write, in order to be free to pray. There is much good moral advice in these letters, and some very frank rebuke:

The only way to profit by the humiliation of our faults is to face them in all their ugliness, without losing hope in God, and without having any hope in ourselves. Never did a person need more urgently to be humiliated by her faults than you do. Only thus will God crush your pride and confound your intellectual conceit. (October 2, 1689)

Fénelon prescribes silence, and restraint of speech, for this witty and "disdainful" woman, who found it hard to leave to others the honors of conversation. Let her speak but little, though without feeling superior about it, and cultivate *le recueillement* (recollectedness) amid the boring anecdotes of others (November 16, 1694). When her face is marred with blotches, Fénelon explains the affliction as a heaven-sent remedy for the leprosy of pride and self-love. "You had need to be stricken down, like St. Paul at the gates of Damascus, and to find no resource in yourself" (November 12, 1692).

In the Countess of Montberon, Fénelon had a difficult case which cost him many letters and much disappointment. She was a nerve-racked, imaginative woman, whose moods fluctuated between enthusiasm and depression. J. Lewis May thinks Fénelon ill equipped, because of a strain of femininity in him, to be her director. But who could have directed this overwrought and unpredictable lady? There were no scientific psychiatrists; and she would have offered a grave problem to the best of them. Fénelon was apparently at first deceived in mistaking her religiosity for true religion, and outgrew this as she resisted his simple remedy of absolute resignation to God. She was wilful in her devotions, and liked to dramatize her piety. "I am told that you were once seen dressed as a nun," he writes. She should let her husband decide on her apparel, and avoid extremes which make her noticeable, thus "leaving no feast [ragoût] for self-love." He continually warns against scrupulosity, which is fed by a too lively imagination. He counsels distrust of both imagination and reason, and an attitude of simple faith and love of God. The letters of 1702-9 show frequent tensions that endangered the relationship. Fénelon assumes repeatedly that obedience to God involves obedience to the director. "I will pursue you relentlessly until you return to humility and to the blind obedience that God asks of you" (November 19, 1704). "You are offended with God and with me. . . . Peace can be found only by yielding without delay" (June 13, 1707). At last he throws up his hands: "Consider me as nothing. Think only of Him. . . . Depart, never return, forget me, condemn all my advice" (February 16, 1709). But he was soon plying anew the well-worn admonitions against her agitations, scruples and delusions. "Accustom yourself then, to see yourself as you are: unjust, jealous, envious, changeable and suspicious, and let your self-love die of vexation." Self-love, with its noisy cries, prevents us from discerning "the tranquil and gentle voice of the holy love of God." Fénelon may have saved the Countess from complete disintegration of personality. But she remained a spiritual invalid.

Fénelon gave advice to men as well as women, though less frequently. His letters to the Archbishop-Elector of Cologne, to members of the Colbert family, to the Chevalier de Ramsay, and to the Marquis de Seignelay, have many striking passages. "Your heart," he says to the Marquis, "must be filled with God or with the world. . . . Abandon yourself without reserve to the mercy of the God of all consolation, who reaches out his hands to you despite your ingratitude." Prayer should be "simple, much from the heart, little from the mind." Distractions will come; they should be taken in our stride. "Disquietude over our distractions is the most dangerous distraction." The Vidame of Amiens, a military commander, was another who took Fénelon's counsel. "There is nothing in his direction," says Cagnac, "incompatible with the soldier's life." Again there is a requirement of morning and evening devotion. The Vidame must dare to take a stand, and not blush for Jesus Christ. On the other hand he should be gay, accommodating, considerate and amiable. "Piety is not grave [triste]." Why seek penances?—each day has its pain. One must not return to the hair-shirt, or flee to the desert (1709-10). It is probable that the Vidame profited much from Fénelon's direction.

Fénelon frequently calls attention to the relation of body and mind. "When the mind is agitated the body suffers," and vice versa. Very frequently he prescribes bodily rest, or warns against activity, in a time of poor health, just as he forbids any major decision during a state of mental distraction. There is in some passages a distinct adumbration of the psychosomatic therapy of today. As a moralist, he extols the old virtues but does not ask us to strain after them. They flow from a loving and total abandonment to the will of God, much as for Luther, good works flow from living faith. In an impressive passage written to Montberon (January 5, 1701) he distinguishes courage in suffering from *bonne volonté*, a superior virtue. This is not good will in the common English sense, but a simple love of and obedience to the will of God. The person who has it so bears his sufferings that "if you told him he was suffering well he would not understand you." This devout and unself-conscious heroism without heroics is the crowning virtue—to which his correspondent could never attain. Another constituent element is suggested by his exhortation to "recollectedness," a calm awareness of spiritual realities which protects the soul from trivial dissipation of its powers. The modern reader may often gain, from his lucid treatment of these themes, lessons of great practical value for life in our age of stress and strain.

VIII

The direction of the Jansenist leader, Jean Duvergier de Hauranne, abbé de St. Cyran (d. 1643), has usually been criticized as unduly severe. The opponents of Jansenism have stressed this in a general attack on the austerity of that movement. Cagnac quotes Bossuet's view that "their severity renders Christianity impossible." But St. Cyran's later interpreters have been more favorable. There is no doubt of his exacting demands upon priests in the confessional and his horror at the offenses of priests. Holding a doctrine of the priesthood of all Christians, he even looked upon all grave sins of Christians as violations of a priestly sanctity. Jean Orcibal, in his elaborate study of St. Cyran's life and times, has balanced the evidence for severity with proofs of the abbé's humanity and consideration especially for the young and the poor, and of his charity and large designs for philanthropy, prior to Vincent de Paul. A profound affection appears in his letters to penitents, and he tenderly consoles those in affliction. L. Fréderic Jaccard, in a scholarly monograph, has examined his guidance of Marie-Claire Arnauld whose condition he too late discovered to be one of sickness rather than of guilt. An interior contradiction in St. Cyran's mental makeup is recognized by Orcibal: it is reflected in his guidance of souls. But his concept of the function of a director has much to commend it. According to Jaccard he regarded direction in the light of "a pair of crutches for the use of minor souls." The function should lapse with the progress of the soul. It was during his four-year imprisonment (1638-42) that he wrote with enthusiasm of that "Christian freedom, which liberates us from all bondage, even bondage to men who serve God." "Though the heavenly way may be narrow," he says in a letter, "it grows broader as we tread it." To a nun who had become blind he wrote:

There is no greater affliction than blindness, according to human ideas, passions and reasons. And there is nothing so sanctifying if we look to God and His eternal designs. (Vol. I, letter v.)

In his own afflictions he showed a saintly charity, even toward those who injured him. In a long letter he holds that the penitential devotion of persons of rank may consist in defending their people from the oppression of the strong (II, xxxii).

It is not possible here to extend to later times our treatment of representative Roman Catholic writers of spiritual letters. The writers are innumerable and, even if space permitted, it would be a hard task to select the best for comment. One of the interesting facts in this connection is that a layman, Baron Friedrich von Hügel (d. 1925), left a remarkable series on religious topics, many of them letters of direction, and all marked by a lofty spirituality combined with a gracious friendliness. Some excellent examples of modern clerical direction by letter will be found in Joseph Gorayeb's *Life and Letters of Walter Drum, S.J.*

Father Drum (d. 1921) accords to those under direction a good deal of freedom of choice.

IX

Leading aspects of the cure of souls in Roman Catholicism have now been examined. We have noted the authoritative insistence upon the sacrament of penance, involving the practice of auricular confession to a priest. And we have observed the widespread use of private spiritual direction, which presupposes attendance at the confessional, but separately undertakes fundamental correction and progressive guidance. The former is a matter of oft-reaffirmed ecclesiastical obligation. There was a tendency among devotional writers to urge the necessity for the services of a director as well as of a confessor. Jacob Merlon Horstius in his *Warnings of Christian Wisdom* (1630), addresses "the Christian reader," and presents a commonly attainable pattern of piety. But of the "three supports [*adminicula*] of wisdom" on which he elaborates (in Chapter V), the last is "a faithful director of life":

> Therefore, have someone pious and grave and knowing, a spiritual father and master or confessor, or a faithful friend and monitor; and love to be directed by his counsel and assistance in the weightier matters of life, and most of all in the affairs of salvation. But beware whom you confide in . . . and to whom you commit your soul, than which you hold nothing more precious.

John Baptist Scaramelli (d. 1752) in his *Ascetic Directory or Guide to the Spiritual Life* (1750) affirms the necessity of a guide as a means of acquiring perfection, and supports his view by quotations from the Fathers. While this view was inculcated, it was frequently stated that only one director in a thousand or ten thousand, was qualified for his task. Direction by letter, as we have any record of it, was mainly of two classes of people, those under vows and persons of high social rank. Fénelon's letters were not written to the struggling poor, but to persons of a limited and socially privileged class. How the common people were served in this respect does not appear from such letters.

To find evidence on this we should have to go to the records of parish life, and the task of research would be enormous. We may permit ourselves a reference to the celebrated parish saint, Jean Marie Baptiste Vianney (d. 1859), curé of Ars, a village in the upper Saône. To this village his pastoral labors brought a new spirit. The Abbé Alfred Monnin in describing his guidance of the people remarks:

In spiritual direction the chief thing is to follow God's call and make others follow it, to keep pace with the Holy Spirit, to proportion oneself to souls in order to make them conform to Jesus Christ.

Neighboring priests were hostile to the ascetic and highly unconventional curé, and for a time he was victimized by eccentric women who, prompted by his enemies, came from other parishes to "fling themselves like demons on the curé's confessional" and demand his direction for their trumped-up scruples. But he overcame this strange persecution and many other difficulties, to win the gratitude of his people and a reputation for sainthood that led to his canonization in 1924.

That the directed person "commits his soul" to his director is sometimes stated, and sometimes implied, in the letters we have examined. This is not a conception of the New Testament or of the early Church, and in theory it has no attraction for Protestants. Yet the fact is that in some instances people crave nothing more than to abandon their wills and consciences to others. Milton was a contemporary of our great seventeenth century directors. As an observer of life in Puritan England, he wrote in his Areopagitica (1644):

There is not any burden that some would not gladlier post off to another than the charge and care of their religion.

Certainly many about us are in this mood today. And because of this attitude the line between a healing and strengthening guidance and an unwholesome and debilitating domination is difficult to draw. Psychiatrists face the same problem, and differ greatly in their approach to it. Whether the guide be priest or minister or lay expert, any method that continually fetters one person's conscience to another's will is totally unsatisfactory both from a religious and from a psychological point of view.

The thoughtful reader will obtain, however, alike in the brilliant letters of the great directors and in the often dreary compilations of casuists, innumerable insights into the states and needs of the soul.

Chapter XIV

THE CURE OF SOULS IN THE EASTERN ORTHODOX AND ARMENIAN CHURCHES

I

WHILE there are similarities between the Eastern Orthodox and the Latin Church in the procedures of confession and penance, marked differences have also been noted. Private confession developed in the East largely from monastic practice and spread through the activity of monks rather than of priests. Vacandard has pointed out the indifference of the Greek Christians to priestly orders in a confessor, and the requirement instead that he be specially qualified by spiritual gifts. He observes that the expression "spiritual father" (*pater pneumatikos*) comes out of Eastern Christianity. It was often applied to others than priests, who became directors of souls. The *Syntagma*, a seventh century compilation, indicates that the priest is not by ordination empowered to remit sins, but must be specially delegated to this office by a bishop. Anastasius the Sinaite (A.D. 700), declares that it is useful to confess to "spiritual men, who have experience of souls," and that we should "find a spiritual man, experienced and able to heal us ... that we may confess to him as to the Lord and not to a man." In another passage he recommends confession to priests "or rather to the Lord through [*dia*] the priests." (From a book of *Questions and Answers* in Migne, *Patrologia, series Graeca*, LXXXIX; 369, 372, 833.) This form of language is frequent in modern Orthodox writings: confession is "through" not "to" a priest; absolution "through" not "by" one.

During the period of the Iconoclastic Controversy the hearing of confessions became almost exclusively the function of monks. As previously noted, there was much of this in early monasticism. In the West the earlier Penitential Books were written by monks, but the whole trend was to make the priest the officer of penance. An Eastern writer known as John the Faster (not the patriarch with whom Gregory the Great was in controversy, but, as Karl Holl has shown, a monk of the eleventh century) says that "Our Lord Jesus Christ has given the prophets, apostles, bishops and priests to teach spiritual doctrine, and monks to receive the confessions of sinners" (Migne, *P.G.* LXXXVIII, 1920). This writer's sermon for those going to confession contains directions for questioning the penitent "with all cheerfulness" on an extended list of abominable offenses.

Professor Fedotov, in *The Russian Religious Mind*, gives information on Russian penitentials of the period before the Mongol invasion (*ca.* 1240). These lay emphasis on sex offenses, and impose severe penalties. One such book (*Preface to Penitence*) is quoted as warning that the spiritual father must be wise and good and experienced. The restitution of unjustly acquired possessions was a primary requirement.

At the time of the Fourth Crusade, Innocent III received complaints of the practice, astonishing to Westerns, of the assumption by monks of "sole authority to bind and loose." Numerous Greek doctrinal writers of the Middle Ages assume that confession is mainly to monks and offer their explanations of this. Thus the Chartophylax (custodian of documents) Neciphorus, writing to one Theodosius a memorandum on binding and loosing (Migne, *P.G.* C, 1065 ff.) understands that the priests and bishops, since they were too busy with public ministries, "handed over the task to the monks." Simeon the New Theologian (d. *ca.* 1040), observes that an authority which priests had abused has been "transferred to the people beloved by God" (the monks), who wear the appropriate vestments of penitence. Vacandard would explain the priests' loss of the function on the ground that being married men they were not in favor as confessors while the celibate monks were regarded as truly spiritual (*pneumatikoi*). In this connection he quotes from a French work by J. Pargoire to the effect that in the Greek Church the hearing of confessions was thought of as "less a prerogative of the priesthood than a charisma of holiness."

In the thirteenth century some advocated a return to episcopal authority and confession to priests. Frank Gavin's quotations from nineteenth century Greek theologians would indicate that this emphasis has triumphed. But the association of fitness to hear confession with the *pneumatikoi*, those of marked spiritual attainment, has been a permanent element in Eastern Christianity, and highly important in Russian piety through the modern era.

Orthodox rituals of sacramental penance, and authoritative doctrinal statements, while employing the expression "spiritual father" usually indicate that this functionary is a priest. In the Confession (1643) of Peter Mogila, Metropolitan of Kiev, a document later accepted by a Council of the Greek Church at Jerusalem (1672), we have the words "the priest, his *pneumatikos*." The latter word is rendered by English translators: "spiritual father" or "spiritual adviser." The admirable treatise *On the Duty of Parish Priests*, compiled by two late eighteenth century Russian prelates, George Konissky and Parthenius Sopkofsky, unequivocally makes the priest the officiant in penance. In the modern Greek rite the penitent is first led by the spiritual father before the holy image of Christ. Psalm 51 is recited, and a prayer follows in which reference is made to the penitence of David and Manasses, and of "the woman who was a sinner." The penitent is then urged to confess his sins, in order to obtain the pardon of Christ. "Lo His holy image is before us," says the priest, "I am but a witness bearing testimony before him of all things that thou dost say to me." He is warned against concealment lest he depart unhealed, and the book directs that he be questioned point by point as in the older rituals.

Actually, however, it is apparent that the old, objectionably suggestive questions are not employed. An English observer in Russia in 1772, John Glen King, states that the catalog of indecent offenses is replaced by an inquiry regarding breaches of each of the Commandments. This method is distinctly enjoined in *The Duty of Parish Priests*, and the confessor there warned against such questions as would make known to the confessant sins with which he is unacquainted. A similar caution is indicated in descriptions of confession in the Greek Church, in which the confessor's concern is not with a full recital of sins but with evidence of sincere contrition. The latter point is stressed, too, in *The Longer Catechism of the Orthodox Catholic Eastern Church* (1839), the work of Philaret, the eminent Metropolitan of Moscow (d. 1867). It is characteristic of these documents that they lay emphasis on the reconciliation of those who have quarreled, the forgiveness of injuries, and the restitution of dishonestly acquired property, as conditions of true penance and absolution.

Absolution in the Greek Church is precatory: "God forgive thee by me a sinner." The Russians, however, under Latin influence, adopted the declaratory form: "I, an unworthy priest, pardon and absolve thee." This is a result of the introduction of Western medieval theology into Russia after the Treaty of Brest-Litovsk (1596). Latin theological studies were promoted by Peter Mogila (despite his opposition to the Papacy), who in his Confession describes penance in these words:

The fifth mystery (sacrament) is repentance or affliction of heart for sin committed, which a man discloses before a priest with firm intention of mind to amend his life, and readiness to fulfil that which the priest, his spiritual adviser, may enjoin him for penance. (Neale's translation.)

In Philaret's Catechism the definition reads:

Penance is a sacrament in which he who confesses his sins is, on the outward declaration of pardon by the priest, inwardly loosed from his sins by Jesus Christ himself.

Stephan Zankov states the essentials of the sacrament of penance simply as:

sincere regret for sin, connected with faith in Christ and hope of His mercy: acknowledgment of sin; if necessary, on the advice of the confessor, a penance consisting chiefly in prayer, fasting, and deeds of self-sacrifice.

It is not the priest, he affirms, but God who forgives sins.

In Eastern Orthodoxy, confession has commonly been a preparation for communion. Philaret repeats an old rite for those who "live religiously" of confession and communion at least four times yearly, adding that all are required to confess once a year at least. Dr. Gavin quotes the Greek lay theologian, Chrestos Androustos, in a work of 1907, to the effect that as thought is fulfilled in words, so true penitence, "by the law of psychological necessity" issues in confession of sins. Along with interior penance, confession is an indispensable condition for "the forgiveness of sins bestowed through a priest." According to Dr. Zankov, there has been a fresh emphasis on confession during the first quarter of the present century. Anthony Bashir, in a book of 1947, stresses the point that the confessor acts also as a director of the penitent's life and conduct, and studies closely the spiritual needs of each confessant. The penances imposed are practically designed "to help the penitent to break himself of a sinful habit, to cure him of carelessness . . . or to calm his conscience."

The *Prayer Book for Eastern Orthodox Christians* (1944) compiled for English-speaking members of the Orthodox churches by Peter H. Horton-Billard and Vasile Hategan, priests respectively of the Syrian and Rumanian branches of Orthodoxy, contains directions for confession, with prayers and questions for self-examination in preparation for it. Eight questions usually asked by priests before absolution are given. These include questions on habits of prayer and forgiveness of offenses. The form of absolution is similar to that used in the Russian Church. The book was circulated among the armed forces.

II

Side by side with this parish ministry of the priestly confessor there has flourished in Russia the work of guidance of a class of devout and spiritually experienced men known as elders (*starets*, plural: *startsy*) many of whom are not in priestly orders, yet exercise an authoritative direction of souls. For Western readers much light has been shed upon this matter by Orthodox Russian scholars in Western countries since the Revolution of 1918, especially Nicolas Zernov, Nicolas Arseniev and George Fedotov. The twentieth century popularity of Dostoievsky's *The Brothers Karamazov* (1880) had already created a Western interest in the class of men represented by the "elder," Zossima, in that book, and numerous Western students of Russia had pointed to the importance of this phase of Russian religious life. Although the *startsy* had their representatives in medieval times (e.g., St. Sergius of Radonezh, d. 1392), they have chiefly flourished in the nineteenth century. Their modern importance is connected with the revival of asceticism, which followed the period of secularization inaugurated by Peter the Great, and was led by Paisi Velichkovsky. This reformer's disciples instituted at the monastery of Optina a fraternity of elders who a century ago were celebrated for their expertness in the guidance of souls. Dr. Zernov says that these wise teachers "attracted a ceaseless stream of visitors from all corners of the land." *Starchestvo*, or the spiritual direction of the *startsy*, has assumed such importance that Brian-Chaninov calls these good men "the natural born guides of the Russian people." All classes of people have visited them, both to confess their sins and to obtain personal advice of all sorts.

Many who consulted the *startsy* belonged to the numerous class of pilgrims. The idea that the spiritual life is a pilgrimage has been prevalent in Russia, and has been lived out by countless wandering seekers. "Here below," wrote Nicolas Berdyaev in *The Russian Religious Idea*, "we are all pilgrims without hearth or home. . . . Spiritual vagabondage is one of the striking features of the national character." George Fedotov in A *Treasury of Russian Spirituality*, furnishes a translation of the anonymous *Diary of a Pilgrim* (*ca.* 1850), a vivid account of the experiences and adventures of one of these devout wanderers. The Pilgrim takes the road with no possessions but some rusks in a knapsack and a Bible in his bosom. It is at a guest house of "elders" that he begins to read the Patristic anthology called *Philocalia* (which Paisi Velichkovsky had rendered into Slavonic) and he finally procures a worn copy of this treasured devotional book. Meanwhile he finds his way to the practice of the life of prayer through the guidance of a *starets*. In some incidents of his travels he himself becomes a guide of distressed souls. This pilgrim tale illustrates both the work of the elders and the "spiritual vagabondage" of pre-Revolution Russia.

Dr. Arseniev emphasizes the moderation and pure simplicity of the Russian *starets*. This aspect is illustrated from the spiritual letters of Makari of Optina (d. 1860) and Theophanus of Wyscha (d. 1894). In a letter of 1858 Makari warns a young woman against intemperate zeal, spiritual pretension and a headstrong course of austerities. "According to the opinion of the holy Fathers," he remarks, "we are not to be the assassins of our bodies but of our passions." From Theophanus comes a word of counsel not unfamiliar in the West, that one should yield oneself into the hands of the Lord, crying for deliverance and zealous to do His holy will. All reliance upon our own resources is to be abandoned. To obtain help from God we must first feel our own weakness. Contrition rather than ecstasy is the most important fruit of prayer. Yet this surrender is accompanied by strenuous effort. "Nothing comes without effort." The body, and its muscles, are to be subjected to a soldierly discipline.

The personal habits of certain of the elders are revealed by Dr. Arseniev's quotations from sources. Tikhon of Zadonsk (d. 1783) resigned his bishopric (1767) and retired to a life of saintliness and charity. While walking he would read aloud or sing from the Psalter. His servant and companion tells how he would throw off his robe and cut wood in the forest, or gather fodder for his old work horse, all the while discoursing on eternity. He gave away all his possessions to relieve orphans and poor folk. Apparently Dostoievsky had Tikhon in mind (as well as contemporary *startsy* of Optina to whom he had paid a visit) in his creation of Zossima.

Dostoievsky makes his guide of souls at times show more spiritual gaiety than sternness. At the peak of religious experience the *starets* may know jubilation and illumination. This is seen in the case of the celebrated St. Seraphim of Sarov (d. 1833): "the joy of the Resurrection permeated his entire being." And the face of Makari of Optina was seen illumined like that of an angel. But there is also a great deal of austerity and struggle in these holy lives. The Altai missionary, Makari Glukharev (d. 1847) is depicted in utter weariness of body refusing to lie down. He argues that he should not do less than the bird sitting on a branch that only naps a little before resuming his praise of God. St. Seraphim, too, performed astonishing feats of abstinence.

Dostoievsky evidently offers no misleading index to the character and work of the typical *starets*. He indicates, in the opposing character of Ferrapont that the guardians of the sacraments, and of church order, sometimes regarded the elder as introducing a pernicious innovation. Certainly their work has been largely independent of the church routines. They bore in their hearts a deep responsibility for all men and for each man, and spread a gospel of unlimited charity especially toward the poor and weak. Zossima says that hell is the suffering of being unable to love. They also assumed a large measure of control over their consultants. An elder, says Dostoievsky (Chapter V)

> was one who took your soul, your will, into his soul and his will. When you choose an elder you renounce your own will, and yield it in complete submission, complete self-abnegation.

The Hindu *guru* could hardly ask more than this. Yet the *startsy* seem to have exercised their spiritual authority generously and in a gentle spirit.

Zernov and Fedotov have called attention also to numerous clerical inspirers of the devotional life in modern Russia. John Sergieff Kronstadt (d. 1908) was a powerful preacher of prayerfulness and piety, a faithful pastor and an adviser of pastors in confession and consolation of the sick. He found his parish too populous, however, to conduct confessions in private, and resorted to the strange method of a simultaneous confession of private sins, all together mingling self-revelations and tearful prayers. Dr. Fedotov calls this "an impressive, even terrifying spectacle." A very different type was the contemplative and saintly priest, Alexander Yelchaninov (d. 1934), a teacher of self-examination and the writer of a diary which Fedotov quotes at some length. Yelchaninov's statement that childlikeness is lost in life and recovered in holiness reminds us of a thought of Mencius quoted above (p. 59); but "holiness" is not in Mencius' thought, and the Russian's source is the Christian Gospel. His reference to "sweat, tears and blood" as symbols respectively of work, penance, and martyrdom has value independent of the context in which these words have since been made familiar.

Assuredly, the religious guides of the Russians have been men of strong fiber and genuine spirituality. What survives of this in contemporary Russia I have no means of knowing. But a tradition so firmly established should prove difficult to eradicate.

III

The practice of discipline in the Armenian Church has undergone a long evolution. In the early fifth century the Canons of St. Isaac (426) laid down rigid rules for clerics and laymen. A summary of these is given by Leon Arpee in his *History of Armenian Christianity*. Drunkards, brawlers and the ignorant, and (for the first time in this Church) soldiers, are excluded from the ordinances, and there are sundry regulations for marriage. Shortly afterward an attempt was made to enforce the rules by heavy fines, and fresh regulations were added against clerical abuses and popular superstitions. Unrepentant sorcerers and apostates were to be stoned; if repentant they must do penance for twelve years. Wailing in pagan fashion for the dead—an offense often penalized in the Western penitential books—is cause for exclusion and fines. The collection of fines for breaches of discipline was soon replaced by voluntary gifts at repentance.

Late in the fifth century John Mandakuni was Catholicos, or Primate, of the Armenian Church. A homily ascribed to him urges hospitality to the poor as the means of obtaining remission of sins. "Hast thou," he asks, "made the poor man physician of thy wounded soul? . . . and hast thou invited [him] to thy house as an expiation of thy sins?" To this prelate is also ascribed, in at least one of the manuscripts in which it is preserved, the Canon of Making a Penitent in the Armenian Euchologion. In this rite, the priest leads the penitent to the door of the church and recites a number of psalms. A long series of prayers and exhortations follows. At one point of interest for us Dr. Conybeare, the painstaking editor of the translation, has some difficulty with the text. But clearly an act of public confession is indicated before the absolution. The words of absolution are in a context of prayer:

I, thy servant, according to thine unerring commandment am emboldened unto remission of sins. For thou art Lord after remission of the sins of this man and of us all. . . . But howsoever he shall have sinned . . . I have according to thy commandment remitted on earth; and in heaven has God remitted the sins of this man and of us all. . . . (Conybeare, *Rituale Armenorum*, pp. 198 f.)

Dr. Conybeare shows (p. xii) that the earliest Armenian forms of absolution expressed "the hope of remission" only, but thinks it possible that the declaratory form may have been introduced independently of Latin influence and even prior to the "I absolve thee" formula in the West. This public act of "making a penitent" included injunctions to maintain a penitential behavior through life: "for he shall not again obtain healing. And this is the medicine of repentance. The penitent must be heartbroken until the day of his death."

The highly esteemed Armenian Church leader Nerses "the Graceful," Catholicos 1166-73, author of doctrinal and devotional works, sought a revival of discipline by issuing, when he took office, a comprehensive pastoral letter. Summaries of its contents given by Nève and Arpee indicate that it contains a vigorous statement of the duties of persons of all classes, clerical and lay. The Church was now being subjected to Latin influence, and at the same time the Tatars were becoming the political masters of Armenia. Nerses gives directions affecting his people's relationships with the invaders; they are to keep their promises to them, and not to baptize the children of Muslims. Kindness to servants, avoidance of profanity, and regulations regarding marriage, are among the topics treated. A synod of 1273, whose decisions had no binding authority, marks a further attempt to promote discipline; it requires priests to hold twice a year assemblies for confession and counsel, and lays down harsh penalties for profanity. A German visitor in 1280 reports the practice of the barbarous penalty of castration for theft and other minor offenses, and on the other hand indicates some commendable activities in the cure of souls. He finds that whenever laymen are in doubt, the monks instruct them, and that all behave with great devoutness in church.

Under the scourge of savage war and the cruel sway of the Ottoman Turks, the Armenians suffered so greatly, and so long, that the maintenance of their distinctive character appears almost miraculous. Revival came in the early seventeenth century by means of a very austere monastic movement within Persia, led by Moses of Datev. The monastic exercises included confession of sins twice daily. The popular teaching of the monks led to ecclesiastical reforms, and the Church enjoyed better days in the later seventeenth and in the eighteenth century.

In 1678 an observant traveler, Paul Ricaut, visited the Armenian churches, and in the following year published an account of his observations. He found poverty and ignorance, but an active church life with many peculiar customs and some that were shared with the Greek and Latin churches. The vigor of the seasonal and penitential fasts impressed him. "They use confession in the ear of the priest, who is for the most part, very rigorous in the penance he imposes." For grave offenses this extends over many years, and, once imposed, cannot be mitigated by the superior clergy. He has seen complete abstinence for a calendar week, broken only by "one draught of sherbet" on Wednesday.

The Armenian Church from early times possessed a rite for public penance by which those guilty of grave sins became penitents for life. But it also employed a system of private confession and penance which followed a routine similar to that in Roman Catholicism, and was obligatory for all members. Some Orthodox Armenian writers hold that auricular confession was practiced from the beginnings of their Church. James Isaverdens, for example, ascribes to a synod of Vagharsabad held under Gregory the Illuminator (d. *ca.* 333) a canon enjoining the seal of confession on pain of deprivation and expulsion. It is highly probable, however, that the writings attributed to Gregory were composed much later. Yet undoubtedly secret confession was introduced, without displacing either public confession or the general confession of the congregation, at a relatively early period.

In modern practice confession is enjoined at five seasons of the year, but required of all at Epiphany and Easter only. The confessant, after previous self-examination, kneels before the priest to confess his sins one by one, and asks absolution. The priest counsels him, and enjoins some work of penance; then pronounces the absolution in a form that combines prayer with authoritative declaration:

May the merciful God have mercy upon you and grant you the pardon of all your sins remembered and forgotten. And I, in virtue of my order of priesthood . . . absolve you from all participation in sin by thoughts, words and deeds. . . .

Western Protestantism entered Armenia early in the last century, and evangelical churches were planted in many parts of the country, carrying the types of discipline of their sister churches in the West, chiefly in America. Sunday observance and abstinence from strong drink were prominent in the codes established; and a great deal of educational work was undertaken. However, the avowed aim of American Board missions has been to help the old Armenian Church recover its spiritual forces. After a period of suspicion, the services of the missionaries, especially in education, won favor from the Armenian Church leaders. At this stage the Armenian people were subjected to a series of tragic experiences that have left them scattered and ecclesiastically weak.

IV

From this elementary account of leading aspects of the cure of souls in the Eastern churches we observe not less than in the West the un-equivocal recognition of the obligation of priests in this pastoral function. We are struck, too, by evidence of the inadequacy with which this duty was often performed. No authority that I have read claims that either the Greek or the Russian Church has enjoyed the services of many well-equipped and devoted pastors, and there have been long periods of deterioration in the Armenian Church. One reason for this condition is undoubtedly the pressure of governments upon the Church, encouraging the appointment of priests ill-fitted for their spiritual tasks, and unfavorable to all autonomous action by church officers. A church favored by a government may be morally and spiritually disabled by political interference, and this condition prevailed for centuries in Czarist Russia. On the other hand, the sufferings of the Armenian Christians under the Turks were too severe to yield the moral advantage that often comes from state hostility in milder form.

These facts should be considered in our judgment of success or failure in pastoral work; and when they are justly weighed it appears remarkable that the ideals of these churches have found as much expression as in fact they have. In each case a traditional discipline has been cherished and retained as normal, and its sacramental aspect has apparently been fairly constant. When this was weakly represented and the local pastors were felt to be inadequate, in the state-dominated Church of Russia, the nonsacramental ministry of the *startsy* sprang into activity and undertook the direction of souls. This spontaneous and informal guidance conducted by spiritual men without reference to clerical status, is undoubtedly the most outstanding fact that emerges in this chapter. It is an aspect of the history of the cure of souls that may well be pondered by Western Christians of all communions. It is unique, but only as the Christian Russian expression of a universal phenomenon. We may appropriately recall the language of Ecclesiasticus quoted above (p. 11):

> Stand in the multitude of the elders,
> And cleave to him that is wise. . . .
> And if thou seest a man of understanding, get thee betimes to him,
> And let thy foot wear the steps of his door.

Chapter XV

CONCLUSION

I

THE physicians of the soul whose work has concerned us in this book would be astonished if they could suddenly enter our world of today. They would find themselves in an environment in which their assumptions are ignored by many earnest and highly trained men who undertake the reconstruction of personalities damaged in the stresses of life. It is only recently that the word "psychiatrist" gained a footing in our language, replacing "psychiater" which came into vogue about a century ago. A competent historian and representative of this new science describes psychiatry as "a highly specialized branch of the practice of medicine." Dr. Nolan C. Lewis, from whose *Short History of Psychiatric Achievement* (1941) I quote this, emphasizes in this informing book the interpenetration of psychiatry with other branches of medicine and its contributory sciences, and its interest in man's cultural and emotional life. In chapters of fascinating interest, he treats the gropings after sound diagnosis and treatment of mental and emotional disorders in the early civilizations. The view of Hippocrates that melancholy is caused by "red bile" (literally it is "black bile," however); the location of the organ of memory in the posterior of the brain by a thirteenth century psychologist; even psychotherapy by charms in ancient China and diagnosis by the signs of the zodiac in the Renaissance, are drawn into this account of "psychiatric achievement." Dr. Lewis also observes that from the beginning of recorded history medicine was associated with religion. He certainly shows no animus against religion. Yet, the type of data found in the above chapters is wholly excluded from his volume. The dissociation of psychotherapy from the theological and philosophical traditions is here complete.

319

The actual absorption of the territory of the old-time guide of souls by the empire of medical science is, however, far from complete. The trend is resisted by religious leaders, and is by no means acceptable to all trained psychiatrists. There is a very real distrust of the absolute claims of science in this field. Freudian psychoanalysis has encountered a terrible demon, the feeling of guilt. It has taken not guilt itself but the feeling of guilt as the enemy to be destroyed. The religious director has commonly distinguished the "scrupulosity" that cherishes an exaggerated sense of sin and guilt from a balanced self-judgment. This is exemplified in writers as divergent as Knox and Fénelon. But these writers have also treated not only the feeling but the fact of guilt as real and serious. Psychoanalysis reaches down into the unconscious mind to draw forth lost memories of guilty feelings that have wrought havoc in the personal life, and thus professes to withdraw the festering thorn.

Moral values are not an issue in this treatment. The tendency is to assume that what is wrong with the client's behavior is not his fault but the consequence of inheritance and of the environment of his early years. It is questionable whether the well-intentioned psychiatrist relieves the patient only at the cost of a repudiation of conscience and responsibility that may readily increase the sum of human misery. Some anxious writers on the care of children seek to terrify parents with the perils of allowing their offspring to feel a twinge of guilt for any misdemeanor. One might infer that if the child should impale his godmother with the carving knife, he should not be allowed to entertain for a moment pangs of conscience lest it do him untold damage. This is in effect to exterminate conscience, that troublesome companion that has attended our fathers through the centuries. Where there is conscience, there will be a sense of guilt when its dictates are violated. Religion has regarded the guilt of conscience as curable by repentance and forgiveness, and has cherished conscience as a not infallible but generally useful index of the need of these remedies. Undoubtedly, religious men have shown a tendency to play unfairly upon the sense of guilt, and here they have much to learn and much to answer for. But the attempt to silence conscience is unrealistic; even if it were successful, man and society would be betrayed.

The ultimate needs of individual humans have not changed since the distant era of "the Dawn of Conscience" which Dr. Breasted linked with ancient Egypt. Century after century, man has to live with his passions, his conscience, his neighbors and his God. Any narrower view of the range of his relationships does not match his real humanity. It is true that he shares many of his ills with the beasts that perish, and here medical psychiatry has a wide service to perform. Lobotomy and shock treatments may remove causes of personal disorder, and in many cases psychoanalysis has proved highly useful. But for the attainment of full health of personality, man must find a harmonious relationship in the realm of spiritual values. The primary obstacle to his entrance into this realm is what the Bible calls sin. When all has been done that science can do to relieve a man's distresses, the pride that protects his other sins may withhold him from his true deliverance, leaving him to live out his days a defeated soul. Man is a child of God, strangely prone to reject the divine Fatherhood; and in this aberration he finds himself frustrated and self-exiled from his true inheritance.

The empiricist has no meager service to render, but the religious guide has no reason to go into retirement. The work of the one should be integrated with that of the other. A mutual acquaintance between the two traditions must first be earnestly cultivated. Certainly the religious *Seelsorger* has much to learn from empirical psychology. It has revealed the vast reservoir of the unconscious mind of which the religious soul-healer of the past had little idea. It has explored the obsessions and phobias that plague the mentally unbalanced, and all the symptoms and varieties of psychopathology. Religion and scientific psychiatry cannot avoid contact, since the religious counselor is anxious to profit by the psychiatrist's knowledge, and both often have to do with the same individual case. The absolute claims of a science intolerant of religion and resenting its intrusion are constantly challenged, and many psychiatrists have no wish to assert such claims.

Vigorous reactions against these assumptions have appeared among the scientists themselves. The revisions of Freudianism made by Otto Rank (d. 1939) are radical and, for their bearing on religion, revolutionary. Rank found himself obliged to challenge Freud's scientific positivism and to affirm the operation of spiritual forces not dreamt of in the Freudian therapy. He turned to Christian origins and saw in St. Paul's discovery of life "in Christ" and participation in the Resurrection as a life-principle, the foundation of "a new psychological type of man" (*Beyond Psychology*, 1941). Rank did not abandon psychoanalysis, but sought to make it instrumental toward a comprehensive spiritual transformation of personality. In effect, psychotherapy here becomes the Christian cure of souls, in purpose if not in method. Rank's insights are being loyally perpetuated. In 1948 there was established in Dayton, Ohio, the Institute for Rankian Psychoanalysis under the direction of William Rickel and Doris Mode.

Dr. Fritz Künkel seeks to promote the development of a distinctively religious psychology. For him the nonreligious psychiatrist is as incompetent to deal with religious experiences as a blind man to interpret a work of art. The Swiss pastor and Freudian analyst, Oskar Pfister, views Jesus and Paul and the leaders and reformers of the Church as in a Freudian mirror, and with Freudian presuppositions studies the relation of their religious ideas to the therapy of fear and guilt. This leads to some very questionable historical judgments. A good deal is made of the point, for example, that Jesus "displaced conscience in favor of love." Naturally Dr. Pfister holds a rather unfavorable opinion of theologians, from Paul to Emil Brunner.

Probably most distinguished among those who from the scientific side have made contact with religion in this area is Carl Gustav Jung, whose repudiation of a materialistic view of the psyche, assertion of the "collective unconscious" re-emerging with every individual, and recognition of the patient's faith as a resource in mental healing, make him an ally of the pastoral adviser. In a book edited by Joshua Liebmann, *Psychiatry and Religion*, Seward Hiltner has strikingly pointed out some common areas of endeavor of the psychiatrist and the pastor. David E. Roberts, in *Psychotherapy and the Christian View of Man* examines the whole problem in relation to current theology, and suggests that theologians incorporate the therapist's conception of conflict in the doctrine of sin and his description of healing in the doctrine of grace.

Whoever may be chiefly instrumental in the effective correlation of religious and scientific psychotherapy, it is a safe prediction that the solution of the tension between these will come by mutual recognition and not by the extinction of either. Difficulties in the way of this lie partly in prejudices on both sides, partly in a lack of the institutional means of co-operation, and partly in the sectarian discords of both religion and psychiatry.

II

Throughout recorded history, in every society, the relief of distressed souls has been a major need of a large class, not all of whom have been aware of their true condition or willing to undergo treatment for it.

Some have failed to seek, or refused to accept, the personal help available to them, and some have sought it earnestly and failed to find it. Job had his "miserable comforters." But the writer of Psalm 142, when in his bitter anguish his fellows failed him, turned to his God:

> I looked on my right hand, and beheld, but there was no man that would know me: refuge failed me; no man cared for my soul. I cried unto thee, O Lord: I said, Thou art my refuge and my portion in the land of the living.

Private prayer in which we abandon ourselves to the will and love of God, shed our wayward impulses, and feel ourselves divinely known, forgiven and revived, often proves a sovereign remedy against the dangerous inward enemies of personality. Other means also may be usefully employed by the individual for himself. Just as a man of good physical constitution may manage for years without a physician, prescribing for his own minor ailments, so intelligent self-examination and resolute self-discipline may alleviate or remove the minor disorders of personality without expert help. Most of us hardly realize the degree in which our daily work keeps us in health of mind and spirit. St. Benedict observed that idleness is the enemy of the soul; and Carlyle in *Past and Present* used some of his finest rhetoric upon the function of work in clearing the jungle of the mind and forcing the helldogs that beleaguer the soul —doubt, sorrow, remorse, indignation, despair—to slink away in defeat, when one "bends himself with free valor against his task." Unfortunately not all work-situations are calculated to produce this result. But a man's work is often a strong security against these disorganizing psychological forces.

It should not be overlooked that there is a vast area in which personal guidance is publicly imparted, or where remedial agencies operate by way of a listening or reading experience in which numbers may share. Teaching or writing that satisfyingly illumines the meaning of sorrow or the course of duty; preaching that enables the hearer to lay hold of liberating and sustaining truth; and public worship when it brings a genuine sense of communion with God and our neighbor, are among the most effective means toward health of soul. The drama, whether tragedy in which Aristotle profoundly saw a "catharsis of pity and fear," or comedy that affords a perspective on life and a playtime for the mind, may help greatly to deliver us from morbid self-concern. Besides these, modern society provides for some of its members a wide range of recreations that in a limited way may truly be said to re-create. The dance has become a prominent feature of group psychotherapy. These varied agencies for the health of personality may be utilized by groups of indeterminate number. While they may be prescribed for those under private treatment, they involve in themselves no special provision for the individual.

III

While we are often maintained in inward well-being by praying or playing together, there are always many who must have private assistance or perish. They have fallen into the Slough of Despond and need the outstretched arm of "the Man whose name was Help." Throughout history, this need has called forth the effort to meet it. Men have felt called upon to yield to their fellows in distress such help as they could render. Most of these have been prompted by religious motives, and have labored in the belief that the fundamental personality problems refuse to be solved outside the realm of religion. If this was a false assumption, then was their calling vain. But the contrary assumption has no support in experience. A generation that turns from religion is more and more productive of psychopathic personalities and victims of psychoneurosis and psychosis, and is exposed to the dominance of fanatical psychoneurotics who use psychology itself to destroy personality. The leaders of society and of the churches need to measure critically and justly the possibilities and limitations of scientific psychotherapy in meeting the terrific forces that ravage the interior life of modern man. It is not less important to weigh with the same critical judgment the methods traditionally employed by religious guides of souls.

One of the frequently recurring differences in method observed in the foregoing chapters is in the relationship between the guide and the guided person. To what degree should that relationship involve the authority of the former over the latter? In ancient Egypt and Israel, the consultant seems to have retained more of choice and self-direction than in India, where unquestioning obedience was exacted and continually insisted upon. Wide variation at this point has also been exhibited in Christianity. A firm control by the confessor was assumed in medieval penance and has been characteristic of modern Roman Catholic practice in the confessional. Protestantism has favored a less intimate supervision, and has usually left consultation involving the secrets of conscience to the free choice of those who felt the need of it. With the degree of authority, the duration of the relationship varies. On the one hand, we have the assumption that all require the services of the confessor periodically, and that they are not free to change their confessor at will. On the other, the conception prevails that private guidance is principally to be given to those in special crises; that it is available rather than obligatory, and for many persons ordinarily unnecessary. Protestant counselors have often shrunk from an intrusive intimacy with the inner secrets of men, and especially from the assumption of authority over any man's conscience. "God alone is Lord of the conscience," said the Westminster Divines.

Yet the difference here is much less than is usually assumed. Most Protestant churches, including those that adopted the Westminster standards, insisted upon clearly defined and exacting codes of behavior for all members, and devised means to assure their maintenance. They also required of their pastors systematic visitation of all the homes of their people, and this task was sometimes interpreted as involving conversations with each individual in the household. The pastor or counselor was exhorted to maintain silence on the secrets divulged in private conference or confession. Fitness to participate in communion was often tested by the personal inquiry of the pastor or other officer of the church. To pass this examination was felt to be a kind of absolution, whether a solemn form of absolution was pronounced or not. Such formal absolution of individuals was employed in Reformed churches in a public rite, in cases where public discipline had taken its course.

The strictly disciplinary factor was stronger in Reformed and Puritan than in Lutheran and Anglican churches. It employed the services of lay elders and followed well-defined procedures. In Scotland, this system was a prominent aspect of the social life. Its framers designed it in a truly pastoral spirit, and were solicitous to induce the sinner to repent rather than to subject him to censures and penalties. Its operation is subject to criticism for manifest defects, but when pastors and elders were wise and faithful, it was capable of a steadying and character-building influence upon persons and communities. Attempting more than it could accomplish, Scottish discipline drifted into legalistic and negative trivialities, and lost its authority. Methods of a more positively religious sort, resting on persuasion, replaced it.

The differences to which we have called attention were associated with the question of sacramental private confession, penance and absolution. The absorption of the private cure of souls in the sacrament of penance was a slow development of the early medieval centuries; and it was never quite complete. In Protestantism, penance was no longer regarded as a sacrament, and absolution was confined to the open rite following the prayer of confession, and the restoration of those under public discipline. In Anglicanism, the visitation service provided a form of absolution that was also used in private confession generally, where this was practiced. Many Anglican writers of the seventeenth century, and of the period since the Oxford Movement, have approached or affirmed a sacramental view of penance. The form of absolution used in the early Scottish Reformed Church for those being restored to communion, asserts the authority of the minister in high terms, using the language, "I absolve thee," but with a qualification that makes absolution conditional on repentance. Protestantism has pretty scrupulously avoided the sacerdotal claims which it condemned in Roman Catholicism, but in the Reformed churches the doctrine of ministerial authority was high. Calvin links ministerial absolution with the mutual consolation and assurance of divine mercy which takes place among laymen, but it is in connection with the minister's pronouncement only that he quotes: "Whose soever sins ye remit." Ministers, he writes, "are said to remit sins and to loose souls." And Knox's absolution form asserts the minister's authority to speak "in the name and authority of Christ."

The question of authority in discipline or direction has great importance on psychological ground. Belief that the ministrant of penance is exercising a power that affects the penitent's eternal state is a strong factor in the latter's willingness to take advice, and in his peace of mind when the absolution is given. But the problem arises also for psychiatry, where authority is often affirmed and obedience demanded. There is undoubtedly a place for authority, and often a stage in treatment where it must be firmly exercised. The danger of its immoderate use lies largely in the readiness with which many people yield to, and cling to, another whom they trust. There is a great difference between the use of a crutch in convalescence from a leg fracture and its habitual use after the fracture is healed. A method that would prolong the duration of treatment stands in contrast to one that aims to release the consultant as soon as possible. Here Rank differs from Freud somewhat as Protestantism has differed from Roman Catholicism.

Vinet, with many others, felt that where authority is strongly asserted in guidance, the danger to the counselor is not less than the possible damage to the consultant, since the experience of control over another's will tends to arouse a domineering temper. Without professing to know how the *guru*, who is sometimes regarded as more worthy of obedience than the celestial deities, feels toward his devotee, it is safe to say that such adulation would not be wholesome for Western clergymen. Yet, a transparently good priest or minister, who bears the marks of saintly humility, or of unusual spiritual wisdom, by his personal qualities invites, where he does not demand or desire, an attitude of reverence from those who are struggling beginners in these virtues. Spirituality inevitably conveys a kind of authority.

Authority in the direction of souls goes behind the person who exercises it to the tradition or ecclesiastical system which he represents. Where the system itself is highly authoritarian, the minister of it is understood, and indeed required, to speak with an authoritative voice. The priest in the confessional expects to be obeyed. In other pastoral relations he need not be similarly authoritative. It is often said that the Protestant minister lacks an authority comparable to that of the Roman Catholic priest. But this was not always the case. The older Protestant writers felt that the words of Scripture gave them a firm authority, and this was true of the Evangelicals of the eighteenth century in a degree that is no longer the case with those nurtured in biblical criticism. Yet, the scriptural theologians of today are helping us to discover anew the authority of the Bible as a guide to the will of God, the nature and the needs of man, and the availability of divine grace in daily living. The churches, too, may gain authority if they first gain depth and breadth of spiritual life. But ecclesiastical or institutional authority should not be overstressed. The authority of the psychiatrist is that of an expert in his growing science. That of the religious counselor must rest primarily upon his spiritual expertness. This involves an understanding of the main elements of Christian experience and historic spirituality, and may be effective with variant adherence to ecclesiastical prescriptions and habits.

IV

Attention has been repeatedly called in some chapters of this book to the mutual exercise of the cure of souls. *Aedificatio mutua* and *correptio fraterna* were principles of the Christian way of life in the New Testament and in the Church Fathers. The idea that every Christian is a priest toward his neighbor was one of the most vivid doctrines of the Reformation. Luther stressed the possibilities of spiritual enrichment by mutual edification. Bucer and Calvin gave the principle some organizational setting. It was stressed in Spener's writings and practiced in the Pietist movement of which he was the principal founder, and was given great prominence in its Moravian branch. John Wesley seized upon it, and its use in early Methodism was remarkably active, both for "edification" and for "correction." In our busy times a similar use of it would be difficult to secure. Yet, it appears in innumerable group movements, retreats, and enthusiastic sects, and people seem inclined to practice it where opportunity is given. "Where two or three are gathered together," it is always possible. But in mutual reproof and correction a marked difference arises with regard to whether the number is two or more. Two persons do not succeed very well, ordinarily, in correcting each other. It was natural that this mutual discipline should have been practiced mainly in groups rather than in pairs. No doubt a great deal of it goes on without the participants being aware that they are engaged in a traditionally honored practice. Like all methods of soul guidance, it is subject to abuses and deterioration, but a well-guarded use of mutual lay guidance would probably prove very valuable, relieving troubled consciences and toning up many feeble souls. It has its scientific counterpart in modern experimental methods of group psychotherapy.

The doctrine of the universal priesthood of Christians does not, of course, carry the implication that all are equally qualified for the functions of the cure of souls. There are differences of gifts. In the modern situation a way should be found to utilize within a religious framework the special skills of trained social workers, teachers and psychiatrists who are themselves religious persons and understand the values of religion for perplexed and disordered personalities. Theirs is a lay priesthood of special significance and promise.

There has always been a great deal of private help imparted outside the framework of ecclesiastical canons and sacraments. Even where sacramental views of penance are assumed, private direction apart from the sacrament has often flourished. In seventeenth century Europe nonsacramental direction was almost a profession in itself. Its nature is now best discovered through the preserved correspondence of great directors. The art of writing letters of counsel was, as we saw, widely practiced in antiquity, and Christianity has made very extensive use of it. All branches of the Western Church that have been noticed here present a considerable body of this material. The study of spiritual letters in Roman Catholicism, Anglicanism, and Protestantism reveals marked differences mingled with close similarities and common elements. The differences lie in the degree of obedience to the director that is asked, and in the prescriptions for devotional routines, and are to some extent related to social responsibility. Many spiritual letters by Roman Catholics pay no attention to specific ecclesiastical attachment and duties, and many make much use of Scripture and strongly urge acquiescence in the dispensations of God's providence (Bossuet), or entire self-abandonment to His love (Fénelon). In Anglicanism we have, in this as in other matters, a wide variety of types. Keble and Pusey are authoritative and ascetic, but differ in the strictness of their demands, while Evangelicals like Romaine and Simeon have the Protestant hesitation about assuming authority over others, and stress the grace of Christ. There are almost equally great variations in Scottish Presbyterian letters of this class, from the luxuriant imagery of Rutherford's poetic mysticism to the earnest evangelicalism of Chalmers. The letters written by Luther, Calvin, and Wesley reflect the qualities of these great leaders, and the variations among them in their methods. A rough generalization would be that Luther is persuasive and sympathetic, Calvin labors to produce resolute decision, and Wesley combines these elements with his own peculiar urgent haste to convert men to the practice of "scriptural holiness."

We have briefly noted some features of the cure of souls in the Orthodox Eastern Church and in the Church of Armenia. In both, the subject takes large importance, and both have practiced sacramental penance. Orthodoxy has always valued the work of the "spiritual father" rather in consideration of his personal spirituality than on grounds of church authority. In Russia this attitude has made possible, without much ecclesiastical objection, the activity of the "elders" who practice direction of souls though not ecclesiastically commissioned to do so. We seem to find here something like a Christian counterpart both of the Wise Men of Israel and of the detached ascetics and wandering holy men of India; but the spirit of the "elders" of Russia has been nourished from the New Testament and the Church Fathers. Western Christianity has not at any period possessed a similar class of spiritual directors.

The consolation of the bereaved and of those under other heavy strokes of adversity has been featured in chapters on the ancient philosophers and on the Patristic period of the Church, and has elsewhere frequently come to notice. Christian conceptions of the life to come were far more vivid and reassuring than those found in the pagan literature of Consolation, but Christian writers utilized, with appropriate changes, much of the pre-Christian material in this field. Similarly today,

Christian guidance is seeking to make use of the findings of psychologists in the treatment of morbid grief. Probably modern scientific and religious counselors alike would find fruitful suggestions in the study of the early Consolation writings, both pagan and Christian.

The private ministry to the sick and the dying has come to our attention at numerous points in this history. From the end of the Middle Ages, the sources for this are fairly ample. Our references to official Visitation directions and rites, and brief reviews of the Art of Dying booklets and of many treatises in whole or in part concerned with this task, are evidence of its prominence in the Christian cure of souls. We have seen, too, glimpses of the labor of numerous individual pastors, and even of laymen, both in this important function, and in the ministry to those in prison or condemned to die.

V

The cure of souls has been a vast historic enterprise. The Christian Church has regarded it in the light of an unending warfare against the sin and sorrow of the teeming human generations, man by man. This book has attempted to place on record the outlines of a singular history of human consecration to a redemptive task. The physician of souls has not taken his duties lightly. His has been the most demanding of all professions. Nobody would engage in it for wages alone. The hirelings in the pastorate have neglected this ministry, whatever else they have been willing to do. Only an inward compulsion drives men to it and holds them in it. Deeply conscious of their own limitations, but sustained by high faith and heroic devotion, countless numbers of our race have spent themselves in this spiritual service to damaged or endangered souls. They are a spiritual *élite*, a fraternity that spans the churches and even the religions. Caught like others in the drives of history, they have differed and quarreled with one another, but looked at by discerning eyes from the vantage of the present, they appear as co-laborers in a single cause. To the shining company of *curatores animarum* whose efforts have claimed our attention, let us accord a reverential salute. May their successors, equipped with new skills, profit by their insights, avoid their mistakes, and surpass their achievements!

BOOKS AND ARTICLES CONSULTED

Chapter I

THE GUIDES OF ISRAEL: WISE MEN, SCRIBES AND RABBIS

Bevan, Edwyn Robert, and Singer, Charles, editors. *The Legacy of Israel.* Oxford, 1927.

Bücher, Adolph. *Studies in Sin and Atonement in the Rabbinic Literature of the First Century.* London, 1928.

———. *Types of Jewish-Palestinian Piety.* London, 1922.

Budge, Sir E. A. Wallis. *The Teaching of Amen-em-Apt, Son of Kanekht . . . with Translations of the Moral and Religious Teachings of Egyptian Kings and Officials . . .* London, 1924.

Charles, R. H. *The Apocrypha and Pseudepigrapha of the Old Testament.* 2 vols. Oxford, 1913.

Dubarle, A. M. *Les Sages d'Israel.* Paris, 1946.

Duesberg, Dom Hilaire. *Les scribes inspirés: introduction aux Livres Sapientiaux de la Bible.* 2 vols. Paris, 1938-39.

Ginzberg, Louis. *The Legends of the Jews.* Translated by Henrietta Szold. 7 vols. Philadelphia, 1909-38.

———. *Students, Scholars and Saints.* Philadelphia, 1928.

Goodrick, A. T. S. *The Book of Wisdom, with Introduction and Notes.* New York, 1913.

Gorfinkle, Joseph I. (translator and editor). *The Sayings of the Jewish Fathers: Pirke Abot.* 3rd ed., New York, 1923.

Gressmann, Hugo. *Israels Sprachweisheit im Zusammenhang der Weltliteratur.* Berlin, 1925.

Griffith, F. L. "The Teaching of Amenophis, the Son of Kanakht." *Journal of Egyptian Archaeology,* XII (1926), 191-231.

Guignebert, Charles. *The Jewish World in the Times of Jesus.* Translated from the French by S. H. Hooke. London, 1939.

Gunn, Battiscombe G. *The Instruction of Ptah-hotep and the Instruction of Kegemmi, the Oldest Books in the World. Translated from the Egyptian . . .* London, 1906.

Herford, R. Travers. *Pharisaism, Its Aims and Methods.* New York, 1912.

———. *Talmud and Apocrypha: A Comparative Study . . .* London, 1933.

Houghton, Louise Seymour. *Hebrew Life and Thought . . .* Chicago, 1906.

Hughes, H. Maldwyn. *The Ethics of Jewish Apocalyptic Literature.* London, 1940.

Humbert, Paul. Article "Weisheitsdichtung" in *Die Religion in Geschichte und Gegenwart.* V. Tübingen, 1931.

Humbert, Paul. *Recherches sur les sources Egyptiennes de la littérature sapientielle d'Israel.* Neuchatel, 1929.

Kent, Charles Foster. *The Wise Men of Ancient Israel and their Proverbs.* Boston, 1899.

Macdonald, Duncan Clark. *The Hebrew Philosophical Genius: a Vindication.* Princeton, 1936.

Montefiore, Claude Goldschmid and Loewe, H. *A Rabbinic Anthology.* London, 1938.

Moore, George Foot. *Judaism in the First Century of the Christian Era. The Age of the Tannaim.* Cambridge, Mass., 1927.

Oesterley, W. O. E. *The Jews and Judaism during the Greek Period.* London, 1941.

———. *The Wisdom of Solomon.* London, 1918.

———. *The Wisdom of Egypt and the Old Testament in the Light of the Newly Discovered "Teaching of Amen-em-ope."* London, 1927.

Radkinson, Michael L., and Wise, Isaac M. *The Babylonian Talmud.* Edited and translated by Michael L. Radkinson. Revised and corrected by Isaac M. Wise. 19 vols. Boston, 1916.

Rankin, O. S. *Israel's Wisdom Literature; Its Bearing on Theology and the History of Religion.* Edinburgh, 1936.

Ranston, Harry. *Ecclesiastes and the Early Greek Wisdom Literature.* London, 1925.

———. *The Old Testament Wisdom Books and Their Teaching.* London, 1930.

Schechter, S. *Some Aspects of Rabbinic Theology.* New York, 1923.

———. *Studies in Judaism.* Second Series. Philadelphia, 1908.

Schurer, Emil. *A History of the Jewish People in the Time of Christ.* Second Division. The Internal Condition of Palestine and of the Jewish People. 2 vols. Translated by S. Taylor and P. Christie. Edinburgh, 1898.

Smith, J. M. Powis. *The Moral Life of the Hebrews.* Chicago, 1923.

Strack, Hermann L. *Introduction to Talmud and Midrash.* Authorized Translation. Philadelphia, 1931.

Zeitlin, S. "The Halaka: Introduction to Tannaitic Jurisprudence." *Jewish Quarterly Review,* XXIX (1948), 1-40.

Chapter II

PHILOSOPHERS AS PHYSICIANS OF THE SOUL

Arnim, H. von. Article, "Krantor" in Pauly-Wissowa, *Real-encyclopädie,* Vol. XI. Stuttgart, 1922.

Bevan, Edwin. *Stoics and Skeptics.* Oxford, 1913.

Boissier, Gaston. *Cicero and His Friends. A Study of Roman Society in the Time of Caesar.* Translated . . . by Adnah David Jones. New York, 1925.

Bréhier, Émile. *Chrysippe.* Paris, 1910.

Brett, George Sidney. *A History of Psychology.* 3 vols. London, 1912-21.

Buresch, Carolus. *Consolationum a Graecis Romanisque scriptarum historia critica.* In *Leipziger Studien zur Classischen Philologie.* Bd. IX. Leipzig, 1886., pp. 1-171.

Burgess, Theodor C. "Epideictic Literature." *Studies in Classical Philology,* vol. III, Chicago, 1902, pp. 89-261.

Caird, Edward. *The Evolution of Theology in the Greek Philosophers.* 2 vols. Glasgow, 1904.

Cicero, Marcus Tullius. *De Officiis,* with an English translation by Walter Miller. Cambridge, Mass., 1947.

——. *Tusculan Disputations,* with an English translation by J. E. King. London, 1927.

Davidson, W. L. *The Stoic Creed.* Edinburgh, 1907.

Dill, Samuel. *Roman Society from Nero to Marcus Aurelius.* London, 1904.

Epictetus. *The Discourses and Manual together with Fragments of His Writings.* Translated with Introduction and Notes by P. E. Matheson. 2 vols. Oxford, 1916.

Fabre d'Olivet, Antoine. *The Golden Verses of Pythagoras* . . . Translated by Nayán Louise Redfield. New York, 1917.

Farrar, Frederick William. *Seekers after God.* London, 1876.

Fern, Sister Mary Edmund. *The Latin Consolatio as a Literary Type.* St. Louis, Missouri, 1941.

Forbes, J. T. *Socrates.* New York, 1905.

Henry, Margaret Young. *The Relation of Dogmatism and Scepticism in the Philosophical Treatises of Cicero.* Geneva, N. Y., 1925.

Hyde, William DeWitt. *From Epicuris to Christ: A Study in the Principles of Personality.* London, 1906.

Jaeger, Werner. *Paideia. The Ideals of Greek Culture.* Translated from the German Manuscript by Gilbert Highet. Vol. II. New York, 1943.

Livingstone, Sir R. W. *Greek Ideals and Modern Life.* Oxford, 1935.

——. *The Mission of Greece: Some Greek Views of Life in the Roman World.* Oxford, 1928.

Lutz, Cora E. *Musonius Rufus: "The Roman Socrates."* New Haven, 1947.

MacCurdy, Grace. *The Quality of Mercy: the Gentler Virtues in Greek Literature.* New Haven, 1940.

Martha, Benjamin Constant. *Études morales sur l'antiquité.* Paris, 1896.

[Moran] Sister Mary Evaristus. *The Consolations of Death in Ancient Greek Literature.* Washington, 1921 (?).

Nilsson, Martin Persson. *Greek Piety.* Translated by H. J. Rose. Oxford, 1948.

Oakesmith, John. *The Religion of Plutarch, a Pagan Creed of Apostolic Times.* London, 1902.

Oates, Whitney J. Editor. *The Stoic and Epicurean Philosophers. The Complete Extant Writings of Epicurus, Epictetus, Lucretius and Marcus Aurelius.* New York, 1940.

Pettazzoni, Raffaele. "Confession of Sins and the Classics." *Harvard Theological Review* XXX (1937) 1-14.

Plato. *Opera omnia, recensuit et commentariis instruxit Godofredus Stall-baum.* 12 vols. in 6. Leipzig, 1841-97.

————. *The Works of Plato:* translated into English with Analyses and Introduction by Benjamin Jowett. 4 vols. London, 1871. 2 vols. New York, 1936.

Plato and Xenophon. *Socratic Discourses.* With an Introduction by A. D. Lindsay. London and New York, 1910. Everyman Series.

Plutarchus. *Plutarch's Moralia* with an English translation by Frank Cole Babbitt. Of the 14 vols. projected, vols. I-VI and X have appeared. New York, 1927.

————. *Plutarch's Morals.* Translated from the Greek by several hands. Corrected and revised by William W. Goodwin . . . with an Introduction by Ralph Waldo Emerson. 5 vols. Boston, 1871. (Revision of a translation published 1684-94.)

Seneca, Lucius Annaeus. *Ad Lucilium epistulae morales.* With an English translation by Richard M. Gunmere. 3 vols. London, 1917-25.

————. *Moral Essays.* With an English translation by John W. Basore. 3 vols. London, 1928-35.

Sihler, E. G. *Testimonium animae, or Greeks and Romans before Jesus Christ.* New York, 1908.

Smith, T. V. *Philosophers Speak for Themselves.* Chicago, 1924.

Thamin, R. *Un problème moral dans l'antiquité: étude sur la casuistique stoïcienne.* Paris, 1884.

Zeller, E. *Socrates and the Socratic Schools.* Translated by O. J. Reichel. London, 1868.

Chapter III

SPIRITUAL DIRECTION IN HINDUISM, BUDDHISM, CONFUCIANISM AND ISLAM

Ahlbert, G. and Ihrahim, M. "Two Moslem Saints and Mystics." *The Moslem World,* XV (1925), 59-65.

Alabaster, Henry. *The Wheel of the Law. Buddhism Illustrated from Siamese Sources.* London, 1871.

Archer, John Clark. "The Bible of the Sikhs." *Review of Religion* XIII (1949), 115-25.

Auvard, A., and Schultz, M. *Bhagavad Gita, traduite et commentée.* Paris, 1919.

Beal, Samuel. *A Catena of Buddhist Scriptures from the Chinese.* London, 1871.

Brown, John P. *The Darvishes, or Oriental Spiritualism.* Edited with Introduction and Notes by H. A. Rose. Oxford, 1927.

Cooke, W. Article "Hinduism" in *Hastings Encyclopedia of Religion and Ethics,* VI. New York and Edinburgh, 1914.

Coomaraswamy, Ananda. *Buddha and the Gospel of Buddhism.* London, 1916.

Confucius. *The Analects of Confucius*. Translated by Arthur Waley. New York, 1939.

Dickson, J. F. "The Patimokkha, Being the Buddhist Office of the Confession of Priests." *Journal of the Royal Asiatic Society*, New Series VIII (1876), 62-130.

Donaldson, Dwight M. "Requirements of the Common People." *The Moslem World*, XXX (1940), 358-74.

Dubois, Jean Antoine. *Hindu Manners, Customs and Ceremonies*. 3rd ed. Oxford, 1906.

Dutt, Nalinaksha. *Aspects of Mahāyāna Buddhism and its Relations to Hīnāyana*. London, 1930.

———. *Early History of the Spread of Buddhism and the Buddhist Schools*. Calcutta, 1925.

Dutt (Datta), Sukumara. *Early Buddhist Monachism, 600 B.C.—ca. 100 B.C.* London, 1924.

Edgerton, Franklin. *The Bhagavad Gita; Translated and Interpreted*. 2 vols. Cambridge, Mass., 1944.

Farquhar, John Nicol. *Modern Religious Movements in India*. New York, 1915.

———. *A Primer of Hinduism*. 2nd ed. London, 1914.

———. *An Outline of the Religious Literature of India*. London and Edinburgh, 1920.

Garland, Mary Tudor. *Hindu Mind Training*. By an Anglo-Saxon Mother. Introduction by S. M. Mitra. London, 1917.

Goldziher, Ignaz. *Mohammed and Islam*. Translated from the German by Kate Chambers Seelye. New Haven, 1917.

Gowen, Herbert Henry. *A History of Indian Literature from Vedic Times to the Present Day*. New York, 1931.

Grierson, George Abraham. Article "Bhakti-Marga" in *Hastings Encyclopedia of Religion and Ethics*, II. New York and Edinburgh, 1910.

Griffith, Ralph T. H. *The Hymns of the Rigveda Translated with a Popular Commentary*. 3rd ed. 2 vols. Benares, 1920-26.

Guénon, René. *Introduction to the Study of Hindu Doctrines*. Translated by M. Pallis. London, 1945.

Hardy, Robert Spence. *A Manual of Buddhism in its Modern Development*. Translated from Singhalese Mss. London, 1880.

Hasluck, F. W. *Christianity and Islam under the Sultans*. 2 vols. Oxford, 1929.

Hayes, Helen M. *The Buddhist Pilgrim's Progress. From the Shi Yeu Ki, the Records of the Journey to the Western Paradise*. London, 1930.

Hume, Robert Allen. *An Interpretation of India's Religious History*. New York, 1911.

Hume, Robert Ernest. *The Thirteen Principal Upanishads*. Translated from the Sanskrit. 2nd ed. London, 1934.

———. *The Religious Heritage of India*. Boston, 1931.

Keith, Arthur Berriedale. *A History of Sanskrit Literature*. Oxford, 1928.

Keith, Arthur Berriedale. *The Religion and Philosophy of the Veda and Upanishads* (Harvard Oriental Series XXXI and XXXII). 2 vols. Cambridge, Mass., 1925.

Lao Tzu. *The Sayings of Lao Tzu*. Translated from the Chinese with an Introduction by Lionel Giles. London, 1911.

La Vallée Poussin, Louis de. *The Way to Nirvana: Six Lectures on Ancient Buddhism as a Discipline of Salvation*. Cambridge, 1917.

Macauliffe, Max Arthur. *The Sikh Religion, Its Gurus, Sacred Writings, and Authors*. 6 vols. Oxford, 1909.

MacMunn, Sir George Fletcher. *The Religious and Hidden Cults of India*. London, 1931.

Massigny, Louis. Al-Hallaj, Martyr Mystique de l'Islam. 2 vols. Paris, 1921-22.

———. *Essai sur les origines du Lexique de la mystique musselmane*. Paris, 1922.

Mencius. *Mencius*. Translated by Leonard A. Lyall. London, 1932.

Müller, Frederick Max, Editor.
The Sacred Books of the East. 50 vols. Oxford, 1879-1910.

Vols. II (1879) and XIV (1882), *The Sacred Laws of the Aryas*, Pts. I and II. (Containing the texts of Apastamba, Gautama, Vasishtha and Bandhayana.) Translated by Georg Bühler.

Vol. VII (1880). *The Institutes of Vishnu*. Translated by Julius Jolly.

Vols. XII (1882), XXVI (1885), XLI (1894), XLIII (1897), *The Satapatha Brahmana*, Pts. I to IV. Translated by Julius Eggeling.

Vols. XIII (1881), XVII (1882), XX (1885), *Vinaya Texts*. (Containing the *Pātimokkha*, the *Mahāvagga* and the *Kullavagga*). Translated from the Pāli by T. W. Rhys Davids and Hermann Oldenberg.

Vols. XXII (1884), XLV (1895), *Gaina Sūtras*, Pts. I and II. (Containing the *Akārānga*, *Uttarādhyana*, and *Sutrakutanga Sūtras*.) Translated from Prākrit by Hermann Jacobi.

Vol. XXV (1886). *The Laws of Manu*. Translated with Extracts from Seven Commentaries, by George Bühler.

Naish, C. G. "Al Ghazzali on Penitence." *The Moslem World*, XVI (1926), 6-18.

Nicholson, Reynold Alleyne. *Studies in Islamic Mysticism*. Cambridge, 1921.

Pettazzoni, Raffaele. *Stori della Religione*. Vol. VIII, *La Confessione dei Peccati*. Bologna, 1929.

———. *La confession des péchés*. Pt. I, Vol. I. Traduit par R. Monnot. Paris, 1931.

Reischauer, August Karl. *Studies in Japanese Buddhism*. New York, 1917.

Saunders, Kenneth James. *Epochs in Buddhist History*. Chicago, 1924.

Shaku, Soyen. *Sermons of a Buddhist Abbot*. Chicago, 1906.

Skellie, Walter James. *The Religious Psychology of Al-Ghazzālī*. A Translation of His Book of the THYA, on *The Explanation of the Wonders of the Heart*, with Introduction and Notes. Unpublished doctoral dissertation, Kennedy School of Missions, Hartford Seminary. Hartford, 1938.

Slater, Robert H. L. *Beyond Philosophy, or, The Paradox of Nirvana.* Unpublished doctoral dissertation. Columbia University. New York, 1948.

Smith, Margaret. *Al Ghazzālī, the Mystic.* London, 1944.

———. *Rābiʻa the Mystic and Her Fellow Saints in Islam.* Cambridge, 1928.

———. *Studies in Early Mysticism in the Near and Middle East.* London, 1931.

Stevenson, Margaret (Mrs. Sinclair Stevenson). *The Rites of the Twiceborn.* London, 1920.

Streeter, B. H., and Appasamy, A. J. *The Message of Sadhu Sundar Singh.* New York, 1922.

Subhan, John A. *Sufism, Its Saints and Shrines.* Lucknow, 1938.

Tachibana, S. *The Ethics of Buddhism.* London, 1926.

Thurston, Edgar. *Castes and Tribes of Southern India.* 7 vols. Madras, 1909.

Venkateswara, Sekharipuram Vaidyanatha. *Indian Culture Through the Ages.* Vol. I, *Education and the Propagation of Culture.* London, 1928.

Wach, Joachim. "Spiritual Teachings in Islam: a Study." *Journal of Religion,* XVIII (1948), 263-80.

Warren, Henry Clarke. *Buddhism in Translations.* Harvard Oriental Series Vol. III, 8th issue. Cambridge, Mass., 1922.

Wilson, Horace Hayman. *Hindu Religions. An Account of the Various Religious Sects of India.* Calcutta, 1899.

Wright, Dudley. *A Manual of Buddhism.* London, 1912.

Chapter IV

The Guidance of Souls in the New Testament

Appasamy, A. J. *The Johannine Doctrine of Life; a Study of Christian and Indian Thought.* London, 1934.

Bultmann, Rudolf. *Form Criticism: a New Method in New Testament Criticism.* Translated by F. C. Grant. Chicago, 1934.

Dibelius, Martin. *From Tradition to Gospel.* Translated in consultation with the author by B. L. Woolf. London, 1934.

———. *The Message of Jesus Christ.* Translated by Frederick C. Grant. New York, 1939.

Dodd, Charles H. *History and the Gospels.* New York, 1938.

———. *The Parables of the Kingdom.* New York, 1936.

Easton, B. S. *Christ in the Gospels.* New York, 1930.

———. *The Pastoral Epistles; Introduction, Translation, Commentary.* New York, 1947.

Enslin, Morton Scott. *Christian Beginnings.* New York, 1938.

———. *The Ethics of Paul.* London, 1930.

Filson, Floyd Vivian. *Origins of the Gospels.* New York, 1938.

Finkelstein, Louis. *The Pharisees.* 2 vols. Philadelphia, 1938.

Glover, T. R. *The Influence of Christianity in the Ancient World.* New Haven, 1929.

Goguel, Maurice. *Jesus et les origines du Christianisme.* Vol. I: *Vie de Jesus;* Vol. II: *Jesus et les origines du Christianisme.* Paris, 1932-46

Grant, Frederick C. *The Earliest Gospel; Studies in the Evangelical Tradition at Its Point of Crystallization in Writing.* New York, 1943.

————. *The Gospel of the Kingdom.* New York, 1940.

————. *The Growth of the Gospels.* New York, 1933.

Hall, G. Stanley. *Jesus the Christ in the Light of Psychology.* New York, 1917.

Heinrici, Karl Friedrich Georg. *Paulus als Seelsorger.* [Biblische Zeit—und Streitfragen. Ed. D. Kropatscheck, 6, 1.] Berlin, 1910.

Kittel, Gerhard. *Jesus als Seelsorger,* Berlin, 1917. [Zeit—und Streitfragen des Glaubens, der Weltanschauung und Bibelforschung, XI, 149-70.]

Klausner, Joseph. *From Jesus to Paul.* Translated from the Hebrew by William F. Stinespring. New York, 1943.

Kuist, Howard Tillman. *The Pedagogy of St. Paul.* New York, 1925.

Lewis, Edwin. *A New Heaven and a New Earth.* New York, 1941.

Mackinnon, James. *The Historic Jesus.* London, 1931.

Manson, T. W. *The Teaching of Jesus.* Cambridge, 1931.

Mavis, W. C. "Jesus' Influence on the Pastoral Ministry," *Theology Today,* IV (1948), 357-67.

McCasland, Selby Vernon. "Religious Healing in First Century Palestine." *Environmental Factors in Christian History.* Edited by John T. McNeill, Mathew Spinka and Harold R. Willoughby. Chicago, 1939, chap. II.

McCown, Chester C. "The Reign of God," *Religion in Life,* XVIII (1949), 211-221.

————. *The Search for the Real Jesus: a Century of Historical Study.* New York, 1940.

Micklem, E. R. *Miracles and the New Psychology.* Oxford, 1922.

Moffatt, James. *An Introduction to the Literature of the New Testament.* New York, 1922.

Otto, Rudolph. *The Kingdom of God and the Son of Man.* Translated by Floyd V. Filson and Bertram Lee-Woolf (1938). New and Rev. Ed. London, 1943.

Rawlinson, A. E. J. *St. Mark; with Introduction, Commentary and Additional Notes.* 3rd ed. London, 1931.

Richardson, Allan. *The Miracle Stories of the Gospel.* New York, 1942.

Riddle, Donald W., and Hutson, Harold H. *New Testament Life and Literature.* Chicago, 1946.

Schlunk, Martin. *Paulus als Missionar.* Gütersloh, 1937.

Schonfield, Hugh Joseph. *The Jew of Tarsus. An Unorthodox Portrait of St. Paul.* London, 1946.

Schweitzer, Albert. *The Psychiatric Study of Jesus.* Translated with an Introduction by Charles R. Joy. Boston, 1948.

————. *The Quest of the Historical Jesus* (German ed., 1906). Translated by W. Montgomery. With a Preface by F. C. Burkitt. London, 1910; Boston, 1948.

Scott, Ernest. *The Ethical Teaching of Jesus.* New York, 1924.

————. *The Kingdom of God in the New Testament.* New York, 1931.

————. *Man and Society in the New Testament.* New York, 1946.

————. *The Varieties of New Testament Religion.* New York, 1943.

Sencourt, Robert. *Saint Paul, Envoy of Grace.* London, 1948.

Smith, B. T. D. *The Parables of the Synoptic Gospels. A Critical Study.* Cambridge, 1937.

Street, T. Watson. *Moral Autonomy in the Gospels.* [Typed S.T.M. thesis, Union Theological Seminary.] New York, 1943.

Taylor, Vincent. *The Formation of the Gospel Tradition.* London, 1933.

Wilder, Amos R. *Eschatology and Ethics in the Teaching of Jesus.* New York, 1939.

Willoughby, Harold R., Editor. *The Study of the Bible Today and Tomorrow.* Chicago, 1947. I am especially indebted to the following essays in this series: iii. "New Testament Criticism in the World-Wars Period" by Merrill M. Parvis; xvii. "The Teaching of Jesus and First Century Jewish Ethics" by Frederick C. Grant; xviii. "Reassessing the Religious Importance of Paul" by Donald W. Riddle; xix. "The Central Problem Concerning Christian Origins" by Floyd V. Filson.

Chapter V

DISCIPLINE AND CONSOLATION IN THE AGE OF THE CHURCH FATHERS

Alès, A. J. L Édit de Calliste. Étude sur les origines de la pénitence chrétienne. 2nd ed. Paris, 1914.

The Ante-Nicene Fathers. *Translations of the Writings of the Fathers down to A.D. 325.* Alexander Roberts and James Donaldson, Editors. American reprint of the Edinburgh edition with prefaces and notes by A. Cleveland Coxe. 10 vols. Buffalo, 1885-96.

Ayer, James Cullen. *A Source Book of Ancient Church History.* New York, 1913.

Benedictus. *S. Benedicti regula monasteriorum.* Edidit . . . Benno Linderbauer, O.S.B. Bonn, 1928.

Budge, E. A. Wallis. *The Paradise, or the Garden, of the Holy Fathers . . . of the Deserts of Egypt . . .* 2 vols. London, 1907.

Cadoux, Cecil John. *The Early Church and the World.* Edinburgh, 1925.

Corpus scriptorum ecclesiasticorum latinorum. Edited by the Vienna Academy of Letters. 69 vols. Leipzig, 1866-1939.

Dobschütz, Ernst von. *Christian Life in the Primitive Church.* Translated by George Bremner. London, 1904.

Duchesne, Louis. *Christian Worship: Its Origin and Evolution . . . to the Time of Charlemagne.* Translated from the 4th French ed. by M. L. McClure. 4th English ed. London, 1912.

Favez, Charles. *La consolation latine chrétienne.* Paris, 1937.

Frank, F. *Die Bussdisciplin der kirche von den apostelzeiten bis zum siebenten Jahrhundert.* Mainz, 1867.

Hannan, Mary Louise. *Thasci Caecilii Cypriani: De Mortalitate.* A Commentary with an Introduction and Translation. Washington, 1933.

Hardeland, August. *Geschichte der speciellen Seelsorge, in der vorreformatorischen Kirche und in der Kirche der Reformation.* I Hälfte. 2 vols. in one. Berlin, 1897-98.

Haslehurst, Richard Stafford Tyndale. *Some Account of the Penitential Discipline of the Early Church.* London, 1921.

Hoh, Josef. *Die kirchliche Busse im II Jahrhundert.* Breslau, 1932.

Kidd, Beresford James. *Documents Illustrative of the History of the Church* (to A.D. 461). 2 vols. London, 1920-23.

———. *A History of the Church to A.D. 461.* 3 vols. Oxford, 1922.

Labriolle, Pierre Champagne de. *History and Literature of Christianity from Tertullian to Boethius.* Translated from the French by Herbert Wilson . . . 2 vols. London, 1924.

———. *The Life and Times of St. Ambrose.* Translated from the French by Herbert Wilson. St. Louis, 1928.

Latko, Ernest F. *Origen's Concept of Penance.* Quebec, 1949.

Lea, Henry Charles. *History of Confession and Indulgences.* 2 vols. Philadelphia, 1896.

Macarius the Egyptian. *Fifty Spiritual Homilies of St. Macarius the Egyptian.* Edited with an Introduction by A. J. Mason. London, 1921.

Marshall, Nathanael. *The Penitential Discipline of the Primitive Church.* London, 1714; Oxford, 1844.

Migne, Jacques Paul. *Patrologiae cursus completus.* Series Graeca. 163 vols. Paris, 1857-66. Index by Theodorus Hopfner. 2 vols. 1928-36.

———. *Patrologiae cursus completus.* Series Latina. 221 vols. Paris 1879-91.

Moore, Clifford Herschel. "The Epicedia of Statius," *Anniversary Papers* by Colleagues and Pupils of George Lyman Kittredge. Boston, 1913, pp. 127-37.

Morinus, Johannes. *Commentarius historicus de disciplina in administratione penitentiae tredecim primis saeculis.* Paris, 1651; 2nd ed., Antwerp, 1682.

Mortimer, R. C. *The Origins of Private Penance in the Western Church.* Oxford, 1939.

Mozley, J. K. "Binding and Loosing." Article in *Hastings Encyclopaedia of Religion and Ethics,* II. New York and Edinburgh, 1910.

O'Donnell, M. J. *Penance in the Early Church.* Dublin, 1908.

Pijper, F. *Geschiednis der Boete en Biecht in de christelijke Kerk.* 2 vols. 's Gravenhage, 1891, 1908.

Poschmann, Bernhard. *Die abendländische Kirchenbusse im Ausgang des christlichen Altertums.* Munich, 1928.

Poschmann, Bernhard. *Hat Augustinus die Privatbusse eingefuhrt?* Brauns-berg, 1920.

Rahner, Hugo. *Griechische Mythen in christlichen Deutung* (Zweites Teil: "Seelen-heilung"). Zürich, 1945.

Roberts, Charles Manley. *History of Confession until It Developed into Auricular Confession, A.D. 1215.* London, 1901.

A Select Library of the Nicene and Post-Nicene Fathers of the Christian Church. Edited by Philip Schaff. 14 vols. New York, 1887-94. 2nd Series. Edited by Philip Schaff and Henry Wace. 14 vols. New York, 1890-1900.

Simpson, Adelaide Douglas. "The Good Citizen of the Second Century." *L'Antiquité classique*, XVI (1947), 59-78.

———. "Epicureans, Christians, Atheists in the Second Century." *Transactions of the American Philological Association*, LXXII, 1941, 372-81.

Taylor, Henry Osborn. *The Classical Heritage of the Middle Ages.* New York, 1902.

Thatcher, Oliver J., and McNeal, Edgar Holmes. *A Source Book for Medieval History.* New York, 1905.

Vacandard, E. *La confession sacramentelle dans l'église primitive.* 8th ed. Paris, 1908.

———. *La pénitence publique dans l'église primitive.* 7th ed. Paris, 1908.

Watkins, Oscar Daniel. *A History of Penance.* 2 vols. Oxford, 1920.

White, Hugh G. Evelyn. *The Monasteries of the Wadi 'n Natrun.* Pt. II. *The History of the Monasteries of Nitria and of Scetis.* Edited by Walter Hauser. New York, 1932.

Chapter VI

THE CELTIC PENITENTIAL DISCIPLINE AND THE RISE OF THE CONFESSIONAL

Boileau, Jacobus. *Historia confessionis auricularis ex antiquis scripturae Patrum Pontificum and Conciliorum monumentis . . . expressa.* Paris, 1684.

Cabral, Fernand, and Leclercq, Henri. *Dictionnaire d'archéologie chrétienne et de liturgie.* Paris, 1907.

The Catholic Encyclopedia. Edited by C. G. Hubermann and others. 17 vols. New York, 1907-22.

Dalleus, Johannes. *De sacramentali sive auricularia latinorum confessione disputatio.* Geneva, 1661.

Duchesne, Louis. *Christian Worship, Its Origin and Evolution.* Translated from the 4th French ed. by M. L. McClure. 4th English ed. London, 1912.

Dudden, Frederick Holmes. *Gregory the Great. His Place in History and Thought.* New York. 2 vols. 1905.

Ellis, Thomas Peter. *Welsh Tribal Law and Custom in the Middle Ages.* Oxford, 1926.

Fearsey, Henry John. *Ancient English Holy Week Ceremonial*. London, 1897.

Fournier, P., and Le Bras, G. *Histoire des collections canoniques en occident, depuis les fausses décrétals jusqu'au décret de Gratien*. 2 vols. Paris, 1931-32.

Friedberg, Emil. *Aus deutschen Bussbüchern: ein Beitrag zur deutschen Culturgeschichte*. Halle, 1868.

Gougaud, Louis. *Christianity in Celtic Lands*. Translated from the author's manuscript by Maude Joynt. London, 1932.

———. *Devotional and Ascetic Practices in the Middle Ages*. English ed. Prepared by G. C. Bateman. London, 1927.

Haddan, Arthur West and Stubbs, William. *Councils and Ecclesiastical Documents relating to Great Britain and Ireland*. 3 vols. Oxford, 1869-78.

Hardeland, August. *Geschichte der speciellen Seelsorge in der vorreformatorischen Kirche und in der Kirche der Reformation*. 2 vols. in one. Berlin, 1897-98.

Holl, Karl. *Enthusiasmus und Bussgewalt beim griechischen Mönchtum*. Leipzig, 1898.

Hopkins, John Henry. *This History of the Confessional*. New York, 1850.

Jungmann, Josef Andr. *Die lateinischen Bussriten in ihrer geschichtlichen Entwicklung*. Innsbruck, 1932.

Kenney, James Francis. *The Sources for the Early History of Ireland; an Introduction and Guide*. Vol. I: *Ecclesiastical*. New York, 1929.

Kirk, Kenneth E. *The Vision of God. The Christian Doctrine of the Summum Bonum*. London, 1931.

Kirsch, Peter Anton. *Zur Geschichte der katholischen Beichte*. Würzburg, 1902.

Kurtschied, Bertrand. *Das Beichtsiegel in seiner geschichtlichen Entwicklung*. Freiburg, 1912. Also: Translated by F. A. Marks. *A History of the Seal of Confession*. St. Louis, 1927.

Lea, Henry Charles. *History of Auricular Confession and Indulgences*. 2 vols. Philadelphia, 1896.

McNeill, John T. *The Celtic Penitentials and their Influence on Continental Christianity*. Paris, 1923.

———. "Medicine for Sin as Prescribed in the Penitentials." *Church History* I (1932), 14-26.

McNeill, John T., and Gamer, Helena. *Medieval Handbooks of Penance. A Translation of the Principal libri poenitentiales*. Columbia University, "Records of Civilization," vol. XXIX. New York, 1938.

Morinus, Joannes. *Commentarius historicus de disciplina in administratione penitentiae tredecim primis seculis*. Paris, 1651; 2nd ed. Antwerp, 1682.

Oakley, Thomas P. *The English Penitential Discipline and Anglo-Saxon Law*. New York, 1923.

Owen, Aneurin, Editor. *The Ancient Laws and Institutes of Wales*. 2 vols. London, 1841.

Poschmann, Bernhard. *Die abendländische Kirchenbusse im frühen Mittelalter*. Breslau, 1930.

Schmitz, Hermann Joseph. *Die Bussbücher und die Bussdisciplin der Kirche*. Mainz, 1883.

———. *Die Bussbücher und das kanonische Bussverfahren*. Düsseldorf, 1898.

Teetaert, Amédée. *La confession aux laïques dans l'église latine depuis le viiie jusqu'a xive siècle*. Wetteren, 1926.

Wasserschleben, F. W. Hermann. *Die Bussordnungen der abendländischen Kirche*. Halle, 1851.

Watkins, Oscar Daniel. *A History of Penance*. 2 vols. London, 1920.

Zimmermann, Charlotte. *Die deutsche Beichte vom 9. Jahrhundert bis zur Reformation*. Weida i. Thür., 1934.

Chapter VII

THREE CENTURIES OF ENRICHMENT AND DETERIORATION, FROM THE COMING OF THE FRIARS TO THE RENAISSANCE

Aron, Marguerite. *Un animateur de la jeunesse au xiiie siècle . . . Jourdain de Saxe* . . . Paris, 1930.

Bowden, Muriel. *A Commentary on the General Prologue to the Canterbury Tales*. New York, 1948.

Caplan, Harry. *Medieval Artes Praedicandi, a Hand-List*. Ithaca, N. Y., 1934.

Comper, Frances M. M., Editor. *The Book of the Craft of Dying and Other Early English Tracts Concerning Death . . . Done into Modern Spelling*. London, 1917.

Connolly, James L. *John Gerson, Reformer and Mystic*. Louvain, 1928.

Conway, Placid, and Jarrett, Bede, Editors. *Lives of the Brethren of the Order of Preachers, 1206-1259*, in the translation of Fr. Placid Conway, edited by Fr. Bede Jarrett. London, 1924.

Coulton, George Gordon. *Five Centuries of Religion*. Vols. I-III. Cambridge, 1923-36.

———. *Life in the Middle Ages*. Four vols. in one. New York, 1931.

Cowley, Patrick. *Franciscan Rise and Fall*. London, 1933.

Cutts, Edward L. *Parish Priests and Their People in the Middle Ages in England*. London, 1898.

Early English Text Society Publications. Original Series:

No. 23. Dan Michel's Ayenbite of Inwyt, 1340. Edited by Richard Morris. 1866.

No. 31. *Instructions for Parish Priests*, by John Myrc. Edited by Edward Peacock. 1868.

Nos. 89 and 159. *Vices and Virtues. Being a Soul's Confession of Its Sins, with Reason's Description of the Virtues . . .* of about 1200. Edited by Frederick Holthausen. Pt. I, 1888; Pt. II, 1921.

No. 118. *The Lay Folks' Catechism, or the English and Latin Versions of Archbishop Thoresby's Instructions for the People.* Edited by Thomas Frederick Simmons and Henry Edward Nolloth. 1901.

No. 123. *Robert of Brunne's Handlyng Synne, A.D. 1303, with Parts of the Anglo-French Treatise . . . William of Waddington's Manuel des Pechiez.* Re-edited by Frederick J. Fournival. 1901-3.

Nos. 126 and 127. *An Alphabet of Tales.* Edited by Mrs. M. M. Banks. 1904-5.

No. 217. *The Book of the Vices and Virtues.* A Fourteenth Century English Translation of the *Somme le Roi* of Lorens d'Orleans. Edited by W. Nelson Francis. 1942.

Extra Series:

Nos. lxxxi, lxxxii. *Gower's Confessio Amantis.* Edited by G. C. MacAuley. 1901.

Falk, Franz. *Die Deutschen Sterbebüchlein von der ältesten Zeit des Buchdruckes bis zum Jahre 1520.* Köln, 1890.

Felder, Hilarin. *Die Ideale des Heiligen Franziscus von Assisi.* Paderborn, 1923.

Freer, Arthur Savile Beresford. *The Early Franciscans and Jesuits: A Study in Contrasts.* London, 1922.

Green, Victor G. *The Franciscans in Medieval English Life, 1224-1348.* Franciscan Studies, XX. Paterson, N. J., 1939.

Hardeland, August. *Geschichte der speciellen Seelsorge,* I Hälfte. Berlin, 1897.

Henson, Herbert Hensley. *Moral Discipline in the Christian Church.* London, 1905.

Howie, Margaret D. *Studies in the Use of Exempla, with Special Reference to Middle High German Literature.* London, 1923.

Huizinga, J. *The Waning of the Middle Ages.* London, 1924.

Jusserand, J. J. *English Wayfaring Life in the Middle Ages* (14th century). Translated by Lucy Toulmin Smith. London, 1891.

Lea, Henry Charles. *A History of Auricular Confession and Indulgences.* 3 vols. Philadelphia, 1896.

Little, Andrew George. *Liber exemplorum ad usum predicantium saeculo xiii compositus a quodam fratre minori anglico de Provincia Hibernia.* Aberdeen, 1908.

————. *Franciscan Papers, Lists and Documents.* Manchester, 1943.

————. *Studies in English Franciscan History.* Manchester, 1917.

The Little Flowers and the Life of St. Francis with the Mirror of Perfection. Introduction by T. Okey. London, 1910. Everyman.

Mandonnet, Pierre Felix. *St. Dominic and His Work.* Translated by Sister Mary Benedicta Larkin. St. Louis, 1944.

Moorman, John Richard Humpidge. *Sources for the Life of St. Francis.* Manchester, 1940.

Mosher, Joseph Albert. *The Exemplum in the Early Religious and Didactic Literature of England.* New York, 1911.

O'Connor, Sister Mary Catherine. *The Art of Dying Well. The Development of the Ars Moriendi.* New York, 1942.

Owst, Gerald Robert. *Literature and the Pulpit in Medieval England.* Cambridge, 1933.

————. *Preaching in Medieval England . . . ca. 1350-1450.* Cambridge, 1926.

Peckham, John Lajmbeer. *Archbishop Peckham as a Religious Educator.* Yale Studies in Religion, No. 7. Scottdale, Pa. 1934.

Perinelle, Georges. *L'Attrition d'aprés le concile de Trent et d'aprés Saint Thomas d'Aquin.* Kain (Belgium), 1927.

Petry, Ray C. *Francis of Assisi, Apostle of Poverty.* Durham, N. C., 1941.

Reeves, John-Baptist. *The Dominicans.* London, 1929.

Rogers, Frederick H. *The Seven Deadly Sins.* London, 1907.

Rütten, Wilhelm. *Studien zur mittelalterlichen Busslehre, mit besonderer Berücksichtigung der älteren Franziskanerschule.* Münster i.w., 1902.

Rylands, W. Harry and Bullen, George. *The Ars moriendi* (Editio princeps, circa 1450). Edited by W. Harry Rylands, with an Introduction by George Bullen. London, 1881.

Sabatier, Paul and Others. *Franciscan Essays.* Aberdeen, 1912.

Schnürer, Gustav. *Kirche and Kultur im Mittelalter.* 3 vols. Paderborn, 1927-30.

Scudder, Vida D. *The Franciscan Adventure.* London, 1931.

Stevenson, Francis Seymour. *Robert Grosseteste.* London, 1899.

Swan, Charles, Editor. *Gesta Romanorum;* translated from the Latin by Charles Swan, revised by Wynnard Cooper. London, 1899.

Walz, Angelus Maria. *Compendium historiae Ordinis praedicatorum.* Rome, 1930.

Zawart, Anscar. *The History of Franciscan Preaching and of Franciscan Preachers* (1209-1927). The Franciscan Educational Conference, Vol. IX. Washington, D. C., 1927.

Chapter VIII

The Cure of Souls in Lutheranism

Bachmann, C. Charles. *The Development of Lutheran Pastoral Care in America.* Unpublished doctoral dissertation, Boston University, 1949.

Bellardi, Werner. *Die Geschichte der "Christlichen Gemeinschaft" in Strassburg* (1546-1550 [Quellen und Forschungen zur Reformationsgeschichte, xviii]). Leipzig, 1934.

Boehmer, Heinrich. *Luther and the Reformation in the Light of Modern Research.* Translated by E. S. G. Potter. New York, 1930.

————. *Road to Reformation. Martin Luther to the Year 1521.* Translated from the German by John W. Doberstein and Theodore G. Tappert. Philadelphia, 1946.

Bucer, Martin. *De vera animarum cura veroque officio pastoris ecclesiastici.*

Strasbourg, 1538. Text in *Buceri Scripta Anglicana fere omnia*, Basel, 1577, pp. 260-356.

———. *Pastorale, das ist von der waren Seelsorge*. Heidelberg, 1574.

Drews, P. *Der evangelishe Geistlicher in der deutschen Vergangenheit*. 2nd ed. Jena, 1924.

Dunkley, E. H. *The Reformation in Denmark*. London, 1948.

Frey, August Emil. *Luther und seine Freunde I Theil. Die Freunde Luthers zum Beginne der Reformation*. St. Louis, 1884.

Hardeland, August. *Geschichte der speciellen Seelsorge*. II Hälfte: *In der Kirche der Reformation*. Berlin, 1898.

Gerberding, G. H. *The Life and Letters of William Alfred Passavant, D.D.* Greenville, Pa., 1906.

———. *The Lutheran Pastor*. Philadelphia, 1902.

Grünberg, Paul. *Philipp Jakob Spener*. Vol. II. *Spener als praktischer Theolog und Kirchlicher Reformer*. Göttingen, 1905.

Halsey, Luther. *Memoirs of John Frederick Oberlin . . . Compiled from Authentic Sources*. New York, 1855.

Harms, Claus. *Pastoraltheologie*, Bk. III, *Der Pastor*. Kiel, 1837.

Harnack, Theodor. *Geschichte und Theorie der Predigt und der Seelsorge*. Erlangen, 1878.

Hartmannus, Johannes Ludovicus. *Pastorale Evangelicum seu institutio plenior ministrorum verbi*. Nuremberg, 1678.

Held, Felix Emil. *Christianopolis, an Ideal State of the Seventeenth Century*. Translated from the Latin of Johann Valentin Andreae, with an Historical Introduction. New York, 1916.

Jacobs, Henry Eyster. *A History of the Evangelical Lutheran Church in the United States*. New York, 1893.

Köstlin, Heinrich Adolf. *Die Lehre von der Seelsorge nach evangelishen Grundsätzen*. 2nd rev. ed. Berlin, 1907.

Luther, Martin. *Correspondence and Other Contemporary Letters*. Translated and edited by Preserved Smith. 2 vols. Philadelphia, 1913.

———. *Works of Martin Luther with Introductions and Notes*. 6 vols. Philadelphia, 1915-32.

———. *Werke. Kritische Gesammtausgabe*. Weimar, 1883-1948.

Luther Speaks. Essays for the fourth centenary of Martin Luther's death by a group of Lutheran ministers with a foreword by the Bishop of Oslo. London, 1947.

Mattson, A. D. *Polity of the Augustana Synod*. Rock Island, 1941.

McNeill, John T. "Personal Counselling in Early Protestantism." *Christendom, an Ecumenical Review*, VI (1941), 364-75.

Muhlenberg, Henry Melchior. *The Journals of Henry Melchior Muhlenberg . . .* Translated by Theodore G. Tappert and John W. Doherstein. 2 vols. Philadelphia, 1942-45.

Mundinger, Carl S. *Government in the Missouri Synod*. St. Louis, 1947.

Nebe, August. *Luther as Spiritual Adviser*. Translated by Charles A. Hay and Charles E. Hay. Philadelphia, 1894.

Rade, Martin. *Das königliche Priestertum der Gläubigen und seine Forderung an die evangelische Kirche unserer Zeit.* [Sammlung gemeinverständlicher Vorträge und Schriften, 85.] Tübingen, 1918.

Ritter, John N. "Muhlenberg's Anticipation of Psychosomatic Medicine." *Lutheran Church Quarterly,* XIX (1946), 181-88.

Schindler, Carl J. "The Psychology of Henry Melchior Muhlenberg." *Lutheran Church Quarterly,* XVI (1943), 50-59.

Spener, Philipp Jakob. *Die Hauptschriften Philipp Jakob Speners.* Edited by Paul Grünberg. Gotha, 1889.

———. *Pia desideria.* Edited by Paul Aland. Berlin, 1940.

Stumpff, Albrecht. *Philipp Jakob Spener über Theologie und Seelsorge als Gebiete kirchlicher Neugestaltung.* Tübingen, 1934.

Tholuck, August. *Das kirchliche Leben des siebzehnten Jahrhunderts.* 2 vols. Berlin, 1861-62.

Walther, Carl Fredinand Wilhelm. *Amerikanisch-Lutherhische Pastoral-Theologie.* St. Louis, 1872.

Westberg, Granger E. "Private Confession in the Lutheran Church." *Augustana Quarterly,* XXIV (1945), 138-162.

Chapter IX

The Cure of Souls in the Continental Reformed Churches

Alsted, Johann Heinrich. *Theologia casuum, exhibens anatomen conscientiae et scholam tentationum.* Hanover, 1630.

Appel, Theodore. *The Life and Work of John Williamson Nevin.* Philadelphia, 1889.

Baur, August. *Zwinglis Theologie, ihr Werden und ihr System.* Vol. I. Halle, 1885.

Benoit, Jean-Daniel. *Calvin, directeur d'âmes. Contribution a l'histoire de la piété Réformée.* Strasbourg, 1947.

———. *Direction spirituelle et Protestantisme. Étude sur la légitimité d'une direction protestante.* Paris, 1940.

Bouvier, André. *Henri Bullinger, réformateur et conseiller oecuménique.* Paris, 1940.

Calvin, Jean. *Letters of John Calvin compiled from the Original Manuscripts . . . by Dr. Jules Bonnet, Translated . . . by David Constable.* 2 vols. Edinburgh, 1855-57. The same, 4 vols., Philadelphia, 1858.

———. *Ioannis Calvini opera quae supersunt omnia . . . ediderunt Guilielmus Baum, et al.* 58 vols. Brunsweig, 1863-1900.

Drelincourt, Charles. *Les consolations de l'âme fidèle contre les frayeurs de la mort. Avec les dispositions et les préparations nécessaire pour bien mourir.* Paris, 1651. *The Christian's Consolations against the Fears of Death: with . . . Directions for Preparing Him to Die Well.* 7th American ed., Philadelphia, 1836.

Frommel, Gaston. *The Psychology of the Christian Faith . . .* Selections from the Writings of Gaston Frommel. Translated by J. Macartney Wilson. London, 1928.

Fuhrmann, Paul T. "Alexander Vinet and His Theology." *Lutheran Quarterly*, XIX (1946), 235-51.

————. *The Theology of Conscience in Pascal and His Swiss Protestant Successors*. Madison, N. J., 1933.

Gunn, Alexander. *Memoirs of the Rev. John Henry Livingston*. New York, 1856.

Harbaugh, H. *The Life of the Rev. Michael Schlatter, with a Full Account of His Travels and Labors . . .* Philadelphia, 1857.

Heppe, Heinrich. *Geschichte des Pietismus und der Mystik in der Reformierten Kirche, namentlich der Niederlande*. Leiden, 1879.

Lane, Laura M. *The Life and Writings of Alexandre Vinet . . .* With an Introduction by F. W. Farrar. Edinburgh, 1890.

Ley, Roger. *Kirchenzucht bei Zwingli*. [Quellen und Abhandlungen zur Geschichte des schweizerischen Protestantismus, 2.] Zurich, 1948.

Monod, Sarah. *Life and Letters of Adolphe Monod*. By One of his Daughters. London, 1885.

Pannier, Jacques. *L'Église réformée sous Louis XIII*. Paris, 1920.

Pestalozzi, Carl. *Heinrich Bullinger. Leben und ausgewählte Schriften*. Elberfeld, 1858.

Pressensé, Edmond de. *Contemporary Portraits*. Translated by Annie Harwood Holmden. New York, 1880.

Schrag, Felix James. "Theodorus Jacobus Frelinghuysen, the Father of American Pietism." Church History, XIV (1945), 201-16.

Strathmann, Hermann. *Calvins Lehre von der Busse in ihrer späteren Gestalt*. Gotha, 1909.

————. *Die Entstehung der Lehre Calvins von der Busse*. [Reprint from *Calvinstudien* by Joseph Bohatec and others.] Leipzig, 1909.

Turretini, François. *Institutio theologiae elencticae*. 3 vols. New York, 1947.

Van Oosterzee, Johannes Jacobus. *Practical Theology*. Translated and adapted by Maurice J. Evans. London, 1878.

Vinet, Alexandre. *Lettres d'Alexandre Vinet et de quelques uns de ses correspondants*. Lausanne, 1882.

————. *Pastoral Theology; or, the Theory of the Evangelical Ministry*. Translated and edited by Thomas H. Skinner. New York, 1853.

————. *Lettres*. Edited by Pierre Bovet. Vol. I, 1813-28. Lausanne, 1947.

Voet, Gijsbert. *Gisberti Voetii . . . Politicae ecclesiasticae pars tertia et ultima*. Amsterdam, 1676.

Zwingli, Huldreich. *Sämmtliche Werke . . .* Edited by Emil Egli, et al. [Corpus Reformatorum ed.] 13 vols. Berlin, 1905.

————. *Selected Works of Huldreich Zwingli*. Translated from the Originals. Edited by Samuel Macauley Jackson. Philadelphia, 1901.

————. *The Latin Works and Correspondence of Huldreich Zwingli . . .* Translations by Henry Preble and Others. Edited by Samuel Macauley Jackson. 3 vols. New York, 1912-29.

Zwingli, Huldreich. *The Ymage of Bothe Pastours.* Translated from the Latin by John Veron Sinonoys. London, 1550.

Chapter X

THE CURE OF SOULS IN THE ANGLICAN COMMUNION

Allestree, Richard. *The Whole Duty of Man.* London, 1715.

Balmforth, Henry, and Others. *An Introduction to Pastoral Theology.* New York, 1937.

Bayly, Lewis. *The Practice of Piety: Directing a Christian How to Walk . . .* London, 1669.

Becon, Thomas. *Prayers and other Pieces by Thomas Becon.* Edited for the Parker Society by John Ayre. Cambridge, 1844.

Blunt, John Henry. *The Annotated Book of Common Prayer.* London, 1903.

Bradford, John. *The Writings of John Bradford.* Edited for the Parker Society by Aubrey Townsend. 2 vols. Cambridge, 1848-53.

Bramhall, John. *The Works of the Most Reverend Father in God John Bramhall.* 5 vols. Oxford, 1842-45.

Brightman, Frank Edward. *The English Rite, Being a Synopsis of the Sources and Revisions of the Book of Common Prayer.* 2 vols. London, 1915.

Brooks, Phillips. *Lectures on Preaching.* Delivered before the Divinity School of Yale University. London, 1902.

Burnet, Gilbert. *A Discourse of Pastoral Care.* London, 1713.

Butler, Dougald. *The Life and Letters of Robert Leighton.* London, 1903.

Carter, Thomas Thelluson. *The Doctrine of Confession in the Church of England.* 2nd ed. London, 1869.

Carus, William. *Memoirs of the Life of the Rev. Charles Simeon . . . with a Selection from his Writings and Correspondence.* (American ed. edited by Charles P. McIlvaine.) New York, 1848.

[Church of England.] *The Doctrine of the Church of England as Stated in Ecclesiastical Documents Set Forth by Authority of Church and State in the Reformation Period.* (1536-1562) London, 1868.

The Two Books of Homilies. Edited by John Griffiths. Oxford, 1859.

Collier, Jeremy. *Reasons for Restoring some Prayers and Directions . . . in the Communion Service of the First English Reformed Liturgy . . .* London, 1717.

Cosin, John. *The Works of the Right Reverend . . . John Cosin . . . Now First Collected.* 5 vols. Oxford, 1843-55.

Cranmer, Thomas. *The Works of Thomas Cranmer.* Edited for the Parker Society by John Edmund Cox. 2 vols. Cambridge, 1844-46.

Cunningham, William. *The Cure of Souls; Lectures on Pastoral Theology.* Cambridge, 1908.

Ferrar, Nicholas, *The Ferrar Papers.* Edited by B. Blackstone. Cambridge, 1938.

Fulke, William. A *Defence of the Sincere and True Translations of the Holy Scriptures* . . . Edited for the Parker Society by Charles Henry Hartshorne. Cambridge, 1843.

Fuller, Thomas. *The Holy State and the Profane State.* Edited by Maximilian Graff Walten. New York, 1938.

Gray, Charles Norris. *Confession as Taught by the Church of England.* 5th ed. Manchester, 1872.

Herbert, George. *The English Works of George Herbert,* Newly arranged . . . by George Herbert Palmer. 3 vols. Boston, 1905.

Hooker, Richard. *The Works of that Learned and Judicious Divine Mr. Richard Hooker* . . . Arranged by John Keble. 7th ed. Revised by R. W. Church and F. Paget. 3 vols. Oxford, 1888.

Jewel, John. *The Works of John Jewel.* Edited for the Parker Society by John Ayre. 4 vols. Cambridge, 1845-50.

Keble, John. *Letters of Spiritual Counsel and Guidance.* Edited by R. F. Wilson. Oxford, 1881.

Kettlewell, John. *Death Made Comfortable; or, The Way to Die Well* . . . London, 1618.

Kirk, Kenneth E. *Conscience and Its Problems. An Introduction to Casuistry.* London, 1927.

Latimer, Hugh. *The Works of Hugh Latimer.* Edited for the Parker Society by George Elwes Corrie. 2 vols. Cambridge, 1844-46.

Laud, William. *Works of Archbishop Laud.* Edited by William Scott. Vol. III. Oxford, 1853.

Law, William. *A Serious Call to a Devout and Holy Life.* With an Introduction by J. V. Moldenhawer. Philadelphia, 1948.

Lloyd, Charles, Editor. *Formularies of the Faith, Put Forth by Authority in the Reign of Henry VIII.* Oxford, 1825.

Marshall, Nathaniel. *The Penitential Discipline of the Primitive Church* . . . A new edition. Oxford, 1844.

Meade, William. *Lectures on the Pastoral Office.* Delivered to students of the Theological Seminary at Alexandria, Virginia. New York, 1849.

More, Paul Elmer, and Cross, Frank Leslie. *Anglicanism. The Thought and Practice of the Church of England, Illustrated from the Literature of the Seventeenth Century.* Milwaukee, 1935.

Pusey, Edward Bouverie. *Advice to Those who Exercise the Ministry of Reconciliation through Confession and Absolution. Being the Abbé Gaume's Manual for Confessors.* Abridged . . . 2nd ed. Oxford, 1878.

————. *Spiritual Letters of Edward Bouverie Pusey.* Edited by J. O. Johnston and W. C. E. Newbolt. London, 1901.

Romaine, William. *Letters on the Most Important Subjects.* Edited by Thomas Wills. New York, 1846.

Scudder, Vida Dutton. *Father Huntington, Founder of the Order of the Holy Cross.* New York, 1940.

Sidney, Edwin. *The Life of the Rev. Rowland Hill.* New York, 1834.

Sweet, Charles R. *The History of the Confessional on the Church of England.* Union Theological Seminary B. D. Thesis, 1947. Typed manuscript.

Taylor, Jeremy. *The Whole Works of the Right Rev. Jeremy Taylor.* With a Life of the Author . . . by Reginald Heber. Revised by Charles Page Eden. 10 vols. London, 1883.

Tyndale, William. *The Works of the English Reformers, William Tyndale and John Frith.* Edited by Thomas Russell. 3 vols. London, 1831.

Wace, Henry. *Confession and Absolution. Report of a Conference Held at Fulham Palace* . . . London, 1902.

Webb, William Walter. *The Cure of Souls; a Manual for the Clergy.* 2nd ed. Milwaukee, 1910.

Williams, Watkin W. *The Moral Theology of the Sacrament of Penance.* London, 1917.

Wilson, Thomas. *Parochialia; or, Instructions for the Clergy.* London, 1708.

Chapter XI

The Cure of Souls in Presbyterianism and Puritanism

Ames, William. *Conscience, with the Power and Cases Thereof.* Translated out of Latine into English for more Publique Benefit. London, 1643.

Andrews, Williams, Editor. *Bygone Church Life in Scotland.* London, 1899.

Barbour, G. F. *The Life of Alexander Whyte.* London, 1924.

Batten, Joseph Minton. *John Dury, Advocate of Christian Reunion.* Chicago, 1944.

Baxter, Richard. *The Christian Directory.* London, 1673.

———. *Gildas Salvianus: The Reformed Pastor.* Edited with an Introduction by John T. Wilkinson. London, 1939.

———. *How to Do Good to Many: or, The Public Good is the Christian's Life. Directions and Motives to it.* London, 1682.

———. *The Practical Works of the Rev. Richard Baxter, with a Life of the Author* . . . by William Orme. 23 vols. London, 1830.

Blaikie, William Garden. *For the Work of the Ministry: a Manuel of Homiletic and Pastoral Theology.* London, 1873.

Bonar, Andrew A. *Memoir and Remains of Robert Murray McCheyne.* (Seventy-second thousand.) Edinburgh, 1864.

Boston, Thomas. *A Soliloquy on the Art of Man-fishing.* Edited by D. D. F. Macdonald. Paisley, 1900.

Clark, Ivo Macnaughton. *A History of Church Discipline in Scotland.* Aberdeen, 1929.

Downame, John. *A Guide to Godlynesse, or, A Treatise of a Christian Life* . . . London, 1622.

Erskine, Thomas. *Letters of Thomas Erskine of Linlathen.* Edited by William Hanna. Edinburgh, 1877.

Fairbairn, Patrick. *Pastoral Theology. A Treatise on the Office and Duties of a Christian Pastor.* Edinburgh, 1875.

Gerard, Alexander. *The Pastoral Care*. Published by his son . . . Gilbert Gerard. London, 1799.

Gouge, Thomas, *Christian Directions, Shewing How to Walk with God All the Day Long*. London, 1664.

Gouge, William. *A Guide to Goe to God: or, An Explanation of . . . the Lord's Prayer*. London, 1626.

————. *Of Domestical Duties. Eight Treatises*. London, 1622.

Hanna, William. *Memoirs of the Life and Writings of Thomas Chalmers*. 4 vols. Edinburgh, 1852.

Henderson, G. D. *The Scottish Ruling Elder*. London, 1935.

Howie, John. *The Scots Worthies*. Revised by W. H. Carslaw. Edinburgh, 1870.

Kemp, Charles F. *A Pastoral Triumph. The Story of Richard Baxter*. New York, 1948.

Knox, John. *The Works of John Knox*. Collected and Edited by David Laing. 6 vols. Edinburgh, 1895.

Mackay, John. *The Church in the Highlands*. London, 1914.

Macmillan, Donald. *The Life of George Matheson*. London, 1907.

McMillan, William. *The Worship of the Scottish Reformed Church, 1550-1638*. London, 1931.

McNeill, John T. "Casuistry in the Puritan Age." *Religion in Life*, XII (1943), pp. 76-89.

Miller, Samuel. *An Essay on the Warrant, Nature, and Duties of the Ruling Elder in the Presbyterian Church*. Philadelphia, 1832.

Moncrief, H. Wellwood. *The Practice of the Free Church of Scotland in Her Several Courts*. 2nd ed. Edinburgh, 1877.

Patterson, George. *Memoir of the Rev. James MacGregor*. Philadelphia, 1879.

Perkins, William. *The Whole Treatise of the Cases of Conscience . . . Taught and Delivered by M. W. Perkins in His Holy-Day Lectures . . .* Published for the Common Good by T. Pickering. London, 1611.

Preston, John. *The Saint's Daily Exercise. A Treatise Unfolding the Whole Duty of Prayer*. 9th ed. London, 1635.

Ross, William. *Glimpses of Pastoral Work in Covenanting Times. A Record of the Labors of Andrew Donaldson, Minister of Dalgety*. London, 1877.

Rutherford, Samuel. *Letters of Samuel Rutherford with a Sketch of His Life and Biographical Notices of His Correspondents*. By Andrew A. Bonar. 4th ed. Edinburgh, 1891.

Shedd, William Greenough Thayer. *Homiletics and Pastoral Theology*. New York, 1867.

Smyth, Thomas. *Complete Works of the Reverend Thomas Smyth*. Edited by J. William Flinn. 10 vols. Columbia, S. C., 1908-13.

Steuart of Pardovan, Walter. *Collections and Observations Concerning the Worship, Discipline and Government of the Church of Scotland*. 5th ed. Edinburgh, 1937.

Stuart, John, Editor. *Extracts from the Presbytery Book of Strathbogie, 1631-1654.* Aberdeen. Printed for the Spaulding Club. 1843.

———. *Selections from the Records of the Kirk Session, Presbytery and Synod of Aberdeen.* Aberdeen. Printed for the Spaulding Club. 1846.

Sweet, William Warren. *Religion on the American Frontier: the Presbyterians.* New York, 1936.

Trinterud, Leonard J. *The Forming of an American Tradition. A Re-examination of Colonial Presbyterianism.* Philadelphia, 1949.

Watson, John. *The Cure of Souls.* The Lyman Beecher Lectures on Preaching at Yale University. New York, 1896.

———. *The Scot in the Eighteenth Century. His Religion and His Life.* London, 1907.

Whiting, Charles E. *Studies in English Puritanism from the Restoration to the Revolution, 1660-1688.* New York, 1931.

Chapter XII

THE CURE OF SOULS IN CONGREGATIONALISM, THE BAPTIST CHURCHES, QUAKERISM AND METHODISM

Anderson, William K., Editor. *Methodism.* Nashville, 1947.

Asbury, Francis. *The Heart of Asbury's Journal.* Edited by Ezra Squier Tipple. New York, 1904.

Bogue, David, and Bennett, James. *A History of the Dissenters 1688-1808.* 4 vols. London, 1809.

Bradford, William. *Bradford's Memoir of Elder Brewster.* (Old South Leaflets II, 48.) Boston, 1896.

Brockunier, Samuel Hugh. *The Irrepressible Democrat, Roger Williams.* New York, 1940.

Brown, John. *John Bunyan 1628-1688: His Life, Times and Work.* London, 1928.

Bunyan, John. *Complete Works of John Bunyan.* Philadelphia, 1872.

———. *Grace Abounding to the Chief of Sinners.* London, 1902.

Carlile, John Charles. *C. H. Spurgeon, an Interpretative Biography.* London, 1934.

Child, Frank Samuel. *The Colonial Parson of New England.* New York, 1896.

Dale, R. W. *History of English Congregationalism.* London, 1907.

Doddridge, Philip. *The Rise and Progress of Religion in the Soul.* Philadelphia, 1843.

———. *The Works of the Rev. Philip Doddridge.* 10 vols. Leeds, 1802-5.

Dimond, S. G. *The Psychology of the Methodist Revival.* Oxford, 1926.

Edwards, Jonathan. *The Works of Jonathan Edwards, with an Essay on His Genius and Writings by Henry Rogers and a Memoir by Sereno E. Dwight.* Revised and corrected by Edward Hickman. London, 1840.

Emory, Robert. *History of the Discipline of the Methodist Episcopal Church.* New York, 1843.

Fletcher, John William. *Fletcher's Appeal to Matter of Fact and Common Sense . . .* To which is now added, *The Life of the Venerable Author* by J. Kingston. Baltimore, 1814.

Garvie, Alfred E. *The Christian Preacher.* New York, 1921.

Gladden, Washington. *The Christian Pastor and the Working Church.* New York, 1898.

Grimes, Lewis Howard. *Making Lay Leadership Effective: a Historical Study of Major Issues in the Use of Laymen in the Methodist Church.* Unpublished doctoral dissertation, Library of Teachers College. New York, 1949.

Jones, Rufus M. *The Faith and Practice of the Quakers.* London, 1927.

Kidder, Daniel P. *The Christian Pastorate, Its Character, Responsibilities, and Duties.* Cincinnati, 1871.

Mather, Cotton. *Dr. Cotton Mather's Student and Preacher, Intituled Manuductio ad Ministerium . . .* Republished by John Ryland. London, 1781.

Morris, J. W. *Memoir of the Life and Writings of Andrew Fuller.* Boston, 1830.

Murdoch, Kenneth Ballard. *Increase Mather, the Foremost American Puritan.* Cambridge, Mass., 1892.

Pierce, Samuel Eyles. *Letters on Spiritual Subjects.* 2 vols. London, 3rd ed., 1836.

Pierce, William. *The Ecclesiastical Principles and Polity of the Wesleyan Methodists.* Revised by Frederick J. Johnson. 3rd ed. London, 1873.

Ryland, John. . . . *Life and Death of Andrew Fuller . . . Chiefly Extracted from His Own Papers.* Charleston, 1818.

Simon, John S. *John Wesley and the Methodist Societies.* London, 1923.

Steele, Ashbel. *Chief of the Pilgrims, or, The Life and Time of William Brewster.* Philadelphia, 1857.

Stevens, Abel. *A History of the Religious Movement . . . Called Methodism.* 3 vols. New York, 1858-61.

Sweet, William Warren. "The Churches as Moral Courts on the Frontier." *Church History,* II (1933), 3-13.

———. *Religion on the American Frontier.* Vol. I. *The Baptists, 1783-1830.* New York, 1931.

———. *Religion on the American Frontier, 1783-1850.* Vol. III. *The Congregationalists.* Chicago, 1939.

———. *Religion on the American Frontier, 1783-1840.* Vol. IV. *The Methodists.* Chicago, 1946.

Terrill, Edward. *The Records of a Church of Christ Meeting in Broadmead, Bristol, A.D. 1640 to A.D. 1688.* Edited by Nathaniel Haycroft. London, 1865.

Tyerman, Luke. *The Life and Times of John Wesley, M.A., Founder of Methodism.* 3 vols. London, 1870.

Waddington, John. *Congregational History, 1700-1800.* London, 1876.

Watts, Isaac. *The Works of the Reverend Isaac Watts in Seven Volumes.* Vol. IV. Leeds, 1800.

Wesley, John. *The Journal of the Reverend John Wesley.* Edited by Nehemiah Curnock. 8 vols. London, 1909-16.

————. *The Letters of John Wesley.* Edited by John Telford. 8 vols. London, 1931.

————. *The Works of the Rev. John Wesley.* Third American complete and standard edition. Edited by John Emory. 7 vols. New York, 1831.

Williams, Roger. *Experiments of Spiritual Life and Health.* London, 1652.

Winthrop, John. *The History of New England from 1630 to 1649.* 2 vols. Edited by James Savage. Boston, 1825-26.

Woolman, John. *The Journal and Essays of John Woolman.* Edited by Amelia Mott Gummere. Philadelphia, 1922.

Chapter XIII

THE CURE OF SOULS IN ROMAN CATHOLICISM

Borromeo, Charles. *S. Caroli Borromaei Pastorum instructiones, monitiones ad clerum atque epistolae.* Edited by E. W. Westhoff. 2nd ed. Münster, 1860.

————. *Pastorum instructiones.* Editio nova. Louvain, 1701.

Bossuet, Jacques Bénigne. *Correspondance de Bossuet.* Nouvelle edition augmentée . . . par Charles Urbain and E. Levesque. 15 vols. Paris, 1909-25.

Brémond, Henri. *Histoire littéraire du sentiment religieux en France depuis la fin des guerres de religion.* 11 vols. Paris, 1916-33.

Brodrick, James. *The Economic Morals of the Jesuits. An Answer to H. M. Robertson.* Oxford, 1934.

Busenbaum, Hermann. *Medulla theologiae moralis.* 8th ed. Padua, 1729.

Cagnac, Moïse. *Fénelon, directeur de conscience.* Paris, 1901.

Calvet, J. *Saint Vincent de Paul. Textes choisis et commentés.* Paris, 1913.

————. *La littérature religieuse de François de Sales à Fénelon.* Paris, 1938.

Clarkson, David. *The Practical Divinity of the Papists. Destructive of Christianity and Men's Souls.* London, 1676.

Fénelon, François de la Mothe. *Oeuvres de Fénelon, archévêque de Cambrai. Précédées d'études sur sa vie,* par M. Aime-Martin. 3 vols. Paris, 1835.

————. *Spiritual Letters of François de Salignac de la Mothe-Fénelon.* Translated by Mildred Whitney Stillman. Cornwall-on-Hudson, 1945.

————. *The Spiritual Letters of François de Salignac de la Mothe-Fénelon.* Translated from the text of Abbé Gosselin. London, 1892.

Francis de Sales. *Oeuvres complétes de S. François de Sales.* Edited by the Abbé de Baudry and others. 9 vols. Paris, 1861-64. (There is an improved edition in 20 vols. Paris, 1918.)

————. *The Spiritual Director of Devout and Religious Souls.* From the writings of St. Francis Sales. New York (undated).

Francis de Sales. *Spiritual Letters to Persons in Religion.* Translated by Henry Benedict Mackey. 'Westminster, Maryland, 1943.

Ghéon, Henri. *The Secret of the Curé d'Ars.* Translated by J. F. Sheed. New York, 1938.

Gorayeb, Joseph. *Life and Letters of Walter Drum, S.J.* New York, 1928.

Horstius, Jacob Merlo. *Monita sapientiae Christianae ad mores, et vitae spiritualis officia.* Cologne, 1630.

Hügel, Baron Friedrich von. *Selected Letters 1896-1924.* Edited with a memoir by Bernard Holland. London, 1928. New York, 1933.

Jaccard, L.-Frédéric. *Saint Cyran, précurseur de Pascal.* Lausanne, 1945.

Lea, Henry Charles. *A History of Auricular Confession and Indulgences in the Latin Church.* 3 vols. Philadelphia, 1896.

Liguori, Alfonso de. *Homo apostolicus instructus in sua vocatione ad audiendas confessiones; sive, Praxis et instructio confessariorum.* 2 vols. Paris, 1684.

Liguori, Alfonso Maria de. *Theologia moralis Beati A.M. de Liguorio.* Paris, 1834.

May, James Lewis. *Fénelon; a study.* London, 1938.

Michelet, Jules. *Le prêtre, la femme, et la famille. Les Jesuites.* Edition definitive. Paris, 1895.

──────. *Priests, Women and Families.* Translated by G. H. Smith. London, 1850(?).

Orcibal, Jean. *Les Origines du Jansenisme. II. Jean Duvergier de Hauranne, Abbé de Saint Cyran, et son temps.* Louvain, 1947.

Pascal, Blaise. *Les lettres provinciales de Blaise Pascal.* Edited by H. F. Stewart. Manchester, 1920.

──────. *The Provincial Letters of Blaise Pascal.* A New Translation with Historical Introduction and Notes. By Thomas McCrie. Edinburgh, 1847.

Robertson, Hector Mentieth. *Aspects of the Rise of Economic Individualism.* Cambridge, 1933.

Saint Cyran, Jean Duvergier de. *Lettres chrétiennes et spirituelles de Jean Duvergier de Hauranne, Abbé de Saint Cyran.* 2 vols. Paris, 1648.

Sanders, Ella Katharine. *S. François de Sales, 1567-1622.* London, 1928.

Scaramelli, Giovanni Battista. *The Directorium Asceticum, or Guide to the Spiritual Life.* With a Preface by Cardinal Manning. 8th ed. London, 1924.

Slater, Thomas. *Cases of Conscience for English-speaking Countries.* 2 vols. New York, 1911-12.

Trent, Council of. *Canons and Decrees of the Council of Trent.* (Latin text, with English translation by J. Waterworth 1848), in Schaff, Philip, *The Creeds of Christendom with a History and Critical Notes,* Vol. II. 4th ed. New York, 1919.

──────. *Catechism of the Council of Trent for Parish Priests . . .* Translated into English with notes by John A. McHugh and Charles A. Gallan. New York, 1923.

Vacant, A., and Mangenot, E. *Dictionnaire de théologie catholique.* See especially articles: "Busenbaum, Hermann" by Joseph Brucker; "Casuistique" by E. Dublanchy; "Confession" by E. Vacandard.

Vincent de Paul. *Saint Vincent de Paul: correspondance, entretiens, documents.* Edited by Pierre Coste. 14 vols. Paris, 1920-25.

Chapter XIV

THE CURE OF SOULS IN THE EASTERN ORTHODOX AND ARMENIAN CHURCHES

Arpee, Leon. *A History of Armenian Christianity.* New York, 1946.

Arseniev, Nicolas. "Le Monde des saints et des starets russes." *Dieu vivant: perspectives religieuses et philosophiques,* VI (1946), 99-119.

Attwater, Donald. *The Catholic Eastern Churches.* Milwaukee, 1935.

Blackmore, R. W. *The Doctrine of the Russian Church. Being the Primer or Spelling Book, the Shorter and Larger Catechisms, and a Treatise on the Duty of Parish Priests.* Translated from the Slavono-Russian originals. Aberdeen, 1845.

Brian-Chaninov, Nicholas. *The Russian Church.* Translated from the French by Warre B. Wells. New York, 1936.

Casey, Robert Pierce. *Religion in Russia.* New York, 1946.

Conybeare, Frederick C. *Rituale Armenorum.* Oxford, 1905.

Dalovich, Sebastian. *The Holy Orthodox Church, or the Ritual Services and Sacraments of the Eastern Orthodox (Greek-Russian) Church.* Wilkes-Barre, Pa. 1898.

Dostoievsky, Fyodor. *The Brothers Karamazov.* Translated by Constance Garnett. London, 1910.

Fedotov, George Petrovich. *The Russian Religious Mind.* Cambridge, 1946.
———. *A Treasury of the Russian Spirituality.* New York, 1948.

Gavin, Frank Stanton Burns. *Some Aspects of Contemporary Greek Orthodox Thought.* Milwaukee, 1923.

Hapgood, Isabel F. *Service Book of the Holy Orthodox Catholic-Apostolic (Greco-Russian) Church.* Boston, 1906.

Isaverdens, James. *The Sacred Rites and Ceremonies of the Armenian Church.* (Armenian Ritual Part IV.) Venice, 1888.

King, John Glen. *The Rites and Ceremonies of the Greek Church in Russia.* London, 1772.

Neale, John Mason. *A History of the Holy Eastern Church.* 5 vols. London, 1847-73.

Nève, Felix. *L'Arménie chrétienne et sa littérature.* Louvain, 1886.

Palmer, William. *A Harmony of Anglican Doctrine with the Doctrine of the Catholic and Apostolic Church of the East. Being the Longer Russian Catechism with an Apepndix . . .* Aberdeen, 1846.

Ricault, Paul. *The Present State of the Greek and Armenian Churches.* London, 1679.

Tolstoy, Count Dmitry. *Romanism in Russia. An Historical Study.* Translated by Mrs. McKibbin. 2 vols. London, 1874.

Torossian, A. *The Divine Liturgy According to the Rites of the Holy Apostolic Church of the Armenians.* New York, 1933.

Vacandard, E. Article "Confession, ii: Du ier au xiie siècle" in Vacant, A. and Mangenot, E., *Dictionnaire de théologie catholique,* Vol. III. Paris, 1908.

Zankov, Stefan. *The Eastern Orthodox Church.* Translated by Donald A. Lowrie. Milwaukee, 1929.

Zernov, Nicolas. *Three Russian Prophets: Khomiakov, Dostoevsky, Soloviev.* London, 1944.

Chapter XV

CONCLUSION

Balmforth, Henry, and others. *An Introduction to Pastoral Theology.* New York, 1937.

Blackwood, Andrew Watterson. *Pastoral Work, a Source Book for Ministers.* Philadelphia, 1945.

Boisen, Anton T. *The Exploration of the Inner World.* Chicago, 1936.

————. *Problems in Religion and Life. A Manual for Pastors.* New York, 1946.

Bonnell, John Sutherland. *Psychology for Pastor and People.* New York, 1948.

Bonthius, Robert Harold. *Christian Paths to Self-Acceptance.* New York, 1948.

Cabot, R. C., and Dick, R. L. *The Art of Ministering to the Sick.* New York, 1935.

Dunbar, Helen Flanders. *Medicine, Religion and the Infirmities of Mankind.* New York, 1934.

Hiltner, Seward. *Pastoral Counseling.* New York, 1949.

Holman, Charles Thomas. *The Cure of Souls, a Socio-psychological Approach.* Chicago, 1932.

————. *Psychology and Religion for Everyday Living.* New York, 1949.

James, William. *Principles of Psychology.* 2 vols. New York, 1889.

————. *The Varieties of Religious Experience.* New York, 1902.

Jung, Carl Gustav. *Psychology and Religion.* New Haven, 1938.

Künkel, Fritz. *In Search of Maturity.* New York, 1943.

Lee, R. S. *Freud and Christianity.* New York, 1947.

Lewis, Nolan D. C. *A Short History of Psychiatric Achievement.* New York, 1941.

Liebman, Joshua Loth, Editor. *Psychiatry and Religion.* Boston, 1948.

Murphy, Gardner. *An Historical Introduction to Modern Psychology.* New York, 1929. Rev. ed., 1949.

Oliver, John Rathbone. *Psychiatry and Mental Health.* New York, 1932.

Pfister, Oskar. *Christianity and Fear. A Study in History and in the Psychology and Hygiene of Religion.* Translated by W. H. Johnston. New York, 1948.

Rank, Otto. *Beyond Psychology*. New York, 1941.

————. *Will Therapy*. Translated by Jessie Taft. New York, 1936.

Roberts, David Everett. *Psychotherapy and a Christian View of Man*. New York, 1940.

Rogers, Carl R. *Counseling and Psychotherapy*. Boston, 1942.

Schaer, Hans. *Religion and the Cure of Souls in Jung's Psychology*. Translated by R. F. C. Hull. New York, 1950.

Seabury, David. *How Jesus Heals Our Minds Today*. Boston, 1940.

Sherrill, Louis Joseph. *Guilt and Redemption*. Richmond, Va., 1945.

Stolz, Karl R. *The Church and Psychotherapy*. New York, 1943.

————. *Pastoral Psychology*. Nashville, 1932.

Symonds, Percival M. *The Dynamics of Human Adjustment*. New York, 1946.

Thurneysen, Eduard. *Die Lehre von der Seelsorge*. Zürich, 1946

Tillich, Paul J. "The Relation of Religion and Health." *Review of Religion*, X (1946), 348-84.

White, William A. *Twentieth Century Psychiatry: Its Contribution to Man's Knowledge of Himself*. New York, 1936.

Zilboorg, Gregory. *Mind, Medicine and Man*. New York, 1943.

INDEX

Abailard, 145 f.
Absolution, 99, 168 f., 213, 218, 227 ff.,
    238; abuses in, 147 f.; comfort of in
    Lutheranism, 170, 175 f.; forms of,
    133, 175, 232, 250, 314 ff., 326; min-
    isterial, 229, 234, 326; precatory, 133,
    232, 309 f.; private, 112, 221, 223,
    229, 260; public, 92, 169, 223, 325 f.
Academicians, 24 f.
Acedia, 106
Āchārya (ākārya), 42, 44, 53
Adam, James, quoted, 20
Adamnan, 122
Adiaphora (things indifferent), 38, 211
Aedificatio mutua, see Mutual edification
Aegritudo, 29 f.
Aelfric, 136
Aeschylus, 28, 30
Agricola, J., 171 f.
Ahikar, Maxims of, 4 f., 70
Ahimsa, 50, 57
Alcibiades, 22
Alcuin, 136
Al-Ghazzālī, 63 f.
Allah, 60; absorption in, 63
Allestree, R., 236
Alsted, J. H., 211 f.
Ambrose, St., 94 f., 100, 102, 233; on
    the virtues, 104
Amen-em-apt, 3 f., 5
American board, missions of, 317
Anabaptists, 193
Anapausis, 78
Anastasius, the Sinaite, 307
Ancyra, Council of, 97
Anderson, O. V., 176
Anglican Church, ix, 325
Anglican Communion, 218-46
Anglicanism, x, 326, 328 f.
Anmchara, 115
Anselm, St., 136
Antoine de Bourbon, 202
Anxiety, 79, 165 ff., 269
Apastamba, aphorisms of, 44-6
Apatheia (apathy), 25, 34

Apollo cult, 17 f.
Aporia, 22
Aquinas, St. Thomas, 142, 145 f., 149
Aristotle, 24, 323
Armenian Church, x, 314-17, 329
Arpee, L., 315
Arreum, 123
Arseniev, N., 311 f.
Art of Dying, 158 ff., 210, 213 f., 233,
    236, 264, 330
Artes Praedicandi, 152
Articles, the Ten, 218; the Thirteen, 225
Arya Samāj, 47
Asbury, F., 282
Asceticism, 19, 47, 53, 60 ff., 65, 105 f.,
    111, 241, 300
Ash Wednesday, 132
Asoka, King, 54
Atonement, day of, 15, 17
Attrition, 145, 287
Augsburg Confession, 175
Augustana Synod, 189-91
Augustine, St., 96, 100, 105, 115
Austerities, 38, 47, 50, 98, 120 f., 299,
    312
Authority, in casuistry, 291; of the direc-
    tor, 53, 62 ff., 295, 313, 324, 326 f.,
    329; of elders, 268; in excommunica-
    tion, 211; lack of, 122, 124, 127; of
    ministers, 199, 250, 326 f.; in psychia-
    try, 326; of Scripture, 1, 111, 208, 219,
    228, 326 f.
Ayenbite of Inwyt, 154 f., 159

Babylon, 2
Bands, Wesleyan, 279
Baptist churches, 247, 270 ff., 284 f.
Bashir, A., 310
Basil of Caesarea, St., 95, 97, 114
Baxter, R., 180, 236, 261, 265 ff.
Bayly, L., 210, 229, 234
Beal, S., 54
Becon, T., 224, 233
Bede, the Venerable, 136, 153, 226

361

362 INDEX